Third World Film Making and the West

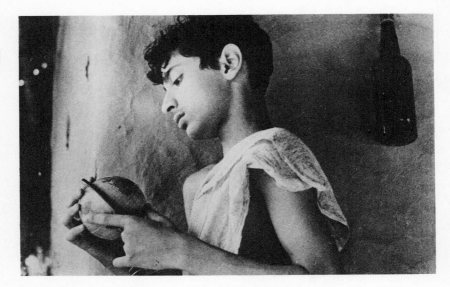

Satyajit Ray: The Unvanquished / Aparajito *(India, 1956)*

Third World Film Making
and the West

Roy Armes

University of California Press
Berkeley / Los Angeles / London

University of California Press
Berkeley and Los Angeles, California

University of California Press, Ltd.
London, England

Library of Congress Cataloging-in-Publication Data

Armes, Roy.
  Third World film making and the West.

  Bibliography: p.
  Includes index.
  1. Moving-picture industry—Developing countries.
2. Moving-pictures—Developing countries.   I. Title.
PN1993.5.D44A76 1987   384′.8′091724   86-11213
ISBN 0-520-05690-6 (pbk. : alk. paper)

Printed in the United States of America

08 07 06 05 04 03 02 01 00
9 8 7 6 5

To Adrienne

A people's history must rediscover the past in order to make it reusable. . . . Such a history must deal with the past with a view to explaining the present. It must therefore be not only descriptive but also analytical; it must deal not only with objective developments but also bring the discussion to the realm of value judgments.

Renato Constantino

Contents

Acknowledgments

During the research for this book I have enjoyed numerous encouragements. Among the many organizations that have made specific contributions I must mention: the Bulgarian Ministry of Culture, which sponsored a number of meetings in Sofia and Varna dealing with the history of world cinema that brought me into contact for the first time with film critics and historians from the Third World; the Universidad Nacional Autónoma de Mexico, which organized the international conference on cinema, culture, and national liberation at which the idea of this book was born; the University of North Carolina at Chapel Hill, where I was able to teach a course at which many of the arguments advanced here were exposed in public for the first time; the journals *Ciné-Tracts, Framework, Films and Filming, Cinema nuovo, London Magazine,* and *New African,* in which first drafts of some of the material contained here first appeared in print; for their hospitality and support, the organizers of the Festival des Trois Continents in Nantes, the Fespaco Festival in Ougadougou, Confrontation in Perpignan, the Pan-African Film Symposium (Mogpafis) in Mogadishu, Filmotsav in Bombay, the Festival du Film Arabe in Paris, the Journées Cinématographiques de Carthage in Tunis, and the Cairo International Film Festival; and for assistance with research and the viewing of films, the Médiathèque des Trois Mondes, the Inter-Service Migrants and the Cinémathèque du Ministère de la Coopération et du Développement in Paris, and the National Film Theatre and the Library of the British Film Institute in London.

Individuals to whom I am variously grateful for assistance, inspiration, and stimulation include: Guido Aristarco, Ibrahim Awed Mohamed, Victor Bachy, Ferid Boughedir, Manuel Gonzales Casanova, Michael Chanan, Malcolm Coad, Pamela Cullen, Uma da Cunha, Haile Gerima, Octavio Getino, Philippe and Alain Jalladeau, Mohammed Jaoua, Catherine Jourdan, Gaston Kaboré, Julie Kitchener, Derek Knight, Ip Kung Sau, A Viren Luther, Fred Marshall, Adrienne Martin, Angela Martin, Donatien Mbaloula, Hashim el Nahhas, Lionel Ngakane, Marcel Oms, Dominique Sentilhes, Gabriella von Schwerin, Nigam Viad, and Paulin Soumanou Vieyra.

For help with obtaining stills I must thank Nigel Algar of the BFI Film and Video Distribution Department, Artificial Eye, Caroline Audemars of the London Film Festival, Michael Chanan, Pamela Cullen of the National Film Development Corporation of India, Ellis Driessen of Cactus Films (rights owner for the Güney films), Haile Gerima of Mypheduh Films, Ben Gibson of The Other Cinema, Charles Hedges of Contemporary Films, Alain and Philippe Jalladeau of the Festival des Trois Continents, Philippe Leray, Lizbeth Malkmus, Tony Rayns, Markku Salmi of the National Film Archive, Dominique Sentilhes of the Association des Trois Mondes, and Paul Willemen.

Above all, I am indebted to Julianne Burton, Hazel Johnson, Lizbeth Malkmus, Richard Maltby, and Ken Short, who read all or part of the manuscript in draft and made valuable comments.

For the funding enabling research to be undertaken I am grateful to the Small Grants Research Fund in the Humanities of the British Academy for a one-year research grant and to the Leverhulme Trust for a two-year research fellowship. I must also thank the Middlesex Polytechnic, and particularly the dean of Art and Design, Professor Peter Green, for consistent support for my research over the years.

Note on Titles

Absolute consistency in the handling of film titles is impossible in a work of this scale. In general, both the original title and an English translation are given on the first reference to a film in any given section, and thereafter films are referred to by the title most likely to be familiar to readers. It should be noted, however, that some films are known in English by titles that are not exact translations of the original. With regard to non-European languages, normally agreed-upon transliterations are used when available (e.g., for Indian films), but in most other instances (e.g., Arabic) there is no single agreed-upon transliteration, and the versions of original titles used here should be regarded as no more than approximations given to assist identification in other research sources.

Introduction

If it is true that no production of knowledge in the human sciences can ever ignore or disclaim its author's involvement as a human being in his own circumstances, then it must be true that for a European or American studying the Orient there can be no disclaiming the main circumstances of his *actuality: that he comes up against the Orient as a European or American first, as an individual second.*

Edward W. Said

This study of Third World film making and the West has to confront a number of obvious hazards:

(i) Firstly, it is a study of Third World film making written from a Western standpoint, with all the implicit assumptions that this carries. As the notes and bibliography indicate, I have tried wherever possible to draw on and refer to the work of Third World theorists and critics in defining the ways in which Third World film making is best approached, but the overall conceptual framework is my own. Inevitably, this book cannot be offered as any kind of "definitive study." It is rather a voyage of discovery through areas of world cinema that remain largely unknown, and it will have succeeded if it allows the reader to experience some of the excitement that went into its writing.

(ii) A work that ventures into areas as diverse as culture and politics, economics and ideology, literature and film must of necessity be a work of synthesis. My debt to the authors on whom I have drawn is self-evident, but I hope and believe that fresh illumination will arise from bringing together strands of analysis hitherto unrelated. The major problem in drawing on this contextual material has been to avoid too gross an oversimplification of arguments developed by their authors through successive books and articles over a period of years.

1

(iii) While the breadth of the issues to be confronted if Third World cinema is to be put into context presents one level of problem, another and hardly less daunting difficulty is posed by the historical span demanded for such a work. Film reached the major cities of Asia, Latin America, and North Africa within a matter of months of the first film showings in Paris, London, and New York, so the history of film exhibition and to some extent film production is virtually as long in the non-Western world as in the West. The pattern of Western dominance—first by France and then by the United States—was established even before the Soviet Revolution of 1917, and this pattern causes problems with the definition of Third World film making. Clearly there was a considerable amount of film production in the non-Western world before the concept of the Third World came into being.

(iv) If the concept of a Third World grouping may be thought to begin, in political terms, with the 1955 Bandung Conference, this meeting of "non-aligned" countries does not offer a basis for selecting countries or film industries to be treated here. Political criteria need to be reinforced by economic definitions, and basically this present study may be said to cover the development of cinema in those countries of Asia, Africa, and Latin America that (a) experienced colonization in the nineteenth and/or twentieth centuries and (b) have not subsequently chosen a socialist path of development that effectively takes them away from the tight economic system that binds the bulk of these countries to the West.

(v) But even this definition begs almost as many questions as it answers. Japan can be safely left aside, since it follows a well-documented alternative pattern of industrial development and hence displays a distinctive approach in its film industry and modes of cinematic representation. But what is to be done with China? Is Turkey to be excluded, since it was never colonized and is a member of NATO? How are the various forms of African socialism to be regarded? Can we ignore Cuba, which has had so potent an influence on the film makers of Latin America and elsewhere? Even if we shelve these fairly fruitless problems of categorization—on the grounds that pre-1949 China is best understood in the context of Western colonial dominance, that Turkey has problems of economic underdevelopment similar to those of its neighbors in the Middle East, that African socialism has not resulted in economic independence, or that Cuban culture can be fully understood only if the influence of proximity and historical links with the United States is taken into account—there are still problems. A broad definition remains dangerous, since it can be taken as implying that it is possible to offer generalizations about the Third World that are equally valid for countries as diverse in history, culture, and resources as Mali and Brazil or Bolivia and India. In specific film terms, it could likewise imply an equation of Ouagadougou, arguably the center of black African film making, with Bombay, the undisputed capital of the Indian film industry.

(vi) Moreover, though an economic definition of the Third World in terms of countries that have been marked by underdevelopment stemming from the dominance of colonial or neocolonial powers offers a reasonable— perhaps the only possible—starting point, there are further complications when one considers specific developments in cinema. Here the dominance of the United States has reached unparalleled dimensions. Tony Garnett's dictum that "to work in the British film industry is to know what it is to be colonized" is well known, and in many ways the struggles of film production in Australia and Canada—which can hardly be considered as belonging to the Third World, however wide we cast the net—offer some of the clearest examples of certain ideological aspects of cultural neocolonialism.

(vii) The problems of tackling the specific issues of film history are in many ways precisely the opposite of those related to research into the con- textual issues of economics and national development. Instead of an over- abundant literature couched in specialist terms, there is a paucity of available source material in English—though this material has increased immeasurably even during the period in which this book has been researched and written— and there remain numerous gaps even when sources in French or Spanish are drawn upon. Moreover, these gaps are not simply in our knowledge of the development of Third World film making but include aspects of cinema in the West as well. There is, for example, no adequate account of the economic organization and rise to world dominance of Hollywood, though various ar- ticles published since the late 1970s do offer clues as to the pattern such an account might take. Because of this lack of preexisting studies, I have been forced on occasion—as in the account of Hollywood's world role—to make assertions and generalizations that themselves really need justification at book length.

Given these practical and conceptual problems and the enormously wide scope of the project, how can the approach adopted here be characterized? Basically, I have attempted in this study to keep the focus broad and to make the issues clear, while outlining an overall development and presenting certain areas of significant achievement. The movement through the successive chap- ters, from context to history and on to the achievements of specific film makers, gives a progression from generality to detail, from theory to realized practice, and, let it be said, from problematics to often dazzling resolution. For though the theoretical issues raised here are extremely complex and the history of Third World film making is one of constant struggle against over- whelming odds, the actual achievements of the film makers have been strik- ingly original and effective.

Part One

The Social, Cultural, and Economic Context

The Indian who goes barefoot but clutching a transistor radio beneath his poncho, runs the risk of getting nowhere, and ending up in no man's land: like a man who has lost his fingerprints. This is the danger we would all risk if, cursing our cultural identity and ceasing to defend it, we blindly accepted the bilateral assistance, foreign technicians and international cooperation which correspond to other mental patterns, other orientations and other objectives.

Oswaldo Guayasmin

The understanding of Third World film making demands consideration of a number of factors—social, cultural, economic—that are customarily ignored in accounts of Western cinemas. This is not because writing about Third World film requires—as the editors of a recent issue of *Jump Cut* assert—"a different methodology and a treatment of other concerns than writing about mainstream film does."[1] Rather, it is an indication of the inadequacy of so much writing about mainstream cinemas, which continues to employ such dubious concepts as autonomous national cinemas and creatively independent "authors," and fails to take into account the economic primacy of distribution for cinema. The following pages therefore look at some of the factors that have defined Third World film making:

> the nature of social structures shaped by the force of tradition and the impact of colonialism
>
> the emergence of Western-educated elites as ruling groups and as the prime movers in cultural production
>
> the problems of defining both a "nation" and a "national culture"
>
> the issue of language and the insights afforded by literature and theater that bridge the gulf between Western and non-Western worlds
>
> the nature of cinema as a product of Western capitalism
>
> the role of U.S.-dominated film distribution as an examplar of the working of the capitalist world system

But our starting point is the personal experience of the colonized, for there is no relevance in arguments about whether "objectively" the Third World has benefited from the impact of the West or whether the possession of colonies was "in reality" a loss-making situation, unless we first take into account the fact that the impact of the West was almost universally experienced as a traumatically destructive force by those subjected to it. As this book will show, Third World film making has the same inextricable mixture of idealism and philistinism as cinema in the West. The finest films display similar qualities of passion and commitment, insight and tenderness. But underlying them all—and crucial to an understanding of their form and meaning—is the often shattering and always dislocating impact of Western values and culture.

Third World Societies 1

On the psycho-cultural level, probably no historical phenomenon of modern times has been so traumatic and so destructive of the mental structures of entire societies. Everywhere, but most especially in nations whose own history dated back to antiquity—China, Egypt, Vietnam, Persia—the onslaught of European colonialism stunned, bewildered, and overwhelmed the traditional elites.

Gérard Chaliand

Though a mere ninety years separate us from the birth of cinema, these years have seen a total transformation of the world political situation. In 1895 the European empires were at the apparent height of their power and influence, dominating between them over three-quarters of the earth's surface. The bulk of Africa and Asia was formally colonized, while most of the Latin American republics, which had achieved their national independence in the early part of the nineteenth century, were still subjected to British economic power. Largely as a result of the two world wars, this pattern was totally destroyed within fifty years or so: the old empires were dissolved—often with surprising ease—and the United States rose to dominance of the "free world." The West was now confronted with new forms of social organization, in the socialist world that came to comprise the USSR, the People's Democratic Republics of Eastern Europe, China, and parts of Southeast Asia. The notion of a "third world" is conceivable only in terms of the opposition of these two power blocks and could come into being only after the move toward post-colonial independence had begun and the countries of Asia, Africa, and Latin America could enjoy a sense—however fleeting and illusory—of achieving an impetus of their own. The Bandung Conference of "nonaligned nations" of 1955 can in this sense be seen as offering a starting point, after which the term *Third World* can be meaningfully applied, though participation in that conference is in no way a limiting definition of the term. The Third World, then, came into existence in the late 1950s, and the term began to enjoy a vogue in the 1960s.

Awareness of this historical time-span allows us to proceed to a definition in geographical terms. Taking the situation in the 1960s, when the concept of a "third world" began to achieve acceptance, we find that the West—that which U.N. statistics define as "the developed countries with market economies" (i.e., the United States, Canada, Western Europe, Japan, Australia, New Zealand, and, arguably, Israel and South Africa)—comprised one-fifth of the world's population but enjoyed almost 60 percent of the world's gross domestic product. The socialist states—which the U.N. documents call "countries with planned economies" (i.e., the USSR, Eastern Europe, China, and the People's Republics of Mongolia, Korea, Vietnam, and Cuba)—contained one-third of the world's population and consumed almost 30 percent of the gross domestic product. This left the Third World—the "developing countries with a market economy" (i.e., Latin America, the remainder of Asia, and all of Africa except perhaps South Africa)—comprising half the land area and embracing half the world's population, while enjoying barely 12 percent of the gross product.[1] The argument for adopting such economic criteria for a definition of the Third World has been admirably summarized by Pierre Jalée:

> To regard the Third World as a single economic entity is, I know, in one sense schematic and arbitrary. But I also know that in a much more important sense this reflects the fundamental reality. Underneath the differences between their natural resources and level of development, the underdeveloped countries of Latin America, Asia and Africa have in common the fundamental characteristics of economies complementary to those of the advanced capitalist countries.[2]

Portrait of the Colonized

The definition offered above presents us with a vast range of differences, all covered by the term *Third World,* and it must be admitted that there is a tendency for discussions to veer between broad generalizations that need immediate qualification (e.g., the Third World is *not* all black, poor, rural . . .) and claims that since all countries are unique, any particular Third World country can be discussed only in terms of its own historical and cultural specificity. The same is true when we come to discuss the impact of the West on these societies.

An initial distinction must be made between colonization (as in the Spanish and Portuguese settlement of Latin America) and colonialism (typified by European rule in Africa from the nineteenth century onward). There are clearly wide divergences of historical and geographical circumstances and great variations in the length and intensity of the foreign impact, but there are also shared characteristics beyond any local particularity. Indeed, as the reception of Albert Memmi's classic study *The Colonizer and the Colonized* shows, a personal portrait that keeps strictly to local observation may take on universal dimensions. The portrait offered may be, in Memmi's own term, a "mythical" one, but it is one key to an understanding of Third World cultural aspirations in the postindependence period. Memmi's analysis demonstrates the way in which the colonial relationship locks the two halves of the equation together, so that the colonizer's privilege and affluence find their counterparts in the deprivation and poverty of the colonized. While the basis of this relationship is economic, it is sustained through ideological means, whereby the "mythical and degrading portrait" created and spread by the colonizer "ends up by being accepted and lived with by the colonized. It thus acquires a certain amount of reality and contributes to the true portrait of the colonized." [3] This imposition is the ultimate aim of the colonizer, whose "legitimacy" is secured only when the colonized accepts not only economic dominance but also the image of the world the colonizer presents to him.

The identity of the colonized depends on a number of sustaining factors—social relations, religion, language, and history—and all of these become the focus of the colonizer's attention. Undermining the economic basis of the colonized's life inevitably serves to disrupt the social relations that bind communities together. Religion is more resistant to outside pressure, but the disruption of traditional family ties resulting from the activities of Western missionaries should not be underestimated. The time-honored way to control language and history is, of course, through the educational system. The reforms of education imposed by colonial administrations often establish a foreign tongue as the language of tuition and employ textbooks imported from the "mother country." Given the colonizer's economic hold over the country, it is possible within a comparatively short time to downgrade native languages and substitute the colonizer's tongue as the language of commerce, law, and government. As a result, all non-European languages are regarded with contempt and deprived of any influence on social or economic life. In Memmi's Tunisia, as in other parts of Africa colonized by France, French became the sole language used by "the entire bureaucracy, the entire court system, all industry," and Memmi laments that "the colonized's mother tongue, that which is sustained by his feelings, emotions and dreams, that in which his tenderness and his wonder are expressed, thus that which holds the greatest emotional impact, is precisely the one which is the least valued." [4]

Literacy itself is not an unqualified boon, if it serves merely as a channel for foreign influences and loosens the links that bind the colonized to their own society and their own history. This was the case in colonial Tunisia where, as Memmi shows, a child fortunate enough to receive a school education was not "saved nationally":

The memory which is assigned him is certainly not that of his people. The history which is taught him is not his own. He knows who Colbert or Cromwell was, but he learns nothing about Khaznadar; he knows about Joan of Arc, but not about El Kahena. . . . The books talk to him of a world which in no way reminds him of his own; the little boy is called Toto and the little girl Marie; and on winter evenings Marie and Toto walk home along snow-covered paths, stopping in front of the chestnut seller.[5]

The universality of Memmi's observation is reflected in Renato Constantino's more detached historical account of the experience of the Philippines, a country twice colonized—first in the sixteenth century by Spain and then in the 1890s by the United States—and still dominated, in its notional independence, by North American business interests. In the Philippines, too, schoolchildren have been taught a distortion of their national history:

Accounts of the years of fierce people's resistance, accounts of the atrocities perpetrated by the Americans in quelling this resistance were suppressed. Instead, the leaders of this resistance were branded as bandits while the early collaborators were presented to the people as leaders and heroes. Of course, the Americans were portrayed in the schools and in media as altruistic benefactors who had been welcomed with open arms by the people. Thus, succeeding generations forgot their people's record of resistance, their history of struggle.[6]

In more general terms, the Americanization of education resulted in a total cultural inauthenticity. As Constantino sardonically remarks, "English opened new vistas of western culture to their dazed eyes and enabled them to write poetry about autumn and winter and snow on the fir trees, to know more of Paul Revere and less of Apolinario Mabini, to sing nostalgically about 'My Old Kentucky Home' and 'White Christmas.'"[7]

The outcome of such policies is that the colonized come to enjoy none of the attributes of citizenship. For Memmi, the most serious blow suffered by the colonized is "being removed from history and from the community."[8] Similarly, Constantino finds that his own people have become habituated "to abdicating control over basic areas of their national life, unaccustomed to coming to grips with reality, prone to escape into fantasies."[9] Perhaps the most cruel and negative fantasy is that which feeds on disunity among the colonized and sees signs of affinity with the colonizer as marks of moral and cultural superiority. Constantino finds examples of this among the Filipinos:

In due course, under a more sophisticated colonialism, the people . . . even came to believe that with their westernized tastes they were better educated and generally better off than most of their Asian brothers. The lack of racial pride produced an inferiority complex towards their conquerors whose every way they tried to ape, while they adopted a condescending attitude towards their neighbours who had not become Christians or westernized and who retained their native culture and identity.[10]

Albert Memmi's remarkable insight into both colonizer and colonized derives from his personal situation as a Tunisian Jew: "The Jewish population identified as much with the colonizers as with the colonized. They were undeniably 'natives,' as they were then called, as near as possible to the Muslims in poverty, language, sensibilities, customs, taste in music, odours and cooking. However, unlike the Muslims, they passionately endeavoured to identify themselves with the French. To them the West was the paragon of all civilisation, all culture." [11]

With this confusion of identities by an individual or group caught between two cultures, we reach one of the crucial problems facing any Third World artist and the starting point for the examination of the psychic damage of colonialism, which Frantz Fanon confronts in the opening chapter of his first book, *Black Skin, White Masks:* "The negro of the Antilles will be proportionately whiter—that is, he will be closer to being a real human being—in direct ratio to his mastery of the French language." [12]

The Postcolonial State

The persistence in postindependence societies of the problems of language, culture, and identity produced by colonialism derives from factors relating to both economic relations and the nature of the colonial state. The economic factors in the incorporation of the countries of Asia, Africa, and Latin America into the capitalist world were themselves sufficient to bring about a lasting distortion of their societies. One does not need to claim that the Third World was highly developed in Western terms—though many more advanced cultures existed than the colonialists' ideology would allow them to perceive—in order to affirm that the impact of the West was in many ways crippling. Incorporation into the capitalist world destroyed local systems of trade and production. Cultivation of the export crops required in the West displaced the growing of food for local consumption, just as taxation under colonialism drew millions from traditional societies into the cash economy, and disruption of traditional agriculture and land ownership patterns provoked the rural exodus that persists to this day.

The urban economy became part of the world system but was unable to offer work to more than a tiny portion of the potential labor force that flocked to it. Its local middle classes were able to occupy only secondary roles in the world system and unable to accumulate sufficient capital to allow industrialization to be undertaken. At the heart of the economic relations between the West and the Third World is a paradox well expressed by Geoffrey Kay: "If we square up to it, we have to face the unpalatable fact that capitalism has created underdevelopment not simply because it has exploited the underdeveloped countries but because it has not exploited them enough." [13] Exploitation has gone far enough to be destructive of traditional economies and to extract valuable surplus, but capitalism has not developed sufficiently to allow the creation and retention of wealth in the Third World.

In the case of those societies that were formally colonized, the situation is made worse by the nature of the state apparatus established under the colonial system and bequeathed to the society at independence. This state apparatus has two aspects that distinguish it from virtually all other forms of social organization. Firstly, it is a form of government designed for one purpose only, the orderly and efficient extraction of wealth and surplus from the indigenous society. Such projects as it finances will be those that produce a realizable profit, a financial gain that can be siphoned off and transferred to the metropolis. While the colonial state controls the economic forces of society to an extent unknown in the West, it has no interest in developing this society except insofar as such development is immediately profitable. Such a state must inevitably thwart the efforts of any indigenous class to acquire and retain capital. A second characteristic of the colonial state is that it is imposed upon native societies from outside. Not being an outgrowth of indigenous society, the colonial state does not reflect or mediate the existing balance of power. Rather, it sets itself against all existing independent sources of power, subverting those that are pliable and destroying the rest.

This attitude is particularly apparent in the ways in which traditional patterns of authority are perverted by the appointment of Western-defined "tribal chiefs." These chiefs, found under all forms of "indirect rule," are used particularly as a means of controlling rural populations remote from the colonial state's urban power base. The existence and undoubted authority of these chiefs—usually drawn from the landowning classes—in no way negate the central power of the state. The terms under which they are appointed and maintained in power make them aware that they draw their authority from the state alone, not from their status in traditional precolonial society. Moreover, the favors they enjoy, their level of material wealth, and the Western education offered to their eldest children all serve to cut them off from the mass of the population, thereby increasing their dependence on the colonial state. After independence, such chiefs may form a significant element in the struggle for power, but they do not have the ability to take over the reins of government unaided (though their Western-educated sons may play a key mediating role).

In view of this inheritance, the application to postcolonial societies of concepts of class formation and class relations developed in the industrialized West is doubly hazardous. On the one hand, such remnants of traditional social organization as have not been eradicated by the colonial state will be precapitalist, if not feudal, and often based in kinship ties rather than individual wealth or class position. On the other hand, the form of the state established during the colonial era and persisting beyond independence is in no way a product of the society. It is an alien structure comprising a form of social organization in which real power lies elsewhere: in the metropolis. Third World social formations are therefore by definition contradictory and fragmentary, distortions of both traditional and modern Western forms. Marxist critics concerned with class analysis in the postcolonial world have also found their efforts hampered by the myth of an overall national unity precluding class divisions, which has commonly been fostered as an ideological justification for the national liberation struggle and the subsequent one-party postindependence state. James F. Petras, in an interesting critique,[14] points to ways in which the accumulation of capital by those in command of the state apparatus—generally dismissed simply as "corruption"—can be positive in giving the leaders a new freedom of action and opening up possibilities for development. He also delineates three "ideal types" of state formation arising from class alliances formed for capital accumulation, of which the neocolonialist model remains only one possibility. In this particular model—characteristic of many of the small states of independent black Africa—the income structure resembles an inverted pyramid, in which power and wealth remain largely in foreign hands, with some limited distribution to the local bourgeoisie but with virtually nothing filtering down to the mass of the work force. As a first alternative to this, Petras points out that certain military regimes in Latin America have been able, under dictatorial conditions, to minimize foreign control while holding the labor force in check, thereby increasing the wealth and power of the narrow bourgeois sector, which is then able to pursue a policy of "national development." Petras's third model, the "national popular" approach, of which he also finds examples in Latin America, is in a sense an inversion of the first, with limitations placed on both foreign and local bourgeois interests, so that wealth and power are largely redistributed to the mass of the working population. He admits, however, that such regimes—of which the first Perón government in Argentina, between 1945 and 1955, is an example—are unstable, both in their foreign relations and in the tenuousness of the class alliance between elements of the national bourgeoisie and workers.

Useful as these broad categorizations are, they still leave us with certain problems if we wish to define the class position of those Third World intellectuals—artists and administrators, writers and film makers—who are responsible for cultural production in the Third World. For this we need a consideration of the role and status of the petty bourgeoisie, a tenuous grouping that is not fully a class and resists precise definition even in Western society and that is, in Abdallah Laroui's words, "even less of a clearly defined class in a fragmented and heterogeneous society."[15] In Third World society such a grouping is a minority in relation to the mass of the peasantry, but it has a key mediating role, since it constitutes the only mode of entry into the modern economy for those who wish to leave the countryside and may indeed—given the numerical weakness of both the proletariat and the national bourgeoisie—represent a majority of the urban population. The petty bourgeoisie is by no means a unified force. Laroui, in his account of Arab social formation, describes it as "an aggregate of groups united by a set of shared values," [16] distinguished from the national bourgeoisie by its lack of real capital and from the proletariat by its possession of the "means of production."

But as Laroui makes clear, these means may comprise forms as divergent as "a piece of land, tools, a herd of animals, a monetary capital or an education." [17] For this reason, the general category of the petty bourgeoisie has doubtful coherence and only limited analytic value. But the specific subsection of the petty bourgeoisie that owes its position to its possession of an education—specifically, a westernized education—constitutes an elite with a crucial role in the operation of Third World societies. Despite the reservations of Marxist analysts like Petras, it is difficult to avoid the use of the concept of an elite when discussing class formation and cultural production in the Third World. Jock McCulloch, for example, in his study of Amilcar Cabral's political theory, talks sardonically of elite theory as being, like underdevelopment, an export from the West. [18] But elsewhere in his book, when he discusses the pattern of four social strata into which the African urban population of pre-independence Guiné can be divided, he observes that Cabral himself came from "an elite which numbered less than twenty." [19] Certainly, the term *elite* does usefully convey both the tiny size and the fragmentary, detached nature of the group. It is also worthwhile to recall Ali A. Mazrui's contention that, in Africa at least, the colonial impact has transformed the traditional basis of social stratification: "Instead of status based on, say, age, there emerged status based on literacy. Instead of classes emerging from the question, 'Who owns what?', class formation now responds to the question, 'Who knows what?' . . . The very process of acquiring aspects of the imperial culture came to open doors first of influence, and later of affluence itself." [20] While it is highly doubtful whether the educated elite can be said to constitute a distinctive social class, westernized education is the source of its particular claim to power.

The Western-Educated Elite

The reasons for the inheritance of power by the Western-educated elite at the moment of independence involve factors of several kinds. Firstly, the colonial state had demanded for its operation increasing numbers of clerks and bureaucrats and was therefore forced to develop policies promoting, or at least allowing, the westernized education of the increasing number of recruits needed to fill the lower ranks of the administration. Eventually the bilingual elite educated in this way—humiliated and frustrated in its everyday contact with the colonial power—came to form an opposition that was a kind of shadow image of the colonial state. Since the elite owed its position solely to its role within the colonial state, of which it was the product, its position at the time of independence was ambiguous. It was ideally placed to seize control, since it was the only group within the nation capable of manipulating the structures of authority bequeathed by the departing colonists. At the same time, the elite had no identity outside these structures—of the kind that would derive from personal wealth, commercial position, or ethnic status—and hence no means of instituting radical changes of the kind that might be expected in an ex-colonial state after independence, since any change that shifted power within the state would inevitably threaten the elite's own position. But the colonial state apparatus, designed to function as a highly developed mechanism of social control, proved to be an ideal power base. It stood above the bulk of society—to which it was not answerable—able to define territorial boundaries, regulate taxes, and control economic development. In the absence of independent counterbalancing forces, which had been largely contained or destroyed by the combination of foreign economic dominance and colonial rule, there could be no effective challenge to the proposition that the state and its new governing elite constituted the focus for economic development.

The prototype of the Western-educated elites were the *criollos*, or American-born Spaniards, who, after long years of being regarded and treated as second-rate citizens by their Iberian-born compatriots, formed the key element in the Latin American wars of liberation between 1810 and 1824. Their principal aspiration—which sets the pattern for subsequent native elites throughout the Third World—has been characterized as "substitution of Iberian dominance and preservation of the colonial heritage of political and social structures. Post-independence criollos to survive had to constrain social change, to prevent the independence movement from turning into a continuing revolution."[21]

The particular social status and role of the criollos, both before and after independence, is a reflection of the archaic nature and values of the Spanish empire in Latin America. Though native-born, they were essentially holders of state office or beneficiaries of state patronage; they may have aspired to ownership of the large estates that formed a key part of the heritage of Spanish colonialism, but they were not self-sufficient, independent settlers in the sense that immigrants and second-generation citizens of North America were. Their existence depended economically on the exploitation of the native American and Negro bulk of the population. For their own self-enrichment the criollos chose methods that increased their dependence on foreign—especially British—merchants and financiers, using their control of the state to enhance the spread of the huge estates growing crops for export, just as their Portuguese-descended equivalents in the newly independent Brazil propped up the plantation economy based on slave labor. In addition to their willingness to serve as the well-rewarded agents of foreign financial interests, the criollos also anticipated later native elites in their cultural policies and attitudes.

The criollos' situation was complicated by the large and increasingly important stratum of people of mixed descent, the mestizos and mulattoes, whose aspirations had to be satisfied, or at least contained. Education became one of the principal paths of upward social mobility for the mestizos and mulattoes who had been, in the local phrase, "whitened by money." But this education, for criollos, mestizos, and mulattoes alike, implied looking abroad for social models and displayed all the symptoms of cultural dependence: "As a bloc the foreign merchants represented what the newly liberated criollo elite considered superior and more enlightened cultures; they provided long isolated criollos a demonstration effect in their standard of living, dress, household furnishings, cuisine, in over-all life-style." [22]

Native elites elsewhere subsequently played a complex mediating role between the opposed cultures of the colonizer and the colonized similar to that of the criollos of Spanish America. The *ilustrados* of the Philippines, for example, have their origins as an elite in the Spanish educational reforms of 1863. These reforms afforded the sons of the prosperous Chinese, mestizo, and native families a solid Hispanic education, which widened their perceptions of the world but imposed a limiting frame to their values, so "they looked at their society and people through the prism of colonial culture." [23] Frustrated in their first aim of cultural assimilation, the ilustrados played a key part in the revolutionary movement that saw the end of Spanish rule. In Renato Constantino's view, the "irreversible gain" history will credit to them was "the acceptance by the people of the idea of equality and the concept of nationhood." [24] But when the movement to independence was preempted by U.S. intervention in 1898, the ilustrados were among the first to collaborate. Eventually they came to add political power to their commercial prosperity, emerging as a ruling elite. "The compromising attitude of the *ilustrados* was soon forgotten. They had now become symbols of success. Self-government could safely be granted to them. Moreover, the type of independence that was later 'granted' not only conformed to American policies; it was also a reflection of the nature of *ilustrado* leadership." [25]

In Calcutta, the headquarters of the East India Company and subsequently the capital of the British colonial administration in India, a similar Western-educated elite had emerged early in the nineteenth century, the so-called *bhadralok*, or "respectable people": "The *bhadralok* were drawn from the dominant Hindu castes who had served in the military and administrative offices of the Moghuls. Collaboration with foreign rule, secured mainly through their mastery of alien languages, formed part of their social and cultural heritage." [26] Accounts of the bhadralok elite stress the common aspiration for an English-language education either in Calcutta or in England itself, followed by white-collar employment at the bar or in the civil service. The most gifted of their number studied French, Hebrew, Latin, and Greek in addition to English, and all were thoroughly westernized in thought and culture. But though the bhadralok constituted an urban elite whose careers were focused on Calcutta, they retained links with rural Bengal, even though in many cases they possessed only small landholdings. They saw themselves not as an uprooted, alienated minority, then, but as a landed Bengali elite. As such, they applied prodigious intellectual efforts to the reshaping of indigenous culture, so as to produce what has become known as the Bengal Renaissance. Politically, however, they reflected "the essential ambiguity of all collaborating classes within Asian communities. . . . Their lack of an *independence* grounded economically in control of capital, or socially in links with the proletarian and peasant masses, strictly compromised their politics and distorted their ideology: despite initiating the anti-Colonial movement, the *bhadralok* ultimately failed to mount a radical challenge and transform Bengali society." [27]

Another remarkable Western-educated elite are the *assimilés,* consciously created by the French in West Africa from the middle of the nineteenth century onward as an elite that would be more attached to its French privileges than to its African identity. French forms of direct colonial rule, unlike British approaches, involved political assimilation, that is, the granting of full French citizenship—including the right to elect deputies to parliament in Paris—to selected groups of the native population. In Africa this reached its greatest extent in Senegal, which was the focal point for French domination of West Africa, and by 1936 citizenship rights had been granted to 78,000 Senegalese (out of a total of 80,000 Africans). Assimilation had a particular effect on the educational system, so that "in the second quarter of this century, black boys sat on their school benches from Dahomey to Dakar, from Conraky to the Congo, reciting their lessons in French: multiplication tables, irregular verbs and the now proverbial history lesson beginning 'Our ancestors, the Gauls, had fair hair and blue eyes.' " [28] The syllabus, which equated education with fluency in French, was in fact "designed to make the child think of himself as French, to admire the colonizing heroes of France (from Napoleon to Faidherbe and Lyauty), and to regard the heroes of African resistance to conquest, such as Al-Hadj Umar and Samory, as so many misguided brigands who impeded the flow of French benevolence and civilisation." [29]

The supreme product of the system is indeed the Senegalese poet, statesman, and member of the Académie Française, Léopold Sédar Senghor. But when Senghor and a number of other francophone intellectuals from Africa and the Antilles sought to rediscover their identity abroad, the movement they founded, Négritude, was an assertion of blackness, made, however, in the intellectual terms and language of the colonizer. Abiola Irele notes the parallel between this concept and European racist doctrines: "As an ideological movement, Négritude is one of the answers to such doctrines, and presents itself, in this light, indeed as a countermyth. But it is important to note that for Senghor, the answer does not consist in a systematic rejection of Western racist theories, but rather a modification of the terms in which they are set out, and in a redefinition of the very notion of race." [30] The limitations in political terms of this redefinition were strikingly revealed in the 1950s, when Senghor and the leaders of other nationalist movements in West Africa were offered a choice between total independence and continued association with France. Only Guinea chose to *demand* total independence; the others allowed it to be granted to them on French terms, which have left them bound, politically and economically as well as culturally, to metropolitan France.

Culture and National Identity   2

> *A national culture is the whole body of efforts made by a people in the sphere of thought to describe, justify, and praise the action through which that people has created itself and keeps itself in existence. A national culture in underdeveloped countries should therefore take its place at the very heart of the struggle for freedom which these countries are carrying on.*
>
> Frantz Fanon

The elites that emerged under colonialism at virtually all the key points of interaction between traditional societies and the West—in Alexandria, Buenos Aires, and Madras, as much as in Manila, Calcutta, and Dakar—are historically unique in terms of their westernization. They owe their power neither to initial wealth (though they may indeed *become* wealthy) nor to direct involvement in production or even ownership of the means of production (though the state they control is likely to become the nation's major economic force). They form a group which has the role of mediating the conflicting interests of both landowning classes and an emerging business class, but which does not owe its position directly to either (though family ties will probably link individuals to one or both of these classes). Their particular position vis-à-vis the West has been characterized by Cedric Robinson as constituting the "conduit through which the technical, political and commercial relations of the technologically sophisticated northern hemispheric people articulate with that vast majority of mankind which supports them materially and economically." These elites are also the stratum through which "the ideological, moral and philosophical traditions of Western civilisation have been transferred, at least superficially, to non-Western societies." [1]

Nationalism and Development

The style of nationalism adopted by the elite was conceived before independence as an opposition to colonialism, and it took Western political forms. It was in fact a search for political independence within a framework of foreign economic and ideological dominance. The concept of the nation was defined in the territorial terms of the colonial state, whose boundaries took no account of social or cultural groupings. The nationalists did not seek to revive a traditional form of society or to mobilize mass support for the independence movement in terms of ethnic identity—denigrated as "tribalism" by the colonizers. Instead, their ambition was to create a modern state, using concepts of democracy, elections, and political parties borrowed from the West. Even the underlying democratic definition of "one man, one vote" conceals a concept of Western origin: individualism.

This modern nationalism has shown the same dynamism as other social and cultural forms derived from the West, but it has done nothing to remedy the elite's inevitable limitations as a force for development and progress. Firstly, since the colonial state is founded on an unbridgeable gulf between rulers and ruled, by taking over the mechanisms of the colonial state, the elite separates itself from the mass of the people whom its nationalist impulse aims to serve. Such a state is designed not to develop the people but to hold them in check. Any move to give real power or representation to the people or to allow the emergence of political opposition parties is a weakening of the structures to which the elite owes its position. Secondly, in moving into the position of the colonial administration, the elite takes on the same subservient role vis-à-vis the Western metropolitan centers, for ultimate power in this structure of government rests not within the colonial state itself, but in the metropolis. The new elite that comes to control the postcolonial state can operate in a wide context only under foreign economic dominance, of which it now becomes the local agent.

This situation is reinforced by the effects of foreign aid. Since far more is extracted annually by the West from the Third World than is returned in the form of aid, the latter can be little more than a cosmetic device. As Pierre Jalée aptly puts it, "It is not the imperialist countries which aid the Third World, but the Third World which aids imperialism." [2] Moreover, even if there were a balance between aid and exploitation, the effect would still be disastrous, since it implies taking money from areas of Third World productivity, such as agriculture and mining, and returning it in the form of "aid" to be used by the westernized elite on prestige projects of "modernization," which are often largely irrelevant to the country's economic development and always carry the invitation to corruption. This is a theme spelled out by Gérard Chaliand, a participant in and observer of Africa's struggles for independence: "The political and social uses of foreign aid in tropical Africa make it an instrument of corruption, a basic neo-colonialist trait. Here it can be seen that aid aims at reinforcing a leadership group linked by self-interest to Western capitalism." [3] Even less can be said in favor of the military aid dispensed with such largesse by the United States to its client dictators in Latin America and elsewhere.

The political complicity of the elite in the economic system underpinning the imperialism from which the elite has claimed or received independence is strikingly illustrated by comparison with another distinctive group created by the colonial system, namely, the settler communities. Once the momentum of decolonization was under way, the old empires were dissolved with quite remarkable speed and with few if any disadvantages to the former colonizing powers. European economic imperialism could come to terms with the political demands of the emergent nationalist elites in most parts of Africa and Asia and still maintain the kind of economic dominance that first Great Britain and then the United States had exercised over Latin America for a hundred and fifty years. With few exceptions, Western-educated elites could move smoothly into place, without disturbing the world system—indeed, major confrontations came only where, as in Nigeria, colonialism had fostered particularly uneven development. By contrast, settler communities have always proved awkward for metropolitan states, since they refuse to accept a subordinate role in the world system, expecting and struggling, rather, to achieve metropolitan status. The process began with the independence of settlers in the United States, who have since been joined in the Western group of "core" nations by settler communities in Canada, Australia, and New Zealand. In the period of decolonization, the Belgians found themselves confronted by their settler communities in the Congo, the British by theirs in Rhodesia, and the French by the *pieds noirs* in Algeria. In each case the Western governments repudiated such communities, sometimes even to the extent of waging war on them.

But insistence that independence be granted only to a native majority was not an act of altruism on the part of the Western governments; rather, it was an example of sound economic sense. From the standpoint of international capitalism, settler communities are, in Arghiri Emmanuel's terms, "a dead weight—if not a parasitic and harmful element" and a "competitive and anarchic sector." The logic of the situation whereby the French first contained the National Liberation Front (FLN) and then fought those who claimed to want a "French Algeria" is clear in Emmanuel's terms: "If the partisans of 'French Algeria' had won, Algeria would have been much less French than she still is today, in spite of the profound breaches made by the revolution and the war. It was so that Algeria might remain as French as possible that [De Gaulle] fought the OAS [Organisation Armée Secrète—the movement within the French army opposing Algerian independence]." [4]

Here we see the central paradox of the postcolonial situation: the settlers, who, aware of their "historic ties," see themselves as part of Europe, are repudiated by Western capitalist interests, while the Western-educated elites, who define their identity in terms of independence from colonialism, are in fact incorporated into the capitalist world system. This progression, worked out in Africa over the past thirty years or so, merely echoes that which has evolved over a much longer period in Latin America. In all Third World countries caught in this way, the state is the crucial element: it is the only potential force for real social change, but at the same time it is "frozen" in an exploitative form, since its present situation is the source of profit and power for those who command it.

National Culture

Within the network of contradictions that characterizes the Third World, there is probably no more problematic area than that of culture. The artistic intelligentsia of Africa, Asia, and Latin America displays the tensions between the forces of westernization and tradition to a particularly intense degree. Even if they are driven to oppose the political and social policies of the ruling elite, they cannot cease to be a part of it, through either shared origins or achieved social status. In respect to the gulf between rulers and ruled, those concerned with culture, whether as politicians and intellectuals, organizers and administrators, or as writers, artists, and film makers, are inevitably closer to the rulers. Yet ultimately in postcolonial society, culture can only be valid if it is the product of individuals able and willing to work against their own narrow class interests.

The position of Third World artists is a unique one. Though often at odds with the ruling members of the elite to which they belong by virtue of their education, they are equally cut off from the mass of the people by the literary forms and language that they choose. Their position could hardly be more different from that of the traditional storyteller or craftsman, whose identification with his audience or clientele was direct and immediate. As Ousmane Sembene noted at the First Festival of Negro Arts at Dakar in 1965, "All of us who are writers are also people who have to some extent lost their roots." [5] A film maker, a radio or television producer, will be using a Western technology; a writer will often be employing the former colonizer's language, in which only a tiny minority of the population is literate. In both cases he or she will almost certainly be using formal structures derived from a foreign source, for all the basic forms of print literature, as well as those of the filmic narrative or television documentary report, are imported.

Perhaps the most valid criteria for the evaluation of work produced under these conditions are to be derived from the national liberation struggles in the Third World over the last thirty years or so. Africa is particularly fortunate in that two of its principal theorists of the national liberation struggle, Frantz Fanon and Amilcar Cabral, have both attributed to culture a key role and offered valuable insights into its priorities. As a starting point, Cabral in his lecture "National Liberation and Culture," delivered in New York in 1970, makes clear that the basis of culture—as of national liberation as a whole—must lie outside the narrow confines of the elite: "Without minimizing the positive contribution which privileged classes may bring to the struggle, the liberation movement must, on the cultural level just as on the political level, base its action in popular culture, whatever may be the diversity of levels of culture in the country." [6] Cabral's definition uses basically Marxist concepts and terminology, and he is at pains to stress the fact that culture "has as its material base the level of the productive forces and the mode of production," whose contradictions, manifested through the class struggle, are "the principal factor in the history of any human group" and "the true and driving power of history." [7] We have seen from Albert Memmi's account of colonization that one of its effects is the elimination of the colonized's culture. As a corollary of this, Cabral points out that "it is generally within the culture that we find the seed of opposition, which leads to the structuring and development of the liberation movement." In fact, for Cabral, "national liberation is necessarily an act of *culture,*" since

> a people who free themselves from foreign domination will be free culturally only if, without complexes and without underestimating the importance of positive accretions from the oppressor and other cultures, they return to the upward paths of their own culture, which is nourished by the living reality of its environment, and which negates both harmful influences and any kind of subjection to foreign culture. [8]

A fascinating assessment of what this process involves is to be found in Frantz Fanon's celebrated essay "On National Culture," contained in *The Wretched of the Earth.* Here Fanon singles out three separate stages: a concern primarily with the culture of the colonizing power; a return to an idealized view of the traditional culture; and a third stage of uniting with the people's struggle in an authentic way. Fanon's definitions are worth quoting at some length, beginning with his initial stage, when the power of attraction of the colonizer's culture is at its strongest:

> In the first stage, the native intellectual gives proof that he has assimilated the culture of the occupying power. His writings correspond point by point with those of his opposite numbers in the mother country. His inspiration is European and we can easily link up these works with definite trends in the literature of the mother country. This is the period of unqualified Assimilation. [9]

Fanon's second stage is one in which the native artist or intellectual attempts to reestablish his links with an abandoned traditional culture:

> In the second phase we find the native disturbed; he decides to remember what he is. . . . But since the native is not a part of his people, since he has only external relations with his people, he is content to recall their life only. Past

happenings of the bygone days of his childhood will be brought up out of the
depths of his memory; old legends will be reinterpreted in the light of a borrowed aestheticism and of a concept of the world which was discovered under
other skies.

In Fanon's third phase, which he calls "the fighting phase,"

the native, after having tried to lose himself in the people and with the people,
will on the contrary shake the people. Instead of according the people's lethargy
an honoured place in his esteem, he turns himself into an awakener of the
people; hence come a fighting literature, a revolutionary literature and a national literature." [10]

The great relevance of Fanon's analysis is not in doubt, though of course
any generalization that in this way divides a complex cultural process into just
three clearly differentiated stages is open to criticism. The three focal points
Fanon picks out are key areas of discussion, even if they cannot be taken to
represent the chronologically successive stages of a single development.

What Fanon's formulation perhaps underplays is the indivisibility of the
three stages, that is, the necessity of both an interaction with Europe and a
concern with local tradition. For many Third World countries, continuing
interplay with Europe provides a crucial and by no means wholly negative
thread. The example of Brazil can stand as a particularly clear example of
trends present to some extent throughout Latin America and continuing across
the divide of political independence. The Brazilian literary historian Afrânio
Coutinho offers a striking definition of the dynamic force that can stem from
the relationship between Europe and Latin America and the effort to create a
local tradition:

Starting with an original stock of notions that had been transplanted with the
first impulses of colonization, Brazilian cultural life went its way in relation to
European culture, sometimes repeating its forms, sometimes reinterpreting
them and adapting them to individual and social native conditions, sometimes
trying to turn its back on them in its anxiety to create a peculiarly Brazilian
tradition. But the persistence and strength of European intellectual influences,
the habit of looking to Europe in search of inspiration, became the fulcrum of
Brazilian mental life, which was marked by an extraordinary capacity for the
assimilation of foreign values. The very idea of Europe was the center of our
concentric waves of culture. [11]

If one had to pick one key aspect of this interplay, it would be that of drawing the Third World culture into the contemporary world, bridging the time
gap that so often exists to separate metropolis and satellite, the giver and the
receiver of cultural influence. In Brazil, for example, the birth of an authentic
national literature is usually dated from the 1920s, which was precisely a time

of strong European influence, typified by the Modern Art Week held in February 1922 in São Paolo. Likewise, it was the impact of surrealism that liberated the Caribbean and African poets of Négritude from the constraints of a borrowed language and enabled them to forge a new and wholly contemporary black poetry.

This sense of entering the present thanks to the assimilated influence of Europe contrasts strongly with the retreat into the past entailed in the confrontation with local tradition, which forms Fanon's second stage. The attempt at a reinsertion into tradition can be extremely difficult for an individual, and one of the central themes of the West African novels published over the last thirty years has been the destructive impact of westernization on an educated person who subsequently finds himself caught between two cultures.[12] Even when this crisis is mastered and becomes the subject of a successfully completed novel, a certain retreat into the past still inevitably seems involved. As Dorothy S. Blair writes in her study of the francophone African novel:

> It is rare to find traces of contemporary European innovations in the structure and style of this African novel in French: no suggestion of a Proust, of a James Joyce, not to mention a Robbe-Grillet or a Claude Simon. By setting out to be the faithful mirror of the African condition of the first half of the twentieth century, the French-African novel remains obstinately based on the French novel of the nineteenth century.[13]

Once more the West African experience can be seen as analogous with a slightly earlier tendency in Latin American literature, where a similar return to the past and to rural life had been attempted by a number of regionalist writers in the latter part of the nineteenth century and the first three decades of the twentieth. Like the francophone African novel, this is essentially a literature *about* tradition *for* a westernized audience. Its self-evident roots in European realist styles allow the customary lines of argument to be effortlessly stood on their head by Jorge Luis Borges in his essay "The Argentine Writer and Tradition": "The idea that a literature must define itself in terms of its national traits is a relatively new concept; also new and arbitrary is the idea that writers must seek themes from their own countries. . . . The Argentine cult of local colour is a recent European cult which the nationalists ought to reject as foreign."[14]

The caution is salutary, for any ostensible rejection of westernized culture in favor of a return to superficially understood traditional roots is hazardous after a period of colonization. As Terence Ranger has demonstrated, those who adopt this strategy "face the ironic danger of embracing another set of colonial inventions instead."[15] Certainly in Africa, much of what passes for "tradition" is

> the result of a conscious determination on the part of the colonial authorities to "re-establish" order and security and a sense of community by means of defin-

ing and enforcing "tradition." . . . The most far-reaching inventions of tradition in colonial Africa took place when the Europeans believed themselves to be respecting age-old African custom. What were called customary law, customary land-rights, customary political structure and so on, were in fact *all* invented by colonial codification.[16]

This reified tradition, which has little historical validity, since it was the product of colonial boundaries, laws, and classifications, continues to color much of the thinking about precolonial Africa. A sense of tradition may be a vital component of a national culture, but it is by no means easily attained, particularly by one whose thought processes have been shaped by a Western education. The kind of intellectual task that the reconstruction of the past after a period of colonization entails is spelled out clearly by the Filipino historian Renato Constantino, in his "Notes on Historical Writing for the Third World":

A people's history must rediscover the past in order to make it reusable. . . . The past should not be the object of mere contemplation if the present is to be meaningful. For if the past were viewed as a "frozen reality" it would either dominate and immobilize the present or be discarded as irrelevant to today's concerns. The past as a concrete historical reality must be viewed as an integral part of the process of unfolding total reality.[17]

Since not only the "new" notions of nationalism, political independence, and the nation-state but also the very definitions of tradition itself are shaped by Western concepts, Fanon's plea for a third stage of political commitment might seem self-evident. Yet even here there are traps for the unwary. At least as far as African leaders are concerned, seeking an alternative in Marxism also implies westernization, since, as Ali A. Mazrui points out, it is for the time being "a socio-linguistic impossibility" for an African to be a sophisticated Marxist without at the same time being substantially westernized. The basic Marxist texts are unavailable in African languages, and "no Africans are ever admitted to Soviet universities directly from some village compound."[18] Political leaders and theorists like Cabral and Fanon acquired their radical views abroad, and considerable care is needed in applying these views to Third World contexts. But such modernizing influences are vitally necessary, particularly in situations where national liberation takes the form of armed struggle. The dual need to draw on the local past while at the same time participating actively in the contemporary world is very clear, but its achievement remains elusive. Albert Memmi, stressing like Fanon the inseparability of cultural development from political advance, asserts that "the most urgent claim of a group about to revive is certainly the liberation and restoration of its language."[19] Certainly many of the paradoxes with which we are confronted in this study are to be found within language itself.

Language, Literature, and Theater

As we have seen, the concept of the nation-state is one that has been inherited from Europe, and a part of this inheritance is the particular role attributed to language. Richard M. Morse has pointed out the inextricable link between definitions of language and national identity: "In nineteenth century Europe the linguistic concerns of the intelligentsia gave predominance to the languages of that continent and how they revealed the 'genius' of nations considered to be world-historical. The identification of 'language' and 'nation' became so strong as to shape the self-image of peoples, ambitions of leaders, and political demarcations of the continent." [20]

Such an identification could not be other than problematic—though to a varying extent—for all colonized countries, beginning with those Latin American states that achieved their political independence in the first quarter of the nineteenth century. Here the crux of the problem was the necessity to express the distinctive identity of the new nation in the language that had been inherited from the colonizer—Spanish or Portuguese. The search for an authentic national language capable of supporting a national literature was enormously long, but the fact that the new economically dominant powers—Britain for most of the nineteenth century and the United States since World War I—used a different language eventually allowed the Spanish and Portuguese languages to become a source and focus of independence and identity. Even so, most critics see the literatures of Spanish America and Brazil as emerging from provinciality only long after political independence, with the Hispanic American modernism of the 1880s and the Brazilian modernism of 1920. Significantly, it was not until the turn of the century that, as George Pendle tells us, reform "had begun to acquire a more radical meaning. Equality in law, free elections, and universal education would not be enough. There was a growing demand for the redistribution of land, and then for the fixing of minimum wages, and for social insurance. Reformers were becoming increasingly insistent, too, that the hold of the foreigner on the national economy must be broken." [21]

It is instructive to compare the delayed growth of this elite culture with the emergence of a national literature in the United States, where political independence was matched by economic independence. The title of Larzer Ziff's book on the generation of writers who, in the fifteen years before the outbreak of the Civil War in 1861, established American literature as "a distinctive way of imagining the world" is itself highly significant: *Literary Democracy: The Declaration of Cultural Independence in America*. In his analysis of Poe, Emerson, Hawthorne, Thoreau, Whitman, and Melville, Ziff shows the close connections between the emergence of the literature they produced and the development of society as a whole. The shift to the new idea that literature was "the voice of the latent forces of the land," which these writers' work illustrates, had to be preceded by "a redefinition of American society," and this redefinition needed a significant economic development to accompany the larger political one: "In the 1820s and 1830s the growth of the factory system produced two new social classes, the industrial capitalists and the factory workers. Strikingly, the major writers came from the economic groups that were the most threatened by the new classes." The result was not a simple opposition but a complex interaction. "The same commercial and industrial developments that dispossessed the classes from which the writers came also provided them with improved means of printing and circulating what they wrote, as well as a widening number of countrymen who had both the knowledge and leisure to read what they wrote." [22]

This complex interplay between an emerging generation of writers and a context of wider economic and political developments is usually lacking in the Third World. While British rule cannot be held responsible for the complexity of India's linguistic problems (some 845 separate languages or dialects were reported in the 1951 census), elsewhere in Asia the colonial era has bequeathed many potentially explosive entanglements of language, religion, education, and status. In Africa it is only in the Muslim north that we find a single unifying language—Arabic—which despite its considerable variations in dialect can to some degree constitute a focus of independence and a rich and viable alternative to the inherited language of the colonizer. South of the Sahara we find an unbridgeable gulf between European and traditional languages. English and French may serve a certain unifying function—as, say, the languages in which a conference on the linguistic problems of Africa may be held—but they remain administrative languages, and their application outside official life remains limited. They are alien to the mass of the people, and, as Abiola Irele puts it in the best discussion of the subject, none of them is able "to carry fully with it the reality of African experience as it exists today. . . . The new literature that is being expressed in them, for all its value and significance, must be seen for this reason, from the African point of view, to be placed in a most ambiguous, not to say precarious situation." [23]

The amount of skill, energy and persistence that has gone into shaping an African literature in European languages is undeniable, but such work is by definition inaccessible to the masses, and it has the added effect of relegating traditional literatures to a marginal position. African writers working in European languages are not in fact bringing modernizing influences and new sources of knowledge to their fellow countrymen, since their readership is, by definition, limited to precisely those whose linguistic abilities allow them immediate access to this knowledge. In truth, as Irele points out, they are merely "carrying over into the European language a whole stock of symbols derived from the African environment," [24] and so the extent to which they are thereby truly enriching these European languages remains, in many cases, doubtful.

In terms of literary expression, there is no single, universal way in which these contradictions of language can be overcome in the foreseeable future. One personal response that may have wider application, however, is that of the Kenyan novelist Ngugi wa Thiong'o. He began his writing career as "James Ngugi," writing in English, but after Africanizing his name in 1970 he began, toward the end of the decade, to write drama and fiction in Gikuyu. By translating his work into English and Kiswahili and encouraging translations into other Kenyan languages, Ngugi is today working toward the creation of a national culture in which indigenous languages play a full part. The political significance of this use of African languages is clear from the reaction of the Kenyan government to this new and vital interaction between an intellectual and the peasant masses. Though his work in Gikuyu is no more overtly political in content than his earlier work in English was, Ngugi was detained without trial for a year in 1977–78, has been prevented from resuming his post as professor of English at Nairobi University, and at present lives in exile.[25]

Even more crucial for future film making than the establishment of the novel was that of a European-style theater. By the beginning of the twentieth century, many local traditions of popular drama had already declined as a result of social changes. In India, for example, "theatre and dance had lost their standing and become a domain of the degraded castes, the occupation of prostitutes. So strong had become the association between the performing arts and the prostitute that measures to combat prostitution seemed likely, for a time, to eradicate what was left of Indian drama, dance and music."[26]

Other popular traditions of dramatic performance did not lend themelves to modern adaptation, however. In black Africa it was well into the twentieth century before theater separated itself from religious ritual, as had occurred in the European tradition as early as Aeschylus. Thus Ola Balogun, himself a dramatist and film maker, observes that

> to speak of the "performing arts" is in a sense a misnomer, since this term is understood in a very different manner in other societies. Perhaps it would be more appropriate to speak of ritual or folk performances or of communicative arts in the African setting, in view of the fact that one does not have in mind theatrical or other entertaining displays performed for the benefit of a passive public, but ceremonies of a social or religious nature into which dramatic elements are incorporated.[27]

The introduction of European-influenced drama was, moreover, initially limited to the urban elites. In the Arab world, in Arlette Roth's view, the appearance of the need for dramatic expression "probably has to be linked to the irruption of Western civilisation," since "theatre was unknown in classical Arabic literature. Though in certain literary genres such as the 'maqāma,' there are dramatic elements, these have never detached themselves or developed to form a distinct dramatic genre."[28] Theater in the modern sense, then, first appeared in the Arab world in Syria during the 1850s—with a translation of Molière into Arabic—and during the latter part of the nineteenth century Syrian émigrés introduced theater into Egypt. But there it remained an imported form, quite distinct from any popular folk tradition and largely derivative of European models, and so could offer pioneer Egyptian film makers no roots for a viable dramatic form that would relate directly to a popular audience.

Western theater was introduced into China even later. There, the first experiments were heavily influenced by Japanese borrowings from the West, and indeed the beginnings of a modern theater movement can be dated to 1907, when a group of Chinese students in Tokyo (where Dr. Sun Yat-sen then had his headquarters) staged a version of Alexandre Dumas's *La Dame aux camélias*. This production was imitated in Shanghai the same year, but it was not until after the overthrow of the Manchus in 1911 that the new ideas of drama began, in a limited way, to establish themselves:

> The new theatre commanded attention as a political and social propaganda medium in these early years, but no significant Chinese playwright appeared to develop it further, and production methods were rudimentary. A play would be prepared, often borrowing freely from other literary sources, and arranged in a number of scenes. It was then presented to the actors, who were relied upon to pull the story together on the stage. Although the substance of the dialogue was decided on beforehand, there was a good deal of improvisation.[29]

This style of performance by students and amateurs for a Western-educated urban audience was common in India, too. But there, as S. Theodore Baskaran has shown, the influence was gradually diffused by traveling groups of actors who shaped a popular form of commercial drama in which mythological subjects were treated with songs and rough comedy. Baskaran traces a continuity between such groups and the Tamil-language sound cinema of South India, which took over the traveling groups' performers and song writers, turned the primitive rural theaters into cinema halls, and prolonged the current of nationalist sentiment that had made itself felt initially within the crude popular drama of the itinerant performers.[30]

Early Chinese cinema shared the confusion of styles to be found in early modern drama in China, for example, in the continuing practice of assigning male actors to play female roles in otherwise realistically intended scenes. But after the upheaval of the May Fourth Movement of 1919 there was an increasing identity between stage and screen, as the new dramatists who emerged in the 1920s and 1930s became heavily involved in the most exciting period of Chinese cinema, between 1931 and 1937, when numerous important left-wing film productions were made in Shanghai.

Though modern theater was slower to establish itself in black Africa, there too it developed political importance as well as popular appeal. The interaction of local traditions, colonial influences, and political aspirations is well illustrated by the career of the Nigerian Hubert Ogunde, a number of whose plays were filmed in the late 1970s and early 1980s. Ogunde began producing as an amateur in a missionary context, as a student teacher and choir master, and his work shows a succession of Western influences. But as a child Ogunde had performed in the Alarinjo Theater (the classical Yoruba theater, in which the players are masked), the influence of which can be seen in his lifelong devotion to researching Yoruba traditions of music and dance. Moreover, he first achieved widespread fame in 1945 with an anticolonial piece, *Strike and Hunger*. His concern to promote a national culture is such that a recent Nigerian critic of his work has claimed that "through his theatre Ogunde was a leading figure in the nationalist movement." [31]

Cinema and Capitalism   3

When one talks of cinema, one talks of American cinema. The influence of cinema is the influence of American cinema, which is the most aggressive and widespread aspect of American culture throughout the world. . . . For this reason, every discussion of cinema made outside Hollywood must begin with Hollywood.

Glauber Rocha

As a modern form of communication, cinema has characteristics that set it off from earlier, traditional forms. Oral communication is universal, and its forms are indigenous, having grown out of specific cultures in which they are rooted historically. Most advanced societies have their own culturally specific forms of written communication, which, even if scripts or alphabets are imported, have usually evolved over hundreds of years. This situation is no longer true, however, when we talk of a modern medium of communication like the cinema. Though now widely distributed throughout the world, the cinema is the product of only a limited number of Western countries at a particular recent point in their historical development. For all Third World countries, then, film is an imported form of communication. Moreover, whatever cinema may have become with the passing of time, its emergence cannot be ascribed solely to artistic aspiration or disinterested scientific endeavor. Unlike the later systems of radio and television broadcasting, the cinema has not been a tool or direct expression of the state: as a "free enterprise" system, its inception and development are closely tied to the profit motive as it is expressed in and through Western capitalism.

The Organization of Film Production

As a product of Western capitalism, the cinema has passed through three broad stages of development as far as the organization of its production is concerned. It emerged in Europe in the 1890s, at a time of small-scale industry. In France, for example, where film was first industrialized and given a world role, Alfred Cobban notes that out of 1,100,000 workshops, 1,000,000 had fewer than 5 employees and only 600 employed over 500.[1] During this period competitive capitalism was at its height, and early film companies fought strenuously to control local and international markets, for despite its modest artisanal beginnings, the cinema saw itself immediately in relation to a worldwide market. Within months of its invention, the cinema was using the whole world as a location for filming and as a source of box office revenue.

The large-scale industrialization of cinema was begun in France by Charles Pathé around 1908, and it reached its high point during World War I with the emergence of the Hollywood studio system. In the postwar period, cinema shared in a general economic move from simple competition to the establishment of monopoly control. The major Hollywood companies, organized as vertically integrated companies uniting production, distribution, and exhibition interests, collaborated to order and control the U.S. domestic market and to exclude outsiders. Their monopolistic practices were allowed—even on occasion encouraged, as under Roosevelt's National Recovery Administration in the 1930s—by the U.S. government.[2]

The Hollywood monopoly system lasted until the 1950s, when it began to crumble in the face of competition from television. After a long period of uncertainty, a fresh definition of film emerged as production companies became enmeshed in huge mass entertainment and leisure service conglomerates. Now receipts from the cinema release of a film are characteristically seen as merely part of an overall package that includes the sale of rights for network and cable television screenings, subsidiary rights to novelization, books about the making of the film, television spin-offs, soundtrack recordings and cassettes, commercially retailed videotapes, and merchandizing tie-ins such as T-shirts, toys, games, comics, and so forth.

The effect of such successive redefinitions of film and reorganizations of production and distribution practices has been to keep Western film interests always a step ahead of potential Third World competitors. By the time some non-Western producers had mastered the basic artisanal technology of film, Hollywood had attained levels of industrially organized production with which no other country could hope to compete. And now that several countries of the Third World have shown themselves able to reach and maintain similar levels and feed a weekly audience in the traditional Hollywood manner, the U.S. film industry has once again redefined the nature and mode of its product's exploitation, attaining levels of investment in individual films (and the attendant package of subsidiary products) that no Third World country can possibly match.

It is the peculiarity of film as a commodity that is bought and sold which has defined the structure of the film industry. Just about all the financial outlay in film production goes into the making of the master negative and the first print. This is not simply the difference between development costs (leading to the prototype of, say, a car) and production costs (of each individual car). In film, all that is required for distribution is a replica—a print costing just a few hundred dollars, even if the production costs have amounted to millions—and it is this mechanical reproducibility of film that is the fundamental source of profit in cinema. The system adopted by Hollywood from the 1920s, when the world market for films began to be systematically exploited, was firmly based on this principle. Production costs were fixed at a level allowing them to be recouped in the U.S. domestic market (the largest and most profitable in the world). Prints sold in the non-Western world therefore yielded almost pure profit, allowing prices to be adjusted so as to ensure the total control of the market. To take an analogy that is in no way exaggerated for the 1920s, it was like being able to sell an imported Rolls Royce for less than the cost of the cheapest locally produced car and still make virtually a 100 percent profit.

The film industry has a three-part structure—production, distribution, and exhibition—but the balance of power between the three is unequal. The producer is forced to cede rights in his film to the distributor, since he needs a distribution guarantee to raise the risk capital. The distributor does not, however, need to yield these rights in turn to the exhibitor, since the latter needs only a regular flow of assorted films on short-term hire. Power in the film industry therefore resides in the distribution company, which, as a purely financial organization, can be located anywhere in the world: it is an intermediary stage not bound geographically to either the studios where the films are produced or the cinemas where they are exhibited. U.S.-controlled distribution companies clearly have no interest in fostering the development of rival film production industries anywhere in the Third World. But even a distribution company controlled by local Third World capital is in no way tied to local production. Able to operate profitably with imported films, such a distributor is likely to be hostile to local film production, since a change in audience tastes would disturb the profitability of his operation. This is a fact often ignored by Third World governments who have taken steps to nationalize the local film industry—that is, to take over production facilities and film theaters—and then found that nationalization is meaningless if power over distribution lies in other, foreign (or foreign-controlled), hands.

Just as the industry underwent several transformations, so too the product itself was radically transformed in the late 1920s. Until that time films were silent (though music of some kind was generally played in the theater) and as such were virtually the ideal capitalist product: infinitely reproducible and having the whole world as their market. The product had a universal appeal, for, at its best, silent cinema could be appreciated by any audience anywhere. As a recent Cuban documentary shows, a Chaplin short can still, even fifty years after it was made, have an immediate impact on a peasant in a remote village who has barely heard of the cinema before. Almost everywhere in the non-Western world, then, the first experience of cinema was an experience of imported silent films. In this way Hollywood introduced to a whole range of societies a new concept: entertainment—that is, a form of performance quite distinct from religious ceremony or ritual, produced by professionals for an undifferentiated mass audience that pays for its pleasure.

From the 1920s to the 1950s—across the synchronous-sound divide— Hollywood continued to offer a product calculated to appeal to a universal audience, though made with the U.S. domestic market specifically in mind. An excellent definition of popular Hollywood movies has been offered by Victor Perkins:

> None of them makes extensive demands on the spectator's intellect. The dialogue and action of each of them is fully understandable without specialized knowledge of political mechanisms, sociological jargon, philosophical concepts or historical facts. None of them employs a form so radically new as to require a substantial readjustment of the spectator's attitude. . . . Where particular knowledge is required—then it is part of the common knowledge of the common man. The spectator does not have to work for his pleasure.[3]

It is this accessibility of the Hollywood movie that allowed U.S. companies to maintain their hold over world distribution even after technological advance and changed market conditions led to the creation in the United States of a radically new product: film with synchronized dialogue. This development gave the erstwhile fully international medium of film a quite new identity, enmeshed in vernacular languages and nascent nationalism. Linguistic barriers, hitherto characteristic only of print and publishing empires, now began to operate in the case of film as well. As a result, although all the impetus for the change-over to sound came from the West, the ability to offer films in local languages, and particularly with local songs and dances, allowed Asian, Latin American, and Egyptian producers to capture the attention of local audiences. Countries with the necessary industrial base began in the mid-1930s to establish the infrastructure for a film industry on the Hollywood model—studios and laboratories, dubbing and editing facilities—though stock and equipment continued for the most part to be imported. In general, however, the result was a commercial cinema destined only for the local populace (and for a few neighboring countries sharing the same language), a confection designed for immediate consumption and with no aspirations beyond that of entertaining its limited audiences. Hollywood's world preeminence remained unchallenged.

Capitalism as a World System

To understand the international development of cinema, it is necessary to see it in the wider context of the world system of capitalism. The notion that capitalism as an economic system seeks its markets worldwide and hence has a global impact has long been commonplace. What is more recent is the assertion that capitalism is therefore analyzable only on a global scale and that the analysis of any of the separate parts of the system—individual capitalist states, for example—that ignores the relationship with the whole is fundamentally inadequate. Such an assertion would once have seemed nonsensical, since both liberal and Marxist approaches tacitly or explicitly assumed that capitalist development was a stage through which all countries would and should pass, and in any case, attention was focused almost exclusively on the more developed countries. Marx himself, in the preface to *Capital,* wrote that "the country that is more developed industrially only shows, to the less developed, the image of its own future."[4]

From this older perspective, individual countries could reasonably be analyzed individually, with studies of the industrially more advanced allowing the plotting of the stages of planned development for their less fortunate neighbors. Modern theorists such as Baran and Sweezy, however, introduce a new note, which breaks with the assumptions of classical Marxism but accounts more closely for the observable facts of developmental change since Marx's day. For Baran and Sweezy, the development of the advanced capitalist countries can only be at the expense of the less advanced, with whom they are locked in a single economic system: "Only a few countries—most of western Europe (including Britain), Japan, Canada, Australia, New Zealand, possibly South Africa—can conceivably follow in the footsteps of the United States. In the rest of the capitalist world scores of colonies, neo-colonies and semicolonies are doomed to remain in their degraded condition of underdevelopment and misery. For them the only road forward leads straight out of the capitalist system."[5] This relationship has been elaborated by a succession of highly individual (and on occasion mutually contradictory) analysts, among whom are Andre Gunder Frank, Immanuel Wallerstein, Arghiri Emmanuel, and Samir Amin. Their work has been the subject of much specialist debate, but a number of the key assumptions of these theorists of what Frank aptly calls "the development of underdevelopment" have a particular relevance to any consideration of the relationship between Third World film making and the West.

The first of these assumptions is that the developed and underdeveloped worlds are indissolubably united. Frank prefaces his study of *Capitalism and Underdevelopment in Latin America* by stating his personal conviction that "it is capitalism, both world and national, which produced underdevelopment in the past and which still generates underdevelopment in the present."[6] He elaborates this view forcefully in the opening essay of the book:

Economic development and underdevelopment are the opposite faces of the same coin. Both are the necessary result and contemporary manifestation of internal contradictions in the world capitalist system. Economic development and underdevelopment are not just relative and quantitative, in that one represents more economic development than the other; economic development and underdevelopment are relational and qualitative, in that each is structurally different from, yet caused by its relationship with, the other. Yet development and underdevelopment are the same in that they are the product of a single, but dialectically contradictory, economic structure and process of capitalism.[7]

If we apply these insights to the cinema, three factors of crucial importance emerge. Firstly, the situation of the countries of the Third World cannot be adequately understood on a country-by-country basis. A consideration of the whole pattern of film commerce in the capitalist world is essential if the mechanisms in operation are to be seen with real clarity. Secondly, there are not two distinct sets of problems, one set relating to Third World cinema and the other concerned with film production in the West. If Hollywood's distribution dominance has stifled the growth of Third World film making, its prosperity has increasingly been made possible only by foreign (including Third World) box office receipts. Thirdly, in all accounts of film production outside the United States, the extent to which the tastes of local audiences have been shaped by foreign imports must be borne in mind. Here the case of Brazil as analyzed by Paulo Emilio Salles Gomes can stand for all Third World cinemas: "During the three generations in which film was the principal form of entertainment, cinema in Brazil was North American and, to a lesser extent, Brazilian. American cinema so saturated the market and occupied so much space in the collective imagination . . . that it seemed to belong to us."[8]

In Frank's account of underdevelopment, the crucial mechanism of exploitation is the chain of interlocking relationships between "metropolis" and "satellite," extending from the principal capitalist centers to regional centers, from regional to local centers, and eventually down to the bottom of the ladder of exploitation, the landless peasant. This formulation, pointing to the universality of exploitation and the difficulty of any individual satellite resisting the power of the metropolis, underlines the virtual impossibility of any single industry in the Third World overcoming, unaided, well-organized and coordinated exploitation by a developed metropolitan center. Only barriers that the state alone can erect—quotas, tariff controls, exchange regulations, and the like—can give a nascent industry any chance of survival.

Thus in the Third World, the development of a national cinema can be a matter only of state policy, not of individual effort, and even here the scope for protection may be limited. Moreover, film fits awkwardly into the state's institutional priorities: it cannot be seen as a governmental achievement in modernization (like the building of a dam or industrial complex), nor is it an aspect of traditional culture, to be promoted internationally along with, say, local carpet making or rural crafts. Films that are not mere imitations of Western styles are all too often socially critical, exploring the human problems rather than the governmental achievements in a developing society. For Third World rulers, who are often Western-educated and always sensitive to the image of their country overseas, the output of a local film industry is the last type of product to be advertised abroad. On the rare occasions when governments have become culturally involved with film (as in India with the National Film Development Corporation), the result is usually the creation of a hybrid product—part-indigenous, part-westernized—that no longer corresponds to local audience tastes. More frequently, Third World governments have simply seen cinema as a source of revenue, through taxes on film imports and box office receipts (often at levels of up to 40 percent), and have ignored the need to offer production support at home and promotion abroad.

Also of considerable interest for an understanding of the development of non-Western cinema is Wallerstein's development of Frank's theoretical model through the addition of a third structural position. If Wallerstein's "core" and "periphery" echo Frank's concepts, the "semiperiphery" is a new category, which Wallerstein sees as necessary for the smooth political working of the capitalist system: "The world-economy as an economy would function every bit as well without a semiperiphery. But it would be far less *politically* stable, for it would mean a polarized world-system. The existence of the third category means precisely that the upper stratum is not faced with the *unified* opposition of all the others because the *middle* stratum is both exploited and exploiter." [9]

This third category, the semiperiphery, helps to explain a seeming anomaly in the one-way flow of film and television material, that is, those Third World countries, such as Egypt and Mexico, that are regional film exporters. Their status stems precisely from the dual situation of exploiter/exploited, which Wallerstein attributes to the semiperiphery. In order to develop a large-scale national film production, a country needs a secure domestic distribution base with well-developed exhibition circuits. Without this, the possibility of a profitable return on investment in film production does not exist. But the very existence of such a base means that the country is more than ever vulnerable to imports from abroad, unless—like present-day India—it can produce on its own the many hundreds of films needed each year to feed such exhibition outlets. With an output of between, say, forty and a hundred films a year, it cannot supply all its own needs and therefore cannot set up effective barriers against foreign—especially Hollywood-distributed—films. But these latter do nothing to support the creation of a *national* film culture: they merely create an audience for more imported foreign films.

Film Distribution in the Colonial Era

Cinema reached the non-Western world during the period of colonialism. As the Tunisian critic Ferid Boughedir points out, it can therefore be seen to have a very definite social role, namely,

> to supply a cultural and ideological justification for the political domination and economic exploitation. . . . The cinema, just like education, archeology, books and newspapers, conspired in the falsification of reality whereby the colonizer was a technician, a man of progress, from a superior culture and civilisation, while the native was a primitive, incapable of technical progress or of mastering his passions, the next best thing to a wild beast (even if he could on occasion be "proud and generous").[10]

Films produced on location by European or North American firms in no sense present a true rendition of the social realities of the countries in which they are shot. Just as European traders sought agricultural produce and raw materials from the colonies, and specialist reporters hunted for marketable stories of riot, flood, famine, and earthquake, so too Western film makers looked only for exploitable landscapes, exotic mountains and deserts, picturesque extras, and of course—like the subsequent tourist industry—sunshine. There are examples of imperialist rhetoric to be found in the 1930s and 1940s film production of most ex-colonial powers, the bulk of them concentrating on their European-born heroes, depicted as dedicating or sacrificing themselves to the good of Asians or Africans who are seen from a totally paternalistic perspective. A stance untroubled by any questioning of European dominance is common to all such works, which fully deserve the strictures of Third World critics.

But this use of location filming constituted no more than a minor facet of the interaction between Western cinema and the colonial world, though the caricature of local life and customs is highly indicative of the West's inherent sense of uncomprehending superiority. The major concern of the European— and later, Hollywood—film companies was to set up structures of distribution and exhibition that would allow the most profitable marketing of Western films. There were two broadly separable strategies adopted, both common to virtually all colonial territories in which films were distributed, and now seen most clearly in black Africa, which still largely lacks an indigenous film production. The first strategy, which stems directly from Lumière's initial marketing approach, is the showing of recent and prestigious films in modern air-conditioned cinemas charging admission prices so high as to limit the audience to European expatriates and members of the westernized elites. Here, cinema forms just one part of that wave of cultural influences, ranging from imported wines and cheeses to airmailed magazines and video cassettes, that serve to separate the elite from the masses. Like the introduction of television transmission in a context where a television set costs more than a peasant family's entire annual cash income, cinema in this form can only enhance social divisions and constitute yet one further aspect of the ideological control of native elites—a key feature of neocolonialism.

The second strategy, which also continues into the present day, is the showing of imported films to a mass audience. The product is generally the cheapest and shoddiest available, reaching the very limit of whatever is allowed by local censors with regard to the depiction of sex and violence. The fact that the old staple diet of Hollywood B-movies has now been largely superseded by cheap Hindu melodramas and Hong Kong karate films in no way changes either the way the system operates or the identity of the ultimate beneficiaries. Such films are seen by their distributors as a purely commercial product, with no attention paid to cultural values, and it is particularly galling to Third World film makers that it is a cinema of this sort that continues to block access to their own national cinema screens.

It is usual for outside observers to take a wholly negative view of film viewing of this kind. An example, taken almost at random, is Alphonse Quenum's account of the unsophisticated mass audience in 1968 in Cotonou (the leading town of what was then Lower Dahomey and is now Benin). The two movie theaters in town invariably presented

> films which, needless to say, are not in the least adapted to local culture, and, in this domain, the word *education* is not even whispered by the civil servants of the Ministry of Education. The movie houses are practically stormed by people of all social categories, especially by a mass of semi-illiterate viewers who use no critical appreciation on the films. The cinema has become a place where they can release pent-up tensions. It is truly surprising to see a whole section of the audience jump and scream every time the hero of some western punches his rival. Doubtless they find some satisfaction here, but it nevertheless remains a socio-cultural problem.[11]

This classic negative account of the consumption of mass culture—which significantly makes no attempt to probe what might be positive in the "release of pent-up tensions"—takes too simplistic a view of how films are read by their audiences, as the accounts by Third World film makers of their childhood viewing reveal.

Three African examples show the range of reaction. Some may draw inspiration from consciously positive depictions of blacks on the screen: the Nigerois film director Djingarey Maiga, for example, was first impelled toward cinema by the role played by Sidney Poitier in Stanley Kramer's classic liberal film *The Defiant Ones*.[12] Others may look back on the experience of moviegoing as a time of cultural alienation. Here we may quote the Ethiopian-born film maker Haile Gerima, whose parents were teachers in the provincial town of Gondar. As a child in the 1960s he was drawn unquestioningly to such heroes as John Wayne, Elvis Presley, and Doris Day, provided by the Holly-wood movies that dominated the local circuits:

> It is as if you accept the heroes and stories of Western society, not voluntarily, but because of the social and political forces you are caught up in. In fact, as kids, we tried to act out the things we had seen in the movies. We used to play cowboys and indians in the mountains around Gondar. . . . We acted out the roles of these heroes, identifying with the cowboys conquering the indians. We didn't identify with the indians at all and we never wanted the indians to win. Even in Tarzan movies, we would become totally galvanized by the activities of the hero and follow the story from his point of view, completely caught up in the structure of the story. Whenever Africans sneaked up behind Tarzan, we would scream our heads off, trying to warn him that "they" were coming.[13]

But even films with negative cultural values can be given a positive reading. Here, the case of Ousmane Sembene is of particular relevance, for he records that he received his key revelation of the power of cinema from a fascist-inspired documentary. It was Jesse Owens's exploits at the Berlin Olympics, as depicted in Leni Riefenstahl's *Olympiad,* that helped shape Sembene's future career, and this film, in which for the first time the young people of Sembene's generation saw a black beating the whites, became *the* film for them.[14]

The depiction of cultural stereotypes, whether of blacks or whites, is highly ambiguous, and certainly if we look back at the response of colonial settlers and administrators to the distribution of films in territories forming part of the European empires in the 1920s and 1930s, we find an immense unease. Far from applauding the "positive" values of an imperially inspired cinema, they were strident in their condemnation of the ways in which West-ern society and its values were depicted, particularly in Hollywood films. To counteract this influence, the Imperial Conference of 1926 proposed that mea-sures should be instituted to ensure that "a larger and increasing proportion of the films exhibited throughout the Empire should be Empire productions."[15]

One result of this proposal was the setting up of the Indian Cinematograph Committee in 1927–28, which launched a detailed investigation of the Indian film industry, some fifteen years after Dadasaheb Phalke had made the first Indian feature, *Raja Harischandra* (1913). Their report is of major interest, since it surveys the early years of the only important cinema to emerge in a colonized country. In his opening statement, the committee's chairman, the South Indian lawyer Diwan Bahadur T. Rangachariar, rejected any notion that they were called upon to "find ways and means for tightening censorship and thereby help the British industry against films from elsewhere, notably Amer-ica."[16] Instead, the committee showed a keen awareness of the realities of world film distribution, particularly the power of Hollywood: "The Indian market is such a negligible factor to America (yielding not more than half of one percent of her cinema revenue) that if she retaliates the Indian film trade is bound to suffer. India gets nearly eighty percent of her imported films from America." [17] Ignoring imperial preference, the committee laid particular stress on the need for measures to foster *Indian* film production, explicitly refusing to differentiate between Western films from different sources: "Unlike the other parts of the Empire, the bulk of the cinema-going public in this country are Indians. . . . American civilisation is as much Western civilisation to them as British civilisation. Both are foreign. . . . If too much exhibition of American films in the country is a danger to the national interest, too much exhibition of other Western films is as much a danger." [18] Unfortunately, the committee's spirited defense of Indian production and its well-reasoned set of concrete proposals were ignored by the Indian colonial government.

Arghiri Emmanuel has argued that the interests and concerns of settler communities and local administrators are quite distinct from those of international capitalism. [19] Certainly in the case of cinema, profitable exploitation by foreign-based distribution companies took preference over the ideological qualms of colonial administrators. In many parts of the colonial world, highly profitable European-owned distribution systems were set up, and in Africa— the one part of the world to escape the attentions of Hollywood exporters until the 1960s—some of these systems persisted far beyond formal independence. The best documented example is the tight monopolistic hold exercised by just two French companies, COMACICO and SECMA (themselves subsidiaries of Monaco-based holding companies), over the market in francophone West Africa. [20] The territory they covered until the early 1970s embraced the fourteen states of what had previously been French West and Equatorial Africa, with a total population somewhat larger than that of metropolitan France. But in terms of film exhibition, this territory constitutes a market only 5 percent as large, with 250 movie theaters compared to the 4,500 in France, and receipts of 120 million French francs compared to 2.5 billion. COMACICO and SECMA not only owned or controlled, between them, over 60 percent of local theaters, they were also sole suppliers of films to the bulk of the remainder. By dividing the territory amicably between themselves, refusing to compete for the purchase of films, and following the same policy of acquiring only the cheapest films, they were able to fix artificially low prices for the acquisition of films in Europe. Their joint monopoly thus effectively precluded the African audience from ever experiencing any other form of cinema.

Naturally COMACICO and SECMA refused to support any film making by Africans or to distribute such African films as were made. The system of low-cost admission for a mass audience accustomed to a weekly or even daily change of program made the two companies virtually invulnerable to a unilateral attempt at nationalization by any of the individual states, since the system required a constant flow of several hundred films a year and was profitable only if these could be circulated in a block of neighboring countries. For many years after independence, francophone African film makers struggled to persuade their governments to wrest power from this duopoly, and eventually in 1974 control was taken over by a pan-African organization, the Consortium Interafricain de Distribution Cinématographique (CIDC), based in Burkina Faso (formerly Upper Volta). Despite this shift of ownership, however, little has changed, and the new company continues to distribute—with no greater degree of efficiency—much the same films to the same audience. Only rarely has space in the programming been found for the promotion of African films.

The local control of just one of the half-dozen or so distribution companies serving the market throughout sub-Saharan Africa in no way alters the realities of the imbalance between Africa and the major film-producing nations. These regional distribution companies are no more than outposts of the multinational interests that control the flow of films throughout the world, and, as CIDC discovered, there is no alternative source for the hundreds of films the cinemas require. In the absence of a shift in the social function of cinema, African-made films still experience almost the same barriers to successful distribution in Africa as in the early years of independence.

Hollywood Dominance

The domination by the United States of world film distribution from World War I onward is best seen as a particularly revealing example of the system characterized by Harry Magdoff as "imperialism without colonies,"[21] established by the U.S. government after 1914 and enhanced after 1945. The invention of the motion picture in 1895 had coincided with the United States' first imperial adventures overseas: the military intervention in Cuba during the Spanish-American War, the diversion of movements for independence in both Cuba and the Philippines, and the annexation of Hawaii. As an American historian notes, the year 1898 "made the nation feel like a world power. It served notice that Europe must reckon with American force in its own dealings."[22] But the United States still had a considerable way to go before it could match the world power of Britain and the other major European states. It was a debtor nation until 1914, and much of its domestic market was controlled by foreign interests—a situation that was echoed in the cinema. American firms had been unable to prevent Pathé's move to world dominance around 1908, at which time Pathé was selling twice as many films in the U.S. domestic market as all his American competitors put together. In the period to 1914, though, control of this enormously rich film market (double that of France, Britain, Germany, and Italy combined) was slowly wrested from foreign hands, in moves aided by a new national awareness on the part of American audiences.

For the U.S. cinema, as for the American economy as a whole, World War I brought a sudden and favorable upsurge in profitability. The major film companies had already completed the orderly monopolistic control of the domestic market when the Motion Picture Producers and Distributors Association (MPPDA) was founded in 1922. The pattern of organization and control established then was to last for some thirty years. During this time the Foreign Department of the MPPDA and its successor, the Motion Picture Export Association of America, were able to operate as a legal cartel under the provisions of the 1918 Webb-Pomerene Export Trade Act, openly coordinating policy and maintaining a united front against foreign interests. In the 1920s, Hollywood, as the world's leading producer of films, with a monopoly control over the world's richest domestic film market, was able to achieve an effortless hold over world cinema—occupying well over 60 percent of screen time in Europe (the richest export market) and up to 80 or 90 percent in parts of Asia and Latin America. This 1920s commercial dominance was achieved with a universally comprehensible product, but without any specific concern for the needs of the export market. Hollywood film production was basically geared to the tastes and needs of the U.S. domestic market, from which the bulk of its profits were derived, and the revenue stemming from Hollywood's vast overseas empire was no more than icing on the financial cake.

The ideology underpinning Hollywood's export effort was the "open door" policy that characterized all U.S. trade strategies of the 1920s. This policy echoed the "free trade" policies employed by Britain to control its nineteenth-century world empire, and its corollary in terms of communication as a whole was the "free flow of information." Only in the 1970s did this "free flow" concept, which for decades had served to underpin the work of UNESCO, begin to receive the critical examination it deserved. Its economic and cultural impact could then be exposed; as Urho Kekkonen, president of Finland, observed at a 1973 conference in Tampere, "More and more it can be seen that a mere liberalistic freedom of communication is not in everyday reality a neutral ideal, but a way in which an enterprise with many resources at its disposal has greater opportunities than weaker brethren to make its hegemony accepted." [23]

Though commercially motivated, Hollywood dominance of film had a cultural impact that extended worldwide. Perhaps the greatest victim in the 1920s was Britain, once a leading force in the development of cinema, which by 1925 was experiencing U.S. control of 95 percent of its home market. Canada and Australia fared similarly; there, the 1920s were a period in which a Hollywood film culture was substituted for the remnants of a European colonial one. In Canada, U.S. domination in the mid-1920s was as great as in Britain—indeed, many Hollywood trade statistics include the Canadian market in calculations of U.S. *domestic* receipts. As late as 1978, Peter Harcourt described Canada's own film production as "the invisible cinema," pointing out that acquainting oneself with Canadian films in Canada is "as 'academic' an exercise as studying Egyptology or learning ancient Greek." [24] Australia, too, provides a striking example of successive colonizations, as Sylvia Lawson explains:

> Australia was still very much a dominion of the British Empire through the first thirty years of film making; British modes dominated its popular theatre, and though strong local mythologies had been established in prose and verse, in the nineties London still constituted a magnetic north for social aspirations and the counter-mythologies of the ruling class. In 1923, however, the control over Australian exhibition-distribution circuits by Hollywood was complete, not through shares and boards, but through the inescapable block-booking system; by then, therefore, the cultural colonization by the United States was accomplished." [25]

In cinema, the pattern of growing U.S. world dominance received a new kind of challenge with the coming of sound in the late 1920s, as film interests in the industrially advanced countries of western Europe could find new allies in national finance and electrical companies. Linguistic differences that came to the fore with sound film also played a crucial role. Only Britain and its anglophone empire were now at the full mercy of Hollywood. Elsewhere, sound provided certain barriers that protected local production, since there would always be an audience for films in the national language. But thanks to the universal comprehensibility of its product as well as government help obtained by emphasizing the harmfulness of all foreign tariff barriers and trade restrictions, Hollywood maintained its position in the world market, and by the end of the 1930s it was drawing a third of its revenue from abroad. [26]

In the short term, the impact of World War II was painful for Hollywood, which found itself excluded from some of its most important export markets. But at the conclusion of hostilities, armed with a backlog of four or five years' worth of old Hollywood movies with which to flood the erstwhile inaccessible markets, the U.S. film industry was in an enormously strong position. In 1945 the MPPDA was renamed the Motion Picture Association of America (MPAA), and its Foreign Department became the Motion Picture Export Association of America (MPEA). This organization maintained very close links with the U.S. government, and both its first heads, Eric Johnson and Jack Valenti, were presidential advisors. Though Valenti was to say so memorably in 1968 that "the motion picture is the only U.S. enterprise that negotiates on its own with foreign governments," [27] many of the industry's negotiations have in fact been carried out for it by senior U.S. government officials. It was, for example, Secretary of State James F. Byrnes who negotiated the Byrnes-Blum agreements in 1948, which threatened to annihilate the French film industry. The motivation for this official involvement is spelled out by Richard Maltby: "The government's principal interest in promoting American film exports was derived from their value in the ideological war it saw itself waging under Truman and Eisenhower. . . . The American film industry, because of its propaganda value, found itself a covert beneficiary of the Marshall Plan." [28]

The film industry presented itself as the flag-bearer of the American way of life in a world torn apart by cold war tensions. Its role in the forefront of the "free market" was, of course, aided by the tacit acceptance of its monopoly position at home, and as the U.S. government remade the "free world" after 1945, so too Hollywood remade, on its own terms, the shattered European film industries.

But even with this dominance, Hollywood cinema was not immutable. As audiences declined from their 1940s peak and television rose in the 1950s to become a major competitor in the entertainment marketplace, film production declined and the industry was convulsed by the breakdown of the traditional pattern of vertical integration of production, distribution, and exhibition. Once indifferent to the needs of audiences outside the United States, Hollywood had by the 1960s come to depend on receipts from abroad for half its revenue. Markets acquired effortlessly in the 1920s were now exploited with a new thoroughness, and those once ignored as too insignificant were now explored through affiliates of the MPEA: anglophone Africa through AMPEC (established 1961) and francophone West Africa through AFRAM (1969). The result of this new aggression in marketing is spelled out in a recent study which suggests that by the late 1970s, "it would seem to be a safe assumption that the U.S. majors and mini-majors account for over seventy percent at a conservative estimate of non-socialist world gross film rentals from cinema." [29]

The new industrial structure of the 1970s, which has seen film companies merged into huge multinational corporations with interests in the whole range of leisure activities, can only enhance the unbalanced flow of communication from the West to the Third World. In considering its implications one cannot do better than echo a recent UNESCO report which observes that "this imbalance can be corrected only by the adoption of national and international policies that strengthen the creation of alternative ways and means of mass communication, especially the creation and promotion of 'national cultural industries.'" [30] But before we look at specific examples of Third World national film industries, we need to look at the general pattern of film production in those parts of the world normally excluded from Western surveys of "world cinema."

Part Two

Theory and Practice of
Third World Film Making

In general, the American, Japanese and European cinemas have never been underdeveloped, while the Indian, Aráb or Brazilian cinemas have never ceased being so. As far as cinema is concerned, underdevelopment is not a stage or a step, but a state: the films of the developed countries never went through this situation, while the others have a tendency to remain stuck there. Cinema is incapable of finding within itself the energies which would allow it to escape from its state of underdevelopment, even when a particularly favourable circumstance provokes an increase in the production of films.

Paulo Emilio Salles Gomes

Western, and later specifically U.S., economic and cultural dominance both in the wider relationship between nations and in the area of cinema itself forms a crucial framework for any understanding of film production in the Third World. But the chronicle of hindrances implied by such a perspective is not the whole story. Bill Warren, in a stimulating polemic, offers a useful reminder that, at certain times and in certain locations, considerable developments in industrialization and in the capitalist transformation of traditional agriculture have indeed occurred in the Third World. Warren marshals formidable evidence to support two main arguments: firstly, "that the prospects for successful capitalist development in many underdeveloped countries are quite favourable," and secondly, "that substantial advances along these lines have already been achieved, especially in industrialization." [1] These counterarguments to the overstatement of the "dependency" theory are useful, since film production on any large scale depends on a degree of industrialization that such a theorization would seem to render unlikely.

Although Warren's determination to see only the positive side of colonialism as "a powerful engine for social change," his assumption that any politically independent state is equally free economically, and his open hostility to national liberation movements (on the grounds that nationalism masks differing class interests) make him an unhelpful guide to Third World cultural production, his views do nevertheless draw attention to the need to include in any overall picture of Third World production the positive, as well as the negative, effects of Western domination. The film makers' involvement with the West—through the use of a Western-originated technology—is by no means exclusively negative. In most cases it was imported films that first fired these film makers' enthusiasm, and many have based their mature styles on a knowledge of Western approaches to cinema, which the international marketing of films has allowed them. The infrastructure on which a potentially profitable local production could be based has in many cases been created by foreign business interests or their local allies. This infrastructure may not be ideal: Third World film makers in the 1960s found that the 35mm exhibition circuits developed by Western capitalist interests precluded the showing of films made with the new, flexible 16mm systems then becoming available unless the resultant films could be blown up to 35mm. But the infrastructure of film theaters and exhibition circuits does provide a starting point, without which a national cinema seems unlikely to evolve. Moreover, it is the evident popularity with Third World audiences of imported films that has allowed film makers to put forward plausible claims both for commercial backing and for aid from cultural organizations and the state to help establish a national film culture.

Part Two offers an overview of the varied development of Third World film making in terms of three often overlapping stages. The successive chapters deal with

> the pioneers of Third World film making, and early efforts to create "national" cinemas on the Hollywood model
>
> the emergence of talented individual film "authors" within these industries in the late 1950s, and the use of basically realist styles to offer a picture of social and domestic life in the Third World
>
> the politically committed cinema of the 1960s and early 1970s, with its important theorizing of "third cinema," and the more diverse but equally lively and exciting contemporary scene.

The aim is to offer an overall picture against which the structures of the various national film industries and the achievements of individual film makers can be better understood.

The Beginnings of 4
Non-Western Film Production

In their factories in Bombay they make films as a factory makes and sells shoes wholesale or retail. They keep saying all the time that the masses want this kind of film—in reality they manipulate the masses to a state of cultural prostration.

Utpal Dutt

The cinematograph, as invented by Louis Lumière in 1895, was very much at an artisanal level. The manufacture of equipment and the production of film stock had, it is true, required capital investment, research, technical know-how, and precision engineering skills. The operation of the equipment at all levels—shooting, processing and printing, projection—needed some dexterity and skill. But Lumière was able to train his team of operators in a matter of weeks, and as cameras were initially handcranked, projection did not necessitate electricity, and film making could be a one-man operation.

To begin with, the cinematograph was just one more commodity that could be made still more profitable by worldwide marketing. In Latin America, the first screenings occurred in 1896, within months of those in Paris, New York, and London. Before the end of the year the Lumière operators had visited Bombay, Shanghai, Cairo, Alexandria, and Tokyo, where they were followed within a few days by a Vitascope representative from New York. In the Philippines, Manila saw films for the first time in 1897; in black Africa, the first recorded screenings were in Dakar in 1900; and in Korea, Seoul had its first film show in 1903.

Despite this geographical spread, cinema at this time was far from being a mass-entertainment medium. The principal audiences for such showings in the colonial world were expatriate administrators and businessmen, together with members of the Western-educated native elites. In the Ottoman and Persian empires, showings were even more restricted, limited to court circles in the capitals. Often these first showings were the occasion for the first shooting of film in the country concerned, for the Lumière cinematograph was both camera and projector, and operators had instructions to shoot interesting local views, for inclusion in the Lumière catalogue in Paris as well as to add novelty to local screenings. Since most of the very earliest films in countries outside western Europe and the United States were shot by foreign film makers or, in the case of Latin America, by recent immigrants from Europe, they belong more to the history of how Europe and the United States have viewed the non-Western world than to an emerging expression of indigenous culture. The situation is encapsulated in Julianne Burton's account of the first four Cuban films, which were shot between 1898 and 1906. The first was a documentary on Havana fire fighters, shot by a Frenchman "who chose and interpreted Cuban reality in his own way"; the second was an example of the fake newsreels on the Spanish-American War, shot by two Vitagraph cameramen; the third and fourth were both publicity films for local products and facilities.[1] Sometimes, as in China, these foreign producers showed no interest at all in arranging local showings for the locally shot material, so, as Jay Leyda tells us, "of the enormous quantity of documentary material filmed in China by foreigners, from the earliest travels of film showmen to the liberation, most of it was never seen by Chinese audiences."[2]

Pioneers

Even before World War I, the initial artisanal level of film making allowed local pioneer producers to make their appearance in places as distant as Brazil and India. Those who imported the cinematograph were usually businessmen who also imported other Western novelties. Thus Albert Samama (known as Chikly), who introduced the cinematograph to Tunisia, also introduced the bicycle, still photography, and the radio, while Ardeshir Khan, who set up one of the first movie theaters in Iran, also imported bicycles and phonographs. Local entrepreneurs in Asia and Latin America could also copy the initial modes of film exhibition in Europe by traveling with tent shows and portable projectors. As early as 1904 we hear of one of the pioneering figures of Mexican cinema touring in this way,[3] and in India all the early producers "travelled far and wide by bullock cart, with projector, screen and films."[4] This low-cost operation can be seen as complementing the activities of the touring dramatic companies, which, in India and elsewhere at this time, were spreading a westernized form of theater from the major urban centers, where it had first been introduced, to the rural masses. Indeed, this style of film making and exhibition persists in parts of Africa even in the 1980s, as with certain films made in Nigeria by Yoruba theater groups, who then take them on tour to local audiences on the theatrical circuit.

In one or two instances, the first local film making preceded the organization of foreign-dominated exhibition circuits. For example, Brazilian film historians speak of a "golden age" (*bela epoca*) between 1908 and 1911: "The first Brazilian films, technically inferior to imported films, were nevertheless more attractive to the still naive spectator unaccustomed to the high-level finishing of foreign products. No imported film enjoyed the box-office triumph of Brazilian films dealing with local crimes or politics."[5] But this popular cinema was wiped out almost overnight when Hollywood began to expand into Latin American markets during and after World War I. As Paulo Emilio Salles Gomes observes, "Brazil, which imported everything—even coffins and toothpicks—happily opened its doors to mass-produced entertainment, and it occurred to no one to protect and foster our own incipient cinematic activity. Early Brazilian films were forgotten."[6]

More usually a foreign hold over distribution, and often over exhibition too, had already been established for many years before local films began to be made. In this respect it is useful to bear in mind Andre Gunder Frank's distinction between "undevelopment" (existence unaffected by capitalist penetration) and "underdevelopment" (incorporation into the bottom of the capitalist world hierarchy). In these terms, the national audience that non-Western film makers began to address with their films was almost invariably an underdeveloped one, which already accepted and enjoyed a Western consumer product and a Western conception of cinema as an undemanding form of mass entertainment—this is a situation that persists to the present day.

No sooner had initial ventures in film making begun in the non-Western world than the cinema in the West was industrialized, first by Charles Pathé in France around 1908 and then, in a more complex way, by U.S. studios during World War I. In this fashion, Western film producers and distributors could derive all the financial advantages inherent in factory-style production methods and worldwide marketing. Even in India, which was later to dominate its own domestic market, 85 percent of screentime in the late 1910s and early 1920s was occupied by foreign imports. As long as films were silent, they formed the perfect product for a capitalist oligopoly intent on establishing a world market. Film making outside the West wishing to compete on equal terms with Hollywood would have needed not only considerable risk capital for investment in studios and high technical sophistication in lighting and shooting, but also a large network of purpose-built film theaters and an urban mass audience already drawn into the cash economy. But nowhere outside Japan and the West had industrialization developed before 1914 to the point where it generated the necessary capital and created the urban mass audience. Among the formally colonized nations, only India had achieved any substantial industrialization, and this was dwarfed by the traditional agricultural sector, which persisted unchanged. Among the politically independent states of Latin America, even Brazil, which was later to become a giant in terms of Third World industry, had abandoned a slave economy only in 1888, just eight years before the coming of the cinematograph.

The disruptions caused to the world economy by the 1914–18 war in Europe relaxed the colonizers' hold on their dependent territories. By providing openings for the making of overnight fortunes through speculation, the war also increased local industrialization, fostering both industries producing goods to aid the war effort and those designed to produce substitutes for manufactures no longer competitively available from abroad. New local capital therefore became available for potential investment in Asian and Latin American film industries in the 1920s, but this was also a period when the U.S. film industry, having ordered its own domestic market, began to look outward and to flood the world with its films. Given the levels of film production in the United States and Europe after World War I, there was no product shortage of the kind that would, of itself, prompt local investment in film production. Inevitably, the bulk of the available capital attracted to cinema outside the West was drawn to investment in exhibition, as a local ally to foreign-based distribution interests: in Cuba—admittedly an extreme example—some two hundred movie theaters had been established by 1910. Only a daring few would risk their fortunes by taking on, through production, the unequal struggle with Hollywood imports, particularly as nowhere in the non-Western world were governments concerned to give support and tariff advantages to film production (or indeed to any other nascent industries).

Nevertheless, "national" film production of sorts began in many countries of Asia, Africa, and Latin America during the silent period. If the films made in both Shanghai and Hong Kong before 1916 were largely the work of foreigners, production by Chinese nationals rose throughout the 1920s, so that some four hundred films were produced by Chinese companies in the years 1928 to 1931. Similarly, although the first pioneer film maker in Turkey was a Westerner—Pathé's Rumanian-born agent Sigmund Weinberg—a first "national" production was shot as early as 1914, and two features were completed and shown in 1917. In the Philippines, too, where the earliest films had all been made by American companies, a first "national" film was made in 1919 by José Nepomunceno. In India, the British undertook no production, so the first feature, made in 1913, was the work of an Indian, Dadasaheb Phalke, who was soon joined by others who addressed themelves to a popular Indian audience: Dhire Ganguly, Debaki Bose, and Chandulal Shah among them. The Tunisian pioneer Chikly, who had arranged the first screenings in Tunis in 1897, made a first feature-length film in 1924, and three years later feature production began tentatively in Egypt. There was some 16mm production in

Burma in the 1920s, and Korea, too, had its 1920s production and its own pioneer film maker, Na Woon Kyu. In Latin America there was, as might be expected, some silent film production in the three more industrially developed countries, Mexico, Argentina, and Brazil, and critics have spoken of the quality of the work of such pioneers as the Argentine José Agustin Ferreyra and the Brazilian Humberto Mauro (who continued working into the 1950s). But there was also production in Bolivia, Chile, Uruguay, Cuba, Peru, Guatemala, and especially Colombia. All this film production occurred at a time when the European empires in Africa and Asia were unchallenged, and long before there was any sense of a distinctive Third World identity let alone any theoretical examination of the potential function of cinema outside the West. But the rediscovery of such pioneer efforts has often gone hand in hand with the creation of national film movements by more politically aware film makers in the 1960s (one thinks of the debt to Humberto Mauro expressed by such a key figure of *cinema novo* as Glauber Rocha).

By and large, early film makers sought in an uncomplicated way to create a mass art that would fill the same entertainment function as imported films, but for a wider and less westernized audience. Most of this pioneer output is now

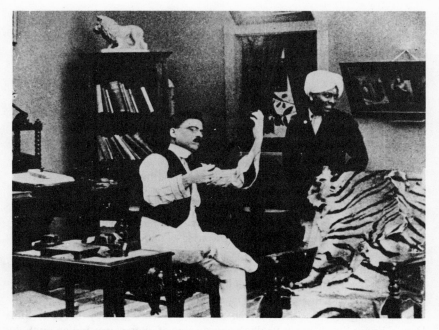

1. Dadasaheb Phalke (1870–1944)

2. *Humberto Mauro (1897–1983)*

lost, but at least fragments of Dadasaheb Phalke's work have been preserved, and these allow us to see the challenges facing early film makers. Phalke received his inspiration from a Western film on the life of Christ, which made him resolve to film similar accounts of Indian religious subjects. After acquiring basic knowledge and equipment on a trip to England, in 1913 he completed India's first feature, *Raja Harischandra,* which was a huge success with Indian audiences and has been partially preserved. From the start, Phalke found a new and responsive public: "The audiences attending the western films in the new cinema palaces paid little attention to Phalke. The English-language newspapers hardly noticed him, and Phalke did not advertise in them. He was reaching, almost at once, a different public."[7]

In creating a distinctively Indian form of cinema, Phalke faced formidable difficulties. His perceptions of the potential of the imported medium to which he was adapting his material could hardly fail to be influenced by the Western films that had given him his first inspiration and continued to dominate the Indian film market. He could not draw on popular traditional forms because Indian drama had become so disreputable that it was many years before Indian actresses could be persuaded to appear before the film camera (most of the female stars of Indian silent cinema were in fact Anglo-Indians, though this was disguised by their screen names: Sulochna—Ruby Meyers; Sita Devi—Renee Smith; etc.). Phalke's chosen area of interest was Indian mythology, but even here he could not fail to be affected by the codification of Indian tradition that had formed part of the British effort to legitimize their own rule. Moreover, the classical drama of India, which might have been expected to assist him—that staged in temples during religious festivals, for example— was not organized into a commercially marketable form appropriate to the new relationship between drama and the mass audience that cinema introduced.

There were, however, other forms of popular imagery and storytelling on which he could draw. These elements have been detailed by the Indian film critic and academic Satish Bahadur:

> The visual values of *Raja Harischandra* were derived, not from the values of Ajanta or Rajput painting, but from the oil paintings of Raja Ravi Varma (d. 1906), who had conceived the Hindu pantheon in the lowest sentimental values of Victorian paintings and popularized it in cheap reproductions through another mass medium, the colour printing press. For dramatics, Phalke drew upon the crude elements of the "Company Navak," not the glories of classical Sanskrit drama or the vital forms of the folk theatre. For story material, Phalke did not delve deep into the spiritual meaning underlying the Hindu epics. Rather, he used their obvious, ritualistic and superficial level, viz., the magical, the miraculous and the spectacular in the exploits of the Hindu gods and goddesses."[8]

In this way, Phalke developed in Indian terms a potential of cinema exploited also in the West, most notably in the slightly earlier work of Georges Méliès.

The Coming of Sound

The interwar years were a difficult time for countries dependent on the export of primary products, following the collapse of prices at the outset of the 1930s and the corresponding rise in the cost of imports. These troubles did, however, give the incentive for the creation of import-substitution industries, which occurred, for example, in a number of Latin American countries. Costs were often high, since equipment and technological know-how had to be imported, but a new stage of industrialization did occur. Though in many cases nationalist impulses lay behind the urge to industrialize, the degree of national economic independence generated in this way was extremely limited.

It was within this general economic context that film makers outside the West had to respond to yet another Western-originated technical innovation: the sound film. From this point on, film making was unambiguously an industry, not an artisanal activity. The equipment required to fit studios and film theaters for sound had to be imported, leading to increased foreign dependence and requiring vast new capital investment. The demands of sound greatly increased production costs of individual films, therefore necessitating different marketing methods in order to make the films profitable. But the barriers of language served to protect the emergent non-Western sound film industries, and local films could begin the slow process of winning from Hollywood movies space on their own cinema screens.

The 1930s drive to achieve self-sufficiency in an ever-widening range of consumer goods received a further boost during World War II, when there was scope for fortunes to be made through speculation and profiteering in India and other parts of Asia, in Latin America, and in Egypt. From the mid-1930s, although many of the smaller, less developed countries were now excluded from film production, we find in those countries that were industrializing the beginnings of the infrastructure required for a sound film industry: studios and laboratories, and dubbing and editing facilities.

Until at least the 1960s, though, cinema was seen by governments throughout the non-Western world merely as a source of tax revenue (at rates far higher than those customary in the West). In India and Egypt the state remained indifferent to the demands of film producers for tariff support. In the three leading film-producing countries of Latin America there was some state support, but the quotas established in Brazil (for short films from 1932 and for features from 1939) fell far below the production capacity of the domestic industry, and protectionist measures under Perón in Argentina seem to have stifled innovation and enterprise. Only in Mexico do we find from the mid-1930s a pioneering state involvement leading to real development.

Sound offered new possibilities to capture a considerable share of a growing home market through films that used local languages and, especially, local music and song. A striking example is India, where sound films in native languages complete with music, songs, and dances were immensely popular, beginning with the very first Indian talkie, *Alam ara,* released in Bombay on 14 March 1931. Indian production rose to new heights throughout the 1930s, with films in half a dozen languages (led by Hindi, with 77 films in 1933), almost all of which made a profit. Though the market was limited to India and government help was virtually nonexistent, big new production companies with their own studios and even laboratories came into existence. A decade later, a new wave of independents with lower overheads took over and brought Indian production from around 171 features in 1940 to some 241 in 1950.

The artificiality of the all-India movie—made in Hindi in Marathi-speaking Bombay—is echoed in China, where production was located in Cantonese-speaking Shanghai but films were made in Mandarin. Shanghai was, of course, the center for foreign investment in trading and for the establishment of foreign-owned industries drawing on low-cost local labor. But from the 1920s Chinese entrepreneurs, too, became active in the modern sector and began "to emulate the foreigner, even to the extent of setting up factories and importing machinery from the West. Native capital could also be mobilised through the banking systems." [9] These developments found expression in the growth of a sophisticated film production showing a keen awareness of Hollywood style before the Japanese invasion of 1937.

In Egypt, Misr Studios, founded in 1935, were the first real production facilities in either Africa or the Arab world. They helped Egyptian cinema, which at the time received little or no government support, to reach a level of around fifteen features a year between 1936 and 1945, climbing to over fifty annually in the early postwar years. These films had wide distribution in the Arab world (though seldom outside it), but at home the industry was very vulnerable to films from the West, which matched the tastes of elite audiences in Cairo and Alexandria, the cities in which the majority of Egyptian movie theaters were located. In the Philippines, too, the advent of sound in 1933 led to the industrialization of cinema, and an output of over fifty features a year was reached by the end of the 1930s, though a great deal of this was the product of U.S.-owned companies. In Latin America, strong production industries emerged in Mexico and Brazil in the 1930s, and to a lesser extent in Argentina as well, but the fortunes of these concerns were more precarious. Their success depended largely on government support—in the form of subsidies, discriminatory taxation, and quota restrictions—but this support tended to be erratic because of the unstable nature of Latin American politics. All three countries had, however, built up considerable industries by the beginning of the 1950s, with between twenty and ninety films a year produced in each country. Latin American ambition to compete with Hollywood on its own terms (a desire shared too by J. Arthur Rank in Britain) led to a number of schemes, of which the most significant was the expensively equipped Vera Cruz studio complex in São Paulo, Brazil, which proved a disastrous failure in the early 1950s.

These major commercial industries established in the 1930s remain the best known and best documented in the West. Most have continued to develop steadily into the 1980s, with India emerging as by far the world's leading film-producing nation (763 films in 1983). Philippine production peaked at 250 films in 1971, and Hong Kong, to which much of the Shanghai film industry was transferred when the communists took power in 1949, was already producing over 200 films by the early 1950s. Mexico reached total of over 120 films in 1970 and stayed at around 100 films a year throughout the decade, while the Brazilian "economic miracle" of the 1970s is reflected in the mushrooming growth of its film production, which had reached 100 films a year by 1978. Brazil's development took place under a military government that established the economic context for a well-protected, state-funded film industry. Similarly, most of the growth of film production in Asia since the 1950s has been in countries that are both rapidly industrializing and ruled by authoritarian regimes able to regulate the market and to control foreign imports. By 1955 the countries producing 50 or more films a year included Burma, Pakistan, and South Korea, and both Pakistan and South Korea had at least

3. S. S. Vassan: Humanity / Insaniyat *(India, 1955)*

*4. Samia Gamal, Egyptian star of the
1940s and 1950s*

doubled this level of output by 1970. The countries producing 50 films a year were joined in the 1970s by Thailand, Indonesia, and Bangladesh. Iranian production reached its peak of 90 films in 1970, and Turkey—by far the largest of the Middle Eastern cinema industries—reached almost 300 features in 1972. This increase in output in the industrializing countries of Asia more than compensates for the sharp decline in output (in numerical terms, at least, though not necessarily in terms of investment) in the two countries that were once the world's leading film producers, the United States and Japan. Indeed, world output is estimated to have risen from under 3,000 films in 1955 to over 4,000 by 1975, over half of this total coming from Asian studios.

Third World Commercial Cinemas

Pioneers like Dadasaheb Phalke can be hailed as innovators, and their work causes no real critical dilemmas. Dilemmas do arise, however, after the coming of sound, when films of a totally undemanding kind begin to pour from the sometimes primitive studios of the non-Western world. The evaluation of the great mass of Arab, Asian, and Latin American films since the 1930s— particularly such forms as the Hindi song-and-dance film, the Egyptian musical (such as those starring the dancer Samia Gamal and the popular singers Farid el-Atrach and Abdel Wahab), or the Brazilian *chanchada* (a combination of comedy and music, often crude)—is enormously difficult, since there exists no accepted critical methodology with which to handle such films. On the one hand, the sheer volume of material is immense: there are literally tens of thousands of such films; on the other, the fact is that very little of this production has ever been shown outside the national or regional boundaries and so tested against standards other than those implicit in its manufacture. It is a local cinema, conceived and made for immediate consumption by local audiences, who have generally shown themselves enthusiastically receptive. But it has given birth to virtually no accompanying critical writing or theoretical speculation of the kind Hollywood has provoked, only to reactions of a thoroughly negative kind. Created for a mass audience and apparently fulfilling no more than an entertainment function, these films are the cause of great unease on the part of Third World critics and film makers, even—and perhaps especially—those concerned to define and promote a "national" cinema.

For these critics and film makers, rejection of the standards implicit in a local cinema is the beginning of an authentic film culture. In judging local products, the critics often reveal most clearly the extent to which they have subconsciously assimilated Western values and modes of thinking about cinema. Such an approach could only be reinforced by the European critical reception of the rare products of Third World industries that received some limited showing in the West. For example, three 1952 films that were

5. *Mehboob Khan:* Savage Princess / Aan
(India, 1952)

6. *Lima Barreto:* The Bandit / O cangaceiro *(Brazil, 1952)*

internationally shown—Mehboob Khan's Indian *Savage Princess / Aan,* Lima Barreto's Brazilian *The Bandit / O cangaceiro,* and Manuel Conde's Philippine *Genghis Khan*—were seen merely as exotic novelties that produced no questioning of Western assumptions of cinematic superiority.

There are three main criticisms leveled at such commercial cinemas in the non-Western world. The first is that the local cinema creates a totally unreal filmic world. This view is most often expressed in terms of denunciation, as in the keynote speech delivered by the Indian actor Utpal Dutt at the opening of an international symposium on cinema in developing countries held in New Delhi in 1979:

> An Indian hero in a blonde wig and latest Bond Street clothes making love to a heroine who seems to have shopped for clothes in New York last week—that's their conception of Indianness! . . . You know, they will not be able to give a local habitation and a name to any of their all-conquering heroes; he has no surname, lest he should be identified with any particular region of India. He dresses as no Indian dresses, he floats on a cloud, it is just not possible to argue and tell the makers of films that only by being intensely and wholly regional can one be truly Indian.[10]

Even where blind imitation of the West is replaced by conscious parody, the unequal relationship persists. The Belgian-born film critic Jean-Claude Bernardet, now a naturalized Brazilian, expresses this second criticism particularly well:

> To parody is to recognize one's momentary inability to replace the imposed model with another. . . . The aggression consists in reducing the model to the level of the underdeveloped. What then happens is a simultaneous devaluation of the imposed model and a self-devaluation. Thus this parody presents an image of the underdeveloped which is perfectly acceptable to the oppressive model, for it seems natural to the latter that the underdeveloped should see themselves as ridiculous, grotesque and cowardly.[11]

Where instead of taking disembodied aspects of Western culture the film makers strive to base their work on traditional themes and ideas, a third common criticism is that this tradition is false. Much of the work of colonizers in India and Africa went into creating an invented tradition that would legitimize Western structures of authority. Even where this is not the case, there is always the danger that the aspects chosen will be precisely those which, even before the introduction of cinema, had already been debased into "folklore," aptly defined by the Moroccan critic Abdallah Laroui as "a sub-expression which perpetuates, in the midst of expression itself, the inferiority of a society which it claims to express."[12]

There is obviously a great deal of truth in these criticisms, and they could be echoed with regard to a great deal of Third World commercial cinema. But

a negative approach of this kind does not exhaust the interest of such productions. An example of the folly of blanket rejections of Third World entertainment cinema, and an indication of what can be discovered when a critic does
investigate his native cinema, is S. Theodore Baskaran's detailed study of
pre-1945 Tamil cinema in South India. His analysis shows that during the first
decade of Tamil sound film making (which began in Madras in 1934), the
strong influence of popular drama led to a cinema that "emerged as a factor in
the political life of the country." [13] Stage performers—especially singers—
who had taken part in direct political action were drawn into the cinema, and
several political figures and intellectuals gave it their support, enabling Tamil
cinema to begin to reflect the patriotic and political aspirations of the people.
While remaining in form and style primarily an entertainment cinema, the
Tamil films of the decade up to 1945 were in many cases patriotic works mer-
iting serious consideration:

> The challenge of foreign rule and the awareness of the need for social reforms as
> a part of the society's efforts to meet this challenge profoundly affected Tamil
> cinema. . . . By supporting nationalistic ideas on the screen, films reflected the
> popular attitude of the times and often gave shape to vague political inclina-
> tions. The cinema lent a new emotional aspect to the political situation by han-
> dling melodramatic patriotic themes on the screen. [14]

The effectiveness of this form of popular cinema, in which patriotically inspired songs played a key role, is borne out by the prompt response of British
censors.

Other positive aspects of Third World commercial cinema are captured by
Paulo Emilio Salles Gomes who, in a discussion of the chanchadas of his native Brazil, notes that the relationship between these films and the spectator
"was incomparably more lively than with the corresponding foreign product,"
involving "an intimate relationship of creative participation." [15] By shifting
the argument to the question of audience response, Salles Gomes throws fresh
light on "the ambiguity of the Brazilian critic's position with regard to his
country's film production":

> The national film is a disturbing element in the artificially coherent world of
> cinematic ideas and sensations which the critic has created for himself. . . .
> Angrily attacking or defending in order to encourage, directed by an awareness
> of a patriotic duty, the critic always reveals the unease which fills him. All these
> attitudes, above all destructive sarcasm, are used to veil the deepest feeling
> which his national cinema provokes in a cultivated Brazilian: humiliation. [16]

A more questionable approach to Third World cinema in Africa and Asia
has been the uncovering—or, more precisely, the construction—of a "realist
tradition" to be set against what is viewed as the mindless escapism of the
popular commercial cinema of the time. In this way, Erika Richter sees Kamal

Selim's *The Will / Al-azima* (1939) as the forerunner of a tradition of realist film making in Egypt that is continued in the work of Henri Barakat, Salah Abou Seif and Tawfik Saleh and perhaps finds its culmination in Youssef Chahine's *The Land / Al-ard* (1969).[17] Similarly, some of the key Indian directors of the 1940s and 1950s, such as Bimal Roy, Guru Dutt and Ritwik Ghatak, have been wrongly viewed as mere precursors of an "Indian neorealism" that finds its fullest expression in the first films of Satyajit Ray, beginning with *Pather panchali* in 1955. Thus we find the French critic Henri Micciolo writing, in his otherwise sensitive and perceptive study of Guru Dutt, that "one can only regret that Guru Dutt was never to make his own *Pather Panchali*."[18] Although Italian neorealism obviously had a great influence on Ray himself, it is becoming increasingly clear as Third World critics and theorists publish their own accounts of their national cinemas that such "realist traditions" constructed by Westerners involve a distortion of both the film maker's relation to his national industry and the particular qualities of his work.

Still another way of dealing with the purely commercial cinemas of Asia and Latin America is to apply criteria developed in the last few years for dealing with Hollywood, since moralizing rejection was until recently as characteristic of critical approaches to American movies as it currently is of analyses of Third World commercial cinema. Both forms of entertainment cinema are products of capitalist systems that reflect certain of the aspirations of the underprivileged members of society who make up their mass audience. With this starting point in mind, a twofold approach can be adopted: firstly, probing the reasons for the evasions that characterize such cinema, and secondly, looking analytically at the imaginary worlds and structures of feeling that the films offer. Richard Dyer, who sees entertainment in terms of "the stuff of utopia"—that is, alternatives, hopes, wishes, dreams—points out that while entertainment "offers the image of 'something better' to escape into, or something we want deeply that our day-to-day lives don't provide," it does not simply present models of utopian worlds; "rather, the utopianism is contained in the feelings it embodies. It presents, head-on as it were, what utopia would feel like rather than how it would be organized. It thus works at the level of sensibility."[19] Dyer's organizing categories of entertainment—abundance, energy, intensity, transparency, community—could certainly be applied to the all-India movie. Dyer links these "utopian" solutions to a series of real social needs, which are themselves created by capitalism: scarcity, exhaustion, dreariness, manipulation, and fragmentation. Since commercial film production in the Third World normally competes with imported foreign films without attempting to change the Western-established social function and definition of cinema, the lines of analysis that Dyer's approach opens up could be extremely fruitful.

But none of these approaches is a substitute for a criticism that will relate Third World commercial films to the issues concerning society and culture raised in Part One. Though these cinemas are "national" in the sense that they are financed by local capital and create products destined largely for a local audience, they have little if any connection to the definitions of the demands of a "national culture" as formulated by Cabral or Fanon. Equally, they are "popular" in the sense of reaching a wide audience, but as examples of mass culture in its most basic sense they have no connection with the term "popular cinema" as used by Latin American film theorists.

One way these Third World national cinemas can be understood is through an examination of their economic and class origins. That is, as an expression of the attempt by local capital to establish commercially viable production structures, these cinemas reveal both the lure of Hollywood as a model to be emulated (but which is all too rarely understood) and the crushing financial power of Western film interests. The limitations of these national industries stem from the overall context in which they are situated, for, as Paulo Emilio Salles Gomes has observed, "Cinema is incapable of finding within itself the energies which would allow it to escape from its state of underdevelopment, even when a particularly favourable circumstance provokes an increase in the production of films." [20]

Approaching the films themselves in class terms, we can trace, beyond the stylistic divergences and differences in surface detail, a unity of approach and conformity of values that relate directly to the petty bourgeois aspirations of the bulk of the film makers. Though occasional film makers working within the commercial industries—Salah Abou Seif in Egypt or Emilio Fernandez in Mexico, for example—come from poor and underprivileged backgrounds, while others—most notably the Indian film maker, Prince Pramathesh Chandra Barua, son of the Rajah of Gauripur—stem from the aristocracy, membership of the urban petty bourgeoisie can in general be taken to describe the film maker's achieved social status.

Petty bourgeois culture does not explore or even acknowledge the contradictions contained in such a concept as nationalism. Instead, nationalism is seen simply in terms of an opposition to a foreign aggressive force (such as the British Empire): this foreign power may not figure explicitly within the text, but it can be held implicitly responsible for all current woes. A national spirit will be seen as inspiring all men of good faith, as a factor uniting rich and poor, and hence as a veil to mask social contradictions. Since such an entity cannot be adequately represented in contemporary terms (its oversimplifications would be too apparent), there is often a retreat into the past, to a tradition seen as incorporating the essence of the "national spirit." But after the dislocations that inevitably arise from Western dominance and colonization, such a "tradition" (where it once existed) is no longer accessible except in terms of the most rigorous intellectual exploration. Too often the "tradition" presented in petty bourgeois culture is at best a debased form of earlier values (often depicted in terms of nineteenth-century commercial imagery and popular literature) or at worst an unwitting echo of a "tradition" in fact invented by the colonizer.

This blurring of the traditional is balanced by an ambivalence toward the modern. Despite the affection with which petty bourgeois artists turn to the past, they themselves are part of the modern sector of society, incorporated into a cash economy, and, in the case of film makers, even using an imported Western technology. The customary response to this threatening ambivalence is to portray society as a given, an entity that is static, unquestionable, and immutable: the depiction of any forward-looking source of social change is impossible. The center of gravity is always the urban petty bourgeoisie itself, from which the bulk of the intended audience will be drawn. Peasant life is as remote as that of the local rulers, and depictions of either are likely to be detached and externally observed (or invented) rather than drawn from inner knowledge. The values celebrated are precisely those of petty bourgeois life: individualism, with an emphasis on stability and order within the family and on material achievement in the world of work outside it. As in so many Western films that share this ideological perspective, rebels will be either reconciled or annihilated, women who assert themselves either tamed or destroyed.

Since this world is itself a fabrication, a construct in which the realities of contemporary society have been reshaped to conform to the structures of a commercial entertainment formula, there is no need for film makers to move outside a studio-created world. Characters in a story can be turned into richly drawn roles for stars, emphasis can be placed on exuberant dialogue and verbal interplay, and, since the end of the narrative is assured, the story's progress can be interrupted to make way for the songs and dances that constitute an essential part of the commercial formula. We have here a form of production that deals ostensibly with the key issues of a true national culture: language, tradition, society. But the approach can be most clearly defined in terms of its multiple refusals: to look directly and critically at contemporary society, to adopt a standpoint rooted outside the particular class position of the artist, to make real use of local traditions of narrative (in terms of the handling of time or the creation of space), or to break with formulas designed to do no more than extract a commercial return from the audience.

It is only when we have a clearer and better documented grasp of the organizational structures and implicit ideological assumptions of Third World commercial film production that it will be possible to begin to evaluate the range of personal achievements to be found there. Despite the limitations of our current knowledge in the West, one can point to a succession of highly talented and successful film makers whose work goes far beyond the constrictions of the individual film maker's class position and calls into question the glib assumptions of petty bourgeois orthodoxy. As examples of work produced over five decades that is as estimable as that of many of the most revered of Hollywood professionals, one might cite the dramas, marked by a mix of commercial calculation and left-wing idealism, produced by Sun Yu in Shanghai before 1937; the romantic melodramas of P. C. Barua in late-1930s

Indian cinema; Emilio Fernandez's sympathetic portrayals of the poor and oppressed in Mexico from the 1940s; the unclassifiable achievements of Luis Buñuel, particularly in the period from *Los olvidados* (1950) to *Nazarin* (1958); Salah Abou Seif's work over two decades, spanning the late 1940s and early 1960s, with its urge to offer a truer portrayal of Egyptian society; the very varied films made within the Indian film industry in the late 1950s and early 1960s by two of Satyajit Ray's exact contemporaries, the romantic idealist Guru Dutt and the grimly intransigent Ritwik Ghatak; the action-packed period films made within the Hong Kong film industry and culminating in *A Touch of Zen / Hsia nü* (1969) by King Hu; the melodramatic flamboyance and commercial calculation of the films of the Filipino Lino Brocka in the 1970s; and the tight narrative control of the work of the Argentinian Adolfo Aristarain in the 1980s. This listing is by no means exhaustive, indicating merely some of the more striking individuals whose work has a personal style and flair that transcends the limitations of the conventional commercial forms in which they are constrained to work and against which their achievements must be judged. These film makers, who have accepted the challenge of working within the industry and who have used its accumulated skills as the basis for conveying their visions, are no less admirable because since the mid-1950s, we have found individual voices of a very different and more westernized kind in Third World cinema. Their work in the mainstream of commercial production, often full of immense visual excitement and always emotionally engaging in its use of melodramatic forms, rewards re-viewing today.

> *Popular and art cinema were falsely made out to be*
> *irreconcilable opposites, when what were actually*
> *being discussed were "commercial" and "elitist"*
> *cinema. Our objective was a realism which would*
> *transcend this tendentious duality. In it we were*
> *joined by other non-cinematic groups all of whom*
> *shared our aspiration towards an art which would be*
> *simultaneously popular and of high quality.*
>
> Fernando Birri

As can be seen from the previous chapter, the emergence of non-Western commercial film industries is not limited to a single period—say, the 1930s to 1950s—and the 1980s problems of self-expression in the newly established cinemas of Asia would seem to be very similar to those experienced decades before in Egypt or India, Brazil or China. While non-Western industrial development does not follow the pattern set earlier in the West, there are certainly marked similarities between individual industries emerging in different countries of the non-Western world over a long period of time but in response to very much the same international economic pressures. Though the impetus toward the industrialization of film production and the creation of a local cinema to fill local needs is far from exhausted, for the past thirty years at least, other possibilities of expression have been at times open to film makers from the non-Western world who wish to take a more individual stance. These openings, which existed nowhere before the mid-1950s, relate very directly to the changes in the balance of world power in the decade following 1945, which allowed the emergence of a distinctive "third world" identity.

World War II was an even greater stimulus to industrialization in Latin America and Asia than was the 1914–18 conflict. Both the allies (in India) and Japan (in Southeast Asia) fostered production that would aid the war effort. Import shortages and the closing of traditional trade routes led to a diversification of local manufacturing, much of it controlled by local capital. As the old empires crumbled in the East, the new sense of nationalism that swept first Asia and then Africa gave a fresh impetus to the drive to industrialize.

One of the striking features of the years immediately following World War II was the dismantling of the European empires and the granting or seizing of independence throughout Asia. The 1947 partition of the Indian subcontinent led to the emergence of the independent states of India and Pakistan. Even more momentous was the Chinese Revolution, completed in 1949 by the communists under Mao Tse-tung. The Japanese occupation of Southeast Asia had weakened colonial ties, and in some cases the occupiers had fostered nationalist movements and granted limited autonomy. As a result, a number of previously occupied countries quickly achieved independence: Indonesia in 1945, the Philippines in 1946, and Burma in 1948. Ho Chi Minh's proclamation of the Democratic Republic of Vietnam in 1945 was followed by the eventual defeat of the French in the first Indo-Chinese War, with the fall of Dien Bien Phu in 1954. Not surprisingly, it was the Asians who were the prime movers in the 1955 Bandung Conference of twenty-nine Afro-Asian states, the first of many such gatherings to assert a Third World identity and to condemn colonialism and racial discrimination. In the Arab world, the overthrow of King Farouk in Egypt in 1952 and the appearance of Gamal Abdel Nasser, first as prime minister (1954) and then as president (1956), seemed to point the way ahead, particularly when Nasser emerged from the Suez crisis of 1956 with strengthened credibility. In North Africa, Morocco and Tunisia both achieved their independence in 1956, while south of the Sahara the first moves were made toward the decolonization that led to independence for Ghana in 1957 and for Guinea in 1958. In Latin America, which had been largely independent for a century or more, there was a setback in 1954 when the democratically elected government of Arbenz Guzmán in Guatemala was overthrown in a coup organized by the U.S. Fruit Company and the CIA. But in compensation, the 1950s saw two rare examples of real social revolution: in 1952 in Bolivia, where the MNR (Nationalist Revolutionary Movement) under Paz Estenssoro set in motion key reforms, and above all in Cuba in 1959, with the overthrow of the corrupt dictator Batista by guerrillas under Fidel Castro.

Independence and After

These events were reflected in a new sense of personal and national identity, shared by film makers as much as by politicians. By 1955, as we have seen, the industrial base for film production existed in many parts of the non-Western world, and in the wake of the increase in levels of film production, individual film makers from Asia, Latin America, and Egypt began to achieve an expression of their national realities in terms that broke with the traditions of the local entertainment-film.

The newcomers of the mid-1950s who achieved this breakthrough all came from countries that had already established a tradition of film making and, in most cases, a strong local industry. The new film makers themselves, however, were generally more strongly marked by films from the West than by local productions. Among names that spring immediately to mind are those of Satyajit Ray (b. 1921) from India, Leopoldo Torre Nilsson (1924–78) from Argentina, and Lester James Peries (b. 1921) from Ceylon (since 1972 the Republic of Sri Lanka). Their work, characterized by social concern, has never been explicitly political. It simply reflects the tensions and contradictions of Third World bourgeois elites from within, posing no radical alternative. Moreover Ray, Torre Nilsson, and Peries are film makers who, for all their very real individual qualities, do not call for a thorough-going redefinition of cinema. All three were able to continue filming prolifically through changing regimes and so build up an oeuvre of fifteen or twenty films in as many years.

7. *Leopoldo Torre Nilsson:* The House of the Angel / La casa del angel *(Argentina, 1957)*

8. *Lester James Peries:* The Line of Destiny / Rekava *(Ceylon, 1956)*

Three other noted film makers active since the 1950s who have shown themselves to be equally proficient and prolific in their personal fusions of Western and indigenous influences are Mrinal Sen (b. 1923) from India, Nelson Pereira dos Santos (b. 1928) from Brazil, and Youssef Chahine (b. 1926) from Egypt. These film makers, however, began within the mainstreams of their respective commercial film industries and perhaps for this reason took longer to establish an international reputation. The sharper political edge apparent in their later work also aligns them more closely to the later 1960s generation. Of course, not all the 1950s film makers who attempted a synthesis of Western and local approaches have been prolific in this way. The Argentine film maker and theorist Fernando Birri (b. 1925) is best known for just two films, the forty-minute documentary *Throw Us a Dime / Tire die* (1958) and the feature-length *The Inundated / Los inundados* (1962). But much of Birri's work has been as a teacher, and his importance lies to a considerable extent in the influence he has had on the younger documentary film makers of Latin America.

In Cuba, where film makers have considerable control over the running of their industry, both Julio García Espinosa (b. 1926) and Tomás Gutiérrez Alea (b. 1928) have combined their film making with administrative activities. This dual role limited Alea's output to just nine features in twenty-five years, while

9. *Mrinal Sen:* The Ruins / Khandar *(India, 1984)*

10. *Nelson Pereira dos Santos:* Barren Lives / Vidas secas
(Brazil, 1963)

García Espinosa has directed only one (unreleased) feature since 1970, though he has combined his duties as vice-minister of culture with practical involvement in production and scriptwriting.

Though the highly individual styles of these film makers allowed them to be, to some extent at least, assimilated within Western critical approaches to film authorship, and their debt to the traditions of Western film making made their work readily accessible, their appearance did create something of a shock in the West with the realization that films of this caliber could be produced in India or Argentina, Egypt or Brazil, Ceylon or Cuba. Working at

11. *Fernando Birri. Throw Us a Dime / Tire die (Argentina, 1958)*

12. Tomás Guitérrez Alea: The Last Supper / La última cena
(Cuba, 1977)

a consistently high level over twenty-five years or more, they have shown that
their particular fusions of indigenous and Western cultures are worthy of the
utmost respect. By their very productiveness, they have begun the long but
vitally important task of reversing the one-way flow of films from West to East,
North to South. Though several of them—Ray, Torre Nilsson, and Peries in
particular—were criticized in the 1960s and 1970s for their lack of explicit
political commitment, they have collectively shown themselves able, against
all the odds, to create a satisfyingly rounded career, to offer unique insights
into their own societies, and to produce work of a truly international standard.
Their example, if not always their particular beliefs and values, has been a
vital lesson for new generations of film makers throughout the Third World.

These film makers' direct heirs among those who have begun their careers
in the 1970s display two marked tendencies. Firstly, they show a similar concern for social depiction rather than for political questioning. Here one might
cite the names of the Bolivian Antonio Eguino (b. 1938), who made two features in the 1970s, and in India, Shyam Benegal (b. 1934) and M. S. Sathyu
(b. 1930), whose work shows a soberly realist approach in which any call for
social change is likely to be fairly muted. A second tendency, which also reveals a reluctance to attach crucial importance to political commitment, has
been the tentative appearance of a self-conscious "art cinema" in the Third
World. In India, for example, an enlightened system of government support in
the 1970s saw the emergence of a New Indian Cinema, which, while drawing
on the lessons of Ray, Sen, and Ritwik Ghatak, offered a wide variety of new
voices. Alongside the sober, naturalistic storytelling of Benegal and Sathyu,
we find other, less accessible, experiments. In the forefront of this esoteric
approach is the work produced under the influence of Robert Bresson by

graduates of the Indian Film Institute at Pune. Many of these films—from Kumar Shahani's *Maya Dapan* (1972) and Mani Kaul's *In Two Minds / Duvidha* (1973) in the early 1970s to Surinder Nath Dhir's *Retaliation / Pratishodh* in 1982—have been shown at festivals and Indian Film Weeks abroad but have received virtually no commercial screenings in India. In North Africa, too, hermetic works have been made in the 1970s by the Moroccans Moumen Smihi (b. 1945) and Hamid Bénani (b. 1940). Even black Africa has an experimental film maker, the Senegalese Djibril Diop Mambéty (b. 1945), whose sole feature, *Touki-Bouki,* is a unique and unclassifiable formal exercise.

Approaches to Reality

One of the major achievements of the mid-1950s generation of Third World film makers—the first to become internationally known—was the pioneering exploration of realist approaches in the fictional feature film. The new approach is very apparent in the writings of Fernando Birri, who advocates a "cinema of discovery" that will offer a "real" image of Latin American reality

> by showing how reality *is,* and in no other way. This is the revolutionary function of social documentary and realist, critical and popular cinema in Latin America. By testifying, critically, to this reality—to this sub-reality, this misery—cinema refuses it. It rejects it. It denounces, judges, criticizes and deconstructs it. Because it shows matters as they irrefutably are, and not as we would like them to be (or as, in good or bad faith, others would like to make us believe them to be).

For Birri, writing in the 1960s, the aim is clear: "To confront reality, with a camera, and to document it, filming realistically, filming critically, filming underdevelopment with the optic of the people." [1]

One source of Birri's enthusiasm for a realist approach to film making is clear: the years he spent studying film at the Centro Sperimentale in Rome. This period—from 1950 to 1952—was the height of the Italian neorealist movement, and it is hardly surprising that Birri should have been deeply affected by the work of Rossellini, De Sica, Visconti, and their contemporaries or that the neorealist approach should have influenced his teaching at the documentary film school he founded at the University of Santa Fe, Argentina.

Two other crucial figures in the resurgence of Latin American cinema in the late 1950s and early 1960s, the Cubans Tomás Gutiérrez Alea and Julio García Espinosa, also studied in Rome alongside Birri in the early 1950s, and a neorealist influence is to be found in their first collaborative effort, the collectively made *The Charcoal Burner / El megano,* shot before the Cuban

Revolution in 1954–55. A fourth key figure of this same generation, the Brazilian film maker Nelson Pereira dos Santos, has also expressed his sense of a debt to the Italians: "Without neorealism we could never have begun, and I believe that no cinematically underdeveloped country would have been able to express itself without this precedent." [2]

Tributes to neorealism have been made by a number of individual Latin America film makers of the 1960s as well, from the Cuban Humberto Solas, who confesses that the early films of Luchino Visconti—*La terra trema* (1947) and *Ossessione* (1942)—had "a formative effect" on him,[3] to Ruy Guerra, a key figure in Brazilian *cinema novo,* for whom "Italian neorealism is one of the great events of the postwar years" and who admits that "a very strong impression" was made on him by Rossellini's *Paisa* (1946) and De Sica's *Bicycle Thieves* (1948).[4] This influence is further echoed in the 1970s work of the Bolivian director Antonio Eguino, who acknowledges that his own film making "utilizes the same methods as the neorealists." [5] Given the acknowledged impact of neorealism on 1950s film makers in other parts of the world—most notably Satyajit Ray, who has explained that *Bicycle Thieves* "exercised a decisive influence" on his first feature, *Pather panchali*[6]—we are faced with an influence, or at least an affinity, that demands closer scrutiny.

The attraction of Italian neorealism for Third World film makers of the late 1950s lies on two levels: the mode of production adopted and the stance of the film makers themselves. The creators of neorealism had all worked in the mainstream of Italian commercial cinema during the early 1940s, and when they began making their own films in the early postwar years, not only did they inherit their equipment and commercial outlets from a fascist cinema they wished to supersede, but they also had to confront an audience shaped by the escapist entertainment cinema of the Mussolini years. Neorealism was a cinema made with limited means: often the rushes could not be viewed because there was no money to pay for prints, and films were shot silent (and post-synchronized) to allow shooting on location in the streets. But the resultant films were neither amateurish nor avant-garde: thanks to their professionalism and artistic quality, they succeeded in conveying the truths of contemporary poverty, unemployment, and old age to audiences throughout the world. Even the language issue—so crucial to Third World culture—was raised by neorealism, with Luchino Visconti making *La terra trema* in a dialect largely incomprehensible to mainland Italians because, as he explained, in Sicily, Italian is not the language of the poor.

All this had considerable relevance for Third World film makers of the 1950s, many of whom had been trained in professional film making techniques at European film schools (Santos and Guerra, for instance, had both studied for a while at the IDHEC in Paris). Returning to their own countries, they found screens dominated by Hollywood entertainment cinema, which also formed a point of reference for existing local commercial film industries (in Brazil and Argentina, for example). To these newcomers working on the fringes of the industry or in very low budget production, the revelation of what could be achieved with limited means was crucial. As Nelson Pereira dos Santos has expressed so forcefully, "the great lesson of neorealism was to produce films without taking heed of the whole material and economic apparatus of the dominant industry of the time, particularly the American industry." [7] Similarly, when first viewing *Bicycle Thieves* Satyajit Ray was "pleasantly surprised to discover that one could work exclusively in exterior settings, with non-professional actors, and I thought that what one could do in Italy, one could do in Bengal as well, in spite of the difficulties of sound recording." [8] Twenty years or so later, the term *neorealism* was explained by Antonio Eguino as "film making with a certain commitment towards the society we are involved in, with little money, shooting with non-actors, mostly outdoors." [9]

As a key figure in Cuban cinema, the documentarist Jorge Fraga, has said, "neorealism played an extraordinary part [as] catalyst" in the emergence of a new Latin American cinema. [10] Particularly interesting in this respect is what the affinity with the neorealists tells us about the class positions of the Third World film makers concerned. The Italian film makers were themselves of urban, largely middle-class origin, socially and culturally remote from the subjects of their work. (One thinks of the aristocratic Luchino Visconti, who came to the cinema after first devoting himself to the breeding of race horses, filming the Sicilian peasants of *La terra trema* and then going on to direct a version of Shakespeare's *As You Like It* with sets by Salvador Dali.) Their aim in choosing as their subject the lives of the poor and underprivileged was to show a reality that had been concealed beneath the official rhetoric of Mussolini's fascism. But this reality was one from which they themselves had largely been sheltered until the upheavals of war and civil war in Italy in 1943–45. The making of the film was itself, therefore, both an act of self-discipline (avoiding the spurious glamor of the entertainment film) and something of a voyage of discovery, literally so for Roberto Rossellini and Federico Fellini when they traveled the length of Italy to make *Paisa*. Though their films were based on careful research, the material was always reshaped into a fictional narrative form that did not deviate from a stance of realistic social observation. This allowed considerable insight and sympathy to be generated for their subjects (a Resistance leader on the run, an unemployed bill poster, or a Sicilian fisherman), but the narrative closure tended to preclude any clear indication of how society could be changed: neorealism remained a social cinema of discovery; it was not a political cinema of confrontation and change.

The social situation of Third World film makers is very much akin to that of the neorealists, although they are likely to be even more detached—by their class backgrounds, their urban upbringing, and their often westernized education—from the bulk of the national population. But the processes of national

independence and popular struggle and a growing awareness of a distinctive
Third World identity can bring them, as intellectuals, into a new relationship
with the mass of their fellow countrymen, and they show in their films a similar desire to uncover a hidden reality—in their case, the world concealed beneath the distortions and lies of colonial or neocolonial cultural dominance.
Realist film making—for which the neorealists in Italy could serve as exemplars—sets itself a number of tasks that distinguish it from mainstream entertainment cinema. As Fernando Solanas and Octavio Getino point out, to
adopt a realist stance is in fact a first political step: "Imperialism and capitalism, whether in the consumer society or in the neocolonialized country, veil
everything behind a screen of images and appearances. . . . The restitution of
things to their real place and meaning is an eminently subversive fact both in
the neocolonial situation and in the consumer societies." [11] The use of local
accents and vernacular languages similarly has a key part to play in "decolonizing" the cinema. Indeed, alongside the appeal of the songs and dances,
Barnouw and Krishnaswamy single out as a key factor in the popularity of
Indian sound films "the status that had suddenly been conferred by film on the
vernacular tongues, in a land in which foreign languages had for a thousand
years dominated the councils and pleasures of the mighty." [12]

But despite the rhetorical stance adopted by Birri in the 1950s and early
1960s, film making—whether in the form of a fictional feature or a documentary study—is never simply a neutral rendering of reality. There is no reality
existing "out there" for the film maker to record, and certainly no way in
which he can easily adopt the "optic of the people." The new image of reality
has to be constructed, not simply recorded, by the film maker. He thereby has
the possibility of conveying an authentic sense of life with its daily dramas
and of reflecting its rhythms of time and sense of space. But to achieve this,
the film maker will need both to question the given forms of Western fiction
and documentary and to define his own relationship with his subject. Often, it
is necessary for the film maker to break out of the narrow confines of an urban
culture to achieve this. For the Senegalese film maker Ousmane Sembene,
whose early work adopts a realist stance, though he has never acknowledged a
conscious debt to the neorealists, it was necessary to show his own early
shorts to village audiences. His viewers asked him why, if the films were for
them, he had made them "in his own language," that is to say, in French. The
experience was crucial for Sembene, as he admitted in 1979: "This was eighteen years ago. I had not at that moment realised how far I had alienated myself from my people. . . . I made a study of our films and then I realised that if
I wanted to make films for my people, then it must be in their language." [13]

It is even possible to argue in retrospect that the lasting importance of these
films is proportional to the extent to which the film maker has acknowledged
his own personal sense of discovery within the stylistic patterning of the text.
Often, as with Satyajit Ray's "Apu" trilogy, it is this evident sense of discov-

ery that gives the films their power, and Ray himself has made explicit the impact of filming on his own life and views:

> Before I made my first film—*Pather Panchali*—I had only a superficial knowledge of what life in a Bengal village was like. Now I know a great deal about it. I know its soil, its seasons, its trees and forests and flowers; I know how the man in the field works and how the women at the well gossip; and I know the children out in the sun and the rain, behaving as all children in all parts of the world do. My own city of Calcutta, too, I know much better now I've made a film about it.[14]

Realist film making of the sort described here marks an advance in awareness relative to the commercial entertainment cinema that preceded it. But it remains confined by the limits of the individual response and the personal discovery. Indeed, at times the work can be seen as much in terms of a self-discovery as of a discovery of a national reality. For many Third World film makers who have come into contact with neorealism, as for the Italian film makers themselves, a realist approach is merely one stage of an overall development, a necessary period of focusing attention, of defining priorities. The Indian film maker Shyam Benegal expressed this aspect well when he spoke of the impact of neorealism as "an element of discipline, of film discipline." It was crucial at a certain point of time but constituted a stage through which a film maker would pass.[15]

Because of its inherent individualism, neorealism proved less than effective as an official approach in postrevolutionary Cuba. Though the two film makers who had studied in Rome and been strongly marked by neorealism, Tomás Gutiérrez Alea and Julio García Espinosa, went on to hold influential positions in Cuba's newly established national film corporation, ICAIC, the attempt to adopt a neorealist approach in the early 1960s proved unsuccessful. In a society undergoing rapid change and defining its revolution, neorealism was as ineffectual as the other imported styles tried out at this time. It is arguable, in fact, that far from helping to create an authentic national cinema in Cuba, it contributed along with other outside influences in retarding the development of Cuban fictional film making.

In conclusion, it is worth stressing that though Third World intellectuals are inevitably, from their class position, susceptible to Western influences, neorealism was very often—as in Shyam Benegal's case—only one of a number of contrasting foreign film influences: Benegal recalls in addition Orson Welles, the Carol Reed of the early postwar years, and a mass of Hollywood films starring Errol Flynn, Tyrone Power, and Paul Muni. Though it is reasonable to talk of influences in the case of those who, like Birri, spent three years in Rome at the height of the neorealist period, in most other instances it is more appropriate to talk of affinities, deriving from similarities of social position and shared ambitions. As an antidote to the Western tendency to see

Third World realist film making as simply a product of approaches pioneered in Europe, it is perhaps worth quoting the Egyptian film maker Salah Abou Seif, who visited Rome in 1950 and has sometimes been described as "the creator of Egyptian neorealism":

> I don't think that neorealism in Egypt was the fruit of Italian influence. In fact this style was already begun in the film *The Will / Al-azima,* which Kamal Selim made in 1939 and of which I was producer and assistant. In addition, I remember very well that Kamal Selim sold a certain Stolof the synopsis of a film which related the misadventures of a poor man who had lost a cow which was his only breadwinner. In my view it was this synopsis which formed the basis of the film *Bicycle Thieves* that De Sica made in Italy in 1948. The cow was replaced by the bicycle, given the difference between Egypt and Italy.[16]

> *The anti-imperialist struggle of the peoples of the Third World and of their equivalents inside the imperialist countries constitutes today the axis of the world revolution. Third cinema is, in our opinion, the cinema that recognises in that struggle the most gigantic cultural, scientific and artistic manifestation of our time, the great possibility of constructing a liberated personality with each people as the starting point— in a word, the decolonisation of culture.*
>
> Fernando Solanas and Octavio Getino

The postwar years saw wide divergences in development in the Third World. The bulk of Africa was hardly touched by industrialization, and Egypt's economy, once a model of westernization, remained largely dormant (as did its level of film production)—only in the oil-rich states was any new industrialization begun. But elsewhere, in Latin America and Asia, the situation was more dynamic, with new industrialization of three kinds.

Firstly, in those countries with a potentially large domestic market, such as India, Mexico, and Brazil, there has been industrial expansion fostered by the state and an elite allied to Western interests, with output aimed partly at the local market and partly at the needs of the top 10 percent of the population. By imposing tariffs and quotas, the state has played a key role in protecting this industrialization from the foreign imports for which it is substituting. This type of development, then, has often gone hand in hand with a massive upsurge in long-established local film industries, regardless of whether these are owned by private capital or controlled through state film development corporations.

A second type of industrialization—characteristic of the "newly industrializing countries" of Southeast Asia, including the Republic of (South) Korea, Hong Kong, and Taiwan—has been built by using cheap local labor for a limited range of products such as textiles and manufactured goods based on labor-intensive assembly. The bulk of this output has been export-oriented (domestic working-class purchasing power being limited by low wages) and hence dependent on dislodging declining Western industries in a chosen area of production. Though generally lacking in a strong film making tradition, these countries, too, developed mushrooming film industries in the 1960s and 1970s, usually related to the entertainment needs of the newly created urban proletariat. While in most cases the aim is self-sufficiency in the provision of films, Hong Kong has built a flourishing export industry, supplying films to Chinese communities throughout the world and even—for a brief time in the 1970s—breaking into Western domestic markets.

The third type of industrialization—that by multinational corporations, which merely transfer to a new and cheaper work force the assembly (and in rare cases the complete manufacture) of goods designed for the world market—is only questionably "Third World industrialization." Capital, technology, and profits are all foreign-controlled, and the factory development has little impact outside the narrow enclave controlled by the multinational corporation. It is perhaps a reflection on the lack of connection between this type of industrialization and its "host" country that Singapore, where multinational control amounts to 70 percent or more of the economy, is the sole Southeast Asian state lacking an indigenous film industry.

The Euphoria of Revolution

This steady development of industrialization, combined with growing national awareness in the Third World during the 1960s, led almost imperceptibly to a belief, which came to be widely held, that an era of socialist revolution was dawning throughout the Third World. The omens seemed good: the 1960s began with the completion of decolonization in Africa—apart from the Portuguese territories and the white strongholds in Rhodesia, South Africa, and South West Africa; the Cubans were successful in resisting the CIA-backed Bay of Pigs invasion in 1961; the Algerians finally achieved independence in 1962, after eight years of armed struggle; and the Vietnamese struggled successfully against seemingly impossible odds and overwhelming U.S. military power. As a result, there emerged what Gérard Chaliand has called "a sort of Third World euphoria."

As Chaliand shows, there were many factors involved in this 1960s mood: the anticolonial struggle, opposition to the Vietnam war, student revolt, a new consciousness on the part of American blacks, the emergence of armed guerrilla groups in Latin America, developments within the communist world opposing China to USSR in terms of revolutionary strategy. From the combination of these factors arose "the myth of a Tricontinental Revolution via the figures of Fanon, Che Guevara, and Ho Chi Minh"[1]—which certainly colored the work of many of the film makers who began in the 1960s. They shared the radical mood and felt the need to take an equally heroic stance in their own work.

In retrospect, of course, much of what passed for political analysis in the 1960s can now be seen to be false. In North Africa, the FLN (National Liberation Front), as a guerrilla force, had been virtually annihilated by the French military by the time that Algerian independence was finally achieved in 1962, and in Latin America, armed struggle in the name of revolution proved far more difficult than had been anticipated. The Cuban and Vietnamese successes were not to be repeated; Che Guevara's failure to spread revolution outside Cuba and his execution in the Bolivian mountains in 1967 certainly indicate that the spread of revolution cannot be achieved by guerrillas who overestimate their own strength and misjudge the situations they wish to transform. Indeed, the 1960s saw not socialist revolution in Latin America, but the 1964 coup (and 1968 "coup within the coup") in Brazil, which heralded a succession of ever more brutal right-wing military coups in the 1970s, most of them with covert U.S. backing. The overthrow and death of the first democratically elected Marxist head of state, Salvador Allende, in Chile in 1973, marks at least the provisional end of an era of hope.

The euphoric mood of the late 1960s is very apparent in the work of many of the film makers who, born mostly in the 1930s, began as feature film makers at this time: Yılmaz Güney (1937–84) in Turkey, Glauber Rocha (1938–81) in Brazil, Jorge Sanjinés (b. 1936) in Bolivia, Ousmane Sembene (b. 1923) in Senegal, Miguel Littin (b. 1942) in Chile, Fernando Solanas (b. 1936), and Octavio Getino (b. 1935) in Argentina. This was the generation that created so many of the "new cinemas" of the 1960s and 1970s, among them *cinema novo* in Brazil, the *nueva ola* in Argentina, and the Cinema of Popular Unity in Chile. These descriptions were often no more than journalistic labels, which many of the film makers grouped under them would reject. But they do indicate how these film makers—unlike their elders of the 1950s generation—could be seen as participating in a collective movement of revolutionary change that had both national and international dimensions.

Belief in the political function of cinema was fundamental to all these film makers. Typical subjects adopted were the workings of justice (Littin's *The Jackal of Nahueltoro / El chacal de Nahueltoro* [1969]), the corruption of the newly emerged black elites (Sembene's *Xala* [1974]), and rural underdevelopment (Rocha's *Antonio-das-Mortes* [1969]). The struggle for national liberation was chronicled in black Africa by Sembene, in Algeria by Mohamed Lakdar-Hamina (b. 1934), and in Tunisia by Omar Khlifi (b. 1934). As the treatment of the subject by the Cubans Humberto Solas (b. 1942) and Manuel Octavio Gómez (b. 1934) showed, this 1960s generation was not content to keep to a surface realism. The Mauritanian Med Hondo (b. 1936) in *Soleil O*

13. Miguel Littin: The Jackal of Nahueltoro / El chacal de Nahueltoro *(Chile, 1969)*

14. Ousmane Sembene: Xala *(Senegal, 1974)*

15. *Fernando Solanas and Octavio Getino:* The Hour of the Furnaces / La hora de los hornos *(Argentina, 1968)*

(made in exile in France) offered an allegory of emerging national consciousness, and a similar tendency toward generalizing abstraction could be found in Sanjinés's indictments of U.S. imperialism, in a study of the internal divisions of a colonized Egypt by Shadi Abdes-Salam (b. 1930), and in Güney's epic script of the clash of cultures *The Herd / Sürü* (1978). For many of these film makers the protective distancing of their work through fiction and imaginary settings was necessary for survival, and it was virtually only in Cuba that documentary could play out its full potential role in the shaping of society. The impact of the Cuban documentarist Santiago Alvarez (b. 1919), like that of Birri, was enormous on the various short-lived and generally clandestine documentary movements that sprang up from time to time in the 1960s and 1970s in Latin America.

Except during brief spells of liberalization, critical attitudes are tolerated scarcely anywhere in the Third World. Cuba is unique in the extent to which its film makers control their industry, and it is no coincidence that it is there alone that a socially critical form of cinema has been encouraged. But even for film makers working within the state-run film industry in a socialist country

16. Shadi Abdes-Salam: The Night of Counting the Years / Al-momia *(Egypt, 1969)*

that, like Cuba, publicly proclaims its desire to change the lives of its people, tensions and difficulties arise when delicate political issues are tackled. (For example, García Espinosa's feature *Son o non son,* shot in 1978–79, was never released, though it is listed in the annual production records.)

Elsewhere in the Third World, though, the situation is very different, and advocacy of change is seen simply as hostility toward the state. In the early 1970s the cost of advocating change proved to be very high for Third World film makers, who suffered censorship, imprisonment, exile, and enforced silence. As a result, the satisfyingly rounded careers achieved by the 1950s generation were no longer possible. At its most extreme, there was no career at all in the case of Abdes-Salam, who was not able to make a second feature to follow his striking debut with *The Night of Counting the Years / Al-momia* (1969). Abdes-Salam was at least able to remain in Egypt, where he could complete a number of documentaries. But elsewhere, film makers were not so fortunate. The emergence of *cinema novo* in Brazil was followed almost immediately, in 1964, by a military coup and a steadily worsening political climate, which by 1968 had driven Rocha and the Mozambican-born director of *The Guns / Os fuzis* (1964), Ruy Guerra (b. 1931), into temporary exile. The

17. Med Hondo: Soleil O *(France/Mauritania, 1969)*

same story was to be repeated throughout Latin America: Bolivia in 1971 (keeping Sanjinés in exile), Chile after the death of President Allende in 1973 (resulting in the departure of Raul Ruiz [b. 1941] to France and of Littin to Mexico), Argentina in 1976 (exiling Solanas and Getino). Similarly, the periodic military interventions in Turkey imprinted themselves on Güney's life, with three successive spells of imprisonment, followed by escape and eventual death in exile. The Mauritanian Med Hondo has made all his films in exile in Paris, and even Sembene, despite his reputation as black Africa's leading film maker, has had a continual battle with the censors in his native Senegal, where *Xala* was released only after eleven separate cuts and where *Ceddo* remained banned for eight years. But this listing of major figures gives only a partial picture, for the various 1970s coups in Latin America led to the exile of virtually everyone, great or small, connected with the film industry. While this had beneficial effects on countries such as Peru and Venezuela who received the exiles, its effect on the work of the film makers was disastrous.

The pressures on this generation have been immense, but its members have persisted with incredible vigor, their efforts symbolized by Güney, who scripted the internationally acclaimed *The Herd* and *Yol* (1982) in a prison

18. Ruy Guerra: The Guns / Os fuzis *(Brazil, 1964)*

cell. These men were often the founders of their national cinemas, and in some cases, as with Sembene and Sanjinés, they worked personally to extend the range and function of cinema by taking their films to remote communities. The profound link that binds each of them to his native country, even when in exile, is very strong and is typified by the treatment of language in their films. Thus, Ousmane Sembene began using Wolof in *The Money Order* / *Mandabi* (1968) before there was an agreed-upon written form for the language, while all Jorge Sanjinés's films have been made not in the Spanish of the educated elite, but in the languages of the Quechua and Amayara Indians who make up the bulk of Bolivia's population. Their inability to continue to reach the national audience with which they had achieved unique links is thus doubly crippling.

Into the 1980s

The period since the mid-1970s is perhaps best understood as a reaction to the exaggerated hopes prevalent in the Third World of the late 1960s. There have continued to be occasional examples of genuine political progress, such as the ending of Portuguese rule in Africa, the independence of Zimbabwe under black majority rule, and the success of the Sandinistas in Nicaragua. But the main beneficiaries of the major economic shift of the 1970s brought about by the enormous rise in oil prices were among the most reactionary of Third World governments: first the shah and then the Ayatollah Khomeini in Iran, together with the various kings and princes of the Gulf States. The instances of rapid industrialization that have occurred—as in Taiwan, Hong Kong, Brazil, and Iran—have been both fragile and tightly controlled by multinational corporations.

While Western advocates of capitalism have pointed to the considerable developments in Asia and Latin America, events in the 1980s—particularly the world banking crisis—have shown that the balance sheet is not wholly positive. Third World industrialization, built largely on foreign loans and directed at export markets, is very precarious and liable to be brought to a halt by shifts in world demand. In almost all cases, industrialization has been fostered by an authoritarian regime (a one-party state or a military government) that is prepared to use force to keep the working class in check. Fundamentals of Western democracy—press freedom, trade unionism, freedom of speech and political assembly—are systematically denied. Always, the state plays a key role—to the benefit of the elite that controls it—in cementing alliances with foreign capital, channeling foreign aid, shaping local investment, and protecting profits. Very little of the gross domestic product so generated finds its way to the mass of the people. Moreover, in virtually no case has industrialization actually lessened foreign dependence. These "developing" countries continue to rely ever more heavily on Japan and the West for technology, capital, and markets, and in most cases the industrial development remains an enclave in a largely untransformed agricultural economy. Local cultural production points to the enormous human cost of this development, with the forms and structures of the violent but introspect cinemas of Southeast Asia offering eloquent testimonials to these societies' lack of human freedom.

It is no longer possible to anticipate world revolution triggered off by Third World developments, and the 1970s and early 1980s have therefore been largely a period of reevaluation for the Third World and its theorists. Among the issues that have had to be confronted are the tendency of political independence, especially in Africa, to lead directly into new forms of neocolonial dependence; the problem of bureaucratization in such cases where social change has occurred; the general failure of the tactics of guerrilla warfare, especially in Latin America; and the dubious results of both the national bourgeois revolutions (typified by Nasser's Egypt) and the various forms of self-proclaimed African and Islamic socialism. In short, what is involved is a fundamental questioning of virtually all the established assumptions of progress that were current in the years preceding and immediately following Asian and African independence. The one certainty now is that there will be no easy answers to replace the lost certitudes of the 1960s. In light of this, it is hardly surprising that a consistent pattern of commitment is difficult to discern in the work of the younger film makers—those born mostly in the 1940s and beginning their careers in the 1970s—who inevitably reflect in their work, though to varying degrees, the prevailing mood.

Perhaps the strongest impression left by Third World film making in the 1970s and early 1980s is its stylistic diversity and geographical spread. Not only are there now film industries in Bangladesh and Thailand, Indonesia and South Korea, and internationally known film makers in virtually all countries with an established film industry, there are also talented film makers working in just about every part of the world. Even if we ignore both those working within the constraints of mainstream commercial cinema and those engaged on esoteric explorations that have yet to find an audience, we are still left with a great number of film makers working individually to express their national social reality. In some cases this means operating on the fringes of a national film industry—in documentary production, for instance; in others it implies initiating film making where no prior local tradition of production exists. The new importance accorded to documentary film making shows that the disillusion with the revolutionary fervor of the late 1960s has not led film makers to turn their backs on reality. Instead, a questioning, probing stance has become common. It is, of course, too soon to offer any definitive evaluation of these younger film makers, most of whom have been unable to make more than a feature film or two, but a brief survey will give some idea of the current diversity of Third World film production.

1971 saw the showing of *The Cruel Sea / Bas ya bahr,* the first of two features by the Indian-trained Khalid Siddik from Kuwait. In 1972 the first of a number of deeply researched documentary studies of the poor and the peasantry was made in Colombia, in close collaboration with their subjects, by Marta Rodriguez and Jorge Silva. In Morocco, Souhel Ben Barka made a fictional study of the commercial exploitation of local craft skills, *A Thousand and One Hands / Mille et une mains* (1972), and in Mexico, Paul Leduc began his career as a documentarist with a study of his country's past, *Reed: Insurgent Mexico / Reed: México insurgente* (1973). A variety of first features appeared in 1974, all with a strong documentary flavor: *Harvest 3,000 Years / Mirt sost shi amit* by the Ethiopian-born Haile Gerima; *Daily Life in a Syrian Village / Al-hayat al-yawmiyya fi qaria suriyya* by Umar Amiralay; *Kafr kassem,* an account of an Israeli massacre, by the Lebanese Borhan Alawiya; and *One Way or Another / De cierta manera,* the only feature-length film of the Cuban woman director Sara Gómez. 1975 was marked by the first part of the masterly documentary trilogy by Patricio Guzmán, *The Battle of Chile / La batalla de Chile,* and by the appearance of two very talented film makers from black Africa: the politically committed Souleymane Cisse, whose first feature was *The Girl / Den muso,* and Safi Faye, whose concerned and questioning study of her native village, *Letter from My Village / Kaddu beykat,* showed her training as an ethnographer. 1977 brought a similar diversity, with

a striking study of the impact of tourism on Tunisia, *Sun of the Hyenas /
Shams al-dibaa* by Ridha Behi, the portrait of a woman active in a macho-
dominated society *Portrait of Teresa / Retrato de Teresa,* by the Cuban Pastor
Vega, and a fresh and uninhibited look at Algerian youth, *Omar Gatlato* by
Merzak Allouache.

In the 1980s, a new personal tone was given to Hong Kong production by
Father and Son / Fuzi qing (1981), directed by Allen Fong. Also, a diverse
array of talent emerged in parts of the world with little or no history of production. Outstanding here are Michel Khleifi, a Palestinian who gives voice to
the Arab minority in Israel, the Syrian Mohamed Malass, who began with a
fictional study of Damascus, *City Dreams / Ahlam al-madina* (1985), and
three directors of enormous potential from black Africa: Fadika Kramo-
Lancine from the Ivory Coast, Gaston Kaboré from Burkina Faso, and Rui
Duarte from Angola. It is impossible to sum up this surge of emerging talent
in a few lines, but the importance of the work produced is more than a sum of
individual achievements. Taken together, these film makers offer a genuine set
of alternatives to North American and European styles. In this way cinema
can cease to be a one-way communication system, imposing stereotypes
"made in Hollywood" indiscriminately on audiences throughout the world:
the possibility of a real dialogue between East and West comes nearer.

Theory and Politics

While earlier developments in Third World cinema had been untheorized,
the 1960s generation of politically committed film makers brought a new, explicitly theoretical, approach, exemplified by two statements published in
1969: "For an Imperfect Cinema," by the Cuban Julio García Espinosa, and
"Towards a Third Cinema," by the Argentines Fernando Solanas and Octavio
Getino. García Espinosa, writing as a Marxist ten years after the Cuban Revolution, is concerned with the role of cinema in consolidating an already
achieved social transformation and with building a new relationship between
culture and society. His starting point is his opposition to the technical perfection of Western cinema, which "is almost always reactionary cinema" and, as
such, represents the greatest temptation facing Cuban cinema.

From García Espinosa's viewpoint—which tallies closely with that of such
theorists of national liberation as Cabral and Fanon—the true aim should not
be to create a new privileged-elite minority of artistic film makers, but to
question radically the separation between such film makers and the mass of
the people, who have access to neither the training nor the facilities required
in film making. García Espinosa attacks the terms in which arguments about
the need for commitment in art are conducted. Though the context of his
thinking is a postrevolutionary society, he rejects the simplistic call for a committed art, asserting that art has its own particular cognitive power: "Every

artist's desire to express the inexpressible is nothing more than the desire to express the vision of a theme in terms that are inexpressible through other than artistic means." [2] From this recognition follows an important distinction between art and science: "Art can stimulate, in general, the creative function of man. It can function as constant stimulus toward adopting an attitude of change with regard to life. But, as opposed to science, it enriches us in such a way that its results are not specific and cannot be applied to anything in particular." [3] But the definition of art as "impartial" or "uncommitted" that follows from this distinction is meaningless, García Espinosa argues, unless the elite isolation of the artist is destroyed. The real task in hand is "to find out if the conditions which will enable spectators to transform themselves into agents—not merely active spectators, but genuine co-authors—are beginning to exist." [4]

What García Espinosa calls "an authentically revolutionary artistic culture" cannot draw on mass art, that is, the kind of art made by a minority for the masses, who are defined as mere consumers or spectators (procedures characteristic of Western "perfect" cinema). But it can draw lessons both from popular art, in which "the creators are at the same time the spectators and vice versa" and art is "carried out as but another life activity," and from the struggles within modern art to democratize art, "combatting the limitations of taste, museum art, and the demarcation lines between the creator and the public." [5] Film presents inherent difficulties—the impossibility in the short run of turning the masses into film makers—but the revolution, defined by García Espinosa as "the highest expression of culture," does offer the context for a new transitional poetics of cinema, an "imperfect" cinema, which "finds its audience in those who struggle" and "its themes in their problems." [6]

For imperfect cinema, the central characters are "lucid" people, that is, "the ones who think and feel and exist in a world which they can change; in spite of all the problems and difficulties, they are convinced that they can transform it in a revolutionary way." [7] In contrast to Western cinema, which concerns itself with the celebration of results and outcomes, imperfect cinema must "above all show the process which generates the problems." [8] To show the process of a problem is not the same as analyzing it.

> To analyze, in the traditional sense of the word, always implies a closed prior judgement. To analyze a problem is to show the problem (not the process) permeated with judgements which the analysis itself generates *a priori*. To analyze is to block off from the outset any possibility for analysis on the part of the interlocutor. To show the process of a problem, on the other hand, is to submit it to judgement without pronouncing the verdict. [9]

In its concern with process, imperfect cinema is indifferent to mere quality or technique—"it can be created equally well with a Mitchell or with an 8mm camera, in a studio or in a guerrilla camp in the middle of the jungle"—and the test of a film maker is quite simply his response to the question "What are you doing in order to overcome the barrier of the 'cultured' elite audience which up to now has conditioned the form of your work?" [10]

Solanas and Getino in their manifesto "Towards a Third Cinema" echo García Espinosa's distrust of Western formal perfection: "The model of the perfect work of art, the fully rounded film structured according to the metrics imposed by bourgeois culture, its theoreticians and critics, has served to inhibit the film maker in the dependent countries, especially when he has attempted to erect similar models in a reality which *offered neither the culture, the techniques, nor the most primary elements for success.*" [11] But their own position is very different: it is one of film makers working clandestinely for social and political change in a hostile environment. Their views are optimistic, however, for they see as the context for the new form of cinema they advocate "the development of a worldwide liberation movement whose moving force is to be found in the Third World countries." [12] Their program—which forms part of a necessary decolonization of culture—proposes a cinema of subversion, aimed at "the *new man* exemplified by Che." [13] For these reasons, their terminology is full of the imagery of guerrilla combat: a film is "a detonator," a camera "a rifle," and a projector "a gun that can shoot 24 frames per second," while the film maker is likened to the guerrilla fighter who "travels along paths that he himself opens up with machete blows." [14]

For Solanas and Getino, the decolonization of cinema involves two complementary procedures: the destruction of the old modes of conceiving cinema and the old image shaped by colonialism and neocolonialism, and the creation of a new cinema, the "construction of a throbbing, living reality which recaptures truth in any of its expressions." [15] They begin their consideration by challenging two existing forms of cinema, both of which are "perfect" in García Espinosa's terms. For them, "first cinema" is Hollywood, and they point out the difficulty of locating, even in the socialist world, examples of work totally outside the Hollywood film model. But this model must be attacked on every level. Since language and ideology are inseparable, even the adoption of the merely formal elements of the dominant Hollywood film language leads inevitably to the adoption of the ideological assumptions, deriving from U.S. finance capital, that underlie them. The only real alternatives to Hollywood cinema that they pick out are those forms of "author's cinema"—from the French *nouvelle vague* to the Brazilian *cinema novo*—which they dub "second cinema." For Solanas and Getino, however, even the advance that these represent is a limited one. Although they do constitute attempts at cultural decolonization and lead their film makers to express themselves "in nonstandard language," they are still contained within the dominant system. Only "third cinema," which they advocate, breaks free of these constraints.

Solanas and Getino, then, see the main basis of revolutionary cinema as the documentary: "Every image that documents, bears witness to, refutes or deepens the truth of a situation is something more than a film image or purely artistic fact; it becomes something which the system finds indigestible." [16] But documentary can only have this impact if it no longer echoes the stance common in the West. Revolutionary cinema "is not fundamentally one which illustrates, documents, or passively establishes a situation: *rather, it attempts to intervene in the situation as an element providing thrust or rectification.*" [17] Thus, it is less a cinema denouncing the *effects* of neocolonialism than one that examines *causes,* "to investigate the ways of organizing and arming for the change."

Solanas and Getino's own stance is based on their confidence in the mass audience, for the effectiveness of the best militant cinema, they claim, has shown that "social layers considered backward" are able "to capture the exact meaning of an association of images, an effect of staging, and any linguistic experimentation placed within the context of a given idea." [18] Film makers are therefore free to be innovative in their use of the resources of cinema, but for revolutionary communication to occur, film makers must discard any preconceptions about their "rights" as artists. They must also disregard the traditional film industry's notions of hierarchy and professionalism and work instead to demystify the medium. Third cinema can only fulfill its role as "the most important revolutionary artistic event of our times" when film makers oppose the cinema of characters, individuals, and authors with a cinema of themes, the masses, and collective work, and when they replace misinformation, escape, and passivity with information, truth, and action—in short, when they build not "a cinema made for the old kind of human being" but "a cinema fit for a new kind of human being, for what each of us has the possibility of becoming." [19]

Neither of these manifestos offers a narrowly prescriptive view of cinema committed to revolutionary change. Solanas and Getino's guerrilla cinema may be defined in terms of documentary, but it embraces a whole host of forms (film letter, film poem, film essay, film pamphlet, and film report), and the richness of their approach is borne out by their own masterly documentary, *The Hour of the Furnaces / La hora de los hornos* (1968). Similarly, García Espinosa's approach implies a breakdown of the rigid categories of documentary and fiction, and this has become a characteristic feature of Cuban cinema since the late 1960s. The relationship between culture and society that these manifestos posit draws its lessons from the liberation struggle and from the writings of such theorists as Cabral and Fanon. To some extent, the optimism of the late 1960s has proved to be ill founded, having underestimated in particular the extremes to which the United States is willing to go to protect its "interests." But the rethinking of cinema undertaken by Latin American theorists will continue to have relevance as long as film is given the function of contributing to social and political change.

Part Three

National Film Industries

It is fruitless to expect the underdeveloped countries of today to repeat the stages of economic growth passed through by modern developed countries, whose classical capitalist development arose out of pre-capitalist and feudal society.

Andre Gunder Frank

The Western dominance of world film distribution is echoed in the almost exclusive attention paid to Western achievements in studies that set out to cover the history of "world cinema." There are honorable exceptions to this generalization (one thinks particularly of Georges Sadoul), but in general the disregard of Third World achievement is such that an awareness of the overall growth of world cinema is very difficult to achieve. Though the present volume can in no way claim to be a comprehensive history of Third World cinema, it does seem appropriate to attempt to redress the balance a little. The chapters that follow, therefore, consider the national film industries of the Third World, in four major groupings: two on Asia, one on Latin America, and one on Africa and the Middle East.

The commercial industries of the Far East, which have given Asia a 50 percent share of world film production for thirty years or more, are—outside India and Japan—as anonymous as they are enormous. Film is a commodity produced for immediate local consumption, with, in most cases, only limited export to neighboring countries sharing a common language. There is no sense of a medium of expression building on its past or constituting the basis of a tradition. Little attempt has been made at film preservation—even in India, which has been concerned about its cinematic past for decades now, barely half a dozen silent films out of perhaps twelve hundred are still in existence. In most parts of Africa a tradition of critical assessment is also largely lacking. Figures whose importance is more than local and who would have given the necessary landmarks have not been picked out, so the task of mapping even the recent past will be difficult. Rooted in decades of low-budget artisanal production, these cinemas may not be national in any true cultural sense, but they are shaped regardless of Western fashion and are largely free to adopt their own rhythms of time and to follow their own predilections in terms of narrative construction.

The perspective changes when we look at the way in which the national cinemas of Latin America, Africa, and the Middle East have developed. Only briefly in Turkey in the early 1970s do we find a huge national industry of the kind characteristic of the Far East. Despite the myth of hundreds of Egyptian, Brazilian, or Mexican films being produced each year, output has generally been far more modest, with the total of a hundred films a year being reached only occasionally by isolated industries enjoying brief spells of intense government support—Mexico in the 1950s or Brazil in the early 1980s, for example. Output in the whole of Latin America has never exceeded 8 percent of the world total (slightly less than the output of eastern Europe and the USSR, and less than half that of western Europe), while the 1 or 2 percent share enjoyed by the African and Arab countries is almost totally accounted for by Egyptian producers—whose industry has, however, never again equaled its peak of eighty films in 1953–54.

From the point of view of the present survey, however, these smaller industries offer fascinating insight into the interplay of indigenous and Western forces, and they provide concrete examples of the often tenuously defined concept of cultural domination. Much of the best Latin American, African, and Middle Eastern work with which we are acquainted in the West has been accomplished within, or in close relation to, these commercial industries—one thinks, for example, of Salah Abou Seif in Egypt or Luis Buñuel for a while in Mexico. But the less industrially developed areas of Latin America, as well as the African and Arab worlds, also offer examples of film making of the very highest quality—from Jorge Sanjinés in Bolivia to Ousmane Sembene in Senegal—that is the result of a struggle to create the basis of a culturally authentic national cinema without an industrial infrastructure, indeed, almost by an effort of will.

The Indian Subcontinent   7

Indian films have been described as "purely escapist," but this is a judgement far beside the mark. The films serve a country marked by deep tensions—between wealth and poverty, old and new, hope and fear. The tensions are the basic material of the medium. Its images and sounds are only the means for playing on those tensions—sometimes subtly, sometimes powerfully.

Erik Barnouw and S. Krishnaswamy

The cinema reached the Indian subcontinent in 1896, at the height of the British *raj,* so the first fifty years of its development took place under a colonial administration that administered the whole territory (including Burma until 1937) as a single unit. The fact that Indian capital "was born and nurtured in the shadow of the colonial state" [1] has important implications for cinema, which is as much a capitalist enterprise in India as in the West. Indian industrialization had begun in the 1850s as part of a wider attempt at modernization, which also included controversial land reforms and led to the first nationalist revolt, the so-called Indian Mutiny of 1857. Some coal was mined, but the key sectors of the industrial economy were jute and cotton. Thanks to the Calcutta jute mills, mostly established by European residents, and the Bombay cotton mills, which were largely Indian owned, India became "a central pillar of the nineteenth century international trade economy." [2] By 1913— the year in which the first Indian feature film was made—the first iron and steel plants had already been set up, and Indian industrialization was very considerable in colonial terms, though limited to just a few products and geographically contained within virtual enclaves around Bombay, Calcutta, and Madras. Though there was no development in the chemical and electrical sectors, which were then coming to the fore in Europe, those industries that did exist were technically efficient and generally well run. Despite a total absence of tariff protection, India was a net exporter of coal, and it "stood as the fourth greatest cotton manufacturing nation" and was "second only to Britain as a world exporter of cotton yarn." [3] Its 34,000 miles of railway network represented over half the total for the whole of Asia.

This industrialization remained one-sided, though. There seems to have been no development of traditional craft industries alongside the industrialization, and financial institutions embracing both modern and traditional capital were not created. Morever, the modern developments were dwarfed by the massive agricultural sector, which continued to dominate the economy as a whole.

India
Silent Cinema

India's first film show took place on 7 July 1896 at Watson's Hotel in Bombay. Other demonstrations by visiting showmen followed, and the cinema gradually established itself. In Bombay, H. S. Bhatvadekar shot little actuality films from 1897 with a camera imported from London, and in Calcutta a year or so later, Hiralal Sen shot theater scenes for incorporation into live performances. A first fictional effort, *Pundalik,* was shot in Bombay with English technicians by R. G. Torney in 1912.

In these early years of the century, exhibition was much more developed than production, and in India, as in Europe, traveling showmen established the first popular audience by taking films from place to place with their tent shows. Among those whose names have survived from this pioneer era are two showmen who eventually established picture palaces, Abdulally Esoofally and J. F. Madan, who was eventually to become India's first exhibition magnate (the Madan company controlled 85 of India's 346 movie theaters in 1927). But the great pioneer of Indian film production was Dadasaheb Phalke (1870–1944), whose work was considered in chapter 4. In a career that extended from India's first feature film, *Raja Harischandra* in 1913, to his last work (and only talkie), *Descent of Ganga / Gangavataran* in 1934, Phalke made over a hundred films of all kinds, including even the 1917 documentary *How Films Are Made.* His contribution was enormous: "Phalke laid the foundation of the film industry, and the countrywide success of his films gave an impetus to many capitalists in Bombay to rush to this industry. Importers of liquor, manufacturers of wooden buckets, hair-oil producers, textile manufacturers and cotton merchants took to producing films. The Indian film industry had arrived." [4]

Phalke arrived at a propitious moment. World War I led to an upsurge in industrialization, triggered by the needs of the war effort and by increased import difficulties. This rapid industrialization led in turn to an enormous

19. Dadasaheb Phalke: Raja Harischandra *(India, 1913)*

growth in the urban working class, which was to form the bulk of the cinema's audience. Indian capital made profits that could be invested in cinema, where popular audience demand outstripped local product availability. When Phalke began, cinema was still in an artisanal state, with the film maker needing to be personally responsible not only for production, direction, and script, but also for processing and even exhibition. Though the Indian film industry itself benefited from no government support or protection and had to assert itself in a context dominated by foreign imports (which reached 85 percent by 1927), the steady expansion of the cinema throughout the 1920s took place at a time when the British authorities were exhibiting a broad willingness to offer support to other local industries through tariffs, quotas, and the like (the Tariff Board was set up in 1923). The diversification of Indian industrialization from its narrow pre-1914 base and the growth toward Indian self-sufficiency in a widening range of consumer goods, then, led to finances generated in the protected industries being reinvested in the film industry. At the same time, the overwhelming predominance of Hollywood in the film industry was balanced by a powerful counterforce, the rising Indian nationalist movement, which took on a new urgency after the Amritsar massacre of 1919 and which, under Gandhi's leadership, became a mass movement in the 1920s. Though mythological subjects remained popular as vehicles for national self-expression, a new awareness of inequalities in society is apparent in the contemporary subjects, known as "socials," that became popular in the 1920s.

Our knowledge of Indian silent cinema is limited by the fact that virtually all the films produced have been lost, but we do know that it spread rapidly. If Bombay, where Phalke set up his studio, remained the center of Indian film production, feature films had begun to be made elsewhere before 1920. In 1917, the first Bengali film was made in Calcutta, J. F. Madan's *Satyawadi Raja Harischandra*. The artist Baburao Painter (1894–1954), whose directing career extended to the year before his death, established a film production company in Kolhapur in 1917 and remained a key figure in film making in Maharashtra, while, in the South, production in Madras began with Nataraj Mudakiar's *Keechaka vadham* (1919).

During the 1920s there was both a doubling in the number of cinemas, located mostly in the main urban areas, and a corresponding rise in film production. Members of the 1927–28 Indian Cinematograph Committee (ICC, whose report is an indispensable source of information on the period) were surprised to discover that, in numerical terms at least, Indian film production already exceeded that of Britain. Figures are uncertain, but the most widely accepted tabulation, listing a total of 1,268 silent films between 1920 and 1934, gives the number of silent films produced in 1920 as 27, rising to 86 in 1925, and peaking at 201 in 1931 (the year the first Indian sound films were released), then falling away to just 7 silent films in 1934.[5]

The Hollywood studio was the accepted model for Indian production and the companies that emerged in the 1920s and 1930s aimed to be totally self-sufficient at all levels of production, including laboratory work. Phalke's organization of his own company of a hundred or so collaborators into a kind of extended family, with himself as the stern father figure, was a much imitated pattern. The studio buildings were "comparatively simple affairs" in the 1920s, "consisting of one or two areas walled with high screens and with a roof of glass or merely of framework, and with an arrangement of curtains for diffusing the light."[6] Only one or two producers used arc lights, and Indian cinema continued to rely on imported equipment, often used foreign technicians, and also drew some of its players—particularly for the big spectacles—from abroad.

Production costs were low and closely related to the potential yield of the 15 percent of the market that Indian films controlled, so a film's cost of around fifteen to twenty thousand rupees was equivalent to the receipts from a four- or five-week run in Bombay.[7] During the 1920s—and indeed until the end of the 1940s—there was little hope of export, but the 1928 ICC report notes that "a good Indian film is extremely profitable to the producer; even an indifferent film generally yields a fair margin of profit."[8] The low level of cost and the possibility of recovering it all in a single run in a major city precluded the emergence of a distribution sector in the industry with a strength equivalent to that in the West. Direct personal negotiations with exhibitors could be undertaken by the producers themselves, who did not normally cede the rights to their productions to intermediaries.[9]

Technically, Indian films of the 1920s were poor, and the ICC report describes them as "generally crude in comparison with Western pictures" and as "defective in composition, acting and in every respect."[10] Since films were designed for an unsophisticated mass audience, there was generally a reliance on action, with players chosen from the ranks of acrobats, stuntmen, and dancers rather than from the stage. The development of a specifically visual storytelling language was hampered by the concentration on mythological subjects (which meant the stories would be well known to audiences) and the use of a "narrator" sitting alongside the screen who "read the title cards for the benefit of the audience, spoke the lines for the main characters, and gave a running commentary on the happenings on the screen." As in Japan at this period, it very often happened that "the performance of the narrator itself acquired an independent value and films which would have otherwise been unsuccessful were often saved by the narrators."[11] The lack of concern with the kind of tight narrative continuity in silent cinema that was evolving in Hollywood helped ease the way for the universal adoption of the distinctive form of the Indian musical after the coming of sound.

In the 1920s, an entertainment tax was introduced—in Bengal in 1922, Bombay in 1923—and censorship control was more formalized. Generally, though, the British were concerned solely with political matters—kissing, for example, was allowed in Indian silent cinema—and were more intent on seeking ways of replacing Hollywood influences with imported British films than with fostering an indigenous film industry. Within this overall pattern, however, a striking array of talents emerged in the last years of silent cinema, most of whom were to find still greater scope in the sound era.

In 1921, Dhiren Ganguly (1893–1978) made his social satire on westernized Indians, *England Returned / Bilat ferat,* the first of over twenty silent films made for the various production companies that he successfully founded. It was with Ganguly that another important film maker of the 1930s, Debaki Bose (1888–1975) made his debut, first as a scriptwriter and then as director, with *The Blind God / Panchasar* (1929). Another prolific director of "socials" was Chandulal Shah (1898–1975), who made dozens of silent films from 1926 onward, many of them featuring one of the leading stars of the period, Miss Gohar. Shah's most celebrated film is *Why Husbands Go Astray / Gun sundari* (1927) and his preoccupations are clearly reflected in his film titles, many of which are in English, such as *Typist Girl* (1926) and *Educated Wife* (1927). The leading proponent of international coproduction was the producer Hinansu Rai, who himself starred alongside the Anglo-Indian actress Sita Devi in three silent films directed by the German Franz Osten, all of which

have been preserved: *The Light of Asia* (1926), *Loves of a Moghul Prince /
Shiraz* (1928), and *A Throw of Dice* (1930).

The Coming of Sound

The 1928 report noted this about the demand for Indian films: "In cinemas
which cater for purely Indian audiences, an Indian film is ordinarily more
profitable to the exhibitor than a Western film. Although the exhibitor pays
more for the Indian film, his gross receipts are greater owing to much larger
attendance." [12] Sound came to Indian film production in 1931, and during the
last sixteen years of colonial rule, production rose from 27 sound features in
1931 to 282 in 1947, while the number of cinemas rose from around 300 to
1,600 in 1938 and over 3,000 in 1948. The second major report on the industry, that of the Film Enquiry Committee (FEC) of 1951, referred with satisfac-
tion to "the changeover of a large number of cinemas from foreign pictures to
Indian pictures," adding that, "in the circumstances, the exhibition of foreign
films is not very significant as far as competition with the Indian industry is
concerned." [13]

This development toward self-sufficiency in film production and exhibition
is part of wider economic changes that made India "self-sufficient in a wide
range of consumer goods" by the 1940s, with "some 60 percent of the market
held by Indian firms." Similarly, in this period Indian banks came to hold over
80 percent of deposits, and Indian firms controlled "around 60 per cent of the
import/export trade." [14] Of equal importance for cultural production, including film, was the fact that throughout the 1930s India was moving toward
greater political control of its own affairs, with eventual dominion status assured by the long-debated 1935 Government of India Act. Although the war
occasioned many British delays and hesitations, the nationalist movement
grew stronger than ever (though there was now a split between the aspirations
of Hindus and Muslims), and by 1945 there could be no doubt that the British
would have to concede full independence.

The coming of sound had the effect of dividing the vast film audience of
several hundred million inhabitants spread throughout India, Ceylon, and
Burma into a dozen or more linguistic communities. It initiated two contradictory tendencies, which continue to dominate Indian film production into
the 1980s. On the one hand, there is the all-India movie: centered in Bombay
and made in Hindi, but without real local roots (since Bombay is in the
Marathi-speaking area), yet nevertheless serving something of a unifying national function, in much the same way as the Egyptian film does in the Arab
world. On the other hand, producers operating in Calcutta, Madras, and other
smaller centers can affirm a regional identity by the use of a local language
and still have access to a potential audience of many millions. The two tendencies are not entirely separate—regional production companies have made

original films in Hindi for the all-India market, and from the start local minority-language successes were often remade in Hindi—but the huge gulf between the big-budget Bombay movie and the small-budget regional cinema has remained.

Though the overwhelming bulk of films up to 1947 were made in Hindi (61 out of 83 in 1932, and 185 out of 282 in 1947), occasional productions were made in most of the other major languages, with a sizable number in Bengali, Marathi, Tamil, and Telegu. The potential Hindi-speaking audience was by far the largest, numbering some 140 million, but it remained less than half the total Indian population. It is perhaps for this reason that producers devised the distinctive form of the Indian song-and-dance film: even if the dialogue was ill comprehended, the music and dance could have a direct impact. Of course, musical films were popular everywhere during the early years of sound (especially in Europe, which had its own language problems). But only in India did this genre become the *sole* form of cinema, so that K. A. Abbas's *Munna*, made in 1954, was apparently only the second film without songs made in India since the coming of sound twenty-three years before. This development set Indian cinema apart from what happened elsewhere in world cinema and no doubt accounts in part for the loyalty of Indian audiences to their own local productions and the increasing difficulties that imported films experienced in reaching a mass audience outside the expensive first-run cinemas in the major colonial cities. The only major film industry to emerge under colonialism thus owes its success to specific film production strategies as well as to the growing sense of an independent Indian identity.

India's first sound film, *Alam ara* (1931), was a mythological tale with a dozen or so songs, directed by Ardeshir M. Irani (who was to make the first Indian color film six years later). Adapted from a stage play, it cost only forty thousand rupees and was an enormous popular success. Its production was lengthy because of technical hazards, which the director himself has detailed:

There were no soundproof stages, we preferred to shoot indoors and at night. Since our studio is located near a railway track, trains would pass every few minutes. So most of the shooting was done between the hours that the trains ceased operation. We worked with single-system Tanar recording equipment, [which is] unlike today's double system which allows a separate negative for picture and sound. There were also no booms. Microphones had to be hidden in incredible places to keep the camera out of range. . . . I chose the lyrics and the tunes. We used only a harmonium and a tabla player, who were out of camera range, and the singer sang into a hidden microphone.[15]

Continuity with the past was assured by at least one of the major companies of the 1930s, Prabhat, which was founded in 1929 and, after the coming of sound, set up studios at Pune. The leading figure among the group that created the new company was V. Shantaram (b. 1901), who had been deeply influenced by Phalke and had begun his career with the Marathi pioneer, Baburao Painter. Shantaram is a major figure in Indian cinema, and his career continued into the 1970s. His 1930s films were mostly mythological studies made in two versions, Marathi and Hindi; they include *The King of Ayoda / Ayodhyecha raja* (1932), *Eternal Light / Amar jyoti* (1936), and *The Unexpected / Duniya na mane* (in Hindi) *Kunku* (in Marathi) (1937). *Eternal Light* and another Prabhat production, *Saint Tukaram / Sant Tukaram* (1936), broke new ground for Indian cinema when they were screened at successive Venice Film Festivals.

If Prabhat's film makers were self-made men with little formal education,[16] a second major company of the period, New Theatres Ltd., was more aristocratic, having been set up in Calcutta by B. N. Sircar, the English-educated son of the advocate general of Bengal. The company employed Dhiren Ganguly, who made a number of comedies, and Debaki Bose, whose films include the Bengali *Chandidas* (1932) and *Vidyapathi* (1937, produced in both Bengali and Hindi). Another New Theatres director was Prince P. C. Barua (1903–1951), son of the rajah of Gauripur. Barua, who graduated from Presidency College, Calcutta, enjoyed all the habitual pastimes of the Indian aristocrat: he was a big-game hunter, sportsman, billiards champion, and playboy. He had already dabbled in acting, produced his own films, and worked with both Ganguly and Bose when he joined New Theatres. Barua's 1930s features— among them the enormously popular *Devdas* (1935), *Liberation / Mukti* (1937) and *Authority / Adhikar* (1938)—are among the most polished of the period, despite the inevitable technical limitations. They focus on a doomed hero (Barua himself) and shape their social themes (such as the problems of caste) into richly romantic melodramas. *Adhikar,* in particular, is a remarkable work: imaginatively staged in art deco sets, fastidiously lit, subtly edited and scored. This is studio film making of the highest order, as striking a work as was produced anywhere in the non-Western world during the 1930s.

A third major company, with even closer links to the West, was Bombay Talkies, founded by Himansu Rai, who with his wife and future star, Devika Rani, had spent many years in Germany and England and had pioneered international coproductions in the late 1920s. The pair returned to India in 1934 with *Karma* (1934), an English-financed feature film shot in England in two language versions, English and Hindi. The following year, Bombay Talkies was set up, and it became one of the leading Indian production companies, making both films on mythological subjects and "socials," such as the celebrated *Untouchable Girl / Achhut kanya* (1936). Bombay Talkies also played a key role in the training of young film makers and among those who began in its studios were such important figures of the early independence years as K. A. Abbas and Raj Kapoor.

The 1930s were a settled and prosperous time for Indian cinema, and these three companies are merely the most prominent of the two dozen or so listed by Barnouw and Krishnaswamy. The 1920s had seen the beginnings of regulated state censorship and taxation; the 1930s by contrast were marked by the emergence of a whole range of trade organizations aimed at regulating the industry for the benefit of producers and exhibitors alike. The market was constantly expanding, and the introduction of the system of filming to playback in 1937 assisted the further development of India's sole film genre, the musical. In financial terms, little had changed since the 1928 report, which noted that "no regular system for financing the producer" existed,[17] but this caused little real problem. Since the stars of the 1930s remained well (but not excessively) paid company employees, production costs could be kept low and producers had little need of outside finance, middlemen, or even distributors.

This cozy system was destroyed irrevocably during the war years of the early 1940s, though, by circumstances that owed little to the internal policies of the film industry. Politically, these were years when the country was stirred by the approach of independence, disturbed by the arrogance with which England had declared war, without consultation on India's behalf, and angered by such avoidable disasters as the Bengal famine (in which several million people are believed to have died). The radical mood of the times was reflected in painting and in new theatrical ventures, such as the Indian People's Theatre Association (IPTA).

Economically, however, the war years were also a period of greed and speculation, as rapidly increasing industrialization led to vast undeclared ("black") profits for the unscrupulous few. A favorite area for the reinvestment of this black money was the film industry, which quickly became a place of secret cash payments and concealed financial deals. The new financiers were naturally uninterested in owning studios or supporting stock companies of actors. They wanted a quick profit on a single venture, and to achieve this they were prepared to pay handsomely for top talent. In the new situation of freelance film making, huge sums were paid to stars, of course, but also to leading directors, musical directors, and playback singers. The star fee in particular began its inexorable climb: two hundred thousand rupees in the 1940s, four hundred thousand in the 1950s, reaching a reputed peak of three and a half million rupees in the 1980s (for superstar Amitabh Bachchan)—all these payments in cash. In this context the settled relations of producer and exhibitor were disturbed, and specialized distributors began to play a role. But these never became the dominant monopoly figures we find in the West: the 1951 FEC report, for instance, notes the existence of no less than 887 individual distributors in 1948.[18]

Another aspect of the disruption of established production arrangements was the emergence of the independent producer-director. Some of those who now worked independently had earlier been stalwarts of the old production system. V. Shantaram, who made the first Indian film to be distributed in the United States, *Shakuntala* (1943), now made the interesting *The Journey of*

20. *V. Shantaram:* Shakuntala *(India, 1943)*

Dr. Kotnis / Dr Kotnis ki amar kahani for his own company in 1946. Similarly, Mehboob Khan (1908–64), who had been active as a commercial director since the early days of sound, set up his own company, Mehboob Productions, in 1942. The same trend can be seen among the directors who made their debuts in the 1940s. If Bimal Roy (1909–66) had begun his career with New Theatres in Calcutta in 1944, it was as an independent producer-director that he embarked on his series of Bombay-based Hindi films in 1952. K. A. Abbas (b. 1914), writer of several of the key films of the period, also worked independently as a director on his own films, such as *Children of the Earth / Dharti ke lal* (1946), the first Indian film to be shown in Moscow, and it was as an independent that Raj Kapoor (b. 1924) began his directing career with an Abbas script in 1948.

After Independence

One striking independent film that did not achieve the hoped-for success was the dancer Uday Shankar's *Imagination / Kalpana* (1948), which was shot in the Gemini studios in Madras, owned by the producer S. S. Vassan (1903–69). The film did, however, inspire Vassan to create, as his own directorial debut, the film that achieved the crucial breakthrough for South Indian cinema, the phenomenally successful *Chandraleka* (1948). This Cecil B. De Mille–style spectacular, the most expensive Indian feature to date, with a budget of four hundred thousand rupees, points to the growing importance of the south in postindependence Indian cinema.

The characteristic works of the Hindi directors of the period have a somewhat different tone, though. Films like Kapoor's *The Tramp / Awaara* (1951) and *Under Cover of Night / Jagte raho* (1956), Roy's *Two Acres of Land / Do bigha zamin* (1953), Abbas's *Munna* (1954), and Mehboob's *Mother India* (1957) all combine an awareness of the requirements of box office success with a clear sympathy for the poor and the oppressed. Social awareness and sentimentality, sincerity and commercial gloss, coexist to give these products of postindependence Bombay cinema their wide appeal and international reputation.

To understand the development of Indian cinema after 1947, one needs to appreciate the nature of Indian independence. The long-drawn-out transition to political independence had allowed the emergence of a strong nationalist elite, politically organized as the Indian National Congress, which had been established in 1885. Reflections of the nationalist feelings that swept the coun-

21. Uday Shankar: Imagination / Kalpana *(India, 1948)*

22. *Bimal Roy:* Two Acres of
Land / Do bigha zamin
(India, 1953)

try during the last decade of colonial rule can be found—as S. Theodore
Baskaran shows—in many of the commercial films of the period. But the
constant delays by the British in granting self-determination during the 1930s
and the war years also caused ruptures in the unity of the emergent Indian
elite, of which the most important was the demand for a separate Muslim
state, leading in 1947 to partition and to the creation of the state of Pakistan.
Within India itself, national unity has been preserved, but the internal tensions caused by regional self-affirmation and separatism—in the north as well
as in the non-Hindi-speaking south—are strong, and they, too, find their expression in the multilingual evolution of postwar Indian cinema.

Equally as crucial as these national and political factors are the extreme
social tensions that the process of independence also brought to the fore. The
communal violence that accompanied independence can only be understood if
we realize that, as Tariq Ali points out, "throughout 1946 India hovered on the
brink of a pre-revolutionary crisis." [19] For the three main parties involved in
the independence negotiations—the Congress, the Muslim League, and the
British—there was a vital need to assure a transfer of power in ways that would
not lead to total social upheaval. This aim was achieved, but only through
political divisions that cost millions of Indians their lives. Within India, political power went to the Congress party, virtually the sole political party, and the

control of the bureaucratic arm of the state passed to the Western-educated administrative elite. In addition, despite Nehru's sincere commitment to socialism and the international policy of nonalignment, the economy was left largely in the hands of a now well established capitalist class, with foreign capital eventually forming "a tiny fraction, not even one percent as a proportion of the capital stock of the country." [20] India—as its films bear out—remains a mass of contradictions: one of the world's poorest states, it has vast natural resources and a large, extremely wealthy bourgeoisie; it supports a mixed economy, with private and public sectors, in which, despite the rhetoric of five-year plans, the private sector is by far the dominant one in terms of size;[21] and it is a country that has made huge strides in industrialization but where all industry is dwarfed by the sheer dimensions of the agricultural sector.

The most striking aspect of Indian cinema since independence has been its ever-increasing growth. From 241 features in 1950, output rose to 305 in 1960, 396 in 1970, 462 in 1975, 710 in 1980, and 763 in 1983. Though there was by the 1980s a large number of schemes at both the national and state levels to foster the development of cinema, the roots of this upsurge lie within the growth of Indian capitalism, as the film industry, with its peculiar financial structure, offered a direct reflection of the amount of risk capital (often illegally acquired, or at least hidden from the tax authorities) generated in the Indian economy.

The capitalist-financed boom in film production should also be seen in the light of the huge expansion of all the modern communication media, both private and state-owned. Though newspaper readership is limited to perhaps a third of the population, the growth of newspaper sales has matched that of the cinema:

> From around 3,000 newspapers and periodicals in 1947, from around 300 dailies, the tally of the early 1980s is 19,000, of them 1,264 dailies. They are published in 84 languages, 16 principal and 68 other languages. The largest number are in Hindi, almost twice as many as in English, with Bengali following a close third. The national total circulation is just over 51 million copies, Hindi at 14 million, English at 11 million and other languages accounting for the remaining 26 million.[22]

Though television is relatively backward in India and videotape was still a cloud on the horizon in the early 1980s, India does possess eleven television transmission stations, which are able to reach nearly a fifth of the population. The spread of radio is more striking still: "In 1947, All-India Radio had only nine stations, of which three went to Pakistan. Today AIR has 85 stations covering 90 percent of the country's population." [23]

The optimism with which the film industry entered the era of independence was shattered not merely by political events (such as the horrors that accompanied partition or the assassination of Gandhi), but by the immediate attitude of the new government. As Barnouw and Krishnaswamy point out, the political leaders quickly showed themselves hostile to the cinema:

> The idea of entertainment as a necessity of life was not familiar to them. If they thought of film, they thought of it as a potential instrument of social reform that was not being used in that way. They thought of it as too much involved with romance and immature hero worship. They associated it with Western influences that needed to be purged. They also saw it as a source of revenue. Not surprisingly, the year 1947 inaugurated a long series of measures affecting film that soon left the film world dazed.[24]

The government was indifferent to the exhibitors' claim that, in 1949, taxes of various kinds amounted to some 60 percent of box office receipts. Instead of offering assistance, the government made matters worse by imposing its own "block booking" system on exhibitors, who were required to show (and pay for) a weekly documentary made by the government Films Division. Though a Film Enquiry Committee was set up to undertake a study of the industry similar to the one done in 1927–28, its recommendations—such as that a government-funded Film Finance Corporation be established—were disregarded for almost a decade. Even the film society movement, which spread after the founding of the Calcutta Film Society by Chidananda Das Gupta and Satyajit Ray in 1947, was subject to all the same rigors of censorship and taxation as the commercial industry.

Contemporary Developments

It was Ray who instigated the major renewal—little less than a revolution—in Indian film production in 1955. Satyajit Ray was just thirty-two when his first feature, independently produced, *Pather panchali,* appeared and established his international reputation. (Ray's unique career, established outside the normal confines of the Indian film industry, is considered in detail in chapter 11.) It is instructive to compare the authority and calm assurance with which he established himself outside the confines of the industry with the troubled progress of his contemporaries who tried to come to terms with the existing structures of the film business. Guru Dutt (1925–64), also educated in Calcutta and steeped in Indian culture through having studied dance with Uday Shankar, directed his first film in the mainstream of the Bombay industry in 1951. In the next thirteen years he directed eight features, produced three, and appeared in six others. His output includes one unsurpassed melodrama that was a great hit, *Eternal Thirst / Pyaasa* (1957), and a moving if extravagant study of a failed film director that was a total flop, *Paper Flowers / Kaagaz ze phool* (1959). But the working conditions of the industry deepened his inbuilt pessimism, and in 1964 he took his own life. Ritwik Ghatak

23.   *Guru Dutt:* Paper Flowers / Kaagaz ze phool *(India, 1959)*

(1925–76), another Bengali, was marked for life by the partition of Bengal, which cut him off from his native Dacca. In a hectic twenty-four-year career littered with abandoned projects, Ghatak completed just eight features, including some of the key works of the Indian 1960s cinema. An uncompromising Marxist whose films are remarkable for the total absence of foreign influences, Ghatak dealt in his major works, especially *The Hidden Star / Meghe dhaka tara* (1960), with human disasters that had their starting point in the division of Bengal. His attempt to create a popular national cinema within the confines of the Indian film industry was, however, a failure, and he died—a bitter, disillusioned alcoholic—at the age of fifty, after completing one of the most harrowing of all filmic self-portraits, *Reason, Debate, and a Tale / Jukti takko ar gappo* (1974). In contrast to these figures, doomed by their romanticism or intransigence, Mrinal Sen (b. 1923), Ray's exact contemporary, is a survivor. But his initial attempt to establish a name for himself within the Bengali film industry, with eight features between 1956 and 1967, met with no success. It was only with *Bhovan Shome* (1969), independently produced with funding from the Film Finance Corporation, that Sen was able to show himself to be a major director and begin the series of films that have made him an internationally respected figure.

Since the early 1960s the Indian film industry has developed in various contradictory ways. The Bombay all-India movie in Hindi has remained the commercial focus, though the number of Hindi films produced (114 in both 1950 and 1980) has not kept pace with the huge overall expansion of production. Bombay remains a high-risk investment area: budgets are normally at least four times as high as those of commercial film making in other regions and may at times be twenty times as high. As elsewhere in a gambling situation, the huge profits of the fortunate few are paralleled by the equally spectacular losses of the majority of investors. It seems generally agreed that the bulk of the risk capital is provided by investors from outside the industry, who frequently end up with an expensive imitation of last year's hit feature that flops at the box office. The difficulties of hitting just the right note for an audience are enhanced by the frequent delays caused by the star appearing in perhaps a dozen other films simultaneously and the experienced producer making the most of a situation that allows him to charge the costs of his expensive life-style to a project funded by someone else.

Bombay is often referred to as India's Hollywood, but despite the deceptive regularity of its output, it has little in common with the heyday the Hollywood studio system experienced from 1930 to the mid-1950s. There the financing was long-term, the control was vested in the New York financiers and the Hollywood heads of production, the stars were kept under tight studio control, and the whole structure was held together through the vertical integration of production, distribution, and exhibition. Despite its size, the Indian film industry has not taken its capitalist methods this far. Its organizational structures still echo those of the chaotic pioneer days of cinema in the West around World War I—when fortunes were made by marketing *The Birth of a Nation*—rather than those subsequently devised by the Hollywood studios. The riches of this overinflated and often formula-ridden cinema still remain to be fully explored, since Indian critics tend to ignore it now that they are offered a choice of "alternative" Indian cinemas.

The first of these alternatives is offered by the regional cinemas, which have developed remarkably in the postindependence era. The Bengali and Marathi cinemas, which were among the first to be established and seem to have had the richest pioneering development, have remained fairly constant in their output, with around forty films a year in Bengal and under twenty in Maharashtra (the Bengali cinema having been particularly stunted by the loss of half its audience through the 1947 partition). But at the same time there has been an explosion of film production in the four southern states of India, to the extent that three of these regional cinemas surpassed Hindi cinema in the numbers of films produced in 1980. In the period from 1950 to 1980, Tamil-language cinema (in the state of Tamil Nadu) rose from 19 to 140 films a year, Telegu cinema (Andra Pradesh) from 18 to 133, Malayalam cinema (Kerala) from 6 to 127, and Kannada cinema (Karnataka) from 1 to 50. Since most of this production is based in Madras, this city has become the most prolific film producing center in India, and indeed in the world. An assessment of this production is far beyond the scope of this book, but a recent study of Malayalam cinema does offer some insight into the organization of regional production.[25]

There was no early film making tradition in Kerala. Only two films were made there during the silent era and just three Malayalam-language films in the years up to 1947. When India was divided into linguistically based states in 1956, production stood at a mere half a dozen films a year. It was not until the early 1960s that output began to rise, reaching 31 in 1965 and 44 in 1970. The late 1970s saw a veritable explosion of film making, which reached a peak of 127 in 1980, and this growth went hand in hand with a similar increase in the number of film theaters. There are a number of factors contributing to this growth. The Kerala state government has given support to the cinema as a means of fostering the Malayalam language, and investment capital has been readily available from locals who have made money working in the Persian Gulf. In the 1970s producers hit on a formula which gave Malayalam cinema a bad reputation but very wide distribution, making a series of "sex" films with titillating titles like *Sexy Dreams / Rathi nirvedam, Her Nights / Avalude ravukal*, and *A Night in the Rest House / Satharathil oru rathri*. But basically, Malayalam films are budgeted to recover their costs from the local market, occupying around three-quarters of the screen time in Kerala's cinemas. In Kerala, a state with high literacy but very little industrialization, film is one of the largest industrial enterprises, and in a way rare elsewhere it has captured a rural audience: in 1978 only 9 of the state's 969 cinemas were located in the capital, Trivandrum. Though the Kerala State Film Development Corporation has worked to develop studio facilities within its own boundaries, most studio work is carried out in Madras, the traditional political capital of the south.

Though working on a far smaller scale than the all-India cinema, the Malayalam film industry is organized along the same lines, with independent producers, investors from outside the industry, a plethora of small distributors, and its own array of stars who appear in film after film. Recent years have seen the growth of a kind of cinema that, while remaining within the commercial format, has begun to treat social themes. In 1984, for example, Kerala contributed six films (more than any other state) to the nationwide selection of twenty-one features that made up the Indian Panorama at Filmotsav '84. These included K. N. Sasisharan's *The Other Shore / Akkare,* a comedy about the impact on local society of returnees from the Persian Gulf; P. Padmarajan's *In Whose Nest / Koodevide,* which looked at the position of women in society; and K. G. George's *Lekha's Death—A Flashback / Lekhayude maranam oru flashback,* an investigation of the suicide of a teenage film star based on a real incident in the early 1980s.

Though Malayalam cinema is typical in its rapid expansion in the 1970s, there is no one pattern of development for India's regional cinemas. What is remarkable is that films are now made in virtually every corner of India and in a staggering range of languages (twenty in 1984, including Malvi, Brijbhasha, and Maithili). In 1982, even the remote state of Manipur, which had made just nine films in all, beginning in 1972, achieved its moment of glory with the international showing of Aribam Syam Sharma's *My Son, My Precious / Imagi ningthem,* a touching drama which stood apart from 1980s trends and adopted a tone and technique that directly recalled the realist film making style of the 1950s.

While much of the impetus for cinema has come from state administrations, there has also been crucial input from the national government. The 1960s saw the setting up of a Film and Television Institute (located in the old Prabhat studios in Pune) and a national film archive. The government took on a direct involvement with the industry through the establishment of the Film Finance Corporation (FFC) and Indian Motion Picture Export Association (IMPEC), whose functions were merged in 1980 under the umbrella of the National Film Development Corporation (NFDC). Thanks to this active government support, international film festivals have become a regular part of India's cultural life, arrangements are made to screen Indian films abroad, and a number of ambitious film projects have been state-funded in whole or in part. Thus, onto the regional pattern of development is superimposed a second "alternative" cinema: the New Indian Cinema, consciously fostered by central government initiative.

Underlying this new cinema is a total hostility toward the commercial industry: the New Indian Cinema is "the creation of an intellectual elite that is keenly aware of the human condition in India."[26] Its forerunners are the Calcutta Film Society and Ray's first feature, *Pather panchali,* which was completed only thanks to a grant from the West Bengal government. This example has now been widely imitated in India, and government and state aid for production has been plentiful, but such initiatives have never been accompanied by a similar development of an art house exhibition circuit. Whereas the qualities of Ray's film allowed it to find its audience, both in Bengal and worldwide, many films of the New Indian Cinema have been esoteric works that never reached any audience, either at home or abroad (apart from isolated festival screenings). The output of the new generation, a dozen years or more after Ray, reflects the dichotomy of the two other founding fathers to whom the movement has looked: the intransigent Ritwik Ghatak and the more flexible and commercially minded Mrinal Sen.

The range of films produced is remarkably wide, and a wholly personal note is to be found in the work of a striking number of the new film makers, many of them graduates of the Film and Television Institute at Pune. In the fifteen years after Sen's *Bhovan Shome* (1969) was financed by the Film Finance Corporation, the rigid separation of film art from the film industry has meant that none of the government-funded newcomers has been able to offer

24. Shyam Benegal: Market Place / Mandi *(India, 1983)*

as rich a flow of films as Shyam Benegal (b. 1934), who made his debut in the new atmosphere created by government intervention but later always found commercial backing—through the advertising company Blaze Film Enterprises. This private support enabled him to make the striking series of ten features beginning with *The Seedling* / *Ankur* (1974) through to *Market Place* / *Mandi* (1983).

More characteristic of the New Indian Cinema, however, is the isolated masterpiece or the tiny handful of artistic successes, followed by long years of silence. Pattabhi Rama Reddy, for example, whose *Funeral Rites* / *Samskara* (1970) inaugurated the new cinema in Karnataka, has never been able to match this first success. His scriptwriter and leading actor, Girish Karnad, further developed Kannada-language cinema with such films as *The Forest* / *Kaadu* (1973) and *Once upon a Time* / *Ondanondu kaladalli* (1978). But the versatile Karnad, a Rhodes scholar, president of the union at Oxford, and one of India's leading young playwrights, was too restless to develop a merely regional cinema. After a spell as head of the Pune Institute, he moved to Bombay, where he worked as actor and scriptwriter with Benegal. B. V. Karanth, Karnad's collaborator on two further films, *The Family Tree* / *Vamsha vriksha* (1971) and *The Cow-Dust Hour* / *Godhuli* (1977), also made one solo feature in the mid-1970s, *Choma's Drum* / *Chomana dudi* (1975), but he has since devoted himself to the theater. The only real echo of what had seemed a breakthrough in Kannada cinema, which in its best work offered penetrating and uncompromising insights into problems of tradition and poverty at the village level, is to be found in such isolated works as *The Ritual* / *Ghatashraddha* (1977), by another Pune graduate, Girish Kasaravalli (b. 1949), or *The Child Widow* / *Phaniyamma* (1983), directed by the woman film maker Prema Karanth, who had worked on Karnad's *Godhuli*.

In neighboring Kerala there was a similar breakthrough of independent talent in the 1970s. The Pune graduate Adoor Gopalakrishna (b. 1941) began his feature career within the context of India's first film cooperative, the Chitralekha. In ten years he completed just three films, which together have given him an international reputation: *One's Own Choice* / *Swayamvaram* (1972), *Ascent* / *Kodiyettam* (1977), and *The Rat Trap* / *Elippathayam* (1981), which won the 1982 British Film Institute award for "the most original and imaginative" film shown that year at London's National Film Theatre. Gopalakrishna's compatriot G. Aravindan (b. 1935) is a more prolific film maker, having completed a stream of five films in as many years, including *The Tent* / *Thampu* and the children's film *The Bogeyman* / *Kumatty,* both in 1978. But none of these obtained a release in India, and indeed, both Gopalakrishna and Aravindan stand aside from the general upsurge of Malayalam-language cinema, with a number of their key films financed privately by a wealthy businessman, Ravi, the "Cashew King" of Kerala. Perhaps more isolated still is the sole representative of Gujerati cinema to become internationally known, Ketan Mehta, who made his first feature, the didactic fable *A Folk Tale* / *Bhavni bhavai,* in 1980.

25. *Mani Kaul:* A Day's Bread / Uski roti *(India, 1970)*

In contrast to the rural and regional inspiration of much of the independent film making in the south, the new cinema in Hindi is more overtly internationally minded. In the forefront are two more Pune graduates, Mani Kaul (b. 1942) and Kumar Shahani, both of whom have expressed a debt to Robert Bresson (with whom Shahani worked as assistant on *Une femme douce*). Kaul's *A Day's Bread / Uski roti* (1970), with its minimal action and long takes, *In Two Minds / Duvidha* (1973), which plays games with temporal and narrative structure, and the austere music study *Dhrupad* (1982) are all uncompromising works that failed to find an audience in India. Similarly, the commercial failure of Shahani's *Maya darpan* (1972) resulted in a twelve-year gap before he could complete *Wages and Profits / Tarang* (1984), a project whose completion had been financially blocked for a number of years.

The intellectual elitism of Kaul and Shahani is counterbalanced in the more commercially oriented work of some of the younger film makers working in Hindi. Key figures here are Saeed Mirza, best known for his lively social study *What Makes Albert Pinto Angry / Albert Pinto ko gussa kyon aata hai* (1980), and the forceful Govind Nihalani, a former cameraman for Benegal, whose own films include *Cry of the Wounded / Aakrosh* (1980) and *Half-Truth / Ardh satya* (1983). In these film makers' work we find the desire to combine treatment of significant social themes with access to a wide audience. This also characterizes the work of Shyam Benegal and the older M. S.

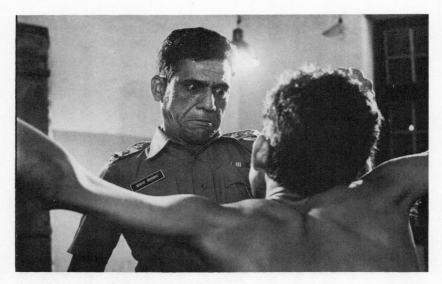

26. *Govind Nihilani:* Half-Truth / Ardh satya *(India, 1983)*

27. *M. S. Sathyu:* Hot Winds / Garm hava *(India, 1975)*

Sathyu (b. 1930), best known for his first feature, *Hot Winds / Garm hava* (1975), an uncompromising look at a Muslim family that stays in India at the time of partition and is gradually destroyed by persecution.

At the beginning of the 1980s there were clear signs of attempts to bridge the gulf between the commercialism of the all-India movie and the esotericism of much of the New Indian Cinema. Several major directors have made films away from Bombay: working in Telegu were both Sen, with *The Outsiders / Oka oorie katha* (1977), and Benegal, with *The Boon / Anugraham* (1978), and in Kannada, Sathyu with *The Famine / Bara* (1980). One of the stars of the Hindi commercial cinema, Shashi Kapoor, has also begun an ambitious production program, backing films by Benegal and Nihalani, the actress Aparna Sen's English-language feature *36 Chowringhee Lane* (1981), and a major new film by Girish Karnad, *Utsav* (1985). Though it seems unlikely that Indian producers will be able to maintain their enormously high levels of output through the 1980s, India's younger film makers seem well placed to continue producing work of a very high standard.

Pakistan, Sri Lanka, and Bangladesh

While India has been able to maintain its national unity and its democratic system of government into the mid-1980s, the other states that became independent on the Indian subcontinent in 1947–48, Pakistan and Ceylon (Sri Lanka), have been torn by violence and political unrest. This is in part a result of the contradictions in the makeup of the states themselves. Pakistan was established as a secular state—though the basis of partition was religious—and as a single state—though it comprised two regions, East and West Pakistan, which were quite distinct in people, language, and history, geographically separate, with a thousand miles of Indian territory between them, and at quite different levels of development, with the military and the bureaucracy (which inherited the control of the postcolonial state) centered in West Pakistan, while East Pakistan comprised a peasantry now deprived of its Hindu ruling and middle-class elites. Ceylon was granted its independence on the basis of a constitution which "contained no law on citizenship, franchise and protection of individual and group fundamental rights," [27] though the state comprised two national groups, whose initial unity in the anticolonialist struggle had been destroyed by British tactics.

In Pakistan the bureaucratic elite proved incapable of creating a nation within the inherited boundaries, and it was replaced by the military, whose brutal incompetence led in 1971 to civil war and the secession of East Pakistan, which formed the independent state of Bangladesh. Pakistan has subsequently been ruled in turn by the charismatic populist Zulfiqar Ali Bhutto and his erstwhile trusted lieutenant, Gen. Mohammed Zia ul-Haq, who in 1977 ousted and later executed Bhutto. Zia's Islamic republic is no more than a grotesque parody of the ideals that attended the birth of Pakistan in 1947. The ruling elite in Ceylon, to whom the state was handed in 1948, comprised a tiny upper-class minority, whose narrow base is shown by the fact that in the first postindependence cabinet only one important post was not held by a member of the prime minister's family. This elite has retained power, but only at the cost of increasing communal violence between the Sinhalese majority and an oppressed Tamil minority, who compromise 20 percent of the population but whose language has been denied national status.

In none of these countries was there a tradition of film making. Pre-1947 Indian cinema had been essentially a Hindu cinema. There were no major figures among the various artists and technicians who emigrated to West Pakistan at the time of partition, and, apart from four small studios in Lahore, the state was without film making facilities. A first sound film had been made in Lahore in 1935, and during the twelve years up to independence some twenty-seven films in Punjabi and a dozen or so in other languages had been produced. But this was not a rich film making tradition, and as the film maker and critic Alamgir Kabir observes, the new state of Pakistan inherited "all that was bad in the film art dispensed from the subcontinent's erstwhile film capital, Bombay."[28] In East Pakistan, the cinema was even less developed. Muslim participation in the Bengali cultural renaissance had been negligible, and at partition the population was cut off from the sources of this tradition when Dacca, previously "a small district town in Calcutta's hinterland,"[29] became the state capital. Only one commercially unsuccessful film had been made by a Bengali Muslim before 1947. No films at all had been made in Ceylon; indeed, until 1956 every Sinhalese film was made in South India, and "local actors were decked out as Indian heroes and heroines who mouthed Sinhalese."[30]

In all three areas, commercial entertainment cinemas based on the Indian music-and-dance model grew up in the 1950s and 1960s. Even before the secession of East Pakistan, it was hardly possible to talk of a unified Pakistani cinema embracing east and west, since the two regions were separated both by language (emphasized by growing Bengali nationalism in the east) and by administrative arrangements. As Alamgir Kabir notes, from the early 1950s "traffic in films between East and West Pakistan was restricted"[31]—thus, for example, the partial ban on the import of Indian films into West Pakistan, introduced in 1952, was not intended to apply to East Pakistan; similarly, while the tax rate at the end of the 1960s was a flat 50 percent in West Pakistan, it ranged from 70 to 110 percent in East Pakistan.

In West Pakistan, then, production rose steadily from about half a dozen films a year in the late 1940s to twenty features in 1955 and forty in 1964. Contemplating what he terms "an impoverished cousin of the Indian commercial system," Javed Jabbar observes that while the import of Indian films was carefully controlled, "the local cinema struggled to evolve its own identity. But, except for the substitution of Muslim character names in place of Hindi ones and occasional references to Hindu/Muslim rivalry and religious differences, any individual identity remained elusive." [32] Freedom from Indian competition after 1965 allowed West Pakistani film production to rise sharply, to eighty and then a hundred films a year, while the number of movie theaters in the region rose from 220 at independence to around 500 on the eve of the civil war. Writing in 1969, Kabir emphasizes the limitations of West Pakistani film production: "Of the 1,000-odd films that have come out of West Pakistani studios since independence, one could not cite more than a handful that contain modest artistic merit. Except a degree of technical sophistication, there has been no improvement in the contents." [33]

Film production was much slower to get under way in East Pakistan, and then thanks largely to the East Pakistan Film Development Corporation, set up in 1957 under Nazir Ahmed, who had done some pioneering documentary film making. A new studio, established in Dacca, allowed output to rise from 3 films in 1959 to 17 in 1964 and to 41 in 1970. Though only six films were completed in 1971, when East Pakistan fought for its freedom, in all some 206 films were made between 1956 and 1971, three-quarters of them in Bengali and the rest in Urdu. Few of these had pretensions to be more than very low budget commercial entertainment-films (even the stars were paid no more than fifteen thousand rupees a film), although Salahuddin's hit film *Roopban* (1965) did, it seems, set a brief vogue for folklore films based on the tradition of the "village operetta" (*jatra*) and strengthened Bengali's claim to be the major, if not sole, language for East Pakistan films. Kabir singles out just three artistically successful films from this mass of production. Two of them, strongly influenced by Western styles and employing Western cameramen, were commercial failures: the documentary feature *Day Shall Dawn / Jago hua savera* (1959), made by the British-trained Ajay Kardar, was the only film of the period to be shown abroad, and Sadeq Khan's *River and Woman / Nadi-o-nari* (1964), the adaptation of a popular novel chronicling the life of the Muslim peasantry of Bengal, is in Kabir's opinion the finest film ever made in Pakistan. Far more popular than these two was Zahir Raihan's *Glimpses from Life / Jibon thekey neya* (1970), apparently the first filmic expression of rising Bengali nationalism.

Cinema was also slow to grow in Ceylon, where output rose from about half a dozen films in 1956, when production was transferred from South India, to around 25 in 1970. By the time the name Sri Lanka was adopted in 1972, the country as a whole had about 300 film theaters, and the film industry could look back on about 250 features produced in the twenty-five years since independence. Moreover, in Lester James Peries (b. 1919) Sri Lanka does possess a film maker of international stature. Peries, who made what is generally regarded as the first truly Sinhalese film, *The Line of Destiny / Rekava* (1956), had close links with the West. Born into a middle-class Roman Catholic family, he was educated at an English-language college; then, after

28. *Ajay Kardar:* Day Shall Dawn / Jago hua savera *(Pakistan, 1959)*

29. *Lester James Peries:* Changes in the Village / Gamperaliya *(Sri Lanka, 1964)*

working as a writer and journalist, he began his film making career with three
short films shot in London in 1949–50. When he returned to Ceylon in 1952 it
was to join the Government Film Unit set up by the British documentarist
Ralph Keene. He left in 1955 to work as an independent feature film maker,
forming a team of collaborators who continued to work with him on subsequent projects. His debut film, *Rekava,* was a conscious revolt against the pre-
dominant style of Indian studio production, showing the clear and acknowledged influence of both British documentary and Italian neorealism, with
which he had come into contact in London. For all its lasting interest, *Rekava*
was not a success with local audiences, and Peries's career was slow in getting
under way. He made only two further films in the first decade of his directing
career, *The Message / Sandesaya* (1960), an epic set at the time of the Portuguese occupation, and *Changes in the Village / Gamperaliya* (1964), a first
literary adaptation. But he was later able to complete thirteen features in the
eighteen years spanned by *Between Two Worlds / Delovak athara* (1966) and
End of an Era / Yuganthayo (1983). In this time Peries has confronted the
problems of the international English-language coproduction (in *The God
King,* 1975), but more often he has filmed literary adaptations, including a
trilogy from novels by Martin Wickremasinghe and Leonard Woolf's colonial
tale *Village in the Jungle / Baddegama* (1980). His characteristic style has
been summed up by Derek Elley: "He lacks the polemic anger which moti-
vates much Third World film making and is clearly uninterested in large tab-
leaux. His is the cinema of simple contrast, subtle shades of feelings and emotions—in short, lives which reflect larger conflicts being played out just out
of view." [34]

The political changes in Pakistan after the 1971 defeat, like the establishment of military rule under General Zia in 1977, appear to have had only a
limited impact on Pakistani cinema, which since 1947 has shown little if any
marked national identity and absolutely no political awareness. Production remains around a hundred films a year, sixty in Urdu and most of the remainder
in Punjabi. Javed Jabbar (writing in 1977) saw no break in Lahore film production in 1971, despite the horrors of the civil war, but rather an unbroken continuity following the exclusion of Indian film imports in 1965. After this ban,
Pakistani cinema "was given the fullest possible protection to develop an artistic and commercial independence," but "twelve years of protection have
had almost the opposite effect: inspired imitation gave way to outright plagiarism; the straitjacket became normal attire." [35]

Administratively, the 1970s saw a variety of developments in Pakistani cin-
ema following the Indian example. In 1973, film was transferred from the
Ministry of Information to the Ministry of Education and Culture, and the
Pakistani National Film Development Corporation (NFDC) was set up. The
NFDC assumed control of the issue of import licenses for the purchase of raw

film stock as well as of the import of foreign films into Pakistan. It also fostered some cultural and film society activities.

Among the NFDC's more interesting attempts to break out of the narrow confines of purely local production was the invitation it issued to Jamil Dehlavi, the Western-educated son of a diplomat, to make a feature film in Pakistan. After studying law at Oxford and film and television in the United States, Dehlavi had attracted some attention at film festivals with a short film, *Towers of Silence*. Returning to Pakistan early in 1977, Dehlavi was able to enjoy considerable freedom during the shooting of *The Blood of Hussein*, thanks to his foreign coproduction funding and connections. But when General Zia seized power, he had to smuggle the negative out of the country, and, his passport having been confiscated by the authorities, it was two years before he could make his own escape. Although the completed film has never been allowed a screening in Pakistan, Dehlavi was able to return in the early 1980s to begin a second feature, *Maila,* which purported to be a documentary on local circuses and folk festivals but was in fact a reflection on the Bhutto years and an indictment of military rule. Dehlavi's intentions were discovered, and again he was able to make his escape with the material already shot. The film, eventually completed with funding from British television, shows all the marks of its disjointed production and Dehlavi's understandable ambiguity of feeling toward Bhutto.

Development was muted too during the 1970s in the newly independent state of Bangladesh. Zahir Raihan, whose *Glimpses from Life* had been a patriotic success in 1970 and who was the main architect of a scheme to develop a truly national cinema in Bangladesh, mysteriously disappeared in the aftermath of the fighting in 1971, and his plans came to nothing. Instead, with film production protected from Indian competition and trade practices as dubious as in India, the Bangladeshi film industry became a favorite focus of investment for war profiteers and speculators. In the early years of independence, production was fairly steady at around thirty to forty films a year (mostly low-budget and in black-and-white, and all made in Bengali). A peak of fifty-one films was reached in 1979, when movie theaters numbered about 290 (an increase of 100 since 1971). Little of this output is of more than local interest, except the Indian director Ritwik Ghatak's sole feature shot in the region where he was born, *A River Called Titash / Titash ekti nadir naam* (1973), five feature films shot between 1973 and 1980 by Alamgir Kabir, and a first feature, made in a style echoing Satyajit Ray and neorealism, which achieved some showing abroad, Shaik Neamat Ali and Mashiuddin Shaker's *The Ominous House / Surja dighal bari* (1979). State involvement has been fairly limited in Bangladesh, apart from the establishment of a National Film Institute and archive in Dacca and some steps to stamp out the more outrageous instances of plagiarism (Kabir estimates that over 70 percent of the films pro-

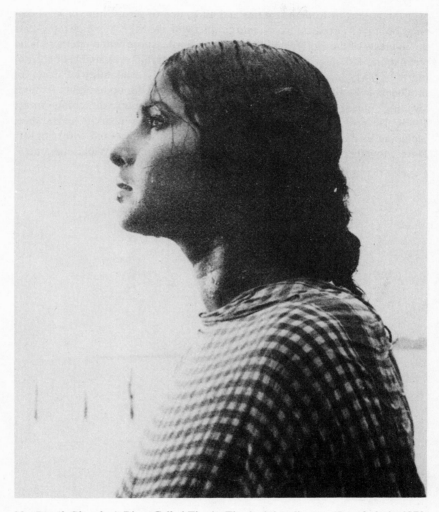

30. Ritwik Ghatak: A River Called Titash / Titash ekti nadir nam *(Bangladesh, 1973)*

duced are plagiarized directly from Indian productions, or even from Pakistani films, which are themselves often copied from Bombay hits).

In Sri Lanka, however, the State Film Corporation began to exercise an increasing array of functions in the 1970s: monopoly control over the licensing of raw stock purchases, responsibility for film export, and encouragement for the use of Sri Lankan locations by foreign production companies. Its control over the import of foreign features and allocation of screen time in local cinemas brought it, needless to say, into conflict with the MPEA, which represents the interests of the Hollywood distributors. Furthermore, although there is no real export market for Sri Lankan films and local circuits are capable of absorbing only thirty locally made films a year, the ready availability of loans for producers led to overproduction in the late 1970s—with up to eighty features awaiting release at one time—and consequent production difficulties in the 1980s. Nevertheless, a new generation of film makers made its appearance, including Sri Lanka's only woman director, Peries's editor (and wife) Sumitra Peries, together with Amarnath Jayatilaka and Dharmasiri Wickremaratne.

East and Southeast Asia 8

A common aesthetic theory governed all the arts, both performing and plastic, in South and South East Asia. Roughly speaking, the common trends may be identified as the negation of the principle of realistic imitation in art, the establishment of a hierarchy of realities where the principle of suggestion through abstraction is followed and the manifestation in the arts of the belief that time is cyclic rather than linear. . . . This tradition of the arts appears to have been persuasive from Afghanistan and India to Japan and Indonesia over two thousand years of history.

Kapila Malik Vatsyayan

Though some fairly detailed research has been published on the cinemas of China and Hong Kong, the national film industries of most of the countries of East and Southeast Asia are virtually unknown in the West, so only the barest sketch can be offered here. It seems that film was comparatively slow to establish itself in countries whose traditions of drama were far removed from the Western notions of theatrical realism that proved so crucial to the development of dramatic film narrative in Europe and North America. Generally, too, initial structures of exhibition in these countries reflected a colonial situation, with expensive luxury cinemas showing recent Western films to an elite audience and a largely despised second tier of cinemas catering to a mass audience and offering older and cheaper Western films and a sprinkling of local productions. But as elsewhere in the non-Western world, the coming of sound gave a fresh impetus for the establishment of production that was "national," in the sense that it received local capital financing and it treated local subject matter in local languages.

The growth of such production beginning in the 1930s reflects the steady advance of industrialization throughout the region. In content, these emerging

135

cinemas also inevitably reflect "the staggering multiplicity of forms and styles of the performing arts in Asia."[1] Since the end of World War II, moreover, there has been a fresh level of divergence. While the 1949 revolution took China out of the capitalist orbit (and so out of the scope of the present study), a number of its smaller neighbors—the so-called newly industrializing countries—have, since the 1950s, become centers of capitalist development. To cater to the needs of the rapidly expanding urban work force, huge local film industries have developed throughout the region, making film one of the most important of Asian mass media. Though generalizations are hazardous, it would seem that Scott Meek and Tony Rayns's statement that it is "impossible to 'read' a Chinese movie without referring to the national situation at the time it was made"[2] applies to the whole of East and Southeast Asia.

Before the Revolution: China and Vietnam

The invention of the motion picture—which was first seen in Shanghai on 11 August 1896—coincided with one of the most disastrous periods of Chinese history. A century of vain resistance to Western and Japanese influence had culminated in defeat in the Sino-Japanese War of 1894 and the secession of Korea, Formosa (Taiwan), and parts of Manchuria from China. The Western powers continued to increase their hold over the commercial concessions and treaty ports, especially after the defeat of the Boxer Uprising in 1900, and the reforms attempted under the rule of the traditionally minded Dowager Empress were timid and ineffective.

Although Western influence had led to some industrialization in the nineteenth century, this was severely restricted. Firstly, the Chinese had attempted to adopt merely the products of Western technology (weapons, railways, steamships, and the telegraph) but to ignore the scientific learning, which alone made such inventions possible. A second important limitation to modernization was that "all was governmental enterprise. No Chinese capitalists entered this field, no companies of free merchants or investors put money into such development." Since much of the finance stemmed from foreign bank loans, "it placed Chinese resources indirectly under foreign control."[3] As Joseph Needham records, "It was not until the First World War, when the European powers temporarily relaxed their profit-making activities in China, that indigenous Chinese capitalist industry got a chance to develop. . . . Even so, it never conquered sectors wider than those of light industry."[4]

This state of affairs is reflected in the history of Chinese cinema. Before the fall of the Manchu dynasty in 1911, little if any film activity was the work of the Chinese themselves. There was not even any interest at court level, since attempts to organize royal showings in 1904 and 1906 had both ended in disaster. The theaters in Shanghai and elsewhere that occasionally presented film programs were all owned by foreigners, and it was these same foreigners who opened the first purpose-built film theaters. The shooting of film before 1911 was also largely the work of foreigners, beginning with James Ricalton, who brought a program of Edison shorts to China in 1897 and shot a dozen short scenes for inclusion in that year's Edison catalogue. The bulk of the films in these early years were documentary or newsreel items, but hardly any of them seem to have been screened in China itself. There was some gradual expansion, however. Peking had its first film show in 1902, and the following year it hosted the first film showing organized by a Chinese (Lin Chu-shau). A few years later, then, the first dramatic films were shot by employees of Peking's Feng Tai Photography Shop. But more important and enduring than any of these initial Chinese endeavors was the Asia Film Company, founded by an American, Benjamin Brodsky, who began production in Hong Kong in 1909 and three years later moved his operation to Shanghai, which was to become the center of Chinese film making.

The 1911 overthrow of the Manchus and establishment of a republic under the presidency of the foreign-educated Dr. Sun Yat-sen did not lead to stability. The presidency was soon taken over by an ambitious general, Yüan Shih-kai, who received foreign support and planned to establish himself as emperor. He died in 1916 without achieving the power needed to fulfill this ambition, and for ten years China fell under the power of provincial warlords who waged incessant internecine war. Even the stability of the foreign-dominated treaty ports was disturbed by strikes, riots, and disorders. The May Fourth Movement of 1919, inspired by nationalist resentment of the Versailles Treaty (which awarded formerly German-controlled territory to Japan), looked forward to the emergence of a new, more aggressive nationalism "which was far less inclined to take democracy as its model or the Western powers as examples."[5] After the Russian Revolution, which had an enormous effect on Chinese intellectuals, Dr. Sun's reformed Kuomintang party began to draw arms and advice from Russia and to work in collaboration with members of the Chinese Communist party, which was founded in 1921. Following Dr. Sun's death in 1925, leadership of the Kuomintang was taken over by Chiang Kai-shek, who by 1927 had launched a successful reunification campaign against the warlords and staged a bloody purge of his erstwhile partners the Communists, who nevertheless continued the struggle through guerrilla warfare for another twenty-two years.

As far as cinema in the period up to the end of the 1920s is concerned, the industry was largely limited to the treaty ports. Control of exhibition, particularly in Shanghai, the center of the industry, remained in foreign hands and adhered to the classic two-tier colonial structure. But despite such hindrances, there was an increase in Chinese involvement in film making. 1912 saw the production of *The Difficult Couple* / *Nan fu nan qi*, "the first Chinese fictional film that did not rely on a mere recording of popular theatre scenes,"[6] made by Zhang Shi-chuan and Zheng Zheng-qiu for the Asia Film Company. Leyda lists eleven further films made by Zhang in 1913–14, most of them set in the present and "made to function as interludes in the theatre of the new drama group."[7] On his way back to the United States after relinquishing control of the Asia Film Company, Brodsky produced a two-reeler starring the actor Li Minwei, *Chuang-tse Tests His Wife* / *Zhuangzi shi qi* (1913), in Hong Kong. Li's wife, appearing in a minor role, was the first Chinese actress to appear on the screen, while Li himself starred in the leading *female* role. In 1916, Zhang set up Shanghai's first (short-lived) Chinese film production company, and 1917 saw the founding of the more solidly based Commercial Press, which in 1920 acquired an enlarged studio "under glass and with artificial lighting."[8] In 1922, Zhang established the Mingxing Company, which remained active as China's largest company till 1937, producing "180 fiction films of various lengths and (in the 1930s) a large number of newsreels and documentaries."[9] A little comedy made by Zhang in 1922 about a fruit seller, *Love's Labors* /*Laogong zhi aiqing*, is the earliest surviving Chinese fictional film.

The revolutionary crisis situations of the early 1920s saw several waves of speculative film financing in Shanghai. In the 1921 boom, 140 companies were founded, but only 12 were still in business by March 1922. The 1925 upsurge, with 175 new companies (including 141 in Shanghai), was more durable, 40 companies producing at least one film by the end of 1926. During this period, up to 1927, Leyda notes that the Shanghai film industry "grew not only less revolutionary, but less real. This was the period of the first attention of the entire industry to Chinese literary sources little noticed before: classical novels and stories, Peking operas, fairy tales, myths, and folklore."[10] One example of this genre that was partly preserved is Hou Yao's *Tale of the Western Chamber* / *Xi xiang ji* (1927), which received some showing in Paris as *La Rose de Pu Chui*. While admitting that on the surface this trend "looks like the escapist tendency of a speculative industry," Leyda notes that "the *other* kinds of films, those of "modern" subjects, had even less connection with their audiences: rarely drawn from modern Chinese life, they were usually content to give Chinese backgrounds and costumes to imitations of foreign, usually American, films."[11]

Despite almost total U.S. domination of Chinese cinema screens (which Leyda puts at 90 percent for 1929), about four hundred films were made by some fifty Shanghai producers in 1928–31, the first four years of Chiang Kai-shek's rule. But this production has little real national interest:

> After the tragedy of 1927 all phases of intellectual life in China went into cautious retreat. Even the cinema, least intellectually demanding of China's arts, found it possible to retreat further from ideas and real life. By the time the new

censorship regulations came into effect in 1930, it is hard to find a concrete tar-
get for the government's fears, for the classical subjects that were in vogue in
1926 had been replaced, and stayed replaced for the next four years, by a Chinese version of the most popular of all American film forms, the "western." [12]

The 1930s were a period of increasing Japanese encroachment on Chinese
territory, beginning with the seizure of Manchuria in 1931 and the bombing of
Shanghai in January 1932, and culminating in the full-scale invasion of China
in 1937. The Kuomintang under Chiang Kai-shek, though receiving support
from the foreign powers with interests in the treaty ports, shied away from
confrontation with the Japanese, choosing instead to turn its weapons on its
own people. Among its principal victims were the Communists, who managed, however, to survive both the suicidal directives of Stalin to collaborate
with their persecutors and the rigors of the six-thousand-mile Long March in
1934, which turned threatening defeat into the basis for eventual victory. It is
not surprising that these conflicts should have found their reflection in the
films of the period, leading two recent critics to claim that "a Chinese film of
the 1930s or 1940s is a site for a clash of ideologies. Every film, like every
novel and every newspaper article, had to have a position on the key issues of
the day: whether or not to resist Japanese aggression, what to do about widespread poverty and corruption." [13]

What is unique at this period, though, is the existence of a politically organized group of left-wing film makers working within the Kuomintang-
controlled and -financed Shanghai film industry throughout the period up to
the 1937 Japanese invasion. Xia Yan, a leading member of the Left-Wing
Dramatists' League, led the group that infiltrated the studios. The League's
"Present Program for Action," adopted in 1931, set out these aims: "Members
must produce scripts for the film makers; join in the film production of the
various companies; accumulate capital for our own film productions; organize
a society for film research; and bring together progressive actors and technicians to form a base for China's left-wing film movement—and we must criti-
cize and analyze the present state of the Chinese cinema." [14]

In the 1930s, Shanghai was at the intersection of a number of worlds: it was
a cosmopolitan city and a focus of national culture, the center for the import
of foreign films and site of China's major film production activities, under
Kuomintang rule (apart from the concessions) and yet possessing a long-
established left-wing underground movement. Shanghai was thus at the center
of China's 1930s crisis and, as Leyda puts it, "these exceptional, bitter, difficult, and often bloody circumstances resulted in the most interesting and lasting Chinese films, superior to what came before, to what was going on above
ground at the same time, and, in many important respects, superior to the
Chinese films made in the years well after the triumph of the Chinese revolution." [15] Although Shanghai cinema continued to be dominated by Holly-

wood—Régis Bergeron puts the U.S. share of screentime in 1934 at 85 percent[16]—production levels were high, with 565 films in all in 1930–37. Almost 70 percent of these were silent, however. Imported sound films were shown in Shanghai as early as 1929, but it was not until 1931 that a successful Chinese experiment with sound on discs could be shown, and it was 1934 before a Chinese film with sound on film could be released. Only in 1935 did sound films exceed silent ones, and even then the changeover resulted in a virtual halving of output (from 101 in 1930 to just 55 in 1935). Recording equipment remained fairly basic, with few possibilities for mixing or laying down sound effects, and films of the late 1930s often have large gaps of silence in their sound tracks.

Equally as striking as this technical backwardness of Chinese 1930s cinema is the extent to which Hollywood served as a conscious model for Shanghai film makers. As Jay Leyda notes, Chinese producers never managed to escape from "their entangling admiration of the efficient American film."[17] Most Chinese films of the 1930s fit into genre categories familiar in the West, and Shanghai cinema does not develop a distinctive dramaturgy of the kind that emerged in Japan and India. Even left-wing film makers offer local versions of Sternberg's *Dishonored* (Sun Yu's *Daybreak / Tianming* [1933]) and *The Prisoner of Zenda* (Ying Yunwei's *Unchanged Heart in Life and Death / Shengsi tongxin* [1936]). Though the young Nie Er, who died in 1935 at the age of twenty-four, wrote a number of stirring songs for left-wing productions (one of which eventually became the Chinese national anthem), many late-1930s films are marred by the insensitive use of Western music in half-comprehending imitation of Hollywood. Leyda maintains, for example, that Cheng Bugao's *Spring Silkworms / Chuncan* (1933), which was shot silent, is best seen without its added musical score, since the "dinner music, Parisian and Viennese operettas, 'Old Black Joe,' Aloha, church hymns make no attempt to reflect or to comment on the film's action or meaning."[18] Likewise, the selection of stars by film companies "must have been a peculiar process. . . . If you seek a film actress who resembles the uniquely Chinese beauty that one can see in ancient frescoes or in the modern countryside, you will find her, if at all, playing 'character' or 'negative' roles."[19] Indeed, most of the stars can easily be related to Western models. Leyda compares Ruan Ling-yu (whom he exempts from his strictures) to Garbo; Tony Rayns sees Li Li-li as a Chinese Dietrich; Han Lan-gen and Yin Xiucen are "the Chinese Laurel and Hardy," and so on.

But if Shanghai cinema was in these ways one of the more imitative of non-Western cinemas in the 1930s, it also expressed a unique political awareness. A left-wing underground survived within the Shanghai industry until the full-scale Japanese invasion of 1937 partly because of its tight organization and ideological awareness but also because the films for which it was responsible were among the most commercially successful of the period. It therefore laid

31. Cheng Bugao: Spring Silkworms / Chuncan *(China, 1933)*

the foundation of a cinema that was both national and popular. As in India, the language question came to the fore as soon as sound arrived, since though Chinese dialects share a common written script, they are mutually incomprehensible in spoken form. A solution akin to that implemented in India was adopted: the bulk of the films were made not in the local dialect of the southern center of production, Shanghai, but in "the language of the north, the Pekin dialect known as 'mandarin,' and politically known as *pai-hua,* the national language. . . . In a period when the nation was in need of all unities, the film industry contributed its mite." [20] This choice of language is merely one aspect of the political involvement that makes the film makers heirs to the intellectuals of the May Fourth Movement of 1919, who had attempted to revolutionize Chinese culture by embarking on "a campaign to publish magazines, newspapers and books" in *pai-hua,* as a first stage in the production of "a new language, a new literature, a new outlook on life and society, and a new scholarship." [21]

But though the new left-wing film makers were deeply influenced by American movies, they were not simply cinephiles. Most came from the modern theater movement and "saw their film work as an extension of their theatre practice." [22] They brought new literary concerns to Chinese cinema, particu-

32. Bu Wancang: Peach Blossom Weeps Tears of Blood / Taohua qi xueji
(China, 1931)

larly a novelistic expansiveness of plot which avoids the tight narrative economy of Hollywood cinema and allows the action to spread over years or decades. An effect of this is the particularly theatrical style of performance
adopted by many players, though some, such as Ruan Ling-yu, have a quin-
tessentially cinematic quality. The use of metaphors from nature is also
general practice, reflected in titles such as that of Bu Wancang's tale of love
thwarted by feudal social divisions, *Peach Blossom Weeps Tears of Blood /
Taohua qi xueji* (1931).

    Shanghai cinema of the 1930s has still been seen only fragmentarily in the
West, and until recently it was highly controversial in China itself. Many film
makers were persecuted during the Cultural Revolution at the instigation of
Mao's widow, Jiang Qing, herself a Shanghai film actress in the 1930s. Although no right-wing films, nor any of those featuring Jiang Qing, have been
made available by the China Film Archive, certain characteristics of this
Shanghai output are now apparent. There was a strong concern for realistic
depiction of both peasants and the urban poor, though often within melodramatic plot structures. As an example of the former, one might cite *Spring
Silkworms / Chuncan,* a strikingly austere study of peasant life. containing a
virtual documentary on every detail of rearing silkworms, made by Cheng

Bugao, whose first film, *Wild Torrent / Kuang liu* (1933) Leyda regards as "the beginning of socially conscious Chinese cinema." [23] Equally impressive as a depiction of urban life—taking the example of a woman driven into prostitution—is *The Goddess / Shennü* (1934), the first feature by Wu Yonggang (1907–82), starring Ruan Ling-yu.

The range of achievement within a leftist approach can be seen by a comparison of the approaches of Sun Yu (b. 1900) and Ying Yunwei (1904–67). Sun Yu, who studied theater and cinema in the United States, made a dozen or so features in the 1930s, among them *Daybreak* and *Little Toys / Xiao wanyi* (both 1933), and *Queen of Sport / Tiyu huanghou* and *The Highway / Da lu* (both 1934, the latter a part-sound film). In these films, a variety of political themes—the rural exodus, the urban proletariat, the need for collective modernization and popular patriotism—are fitted into lively and extrovert dramatic or melodramatic forms. Sun offers vigorous action sequences combined with farce and eroticism (in the form of Li Li-li) and echoes of Sternberg and expressionism alongside emphatic straight-to-camera Chinese patriotism (with sympathy for the 1930s leftist struggle masked as support for Chiang Kai-shek's mid-1920s "revolution"). By contrast, the films of Ying Yunwei, such as *Plunder of Peach and Plum / Tao li jie* (1934) and *Unchanged Heart in Life and Death,* are somber works starring the brilliant Yuan Muzhi and his

33. Wu Yonggang: The Goddess / Shennü *(China, 1934)*

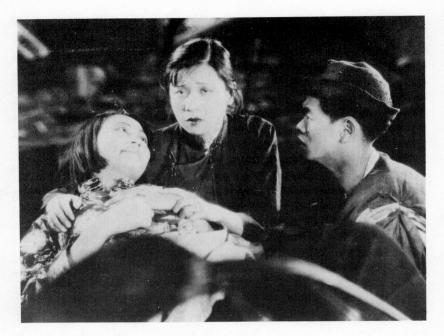

34. Sun Yu: Little Toys / Xiao wanyi *(China, 1933)*

35. Ying Yunwei: Unchanged Heart in Life and Death / Shengsi tongxin
(China, 1936)

wife Chen Bo'er. This couple were real-life political activists who joined Mao in Yenan after 1937 and went on to occupy key posts in the Ministry of Culture after the Revolution. Their commitment gives added weight to the melodramatic stories, which Ying handles with a style using the full visual and editing resources of the cinema to drive home the message that society must be changed.

Given the divisions of China caused by occupation, war, and civil conflict, Shanghai's 1930s cinema is merely one of a number of strikingly different cinemas coexisting in China before 1949. With the 1937 Japanese invasion, the Shanghai left-wingers were dispersed, either to other production centers, such as Hong Kong, or to various politically committed theatrical groups. Though there was some limited production in the Communist-held areas, the major importance of Yenan to Chinese cinema lies in the debates on art and literature conducted there in 1942, which laid the basis for future policy after the Revolution.

The period of the Japanese occupation of Shanghai (1937–41) is viewed unfavorably by Chinese historians, since, like the German occupation of France, it constitutes a problematic chapter in the national history. The Shanghai industry "regarded itself as in an 'orphan island.' . . . In this period Japanese pressure was constantly felt by the film studios in the enclosed city, but semi-independent production continued." [24] The films produced, however, seem to have shown little sign of quality or commitment, perhaps because so many of the best talents had already fled to Chungking or Hong Kong. Also partly on the negative side is the film industry the Japanese established in 1938 in the puppet state of Manchukuo (the occupied province of Manchuria) as part of their general program of industrialization. About 200 films were produced—among them 120 entertainment feature films—in the eight years of this industry's existence, all to fulfill a clearly defined propaganda function: "They were intended to show the world (or the Asian world) a stable, self-confident, unworried regime." [25] Despite Chinese reservations, however, Leyda is convinced that contact with the more sophisticated Japanese film makers had positive effects that became visible in Chinese cinema after 1945.

In Hong Kong, away from the fighting, a very different cinema emerged in the period up to the Japanese invasion, reinforced by successive waves of refugees fleeing the bombing of Shanghai in 1932 and the outbreak of war against Japan in 1937. Beginnings had been tentative in the silent period, when the colonial authorities proved hostile to the establishment of film studios, but by the late 1930s "Hong Kong was the established centre of Cantonese film production. . . . Some of these films were Cantonese operas, others were comedies, dramas, sword-play epics, and so on. All, one gathers, were prone to stop for a song or two. Through the medium of these films, Cantonese popular culture maintained a network connecting dispersed overseas Chinese to their southern homeland." [26] In all, an estimated four hundred features—about forty-four a year—were made between 1933 and 1941, when the Japanese invasion brought production to a halt. I. C. Jarvie's view of this cinema is positive: "Doubtless Cantonese films were far from sophisticated by the standards of Shanghai, and they betrayed their shoe-string budgets. But they were a genuine response to popular demand, an outgrowth of a traditional folk subculture." [27]

From 1941, with an uneasy truce arranged between the Kuomintang and the Communists, China fought as one of the Allies against the Axis powers. But its fragile internal unity barely survived the end of the war, and by 1947 a full-scale civil war had been resumed. During the period 1945–49, Shanghai was again dominated by the Kuomintang, but once more Communist artists and film makers, who were untainted by collaboration with the Japanese, found employment and scope for the underground expression of their ideas. There is indeed a certain continuity with the period after the Revolution, since five independent companies were allowed to continue in operation until the industry was completely nationalized in 1953. Looking back on this varied history of Chinese cinema in the forty-five years or so before the Revolution, one cannot do better than repeat Tony Rayns's conclusion: "The Chinese cinema has produced a body of work that is richly accomplished, politically and aesthetically sophisticated and distinctively of its own culture. The western film establishment has remained ignorant of it for too long." [28]

If the history of Chinese cinema offers an example of success in overcoming some of the innumerable difficulties that have faced all non-Western cinemas, that of Vietnam shows the more customary inability to establish any kind of national film output under colonialism. [29] At the time of the French arrival in the mid–nineteenth century, the Vietnamese "possessed a reasonably homogenous cultural tradition, a well-defined political structure and immense pride at having been able to stave off numerous Chinese encroachments from the north while simultaneously seizing territories from other ethnic groups to the south." [30] But none of this found expression in the structures of film exhibition or production. Early screenings, we are told, "were intended solely for the entertainment of administrative personnel, for the recruitment of expedition and army units in the French colony, for the diffusion of missionary propaganda, and for the derision of the mandarins who prided themselves in having 'progressed intellectually.'" [31]

Though documentation is scarce and contradictory, it would seem that the first cinemas were established before or during World War I. There was the usual two-tiered structure of purely urban exhibition, with French-owned cinemas showing French, and later predominantly American, imports, while the theaters run by Chinese showed films from Hong Kong and China.

Feature film production in the interwar years came in two waves, provoked by the steady expansion in the number of cinemas (there were sixty-three in 1939). In the mid-1920s the Société Indochine Films et Cinéma, which also owned a number of cinemas, produced several dramatic films, beginning with *Kim van Kieu* in 1923. After the coming of sound, the Society of South Vietnam (Asia) produced a further half-dozen films, the first of these being *The Flower from the Cemetery* (1937). Most of these were based on Vietnamese literary sources and were presented as Vietnamese productions, but "in reality, the Vietnamese were only a minority amongst the film crew. The basic work, shooting, editing, sound, making copies, series production, etc., was undertaken by foreigners through their organisations." [32] There were several other ill-documented attempts at film production by amateur groups in the late 1930s, but all this activity came to an end with the French surrender to the Japanese in 1940. Vietnamese film making was reborn as a guerrilla cinema during the struggle against the French, and Vietnamese critics date the birth of an authentic national cinema at Ho Chi Minh's Decree of March 1953, which set up the National Society for Film and Photography.

"Traditional" Societies of Southeast Asia

The cultural disparities separating the various nation-states of East and Southeast Asia are enormous. Even if we ignore those which have quit the capitalist orbit, leave for later consideration the generally smaller "newly industrializing countries," and consider only the Southeast Asian sweep from Burma, Thailand, and Malaysia through Indonesia to the Philippines, we are still faced with staggering diversity. The Philippines, colonized and converted to Catholicism by the Spaniards, did not share the other countries' experience of Indian trading influence or the religious impact of Hinduism and Buddhism. Of the remaining four, only Indonesia was converted (in the fifteenth century) to Islam, which is presently the religion of over 90 percent of the population. While the experience of colonialism is crucial to most Asian societies, Thailand was never formally colonized. Finally, whereas most of these nation-states occupy the boundaries of long-established traditional societies, "the very concept 'Indonesia' is a twentieth century invention, and most of today's Indonesia was only conquered by the Dutch between 1850 and 1910." [33] The manner in which the four former colonies achieved their independence varied from a peaceful transfer of power from the colonizer to a trusted local elite, in the case of the United States and the Philippines, to armed struggle between the colonizers and an emergent revolutionary nationalist movement, in the case of the Netherlands and Indonesia.

Such differentiations could be extended almost infinitely, but there are certain common factors that unite these countries in the twentieth century. In most cases the emergence of a nationalist elite was greatly influenced by major global events such as the first Asian victory over a European power (in the 1904–5 Russo-Japanese War) and the October 1917 revolution in Russia. With the colonizers' hold relaxed during World War I, the elite nationalist groups were in several instances able to widen their appeal and create mass movements on the Indian pattern in the following decades. Such movements usually faced harsh imperialist opposition, but in most instances they served to undermine the overtly collaborating groups (though not in the Philippines, which as a consequence "continued to have one of the most unreconstructed social orders in Asia").[34] The Japanese occupation of Southeast Asia in 1942–45 fatally weakened the Europeans' last hold on their Asian colonies, and opposition to the Japanese invaders—such as that of the communists in China—generally strengthened the nationalists' claims to recognition. By 1949, then, the Philippines, Burma, and Indonesia had joined Thailand as independent states, though Malaysia had to wait for the British to first defeat the largely Chinese Malayan Communists before handing power to a more right-wing Malayan elite in 1957.

Comparatively little is recorded, in English at least, about the various national cinemas of these states, though in most, production of at least a primitive kind dates back to the silent period.[35] Burma, for example, began making films—in 16mm it seems—in the early 1920s. Until 1937, Burma was linked to India, and Rangoon was, after Bombay and Calcutta, one of the major Indian film markets. The members of the 1927 Indian Cinematograph Committee did not visit Burma, but their report tells us that the province had fifty-eight permanent film theaters and seventeen "producing agencies," though only four of these had a steady output. Distribution often took the simplest possible form, with the producer himself hiring a hall in which to exhibit his film. Comments on the quality of late-1920s Burmese films show that the committee regarded them as primitive and provincial. Burmese films, we are told, were "altogether excessive" in length "and the action accordingly protracted," while the high rate of Burmese literacy resulted in "an abundance of captions." As for style, "The commonest type of Burmese film is a kind of fairy tale with a lavish indulgence in the supernatural and a variety of demons. Though novel and fantastic on the first acquaintance, these films are very stereotyped, and the same sort of stories, incidents, and costumes are endlessly repeated. In the Burmese social dramas the mimicry of the west is particularly pronounced."[36]

A first 35mm sound film was produced in 1934, and output had reached fifty films a year by the late 1950s. This level was maintained over the next two decades, with output varying between forty-three and ninety films a year between 1960 and 1979 and falling back to around fifty in the 1980s. By 1977, Burma had 422 movie theaters and some 16 studios and laboratories for black-and-white cinematography. The Motion Picture Corporation, under the Ministry of Information and Culture, is responsible for the production of newsreels and documentaries, for the import of foreign films "which enjoy a good demand," and for running the laboratories and the 180 state-owned theaters (nationalized in 1968). With an entertainment tax of 40 percent and hall rentals of 30 percent, only 30 percent of gross earnings are returned to producers, who, still working in black-and-white in the 1980s, have yet to break into export markets.

Another national cinema which until very recently has been making films purely for its domestic market is that of Thailand. Though a distribution network of over three hundred theaters had been built up by 1960, production remained on a very primitive level: "The Thai film industry dates from 1936, although it is only since about 1970 that production has been organised on anything resembling the western model. For reasons of economy, Thai films of the 1950s and 1960s were shot silent, on 16mm, live 'soundtracks' being provided in each theatre. The first Thai feature with married sound was made in 1971." [37] But the early 1970s saw both an increase of more sophisticated 35mm features using Western-style narrative structures and the emergence of a number of Western-trained directors. In the late 1970s, the Thai film industry, which was making around fifty color feature films a year, received support from the government in the form of a heavy import duty on foreign films, which resulted in an MPEA boycott. A limited number of films by Thai directors have received showings in the West.

Among the veteran film makers is Vichit Kounavudhi (b. 1922), who entered the film industry as a scriptwriter in the 1940s and has made some thirty features since his debut in 1953. Among his critical and popular successes are *The Mountain People / Khon phuu kaow* (1980) and a more recent study of rural life, based on an autobiographical novel, *Son of the Northeast / Luk E-San* (1982). A representative of the younger generation is Cherd Songsri, who made seven 16mm features from 1966 to 1971 before going to study film at UCLA. Among the half-dozen 35mm features he has made since his return to Thailand is the industry's biggest success ever, *The Scar / Prae kaow* (1978). Aside from the mainstream of Thai commercial production there have been occasional films that have looked critically at Thai society; among the ones in this category that have been shown in the West are *Tongpan,* made by the Isan Film Group during the period preceding the 1977 coup, and *On the Fringe of Society / Prachaohon nork* (1981), made by the twenty-five-year-old poet and short-story writer Manop Udomdej.

In Malaysia the control of distribution by Chinese business interests has its origins in 1926, when a first cinema was set up by the Shaw Brothers. Eventually the Shaws, together with the Cathay Organization, were to exercise an almost total hold. From 35 cinemas in 1929, the number had grown to some 368 cinemas by 1975. There were also several hundred mobile cinema units. [38] Malay film production began in the 1930s, when films financed by Chinese tycoons and written and directed by Indian expatriates, but with Malay actors, began to be made. This pattern of production persisted into the 1960s, and Malay production remains today at under a dozen films a year.

Few Malay films are shown abroad: in relation to the most popular imports

36. *Vichit Kounavudhi:* Son of the Northeast / Luk E-San *(Thailand, 1982)*

to overseas markets, Indonesian films, the proportion remains one Malay export for every ten Indonesian imports. With production directed at the needs of the domestic market, no directors of international standing have emerged, though a London International Film School graduate, Jins Shamsuddin, has made two popular hits since his return in 1973, *Waiting for Tomorrow / Menanti hari esok* (1978) and *Bulit Kepong* (1981). A report commissioned in 1974 recommended the establishment of a Malay Film Development Corporation, FINAS, but this was not set up until 1981, and to date none of its ambitious projects (a studio complex, credit facilities, training) have been realized.

An indication of what can be achieved by a sustained policy of government support is shown by recent developments in Indonesia. Though Indonesia has for a long time had a highly developed distribution network—with well over six hundred movie theaters at the beginning of the 1960s, rising to over a thousand in the late 1970s—its film production was slow to develop. Averaging around three features a year in the 1950s, it had still not reached twenty films a year in the course of the 1960s. Then, at the beginning of the 1970s, government assistance in the form of import restrictions and tariffs, together with the provision of credit facilities for producers, raised output to between fifty and eighty features a year. At first this production was directed solely at the domestic market and those neighboring countries, such as Malaysia, where Indonesian is understood. But in the 1980s the government has begun to seek wider recognition for the national cinema through active participation in foreign film festivals. In this way the names of certain film makers have begun to be known in the West, even if few of their films reach Europe. One group comprises those who were sent to study at the Moscow National Film Academy in the 1960s: Wim Umboh (b. 1933), whose films have won more national awards than any other director, Syuman Jaya (b. 1933), and Ami Priyono (b. 1939). A second trio of directors, whose roots lie in developments in Indonesian theater, comprises Teguh Karya (b. 1937), who made his debut in 1971, Arifin C. Noer (b. 1941), who wrote prize-winning scripts before making his directorial debut in 1977, and Slamet Rahardjo (b. 1949), a prominent actor who has appeared in all Karya's films and who began as a film director in the 1980s.

The most important cinema in Southeast Asia is that of the Philippines, which offers a full reflection of that country's troubled past and serves as a striking example of the difficulties of establishing a national cinema under colonialism or neocolonial dominance. The Lumière cinematograph was brought to Manila by Antonio Ramos (who was later to play a key role in establishing cinema in Shanghai) in 1897, the last year of Spanish rule before

37. *Slamet Rahardjo:* The Moon and the Sun / Rembulan dan matahari
(Indonesia, 1979)

control of the Philippines was transferred to the United States. A first regular
movie theater was established in 1898, and distribution was well established
by 1910, when American firms, which were to dominate until the end of
World War I, began regular film production. It is fascinating to note that the
commercial rivalry of U.S. production interests was expressed through two
simultaneous films about the national hero José Rizal, of whom the Filipino
historian Renato Constantino observes that he was used by the American
colonizers in "moulding the desired colonial consciousness. . . . José Rizal
was a safe hero. He condemned the Revolution and refused to join it; he was a
reformist and a great believer in education; and most important, he was shot
by the Spaniards in 1896 and therefore had nothing to do with the Americans." [39] True Philippine national production began in 1919 with the feature
film *A Girl from the Country / Dalagang bukid,* directed by José Nepomu-
ceno, the "father of Philippine cinema," who later made the first local sound
film. As in India, silent production was artisanal and organized through small
production companies, which were often family concerns. This era came to
an end with the advent of sound in 1933 and with the foundation the following
year, by the American Stewart Eddie Tait, of a major production company,
Filippin Films, which used American technicians and by 1938 was producing
twenty films a year. Other production companies organized on modern industrial lines were founded in the late 1930s, and by 1939 overall output was fifty
to sixty features a year.

Production stopped during the Japanese occupation in 1942–45, but after
independence, film making slowly got under way again, with five films in
1946 and twenty-eight in 1947. The immediate postwar period up to the early
1960s—marked by the productions of Lamberto V. Avellana, Eddie Romero,
and Gerardo de Leon—is generally regarded as a time of major achievement.
But Max Tessier captures the precise quality of this achievement when he
compares a striking film like *48 Hours / 48 oras* (1950) by Gerardo de Leon
(1913–81) not with the work of major directors of Hollywood *film noir* but
with contemporary work in another country culturally dependent on the
United States, Mexico (citing as an example Emilio Fernandez's *Salon México*).[40] But despite its achievements at this time, Philippine cinema remained
largely unknown outside its domestic market, with only an occasional film,
such as Manuel Conde's *Genghis Khan* (1952), distributed abroad as an exotic
oddity. For the Filipino film historian Agustin Sotto, the period 1962–74—
the years dominated by Ferdinand Marcos, who declared a state of martial law
in 1972—marks a decline in the quality of Philippine film making "with a
type of populist cinema directly serving the needs of the lower classes" coming to the fore.[41] In commercial terms, however, these are years of expansion
for an industry serving a network of well over seven hundred movie theaters,
with production that was under 100 films a year in the 1950s rising to a peak of
250 in 1971 and remaining above 150 films a year into the 1980s.

International awareness of Philippine cinema has coincided with the emergence in the late 1970s of a younger generation of film makers—Lino Brocka, Ishmael Bernal, and a former director of photography, Mike de Leon—whose work constitutes a new chapter in Philippine film history. The most forceful and dynamic of these younger film makers is Lino Brocka (b. 1940), who made his debut in 1970 and had completed around forty features within a decade or so. Brocka is a complex figure who experienced a religious crisis while a university student and became a Mormon missionary before turning first to theater and then to the cinema. His stance has been to work resolutely within the confines of the industry, despite its purely commercial aspirations and values and the increasing weight of censorship and oppression in Philippine society as a whole under President Marcos. As a result, his films, which include *Manila / Maynila, sa mga kuko ng liwanag* (1975), *Insiang* (1976), *Jaguar* (1979), and *Bona, Kontrobersyal,* and *Angela Markado* (all 1980), are contradictory works. They show a powerful imagination and a fine plastic sense, as well as a willingness to treat controversial aspects of society and to create powerful effects. But always there is the tendency to offer a cleaned-up version of poverty and to treat the setting as no more than a location for the action, to shape all emotion into a straitjacket of melodrama and to maintain complicity with the worlds the films ostensibly denounce. *Bona* uses stars to denounce the excesses of the star system, *Kontrobersyal* is a porn movie as

38. Lino Brocka: Manila / Maynila, sa mga kuko ng liwanag *(Philippines, 1975)*

39. Lino Brocka: Angela Markado *(Philippines, 1980)*

well as a denunciation of porn movie making, and *Angela Markado* attacks rape in the form of a vigilante-style revenge movie that is as exploitative as anything by Michael Winner. In Brocka's work the violent contradictions of Asian societies find a powerful expression.

The "Newly Industrializing Countries"

Four comparatively small countries of East and Southeast Asia—the Republic of China, or Taiwan (formerly Formosa), the Republic of (South) Korea, Hong Kong, and Singapore—have collectively contributed well over half the great surge of Third World industrialization in the 1960s and 1970s.[42] Frequently used as exemplars in the arguments against the dependency theory, these "newly industrializing countries" are in fact very special cases. All four are fragmentary states produced by the vagaries of war, colonialism, and decolonization: Hong Kong remains a British crown colony, without even a semblance of elected self-government; Singapore is cut off from its Malaysian hinterland; Taiwan is the last outpost of nationalist China; and South Korea came into separate existence when Korea was truncated by civil war and foreign military intervention in the 1950s.

There are, of course, considerable differences in the form capitalist development has taken in these countries. Singapore's industrialization is largely the work of transnational corporations, while the economies of the other three have been developed by local capital. But in each case the roots of economic development lie in the period before 1945. Then, Korea and Taiwan were established by Japan as colonies to provide agricultural surplus and developed in ways that destroyed traditional social bonds, while Hong Kong and Singapore were created as imperial trading posts and administered in ways that favored European interests in banking, shipping, and big business but were not hostile to Chinese control of local trade, transport, goods handling, and so on. After 1945, anticommunist governments and an emergent United States–linked bourgeoisie were fostered in Taiwan and South Korea by massive U.S. aid (forming the largest part of the national budget for many years), administered and distributed through the state, which became the major driving force in industrialization. Both the refugee Chinese capitalists fleeing the 1949 revolution for Hong Kong, where British rule was reestablished immediately after the war, and the emergent westernized elite in Singapore committed themselves to a shift from merchant activities to industrial development. Beginning in the late 1950s, then, and gaining momentum throughout the 1960s and 1970s, there came a great surge of industrialization, export-oriented and limited to a range of industries that did not require either huge capital investment or extremely advanced production technologies. Remarkably, much of this massive development was the work of small firms, often organized as family businesses. Such developments obviously created the conditions in which film industries could be expected to grow. On the one hand, film production requires capital investment of a kind familiar to local entrepreneurs (that is, it can be organized on a large scale through family-owned corporations and requires a comparatively unsophisticated technology), and on the other, industrialization provides an urban mass population, whose entertainment needs create a market for a local-language commercial cinema.

The history of film production in Korea exemplifies the shifting forces at work in East Asia. The first film show occurred in 1903, and theaters began to be set up in Seoul between 1910 and 1920. A first fragmentary Korean-made film appeared in 1919, and the first complete film four years later, by which time the profitability of the cinema was established. The period 1926 to 1934 is regarded as "the golden era of silent movies in Korea," with its own national pioneer film maker, Na Woon Kyu.[43] In all, some eighty silent films were produced. Sound, introduced in 1935, increased production costs, so only the larger, better financed companies could survive. A period during which producers, "using new able directors and fine new stars, made good melodrama films and amusing action films with newly polished technique" followed.[44] Korea, a Japanese protectorate since 1905, had been formally annexed in 1910. When Japan allied itself with the Axis powers of Germany and

Italy in 1940 prior to its invasion of Southeast Asia, Korea was subject to fresh pressures. In terms of the film industry, the Japanese "confiscated by force all Korean motion picture facilities, equipment and related assets, and closed more than 10 production companies."[45] In the years 1940–45, only twenty-five feature films were produced, "most of them propaganda for the Japanese imperialism."[46] The immediate postwar situation was one of confusion, and for a time Korean film making regressed to 16mm productions, shot silent and postsynchronized. Hardly had stability of sorts been achieved, than the country was plunged in 1950 into civil war and international military conflict, and only eight films could be made in 1950–54.

With the end of the war and the beginning of the "economic miracle" in the south, Seoul was reestablished as Korea's film capital. Films were exempted from tax, and both audiences and output grew rapidly, with production rising from just nine features in 1955 to over a hundred in 1959. There was a corresponding rise in the number of movie theaters, from around 120 in 1955 to some 265 in 1960. The 1960s were boom years for the privately financed film industry. The number of theaters increased to a peak of about 700, output passed three hundred features a year, and audiences were huge. But the advent of television began a decline in audience levels that by the early 1970s had halved output and threatened the industry with bankruptcy. The government, which had begun to regulate the industry in the early 1960s, gradually took control of film production. By the early 1980s, the industry was fully regulated, with the government allowing twenty feature film producers to make about a hundred films a year. Film imports, too, are tightly controlled, with the government setting quotas for foreign film, allowing only those Korean producers who have made good-quality feature films to import from abroad. These producer-importers distribute their films directly to Korean theaters (300 in urban areas and a further 170 or so scattered through the country).

Hardly any of South Korea's huge output is shown abroad, and there are no internationally known film directors—the handful of films shown in London in 1984 were violently introspective melodramas, often ending in spectacular self-immolation. Evaluation of Korean film production tends to be severely critical. Kai Hong, for example, points out that

> Korean society and government is determined to keep Korea as insular as possible and turn its citizenry into well-behaved conformists. This deliberate policy is applied with particular high-handedness in the strict regulation of the film industry, perhaps in recognition of the democratizing and liberalizing tendencies of the film medium. No country has a stricter code of film censorship than South Korea—with the possible exception of the North Koreans and some other Communist bloc countries. Each line of a screenplay must be approved by the government agency before production can begin. There are also taboo subjects—anything with even a remote political connotation, for example, meaning that you cannot deal with the present in any serious way.[47]

40. Chang-Ho Bae: Warm It Was That Winter / Kuhe kyulun taduthenne
(Republic of Korea, 1984)

The cinemas of Hong Kong, Singapore, and Taiwan are so variously inter-meshed—by the shared background of colonialism and Japanese occupation, by ongoing capitalist development, by the Chinese language and the shared impact of developments in mainland China, and by financial control and dis-tribution networks and exchange of personnel—that in this very brief survey they are considered together. They are, however, essentially individual and show constant shifts both in level and type of output and in relative impor-tance as local capitals have maneuvered for best advantage, first in the expand-ing market of the early years of economic growth and then to face the suc-cessive impacts of television and video. In Singapore, where well-organized exhibition circuits linked to Malaysia were in existence before 1945, produc-tion was around twenty features a year (some Malay, but mostly Chinese) by the mid-1950s but declined to nothing in the 1970s. Singapore is thus the only country in East or Southeast Asia without a local film industry—perhaps a reflection of the relative weakness of indigenous capital in Singapore's eco-nomic development. In Taiwan, in contrast, the film industry was slow to de-velop after 1945, despite the relatively large market of some five hundred movie theaters. Though Taiwan's output, including productions by Hong Kong–based firms, has since overtaken that of Hong Kong in numerical terms, its film producers find it more difficult to break into foreign—even overseas Chinese—markets. Taiwanese production continues to nurture "those Chinese values either thrown to the winds in Hong Kong's commercial hothouse or buried in politics on the Chinese mainland"[48] and so exhibits the inward-looking stance characteristic of the bulk of the large Asian cinemas.

More interesting in the present context is Hong Kong cinema, which has experienced a variety of significant developments virtually unique in the Third World. Film production there got quickly under way after 1945, reached 200 features a year by 1951, peaked at over 300 a decade later, and subsequently declined sharply but still remained at around 150 films a year into the 1980s. As elsewhere in the Third World, even this high level of output did not mean control of the domestic market—"in Hong Kong no Chinese films outgrossed the top American film until 1968–69."[49] Hong Kong cinema does not exist as an outgrowth of local demand (though this demand grew sharply in the late 1940s from a very low level); rather, it is a result almost exclusively of Hong Kong's financial and trading advantages. This was true even before 1941, when Hong Kong, not mainland Canton, became the center for Cantonese film making:

> Raw film was freely importable. Land for studios was cheap. Taxes, duties, licenses and regulations were minimal; there was no precensorship of scripts. Export, like import, was without restriction. Furthermore, Hong Kong was a British colony, and many of the overseas Chinese to whom the films would be shown also lived in British colonies or British areas of influence: Singapore, Malaya, Borneo, and Burma. Trade between British possessions was fostered.[50]

Cheaply made Cantonese-language films continued to be produced in great numbers after 1945, but this local industry was not geared to the Hong Kong market, which accounted for no more than a third of the required returns. Even the most basic Cantonese production had an outside dimension: "Finance for such movies was usually obtained abroad. The producer would raise money in Singapore by proposing a cast and sometimes a story. With this he could start filming, and then sell further stakes in the completed film to other areas."[51]

Of the three big companies that have successively dominated the Hong Kong industry, only one was truly local. Cathay, the major force in the 1950s, was run by a Cambridge-educated magnate resident in Singapore, and its organizational weakness stemmed from the fact that "theatres and power were in one place (Singapore-Malaya), production was in another (Hong Kong)."[52] The financial roots of the huge Shaw Brothers organization also lay in Southeast Asian film theater chains, and the company became a dominant force only in 1958, when Run Run Shaw arrived from Singapore (where he had lived for thirty years) to take over production. Only Golden Harvest, founded in 1970 and celebrated for its Bruce Lee films, is run by a native of Hong Kong (Robert Chow) and exists purely as a production company.

The second anomaly of the Hong Kong industry is revealed in the language of the films produced. Though the residents of Hong Kong are Cantonese-speaking, after 1945 an increasing proportion of films were made in the Mandarin Chinese of the northern mainland. Though initially Mandarin movies "had no natural home in Hong Kong, no audience interested in them,"[53] and constituted under a third of the output in the early 1950s, Mandarin cinema increased steadily until it actually extinguished Cantonese cinema for a while in the early 1970s. The initial development of the Mandarin film was the work of refugees from Shanghai, both capitalists fleeing the 1949 revolution and left-wing artists. As in the Shanghai industry under the Kuomintang, of which it was the heir, there was a bewildering amalgam, a "co-existence of capitalist backers, communist film people, neutral film people, propaganda films and commercial films all within the same company."[54] But the sustained growth of Mandarin cinema points less to continued links with the mainland than to the production of a new, universally acceptable product (akin to the Hindi movie produced in Marathi-speaking Bombay). In this connection, I. C. Jarvie offers a useful distinction between two types of cinema: Cantonese movies, which are "above all Chinese movies, westernized almost as little as possible,"[55] and Mandarin movies, which "stem from the emerging modern national consciousness [and] tend to be produced in sophisticated urban surroundings . . . by culturally cosmopolitan Chinese and to treat stories and use the movie medium in a way that comes to some kind of terms with progress and the modern

41. King Hu: A Touch of Zen / Hsia nü *(Hong Kong, 1969)*

world."[56] It is this outward-looking Hong Kong cinema that has captured world attention, from the cheaply made *kung fu* films of the early 1970s, with their visually sophisticated and balletic use of the traditional martial arts, to the subsequent and more substantial works of King Hu, such as *A Touch of Zen / Hsia nü* (1969–75), the Cannes Grand Prize winner of 1975.

A third feature of particular interest is the relation of film to television in Hong Kong. Hong Kong, which adopted color in 1971, has one of the freest and best-developed television systems in Asia. It was television that was largely responsible for the virtual extinction of Cantonese film making in the early 1970s (only one Cantonese-language film was made in 1971–72), when "audiences of Cantonese films had turned to television to watch re-runs of old Cantonese features and television dramas." But within a few years television could be seen to be having a positive effect, as it "brought new ideas to the film industry through its social satires and crime thrillers, and it also served as training ground for new film makers who would become the forerunners of Hong Kong's 'New Wave' cinema in the 1980s."[57]

The rebirth of Cantonese cinema began with a Shaw Brothers television coproduction using television players, Vhu Yuan's *The House of 72 Tenants*

42. *Allen Fong:* Father and Son / Fuzi qing *(Hong Kong, 1981)*

(1973)—adapted from a play popular in prerevolutionary Shanghai—which outgrossed the films of Bruce Lee. The biggest star of the mid-1970s, the comedian Michael Hui, came from television, as did most of the sixty or so new directors who made their debuts in the late 1970s. But the films of these newcomers, prominent among them the Western-trained Allen Fong and Ann Hui, show an increasing mastery of purely cinematic styles as their makers have established themselves within the film industry. It would be foolish to generalize from the particular experience of Hong Kong, but developments there do indicate that the likely spread of television through Asia in the late 1980s need not necessarily be a disaster for existing Asian film industries—though it may prompt new styles and approaches.

To the extent that the history of our cinema is that of an oppressed culture, the elucidation of each of its stages or of its dimensions is transformed into an act of liberation.

Paulo Emilio Salles Gomes

Latin America is a region of enormous contrasts in terms of geography, population, and culture. But the societies that have emerged there share an economic backwardness—despite rich physical resources—that can be traced back to the early sixteenth century, when they became the ruthlessly exploited colonies of Spain and Portugal. Their underdevelopment can be seen to arise from the fact that the colonizing powers were themselves economic dependencies of other European powers. The situation remained unchanged throughout the three centuries of colonial rule, since the wealth extracted from Latin America was never applied in such a way as to turn Spain and Portugal into modern industrialized nations. The economic subordination of the Iberian peninsula within Europe persisted, and as a result, the exploitation of Latin America brought no accompanying economic or social development, merely the transfer to the New World of those very same archaic social forms and attitudes that were preventing development and industrial growth in Spain and Portugal themselves.

Political independence in the first quarter of the nineteenth century made little impact on this situation. In Spanish America, the impetus for change came less from internal social developments than from events in Europe stemming from Napoleon's seizure of the Spanish throne. Political independence was not part of a social revolution and resulted merely in the seizure of power by a tiny *criollo* elite, jealous of its own wealth and privileges and hostile to social transformation. There was little connection either between the idealistic European-style constitutions and the actual living conditions of the mass of the people or between the passionate proclamations of freedom and the actual tyranny of the brutally dictatorial *caudillos* who took power. Independence came before there was any infrastructure of communications within Spanish America, and instead of a development toward a unified federal structure of the kind achieved in North America, there was a disintegration into seventeen separate republics (joined later by Panama and Cuba). These republics were linked by little more than mutual dislike, rivalry, and open hostility—often exacerbated by foreign commercial interests for their own ends—and five major wars were fought in Spanish America between 1825 and 1935. The Portuguese empire in Brazil avoided the bloodshed and political divisions that marked independence in Spanish America, but the transfer of the Portuguese court to Brazil in 1808 and the eventual proclamation of independence under the monarchy in 1822 marked the continuity of even more archaic social structures (slavery, for example, was not abolished until 1888), which persisted even after the republic was established in 1889.

The social and political contradictions within Latin America left its vast resources open to exploitation by foreign—largely British—capital, which rewarded its allies among the merchant and landowning classes with vast wealth while holding the mass of the population in poverty. The nineteenth century brought wave after wave of migrants from Europe—when the cinema reached Argentina in the 1890s, for example, a quarter of its four million inhabitants were recent arrivals from Europe. But power remained in the hands of the tiny elite allied to foreign capitalist interests. Economic development took the form of the creation of one-product export economies: beef and agricultural products from Argentina, minerals from Chile, first coffee and then rubber from Brazil. While foreign capital modernized Latin America, in the sense of creating a communications and industrial infrastructure, its demands for a high return on investment and a quiescent work force left the mass of the people impoverished and strengthened the authority of the local oligarchy. Even the crucial shift during the first decades of the twentieth century from British to U.S. economic dominance was not accompanied by any move toward democracy or social justice; rather, traditional local tyrants like Porfirio Diaz in Mexico or Juan Vicente Gómez in Venezuela were merely supplemented by a new breed of U.S.-trained military henchmen on the model of Trujillo in Panama and Somoza in Nicaragua.

This, then, was the social context into which the cinema was introduced in Latin America. The very first showings in July 1896 in Rio, Montevideo, and Buenos Aires were soon followed by others in Mexico City (14 August 1896), Guatemala (26 September 1896), Maracaibo (28 January 1897), and Lima (2 March 1897). The year 1897 also saw film exhibitions organized by both the Lumières and Edison in Havana. Similarly, the first shooting of film, in Venezuela in 1897, was quickly echoed—in Argentina, Brazil, Cuba, Mexico, and Uruguay during the 1890s, in Chile in 1902, and in Colombia in

1905. Initially, cinema was very much a scientific novelty for an urban elite audience, with the showing of films so soon after their debut in Paris and New York being hailed by the local bourgeoisie as a mark of Latin American progress and modernity. But in fact, film was essentially just one more product marketed to European-oriented consumers for the greater profit of European manufacturers. The extent of European involvement in the beginnings of Latin American cinema finds its most extreme expression in Argentina, where the first importer of equipment was a Belgian, Henri Lepage; the first film, *The Argentine Flag / La bandera argentina* (1897), was shot by a Frenchman, Eugène Py; the first dramatic film, *The Execution of Dorrego / El fusilamiento Dorrego* (1908), was realized by an Italian, Mario Gallo; and the first producer to begin industrializing the cinema was an Austrian, Max Glucksmann. But in a less intense form, this European influence permeated the early years of the twentieth century throughout Latin America, as spectators were introduced to the short films distributed by the French company Pathé and were later enthralled by the first feature-length Italian epics. These early European works offered early models for many Latin American film makers, so that Gallo's film was a transposed version of the French *L'Assassinat du duc de Guise,* and the first Mexican feature film, *The Light / La luz* (1917), was openly based on Fosco and Pastrone's epic *Il fuoco,* even to the extent of starring an actress with a startling resemblance to the Italian diva, Pina Menichelli.[1]

Cinema very quickly widened its audience so as to become a popular entertainment medium. In Mexico, where some early exhibitors had moved out of the big cities to capture a rural audience, we find as early as 1906 an example of one of those denunciations of the medium that were later to become so common:

> The popular masses, uncouth and infantile, experience while sitting in front of the screen the enchantment of the child to whom the grandmother has recounted a fairy tale; but I fail to understand how, night after night, a group of people who have the obligation of being civilized can idiotize themselves at the Salon Rojo, or in the Pathé, or the Monte Carlo, with the incessant reproduction of scenes in which the aberration, anachronisms, inverisimilitudes, are made *ad hoc* for a public of the lowest mental level, ignorant of the most elementary educational notions.[2]

Certainly the entertainment function of cinema was taken over unquestioningly from the West, though early European command of Latin American film distribution—such as that achieved by Pathé through its branches in Rio de Janeiro, Buenos Aires, Havana, and Mexico City—seems to have been fairly unsystematic. In Brazil, at least, it was possible for local film production to capture local audiences and enjoy a brief "golden age" (*bela epoca*) before 1911. But such possibilities came to an end with World War I, when the Hollywood companies moved in to take over the market. The whole history of Latin American film production up to 1930 and beyond has to be seen against a background of overwhelming Hollywood superiority, against which no governmental barriers were raised. Since films were silent, with the substitution of Spanish or Portuguese subtitles a simple matter, foreign films spoke directly to Latin American audiences. Often 80–90 percent of local screentime was devoted to Hollywood films, which were supported in their impact by increasing U.S. involvement in the other new media of mass communication: newspapers, magazines, and later, radio.

The eighty years or so since independence had seen the emergence of commercial bourgeoisies in Latin America, and it was these who furnished the capital for the local infrastructure on which this system of Hollywood dominance was based. Two potential forms of investment were open to these bourgeoisies: film production or film distribution and exhibition. Not surprisingly—since their backgrounds tended to be more mercantile than industrial —they chose the latter, particularly as they were quick to note the very different rewards the two activities afforded. Outside the United States, production has always been hazardous, whereas distribution consistently brings a steady profit, though at the cost of dependence on imported products. Distribution profits continued to be derived from imported films regardless of whether there is any local production or not, and there has therefore been a natural reluctance on the part of distributors to plough their profits back into production that is, in the best of cases, speculative.

Despite this background of U.S. economic and cultural dominance, silent feature films were produced in at least ten Latin American countries, though in only three of these were the bases of an industry developed. For example, some fifty-four silent films were made in Chile between 1902 and 1932, and there was also production in Uruguay (with a first feature in 1919) and Cuba, where cinema rapidly established itself as an enormously popular medium, with some two hundred cinemas in existence by 1910. Bolivia began production in 1912 and ten years later produced the first of five silent features. There was some (ill-documented) production in Venezuela from 1902, in Peru from 1911 (with a first feature two years later), and in Guatemala, where the first feature was made in 1912. Colombia even enjoyed its brief "golden age" with the making of a dozen silent features between 1921 and 1927.

In Mexico, the years up to 1917 were dominated by documentary production, including some fascinating footage of the Mexican Revolution, while about a hundred silent feature-length fictional films were made between 1917 and 1930. Many of the latter were escapist melodramas set in a dream Mexico, but a few showed a blend of documentary and fiction. Among these is the fourteen-part serial *The Grey Motorcar / El automóvil gris* (1919), directed by Enrique Rosas, Joaquin Coss, and Juan Canals de Homes, which the Mexican film historian Emilio García Riera considers the most ambitious and important of Mexican silent films.[3] In Argentina, too, the beginnings of a more authentic national production were made during the silent years, with the enormously successful *Gaucho Nobility / Nobleza gaucha* (1915), directed by Eduardo Martínez de la Pera and Ernesto Gunche. This period also saw the emergence of the important director José Agustin Ferreyra, with *The Tango of Death / El tango de la muerte* in 1917.

The most important silent cinema in Latin America was that of Brazil, where some 1,685 films were made between 1898 and 1930. Even after the short-lived *bela epoca,* a mass of newsreel and documentary films were produced, along with a few strikingly individual features. Among the latter are Giuseppe Rossi and José Medina's *Fragments of Life / Fragmentos da vida* (1929), set and filmed on the streets of São Paulo, and the first works of Humberto Mauro, the great pioneer of Brazilian cinema, whose career extended from 1925 to 1952 and included such films as *Extinguished Embers / Braza dormida* (1928) *Blood of Minas / Sangue mineiro* (1930), and *Ganga bruta* (1933). Brazil is also unique among Third World countries in that it had its own silent avant-garde to set against that of Europe. The most remarkable example of this is Mario Peixote's only film, the feature-length *Limite* (1930), a striking experiment in narrative rhythm and structure, which has been preserved.

The advent of sound around 1930 offered new potential in the larger coun-

43. *Mario Peixote:* Limite *(Brazil, 1930)*

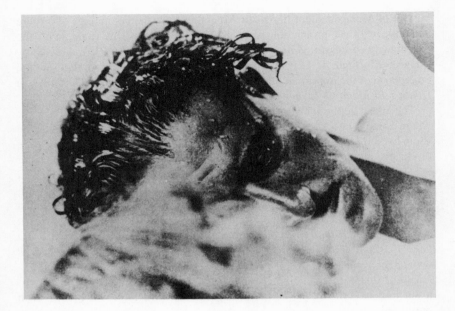

44. Humberto Mauro: Ganga bruta *(Brazil, 1933)*

tries, such as Mexico, Argentina, and Brazil, but it destroyed for half a dozen years or so all possibility of production in the smaller and less developed countries, such as Peru, where optical sound was not introduced until 1935. In Colombia and Venezuela, too, production did not resume until 1938. In general, though Latin American production tended to grow during the 1940s and 1950s, the concept of a national cinema remained elusive in the absence of favorable political changes. Thus Colombia, according to Hernando Salcedo Silva, had to wait until the 1970s for the growth of "a truly critical cinema which analysed reality and its problems, along with their causes and consequences."[4] In Chile, the 135 films made before 1966 likewise belong to a "prehistory" of Chilean cinema, "as they reflect nothing of a truly national history and culture."[5]

The cultural dominance of the United States is nowhere more apparent than in the tiny states of Central America, where U.S. economic links with local dictators and ruling elites are strongest. Feature film production of any kind is still virtually nonexistent in Panama, Honduras, and Costa Rica, and nothing that could remotely be described as a national cinema had been created in Nicaragua before the 1979 Sandinista takeover from the corrupt Somoza regime or in El Salvador before the guerrilla struggle. Guatemala has perhaps the most developed history of film production in the region, but even during the crucial decade of democracy between 1944 and 1954 this "finally comes down to the efforts of isolated individuals who have realised projects which they have financed themselves. There has never been any collective effort emanating from the government or any private enterprise to aid production." [6] Indeed, except for clandestine or guerrilla film making, film production can come into existence only where and when governments give it support. Rodolfo Izaguirre, commenting on the difficulties in his native Venezuela, is also describing the situation in many Latin American countries when he writes that "the main obstacle remains the non-existence of legislation protecting, encouraging, controlling and directing the activity of a cinema conceived as a cultural industry. The absence of a solid infrastructure, indispensable for the development of this industry, can be explained in part by the inability of the legislative machinery to limit the excessive penetration of foreign—and especially American—cinema." [7]

When cinema first reached Latin America, the underlying impetus there was the struggle to achieve economic development, of the kind that had occurred in North America and Europe, by an evolutionary process and through an economy based on the export of primary products and foodstuffs. The contradictions of this approach were not immediately apparent, and indeed the strategy seemed to be working. Certain elite groups achieved the kind of economic success that allowed, among other things, visits to Europe and the import of European luxuries and novelties (such as the Lumière cinematograph in the 1890s). They also accumulated through mercantile activities sufficient capital to allow—in the case of the cinema—the investment in the distribution and exhibition infrastructure necessary to make the import of foreign films profitable. The Depression and World War II shifted this economic pattern considerably. While dependence persisted and U.S. involvement was in many ways increased through investment under the "good neighbor" policy, new strategies were needed to cope with the worsening economic situation. Within the varying degrees of autonomy accorded them, Latin American governments began to take a more active role in industrial development:

> To facilitate the supply of consumer goods which could no longer be obtained from foreign producers because of exchange shortages, governments assisted directly or indirectly the maintenance and expansion of established industrial units, financed the creation of new ones, and provided all the solicited levels of protection in the form of tariffs and exchange and import controls. These emergency measures, continued through the war years and afterward, were presumed part of the process of import-substitution, hopefully an acceleration of Latin America's unilateral evolution towards full industrialisation, economic independence, and social change. [8]

This overall climate provides the economic background for the new impetus given to film production in the larger and more industrially advanced countries of Latin America from 1930 onward. Although the cinema would seem to have been accorded very little importance by governments in the 1930s and 1940s, and its cultural value was ignored as much by intellectuals as by industrialists, important developments did occur in both the level of financial investment and the quantity of films produced. This was particularly the case following the advent of sound (coincident with the Depression), which gave local productions a new economic potential thanks to the ability to use local accents, rhythms, music, and vocabulary with a subtlety impossible to achieve in Hollywood multilingual productions or even dubbed versions. It was industrialists, rather than governments, who were initially drawn into film production, and the films made in the twenty-five years after 1930 in Argentina, Mexico, and Brazil bear the imprint of their producers' petty-bourgeois concept of a "national" cinema. But subsequent developments show that, eventually, it was only insofar as the producers were able to induce the government's support that the emerging film industry's viability could be assured.

Throughout Latin America, the mode of production during these years was modeled on the Hollywood studio, and the basic stylistic strategy was the imitation of Hollywood movies. The contradictions of such an attempt to reproduce metropolitan forms in periphery countries are all too apparent in the years up to the mid-1950s. In Argentina, the 1920s had already seen a certain effort to conquer other Latin American markets, and this tendency increased as sound film production, which began with Ferreyra's *Munequitas portenas* in 1931, rose steadily from two features in 1932 to fifty in 1939. A major production organization—Argentina Sono Film, founded by Angel Mentasi—led the concentration on studio filming, aiming its productions particularly at the masses increasingly drawn by industrialization to the urban centers. A number of directors important in Argentine cinema emerged to make these commercial entertainments, but direct state involvement in the industry was not forthcoming in the early 1940s, and the protectionism instituted under the Perón regime of 1945–55 failed to stimulate the emergence of more vigorous national film production.

This comparative stagnation of Argentine production contrasts strikingly with the situation in Mexico. There, the year 1929 saw important political developments with the founding of the Mexican Revolutionary Party and a new social climate that fostered important artistic developments, including the burst of socialist mural painting associated with the names of Rivera, Orozco, and Siqueiros. Progress in the cinema during the early 1930s was more circumspect, however, in face of the commercial competition from Hollywood, where numerous Spanish-language films, including a handful financed by Mexican producers, were made during these years. Mexican sound film production itself, which began with Antonio Moreno's *Santa* in 1931, had risen to 25 films a year by 1934, when the Cardenas government initiated the support for the film industry that was to continue into the 1980s. With the international success in Latin America of Fernando de Fuentes's *Down on the Big Ranch / Allá en el rancho grande* (1936) and the introduction of a quota system (initially compelling all cinemas to show at least one Mexican film a year), production levels began to climb steeply, to 57 in 1938, 82 in 1945, and 124 in 1950. Amid this great mass of production—dominated by such stars as Pedro Infante, the comedian Cantinflas, and, after her return from Hollywood, Dolores del Rio—a number of new film makers emerged. The most important and internationally known of these is the actor and director Emilio Fernandez (b. 1904), who made his reputation with *Maria Candelaria* (1943), which was photographed by his regular collaborator, Gabriel Figueroa, and went on to make a series of popular melodramas, including *Salon México* (1958). The 1940s also saw the reemergence as a director of the Spanish-born surrealist Luis Buñuel (1900–1983), renowned for *Un chien andalou* (1929) and the banned *L'age d'or* (1930), both made in Paris at the height of the avant-garde movement. In all, Buñuel directed some twenty-one films in Mexico between *Gran casino* (1946) and *Simon of the Desert / Simon del deserto*

45. *Fernando de Fuentes:* Down on the Big Ranch / Allá en el rancho grande
(Mexico, 1936)

46. Emilio Fernandez: Salon México *(Mexico, 1958)*

47. Luis Buñuel: Nazarin *(Mexico, 1958)*

(1962). Among these, at least three—*Los olvidados* (1950), *Nazarin* (1958), and *The Exterminating Angel* / *El angel exterminador* (1962)—rank among his major works.

The ambivalence of all Latin American cinema of this period is very apparent in the *chanchada,* the cinematic form that dominated Brazilian commercial cinema from the 1930s through to the 1950s. This "very Brazilian genre" has mixed origins, as the definition by Randal Johnson and Robert Stam makes clear: "Partially modelled on American musicals (and particularly on the 'radio-broadcast' musicals) of the same period, but with roots as well in the Brazilian comic theatre and in the 'sung films' about carnival, the *chanchada* typically features musical and dance numbers often woven around a backstage plot." [9] Production in Brazil did not reach Mexican proportions at this period, but the steady increase from half a dozen films in the mid-1930s to around thirty-five to forty by the end of the 1950s is indicative of a continuing desire by Brazilian producers to establish a commercial industry. The characteristic attempts to develop production in the 1930s and 1940s—with the founding of such companies as Cinedia (1930), Brasil Vita Filmes (1933), and Atlantida (1943)—all set out to rival Hollywood without a full comprehension of the issues involved.

This tendency reached its peak with the Vera Cruz company, founded in 1949, which completed seventeen features before going bankrupt in 1954. As Maria Rita Galvão observes, "Vera Cruz was historically the most complete realisation Brazil has known of the film industry myth." [10] The São Paulo industrialists who financed Vera Cruz took as their model the 1940s renovation of Brazilian theater and set out to rival Hollywood on its own terms. They built huge studios, appointed foreign technicians in key posts, and hired large permanent technical crews. As head of production they appointed the most celebrated Brazilian-born film director, Alberto Cavalcanti, whose reputation had been made in France and Britain. But the distribution of their product was entrusted to Columbia Pictures with predictable results: though technical quality was high, and a few films—such as Lima Barreto's *The Bandit* / *O cangaceiro* (1953)—were widely shown and won awards at foreign festivals, financial viability was never achieved.

Another aspect of this admiration for foreign models of cinema characterizes the very different work of an important Argentine film maker who emerged in the 1950s and is generally recognized as a precursor of the "New Latin American Cinema," Leopoldo Torre Nilsson (1924–78). Son of the director Leopoldo Torres Rios, he made a succession of striking films, particularly in the period from *The House of the Angel* / *La casa del angel* (1957) to *Summer Skin* / *Piel de verano* (1961). As Octavio Getino notes:

In a period when Argentine films—and indeed Latin American cinema in general—had not yet acquired an international reputation (the Brazilian *cinema novo* had not yet made its appearance), this first stage of Torre Nilsson's had an important and unforeseen impact. Many Euro-centric critics must have been disconcerted to be faced with films made in a modern and "civilised" language, particularly as they came from a virtually unknown continent.[11]

The example of Leopoldo Torre Nilsson—who presented himself as an "author" who had assimilated the latest developments in European cinema and aimed his films, at least in part, at the international audiences of the film festivals and the European art-house market—constitutes one strand of developments in the late 1950s and 1960s. It finds its echo in aspects of the Brazilian *cinema novo,* and indeed of all the "new cinemas," in Argentina and elsewhere.

A further European importation was the lesson of neorealism, which also made its impact at this time. Key examples of this are the forty-minute documentary *Give Us a Dime / Tire die* (1958), by Fernando Birri (b. 1925), the clandestinely made *The Charcoal Burner / El megano* (1955), by the Cubans Julio García Espinosa (b. 1926) and Tomás Gutiérrez Alea (b. 1928), and two early features by the Brazilian Nelson Pereira dos Santos, *Rio 40 Degrees / Rio 40 graus* (1954) and *Rio Northern Zone / Rio zone norte* (1957). These four film makers are undoubtedly among the founding fathers of a "New Latin American Cinema": though strictly realist feature film making is comparatively rare in subsequent Latin American cinema, their range of achievements—from Birri's imaginative Argentine echo of *Miracle in Milan, The Inundated / Los inundados* (1962), to Santos's bleak and uncompromising *Barren Lives / Vidas secas* (1963)—is highly impressive. The impact of realist approaches also made itself felt in documentary film making, particularly the work done, under Birri's influence, at the film school he founded within a university context at Santa Fe, Argentina.

A further lead was given by the documentary and newsreel sections of the Cuban Film Institute (ICAIC), which was founded immediately after the revolution in 1959. Work there was dominated by the personality of Santiago Alvarez (b. 1919), who made, in a masterly series, such films as *Now* (1965), *Hanoi Tuesday 13th / Hanoi martes 13* (1967), *Always Until Victory / Hasta la victoria siempre* (1967), *LBJ* (1968), *79 Springs / 79 primaveras* (1969), and *The Tiger Leaps and Kills, But It Will Die . . . It Will Die / El tigre salto y mato, pero morirá . . . morirá* (1973), a tribute to the murdered Chilean singer Victor Jara. Santiago Alvarez pioneered an economical but inventive and committed film making that never loses sight of the need to remain close to its audience, the people.

Alvarez's lessons found their echo elsewhere in Latin America as well. In Colombia, for example, the former critic Carlos Alvarez made a lucid analysis of the national situation in *What is Democracy? / ¿Qué es la democracia?* (1971). Then, despite a year in jail during 1973–73, Alvarez continued his testimony about exploitation with *The Sons of Underdevelopment / Los hijos del subdesarrollo* (1975). In Central America, one of the few glimmers of

48. Santiago Alvarez: The Tiger Leaps and Kills, But It Will Die . . . It Will Die /
El tigre salto y mato, pero morirá . . . morirá *(Cuba, 1973)*

light is to be found in Costa Rica, which enjoys the rare privilege of a parliamentary democracy. There, within the context of the *departamento del cine* within the Ministry of Culture, some forty-five short films were made in the course of five years, many of them of a genuinely progressive kind, though the government intervened to ban the few examples of really outspoken social criticism, such as Ingo Niehaus's *Costa Rica, Banana Republic* (1976). In Uruguay, in a burst of creative activity preceding the 1971 coup, the Third World Cinémathèque was set up, and Mario Handler directed a number of excellent low-budget documentaries.

49. Carlos Diegues: Ganga Zumba *(Brazil, 1963)*

In the area of the feature-length fictional film, the decisive breakthrough in Latin America came with the emergence of the Brazilian *cinema novo* with *Barravento* (1962), directed (as his first feature) by Glauber Rocha (1938–81; see chapter 13) and edited by Nelson Pereira dos Santos. The existence of a new Brazilian cinema was further confirmed by such brilliant first features as *Ganga zumba* (1963), a forceful study of slavery by Carlos Diegues (b. 1940), and *The Hustlers / Os cafajestes* (1962), by Ruy Guerra (b. 1931). This last film—a complex study of disillusioned youth that achieved notoriety thanks to a five-minute sequence in which Guerra's handheld camera circles endlessly around his naked actress, Norma Benguel—showed the impact of the French *nouvelle vague* as strongly as did Rocha's theorization of cinema.

The first full flowering of *cinema novo* came in 1963–64 with three masterly but very different films set in the barren Nordeste region, the most underdeveloped part of Brazil: Pereira dos Santos's sober and realistic *Barren Lives,* Rocha's mythical study of banditry and superstition *Black God, White Devil / Deus e o diabo na terra do sol,* and Guerra's more directly political picture of oppression and starvation, *The Guns / Os fuzis.* But these films were followed almost immediately by the 1964 military coup, overthrowing President Goulart's democratically elected government. The confusion of the young film makers and intellectuals at this development is very apparent in the contradictory ways in which *cinema novo* subsequently developed—toward films treating the problems of the city, notions of political self-questioning, and what

Rocha termed "tropicalism." Characteristic of the new developments are Leon Hirszman's *Death / A falecida* (1965), Paolo Cesar Garaceni's *The Challenge / O desafio* (1965), Rocha's *Land in Anguish / Terra em transe* (1967) and *Antonio-das-Mortes* (1969), and Guerra's *The Gods and the Dead / Os deuses e os mortes* (1970). These latter films were made in the atmosphere of intensified repression and censorship, which culminated in the "coup within the coup" of 1968. The following year, Rocha and Guerra went into temporary exile, and with their departure from Brazil, the *cinema novo* movement virtually ceased to exist as a coherent force. The contradictions of *cinema novo* are as real as its achievements, but for all this, the major works stand out as films of a new kind in Latin America, even at a distance of twenty years.

Before the wave of enthusiasm provoked by *cinema novo* had subsided, another new Latin American cinema was born out of the political developments in Chile. Though sometimes referred to as the "cinema of Allende," this new cinema in fact has clear roots in the presidency of Allende's predecessor, Eduardo Frei. It was in 1968–69—during Frei's term in office—that the major Chilean film makers made their debuts: Aldo Francia (*Valparaíso mi amor,* 1969), Miguel Littin (*The Jackal of Nahueltoro / El chacal de Nahueltoro,* 1969), Raul Ruiz (*Three Sad Tigers / Tres tristes tigres,* 1968), and

50. Aldo Francia: Valparaíso mi amor *(Chile. 1969)*

Helvio Soto (*Caliche sangrieto*, 1969). All four had previously made short films and documentaries, but their attempts to found a national cinema in 1970 were faced with formidable odds. In Santiago, for example, twenty-seven of the thirty-one first-run movie theaters and eight of the twelve distribution companies were in North American hands, and the 98 percent foreign dominance of cinema screens was echoed by 95 percent American programming on television. This overwhelming economic and cultural dominance was used in the early 1970s against the Chilean cinema—as against other aspects of the economy—in the U.S. response to President Allende's policy of nationalization. The plans of the revitalized national production company, Chile Films, under the leadership of Littin, were ambitious. But the company was underfinanced and never came close to producing the eight features a year that were announced, though it did stimulate short and documentary production, including the first documentary records of the new political situation, made by Patricio Guzmán. Raul Ruiz was able to work prolifically, making eleven films of various lengths and styles between 1970 and 1973, but the time-span available before the coup did not permit a radicalization of the feature film. Symbolic of the failure is the case of Littin, whose masterly revolutionary epic *The Promised Land* / *La tierra prometida* (1973) was not completed in time to have its Chilean release before the Allende government was so brutally overthrown in September 1973 and Littin and most of his colleagues were driven into exile.

Another emergent national cinema throttled at birth by political intervention from the army was that in Bolivia. There, Jorge Sanjinés (see chapter 16) and a few friends—particularly Ricardo Rada and the writer Oscar Soria, joined a little later by the cameraman (and subsequently director) Antonio Eguino—struggled to create the basis of a valid national cinema. Before the 1965 military coup, they had completed a number of documentaries, including *¡Revolución!* (1965), a ten-minute celebration of the return to liberal government on 9 April 1952—one of the few changes of regime in Bolivia to bring with it genuinely positive reforms. The same year, 1965, Sanjinés was appointed to head the Bolivian Film Institute, and during the next two and a half years he produced over two dozen newsreels, four documentaries, and a medium-length study of miners, *Aysa*. He also made a first feature, *Ukamau* (1966), a tale of revenge done in one of the two main Indian languages of Bolivia, Aymara. The following productions of what became the Ukamau Collective increased the political emphasis of Sanjinés's work: *Blood of the Condor* / *Yawar mallku* (1969), an attack on the activities of the Peace Corps, shot in Quechua, and *The Courage of the People* / *El coraje del pueblo* (1971), a vivid record of the massacre of tin miners in June 1967, at a time when Che Guevara was still active with his guerrilla group in the Bolivian mountains.

Throughout the period from 1965 to 1971, Bolivia was at the mercy of a succession of military governments, as generals struggled for power through

51. Antonio Eguino: Chuquiago *(Bolivia, 1977)*

coup and countercoup. The arrival of the brutal General Banzer Suarez in 1971, while Sanjinés and Rada were in Italy finishing postproduction on *The Courage of the People,* led the pair to decide not to return to their native country. Eguino, however, remained in Bolivia and, despite a spell in prison, was able to complete three features in the following decade: *Pueblo chico* (1974), the widely seen study of life in La Paz, *Chuquiago* (1977), and *Bitter Sea / Amargo mar* (1984), a fictionalized account of late-nineteenth-century struggles for Bolivia's national identity. Sanjinés meanwhile continued to work on themes of wide Latin American significance, completing *The Principal Enemy / El enemigo principal* (1973) in Peru and *Get Out of Here! / ¡Fuera de aquí!* (1977) in Ecuador. The brief Bolivian restoration of democracy in 1978 allowed him to return and stage showings of his films at the Bolivian Film Institute, but within a year he was once more in exile, and it was only in the 1980s that he was able to resume work in his native country.

A similar fate awaited those young Argentine film makers who, in the late 1960s, responded to the changing mood of their country and tried to create a cinema more integrally Argentine than that of Torre Nilsson and to take the social commitment of Fernando Birri a stage further. Octavio Getino and Fernando Solanas's proposal for a "Third Cinema," to replace the forms of the dominant Hollywood cinema and the Latin American "authors" cinema, was

exemplified by their masterly documentary study *The Hour of the Furnaces /
La hora de los hornos* (1968). This work was planned explicitly as a reaction
against the film author's perennial quest for technical perfection (typified by
Torre Nilsson), and it implied a new form of distribution, outside the circuits
still dominated by Hollywood products. Nothing Getino and Solanas have
made since had the same impact, though they did complete two long filmed
interviews with General Perón in Madrid prior to his return to power in 1973.
By 1975 they had both been driven from Argentina by the military coup,
which compelled them to continue their film making and theoretical work in
exile. The fate of some of their equally politically committed contemporaries
of the late 1960s was even worse: the Marxist Raymondo Gleyzer was arrested, tortured, and presumably killed in an Argentine prison in 1976, while
Jorge Cedron, maker of the remarkable *Operation Massacre / Operación
masacre* (1972), died in mysterious circumstances in a French police station
in 1980.

The 1960s and early 1970s were marked by attempts to create new forms of
feature film making throughout Latin America, but nowhere were the achievements in Brazil, Chile, and Bolivia equaled. The problem lay largely in the all
too prevalent tendency to imitate Western styles of film making and to adopt
European conceptions of film authorship. For example, a strategy similar to
that of Leopoldo Torre Nilsson was adopted by a number of his Argentine
contemporaries, such as Rodolfo Kuhn and David José Kohon. After initial
involvement in film club activities and short film making, both made features
in the early 1960s. But as Octavio Getino points out, they showed themselves
concerned merely "to bring to the screen, with all the techniques learned from
European cinema, the world and ideas arising from the individual experience
of the Buenos Aires middle classes, traditionally cut off from the reality of the
country." [12]

The same tendency is to be found in the smaller national cinemas as well.
In Peru during the late 1950s and early 1960s, the films of what Georges
Sadoul called the "Cuzco school" did represent an attempt to develop a national cinema. The intense, if artistically limited, effort—reflected in a handful of documentaries and two feature-length films mixing documentary and
fiction, *Kukuli* (1961) and *Jarawu* (1966)—was a laudable attempt to free
Latin American cinema from foreign models and to pioneer the use of the
language of the Quechua Indians. But this approach was not followed up; indeed, the critic Isaac Leon Frias is forced to conclude, with regard to the work
of Peru's best-known director, Armando Robles Godoy, that "the alibi of an
'author's cinema' has served as a shield for the director to justify what is only
a tenuous version of a so-called innovative cinema, which is no more than
pretentious and certainly ill-adapted to the cinematic activity of Peru." [13] This
is film making conceived not for a national audience but according to the
norms of the international market of the film festivals. The complaint is put in

more general terms by Rodolfo Izaguirre, in his analysis of contemporary trends in Venezuelan cinema:

> Some young film makers, better prepared in technical and cultural matters and returning to their country after studying in the major film centres (London, Rome, Leipzig, Los Angeles and Paris) have tried to alter the situation. But, carried away by their enthusiasm and determination to oppose traditional cinema, these new directors have defended a cinema which in the last analysis results in an equally negative attitude. Indeed their reaction against the prevalent folklore, crude humour and futile melodrama has produced a cinema of authors: symbolic, intellectual, confused. . . . This cinema has not succeeded in establishing contact with spectators suspicious of over-intellectual productions.[14]

In addition to the need for the Latin American film maker to free himself from the dominance of foreign cultural models, there is also the problem of his relationship with the state, which everywhere controls cinematographic activity. This situation is very apparent in the case of Mexico, where state support, first established in the 1930s, had by the 1970s come to constitute total state control. As a result, high levels of film production have been maintained, but the quality of these films has not been outstanding, and the Mexican *nuevo cine* of the 1960s and 1970s had only a muted international impact. The conclusions of the Mexican film historian Emilio García Riera are severe:

> In the last analysis, the new Mexican cinema has served the official ideology, and its supposedly militant character, the political commitment claimed for it, [and] its revolution from within were never more than an imposture. It is more exact to give it the label which suits it: that of a cinema of authors. Not a stylistic revolution, a collective project, a group social commitment, nor even a movement, the new Mexican cinema can only be judged in the light of the individual talent of its members.[15]

Only the work of the talented Paul Leduc, author of just three feature-length documentaries in ten years—*Reed: Insurgent Mexico* / *Reed: México insurgente* (1973), *Ethnocide: Notes on Mesquital* / *Etnocido: Notas sobre el mesquital* (1976), and *Historias prohibitas del Pulgarito* (1980)—is immune to such strictures.

The same factors are at work in Brazil. From only four films in 1941, Brazilian output has progressed steadily, reaching twenty-two in 1951, thirty in 1961, ninety-four in 1971 and over one hundred in 1981. One reason for this growth has been the government-imposed quota, which rose from one day a year being reserved for Brazilian films in 1939 to 133 days a year in 1978 and 185 days (i.e., half the screen time in every cinema) in 1980. This assured home market allowed the development of the chanchada in the 1940s and prompted the overambitious attempt to rival Hollywood, with the Vera Cruz company in the early 1950s. Subsequent developments have been paradoxical.

After the brief flowering of *cinema novo* in the 1960s, the harsh military repression and institutionalized torture of the early 1970s seemed for a time likely to crush irrevocably all possibility of creative film making. But in fact, the military government virtually doubled film production between 1969 and 1978, thanks largely to the creation of the massive state production and distribution company Embrafilme. Since this organization is very much concerned with international prestige—as measured by prizes won at foreign festivals— its policies are to some extent a continuation of those adopted by *cinema novo*. As a result, film makers prominent in the 1960s were able to make their mark within Embrafilme: "By 1973 *cinema novo* had ceased to exist as a coherent or unified movement. . . . And yet the historical cycle of *cinema novo* has not yet ended, for its major practitioners not only maintain intellectual hegemony within Brazilian cinema, but they also are the dominant force within Embrafilme and help determine the nature of state aid to the industry." [16]

Nevertheless, as in Mexico, this state intervention has had its cost in creative terms. As Jean-Claude Bernardet observes,

> The impact of the government on the cinema has gone in the direction of using it as a sort of trial balloon for the constitution of a semi-official cultural production, given a collection of favourable conditions. Without totally assuming responsibility for production, but through a complex system of legislative measures and incentives, the state has acquired an immense control over the evolution of cinematic production, not only on the industrial and commercial plane, but also on the ideological plane. [17]

This view is echoed by the film maker Ruy Guerra, who returned to Brazil after a period of exile in the late 1960s:

> Embrafilme reflects the political and economic system. We cannot expect— once again it would be utopian—a state organ to act against the ruling classes and the official government line. A popular cinema would go against the interests of the current government, because today every economic programme is directed towards increasing the wealth of the few and maintaining great social inequities, and it is hard to imagine that Embrafilme would oppose such a programme. It tries at best to be liberal within this context. [18]

Obviously, occasional films of real commitment, such as Guerra's own *The Fall / A queda* (1976), can be made within this context, just as a strikingly honest expression of the effects of oppression such as Adolfo Aristarain's *Time for Revenge / Tiempo de revancha* (1981) can, thanks to its *film noir* form, be made under the military dictatorship in Argentina. But such efforts are bound to be rare. What is more characteristic of Brazilian cinema of the 1980s is the development of a cinema that uses sex as a metaphor to raise certain issues too controversial for the authoritarian regime. The new explicitness, combined with a willingness to adopt purely commercial criteria, has produced a cinema—typified by Hector Babenco's *Pixote* (1981) and Carlos Diegues's *Bye Bye Brazil* (1980)—that is both popular at home and successful in the international market.

In a totally opposing ideological perspective, Cuba, too, has a cinema structured so as to serve the wider needs of the state. One of the first acts of the Castro government in 1959 was to set up the Cuban Film Institute (ICAIC), the aims of which were both industrial and cultural. After a rather hesitant start, Cuba developed an innovative and socially critical style of film making in the late 1960s. But all this activity occurred within the ideological context of the revolution and in accordance with notions of artistic rights and freedoms very precisely defined by Castro in 1961: "Within the Revolution, everything; against the Revolution, nothing."[19] Although some film makers and intellectuals eventually turned against the revolution and chose exile, Cuban cinema—thanks in part to the prestige of its documentary production—came to exercise an influence far in excess of what might be anticipated from an output of just four or five feature-length films a year.

The growing confidence of Cuban cinema and the gradual loss of that sense of neocolonial dependence so characteristic of Latin America can be seen in the total transformation of the kinds of coproductions ICAIC has funded. In 1963, the four coproductions were all superficial, derivative, and often preten-

52. Patricio Guzmán: The Battle of Chile / La batalla de Chile *(Chile / Cuba, 1973–79)*

tious works directed by Europeans, whereas during 1973–78 the characteristic ICAIC coproduction effort was directed toward authentically Latin American subjects and film makers. This support is typified by the project that enabled the Chilean documentarist Patricio Guzmán to complete his masterly three-part study *The Battle of Chile / La batalla de Chile* (1973–79).

Similarly, while the first directors, such as Gutiérrez Alea and García Espinosa were trained abroad, later film makers have all learned their craft within ICAIC itself. In over two decades of continuous production, more than a hundred long or medium-length features have been made, and the general impression is of an eclectic range of approaches and a lack of heavy bureaucratic control. While Santiago Alvarez has kept almost exclusively to documentary, other feature film makers have moved freely between documentary and fictional subjects. In prerevolutionary days, Cuba was used as something of a testing station for U.S. communication industries, with pioneering work done there with telephones and television, advertising and music recording, radio and cinema. Cuban filmgoers were among the most assiduous in the world, and revolutionary film makers have used this media sophistication to create films that combine a revolutionary message with consciously chosen elements of traditional movie entertainment. The enormous stylistic range of Cuban cinema is exemplified by the work of Humberto Solas, which embraces both the exuberant black-and-white audacities of *Lucia* (1968) and the colorful operatic representation of *Cantata de Chile* (1975).

Perhaps more typical of Cuban cinema in the decade after the crucial breakthrough in fiction film making made by Tomás Gutiérrez Alea with *Memories of Underdevelopment / Memorias de subdesarrollo* (1968), however, are the works that ask the more sober social questions. Examples of this approach are Sara Gómez's only feature film, *One Way or Another / De cierta manera* (1974), and Pastor Vega's first feature, *Portrait of Teresa / Retrato de Teresa* (1977). One characteristic of these films is that they relate clearly to certain of the ideas advocated by García Espinosa in his essay "For an Imperfect Cinema." In particular, they adopt an approach that entails showing the *process* that generates problems in society, rather than simply singling out specific problems for depiction in the abstract. This approach allows the ambiguities of a changing society to be more adequately conveyed and leaves the possible resolution open to the viewer, thereby avoiding the twin traps of a conventional left-wing didacticism and a dull socialist realism.

The kind of film making to be found in Cuba is possible only in a country that has achieved its revolution. Developments elsewhere show the darker side of state involvement, for in few countries of Latin America do film makers operate with any real freedom. The repression is often complete, and at the start of the 1980s, many of the Latin American states where real progress toward an authentic national cinema had earlier been made were again in the hands of military regimes. Yet the overall vigor of Latin American cinema

53. Sara Gómez: One Way or Another / De cierta manera *(Cuba, 1974)*

remains. Exemplary in this respect is the Chilean cinema in exile, which comprises over a hundred films made since the overthrow of Allende, with exiled
film makers working in a variety of contexts throughout the world: Guzmán in
Cuba, Littin in Mexico, Ruiz in Paris, Soto in Spain, and so on. A similar, if
smaller, cinema in exile exists for the Argentine-born film makers now resident in Paris. To emphasize these achievements is not to underestimate the
impact of exile on a film maker: the choices facing Latin American film
makers are often excruciating. If the later work of Glauber Rocha, after he had
made his peace with the Brazilian military regime, shows the debilitating
effect of compromise and self-censorship, much of the work in exile of
Rocha's contemporary in the *cinema novo,* Ruy Guerra (*Sweet Hunters,* for
instance), shows the empty rootlessness that can enter an exile's work, however talented his collaborators may be and however gifted his performers.

Within Latin America itself there has been a range of encouraging new developments in the 1970s and 1980s. In Venezuela, with its long tradition of
documentary film making (in which the film department of the University of
the Andes has played an important part), a new government initiative in the
mid-1970s offering loans to cover 60 percent of the production costs for up to

twenty-five features a year led to a striking, if short-lived, surge in production. Before the state scheme was ended and feature production fell back to its earlier fairly minimal level of output, Venezuelan films had shown themselves able to capture an important share of the domestic market. Though these films are little known abroad, Latin American critics (writing in 1979) have described them as showing "a firm commitment to the real life and history of the country and the building of an authentically national culture by exposing and standing against oppression and dependency." In treating these social issues,

> the "classic" themes dealt with continue to be those concerned with the country's recent history and its social reality as an underdeveloped country which is also the possessor of the massively valuable natural resource of oil: life in the "marginal" shanty-town areas around the big cities and the violence inherent in their situation, the dictatorships under which the country lived until recently, the failure of the guerrilla struggle of ten years ago and the new political era which opened with their defeat.[20]

In Colombia, too, there have been important developments. The team of Marta Rodriguez and Jorge Silva has been able to follow such remarkable documentaries as *The Brickmakers / Chircales* (1972) and *Peasants / Campesinos* (1976) with a striking feature-length exploration of popular memory, *Our Voice of the Earth, Memory, and Future / Nuestra voz de tierra, memoria y futuro* (1981). In Bolivia, even under the extreme military repression, film makers were able to make clandestine but innovative use of the potentials of Super 8 filming,[21] and the somewhat tentative restoration of civilian rule has allowed Jorge Sanjinés to begin work again.

As always in Latin America, the liberation struggle has been accompanied by a cultural upsurge, which, in the 1980s, has found expression in film making. The guerrilla war in El Salvador led to two important developments in 1980. The first was the formation of the Cero a la Izquierda Film Collective, responsible for two 1980 studies of the liberated areas: *Morazan* and *First Fruits / Los primos frutos* (also known as *The Decision to Conquer / La decisión de vencer*). The second was the establishment, with the backing of the liberation movement, of the El Salvador Film Institute, the first project of which was the eighty-minute documentary *El Salvador—The People Will Win / El Salvador—El pueblo vencerá* (1980), directed by the Puerto Rican film maker Diego de la Texera. Subsequently, another collectively made film, *Tiempo de audacia* (1982), by the Radio Venceremos Film and Video Collective, has emphasized the importance of developments in El Salvador.

Nicaragua, though it has been the subject of numerous foreign-made documentaries, had no history of film making prior to the victory of the Sandinist National Liberation Front (FSLN). In 1979, the Nicaraguan Film Institute (INCINE) was set up under the supervision of the Ministry of Culture "to establish and develop the Nicaraguan film industry, restoring its national and

54. *Cero a la Izquierda Film Collective:* The Decision to Conquer / La decisión de vencer *(El Salvador, 1980)*

cultural identity, seeking a cinematic language which draws inspiration from our reality and finds a form of artistic expression belonging to our national and Latin American culture." [22] The immediate result was a series of news-reels and a few short documentaries. Then in 1982 a first fictional feature, *Alsino and the Condor / Alsino y el condor,* was released, directed by the Chilean Miguel Littin with the collaboration of Nicaraguan, Cuban, Mexican, Costa Rican, and Chilean film makers—this film, which blends actuality and myth, oppression and aspiration, and embodies a poetic imagination akin to that of Gabriel García Márquez, is a truly striking effort. The ambition of all these varied endeavors in Colombia, Bolivia, El Salvador, and Nicaragua can be summarized in terms of the four general principles underlying the formation of the Salvadorean Film Institute: to respond to the interests of the working class and peasants by providing them with a cinematic instrument of expression; to produce films that will publicize the people's struggle; to contribute to raising the level of political awareness of both the masses and the peoples and governments of the world concerning the struggle; to combat disinformation and to contribute to the reordering of the international information network. [23] Always, the aim is to forge new bonds between film makers and the people— the film makers then become one with the people, and the people become the true authors of their own national cinema.

*Cinema is one of the manifestations of culture and it
must be put to the service of man and his education.*
Ayatollah Khomeini

If there is a risk of distortion inherent in treating the national cinemas of
Latin America as aspects of a single development, the danger is far greater
when we turn to those geographically contiguous areas that form the subject
of discussion in the following pages. Here the various unifying factors—a
Pan-African identity, Arab nationalism, Islam—are only partial grids, each of
which implies a sharply differing set of divisions, meaning that multiple identity is characteristic of the area: Islam extends beyond the Arab world into
Iran and black Africa, Egypt is a key state in both Africa and the Arab world,
Senegal is French-dominated but also predominantly Islamic, and so on. The
rare instances in which important film industries have emerged in Africa and
the Middle East—Egypt, Turkey, Iran—follow patterns already familiar in
other parts of the Third World, both in their relationship to the progress of
local industrialization and in their cultural ambiguities. What is particularly
revealing of the importance of cinema in contemporary culture in the region is
the emergence of talented individual film makers almost everywhere—from
Mali to Afghanistan, from Morocco to Kuwait—even where indigenous film
making traditions are lacking. Africa and the Middle East may be poor in
terms of the industrial production of films (as of other commodities), but they
offer a wealth of thoughtful and carefully realized works that reflect and
speculate upon the various national issues and problems of the region.

The Non-Arab Middle East

The three very diverse countries stretching from the northern tier of the Middle East to the Indian border—Turkey, Iran, and Afghanistan—have certain characteristics in common. All three are predominantly Muslim but non-Arab, and although none was formally colonized by European powers, the modern history of all three has been shaped by their strategic location as "buffer states" between Europe, Russia, and India, which has led to their being, at times, variously divided into "spheres of influence" by Russia and the European empires. The 1952 attachment of Turkey to NATO and the 1979 Soviet invasion of Afghanistan are the more recent manifestations of this traditional tension between East and West.

Afghanistan is by far the least developed of the three countries, with 90 percent of the population rural, 15 percent of which is still nomadic. Nevertheless, a state film corporation, Afghan Films, was set up within the Ministry of Information and Culture in the 1960s, and in all, nine features were made between 1968 and 1980. The 1970s even saw the emergence of the first Afghan director to become known abroad, Toryali Shafaq. Born in 1947 and trained at the Indian Film and Television Institute in Pune, Shafaq worked for the Ministry of Information and served as local assistant to various foreign film companies shooting on location in Afghanistan. After working as co-director on two 1974 features, Shafaq went on to make three independent features in the years 1976 to 1980, but showings abroad have been severely restricted. In the 1970s the bulk of the films shown in local theaters (which numbered forty-five in 1978, with thirteen of these in the capital, Kabul) were imported Hindi, Iranian, and Egyptian features, plus a limited number of severely cut and dubbed American films. This market, together with the tentative beginnings of feature production, was disrupted by the Soviet invasion of 1979, which followed a series of left-wing coups and countercoups that had left a split and highly unstable Communist government.[1]

For the first four decades of this century, Iran shared Afghanistan's lack of development. Nineteenth-century incorporation into the world market had caused a decline in local artisanal production, and some 90 percent of the working population was active either in agriculture or in the nomadic sector.[2] There was almost no industry in 1900 when a cinematograph, acquired in Europe and operated by the court photographer, was introduced as a royal entertainment for the Qajar dynasty in Tehran. Until 1905 it was reserved for an elite public: "Film projectors are circulated within the palace and the residences of dignitaries and important state figures on such festive occasions as weddings, births and circumcision ceremonies."[3] But before World War I a certain number of public cinemas were established, including one set up by the Armenian Ardeshir Khan, who also imported the phonograph and the bicycle. A few newsreel items and the occasional comedy were shot in the late

1920s and early 1930s. *Abi and Rabi* (1931), an imitation of a Danish silent comedy, shot by an Armenian, Avans Ohanian, seems to have been the first Iranian fictional subject. But development was slow, and by 1932 there were only eight movie theaters in Tehran and a few in provincial cities. The exploits of the military leader Reza Khan, who seized power in 1921, established the modern Iranian state, and made himself shah, were celebrated in the first of four Persian-language musical films shot in Bombay in the early 1930s by Abdol Hoseyn Sepenta (1907–69). Farrokh Gaffary describes these films as possessing "a tone of simplicity and sincere naivety and an unpretentious quality," [4] and they had a great success in Iran.

But these first efforts had no immediate succesors. Economic development in Iran was slow, even though some industrialization did occur between 1934 and 1940, leading to the establishment of some two hundred private industrial plants, mostly producing textiles and employing fifty to sixty thousand workers. The state itself "owned an arsenal and factories producing sugar, cement, tobacco and textiles." [5] Little changed initially under Reza Shah's son, who succeeded him in 1941 and ruled until his expulsion in 1979. Though there was a second wave of industrialization during the two years that Mossadegh was prime minister (1951–53), "when lack of foreign exchange promoted import substitution by private entrepreneurs," the major growth did not come until the oil boom in the decade from 1965 to 1975. In 1977, on the eve of the disturbances that were to lead to the shah's overthrow, "there were 2.5 million people employed in manufacturing, and another 1 million in construction, out of a total economically active population of 10.4 millions." [6]

The growth of an Iranian film industry followed this overall pattern of development. The first Persian-language film realized in Iran was *The Whirlwind of Life / Tufane zendegi* (1947), made by the theater director Mohammad Ali Daryabegi. By the mid-1950s, production was around fifteen features a year, rising to pass thirty films in 1961 and to peak at ninety features in 1972. The number of movie theaters rose correspondingly: from 80 in 1950 to 237 in 1960 and 470 in 1970. Though much of the output was mediocre, the year 1970 did see the appearance of a New Iranian Cinema (*cinema motefävet*), created by a fairly heterogeneous group of young intellectuals, many of them foreign-trained, and receiving some support from the Ministry of Culture and the state television service. Among the 1970s films noted in the west were Dariush Mehrjui's *The Cow / Gav* (1970), *The Postman / Postchi* (1972), and *Mina Cycle / Dayera-e-Mina* (1974) and works by Parviz Kimiavi, Sohrab Shahid-Saless, and Bahram Beyzai. In 1974, many of the most important younger film makers left the official film workers' union to set up the New Film Group, a leading figure in which was Parviz Sayyad, an actor-director best known for his later American-made feature *The Mission / Ferestadeh* (1983).

But the shah's government kept cinema taxes high and refused to give the

55. Dariush Mehrjui: Mina Cycle / Dayera-e-Mina *(Iran, 1974)*

local production industry any protection from foreign imports. As a result, the economic basis of the film industry proved as vulnerable as the political basis of the shah's regime, and by 1977–78 production was reduced to a mere half-dozen or so films a year. The films of the young directors had given Iran an international reputation, but they failed to reach a mass audience within their own country. Hampered by censorship restraints and cut off from popular taste by their experimental techniques, they made little impact on Iran's five hundred or so theaters, which continued to screen Indian and U.S. imports alongside locally produced Indian-style comedy musicals.[7]

Most of the young film makers welcomed the overthrow of the shah, anticipating new freedom of expression and a new relationship with the people. With the establishment of the Islamic Republic in February 1979, however, they found instead a cinema far more tightly controlled and rigidly precensored. Within a short time most were forced into exile—Kimiavi to France, where he had studied at the IDHEC, and Shahid-Saless to Germany, where he had earlier made his well-known study of migrant workers *Abroad / In der Fremde* (1975). Those who remained in Iran—Beyzai, for example, and, for a while, Mehrjui—were reduced to silence. In its official statements at least, the new regime recognized the efforts of the young intellectuals of the 1970s "to start a kind of sober and meaningful cinema" but found that "the themes and approaches of these avant-garde film makers were too abstract to attract the masses of filmgoers." Particular venom was reserved for the routine production of the shah's era, "a commercial film making of the lowest order. Film after film dealt with the lives of thieves, prostitutes, plunderers, drug dealers, etc., and sought to attract and entertain an illiterate audience by presenting scenes of sex, violence, dance and music. The low cost of this type of films aroused the interest of many profiteers who were in fact illiterate persons running brothels and cabarets." [8] The new regime was not, however, against the cinema as such (described by Khomeini as "one of the achievements of civilization"), and production resumed at around a dozen films a year, mostly, it seems, tales of the revolution shaped as adventure stories.

There is a close connection, too, between political and economic changes and the development of cinema in Turkey. The Lumière representatives visited Istanbul to demonstrate the cinematograph at the Imperial Palace in 1896, and public screenings occurred in a cosmopolitan district of the city the following year. But cinema was slow to establish itself in the Ottoman Empire. It was not until 1908—the year of the revolution by the Young Turks, which led to constitutional changes and far-reaching modernization—that a permanent cinema was established in Istanbul by a Rumanian, Sigmund Weinberg, the local agent of Pathé. Although Weinberg shot some documentary footage before World War I, the film generally regarded as the first national production (and a reflection of the growing strength of Turkish nationalism) is the 104-meter documentary *Demolition of the Russian Monument at Ayastefanos / Ayastefanos'taki Rus abidesinin yıkılışı*, shot in 1914 by a Turk, Fuat Uzkinay (1888–1956).

During 1914–18, much of the impetus for film making came from one of the country's major modernizing forces, the army, and when the Army Film Center was established on the German model in 1915 by Enver Pasha, Weinberg became its first head. In 1916 he began shooting what was intended as the first Ottoman feature film, *Marriage of Himmet Aga / Himmet Ağa'nin izdivacı*, but at the outbreak of war he was expelled as an alien, and the film was not finished until 1918 by his successor, Fuat Uzkinay. By then two other feature-length films, *The Claw / Pençe* and *The Spy / Casus*, had been made by Sedat Simavi (1896–1953) for the National Defense Association. 1918 saw the fall of the Ottoman Empire, which had entered the war on the side of the Germans, and the state was threatened with dismemberment by the victorious allies. There continued to be limited film making during the struggle for independence (1918–23), and the first private film company, Kemal Films, was established briefly in 1922. But the first five years of Kemal Atatürk's secular republic saw no film production at all in Turkey.

The revival of Turkish film making after the founding of Ipek Film in 1928 coincides with a period of economic growth in the country as

> the petty-bourgeois Kemalist forces began to build the basis of a state-capitalist economy during the 1930s. Under the leadership and control of the rising national and petty bourgeoisies, the state's resources were directed towards the development of an industrial economy that would open the path to an "independent" national capitalism. Throughout this period, Turkey's economic position improved substantially—foreign firms were nationalized, capital goods–producing manufacturing industries were set up and efforts were made to mechanize the agricultural sector.[9]

The principal film maker for Ipek was Muhsin Ertuğrul (1892–1979), director of the Municipal Theater in Istanbul, who made twenty films between 1928 and 1941, including the first Turkish sound film, *The Streets of Istanbul / İstanbul sokakların*, in 1931. Ertuğrul's theatrical style set the pattern for younger directors, but production remained low—under six films a year throughout the period up to 1948, when changes in taxation began to make local production profitable. This was also a time of great prosperity for some, as $1 billion of U.S. aid was poured into Turkey between 1948 and 1952 (Turkey joined NATO in 1952).

The 1950s were a period of rising production—from two films in 1947 and nineteen in 1949 to between thirty and forty a year by the early 1960s. This growth provided the basis for the emergence of Turkish cinema at international film festivals in the 1960s, as when Metin Erksan (b. 1929) won the Golden Bear at Berlin in 1964 with *Dry Summer / Susuz yaz*. In addition, the 1950s were an important decade; the political change of 1950 (the election of the Menderes Democratic government) "led to big changes in art, cinema and culture generally. Broadly speaking, Turkish movies up to that time had been dominated by people from the theatre. In the 1950s, directors like Atıf Yılmaz and Lütfi Ö. Akad started rejecting theatre actors and using people from the street. They also started choosing subjects from real life, everyday subjects."[10]

It was these changes that drew Turkey's best-known director Yılmaz Güney (see chapter 14), into the cinema in 1958 as a writer and actor for Atıf Yılmaz. When, after a spell in prison, Güney turned to directing in the late 1960s, the Turkish social scene was undergoing fresh transformations, many of which served to support an expanding film industry. As two U.S.-based critics point out,

> The 1960s saw a rapid transformation of both the economy and social life, echoed by a vigorous intellectual debate concerning the directions and goals of both the economic base and ideological formations (e.g., politics, literature, cinema) of Turkish society. The decade was dominated by a massive influx of international capital, a rapid increase in urbanization, and a political enfran-

chisement of the masses according to the liberal terms of the 1961 Constitution. Between 1960 and 1970, urban population increased by 5 million.[11]

Film output reached its peak in 1972, when no less than 298 feature films (mostly quickly shot on low budgets in as little as five days) were made. Young Turkish film makers began to make international reputations, including two collaborators of Yılmaz Güney, Zeki Ökten (b. 1941) and Şerif Gören (b. 1944). The domestic audience numbered one hundred million, and there were fifteen hundred indoor theaters and seventeen hundred open-air ones (used only in summer). As a cheap and accessible form of entertainment, Turkish films were very popular with the mass of the population and sold well abroad. Though there was political censorship (intense at times), the censorship code in other matters (based on that in Mussolini's Italy) was interpreted sufficiently liberally to allow a proliferation of pornographic films (variously estimated as a third or a half of the total output), a situation virtually unique in a country where the principal religion is Islam. Throughout the 1960s and 1970s, film production was an area of activity neither dominated by direct investment by foreign companies nor supported or tightly controlled by the state. But the market was still dominated by the four or five hundred imported films (mostly

56. *Şerif Gören:* Derman *(Turkey, 1983)*

Hollywood movies) and, as Güney explains, "When a foreign film was particularly successful, Turkish imitations of it would inevitably follow. The number of films that could be called ethnically Turkish was very small. Most movies were copies." [12] Of the 105 films in which Güney himself acted, he reckons 15 were direct imitations, 50 were not particularly Turkish—"they might equally have been North African, for example"—and only 40 could be called "distinctively Turkish." The spread of television in the 1970s reduced the level of output over the decade, and with the political repression of the early 1980s, production fell to around 70 features a year.

Egypt and the Arab World
Egypt

The development of industrialization in Egypt differs from that in most of the Third World, principally because, as Samir Amin maintains, the initiatives of Muhammad Ali in the early 1800s were such that Egypt might conceivably have become an autonomous capitalist power:

> The material progress achieved during the first forty years of the century was prodigious. Egypt had launched a process of modern industrialization and economic diversification. The state workshops and manufactories employed hundreds of thousands of workers, they produced more cotton goods than most European countries, worked iron, produced steam engines and cannons, etc. All this was achieved with exclusively indigenous national managers in national industries. [13]

But the period after 1840 saw a sharp decline under the influence of European powers who were able not only to produce goods more cheaply, but also to impose free trade on Egypt. As a result, "industry disappeared, not to reappear until the 1920s." [14] Though the British protectorate was not established until 1914, Britain was the effective ruling power in Egypt from the latter years of the nineteenth century, that is, during the period in which Egypt was incorporated into the world market and its agriculture was reorganized, so that it became a producer of raw materials for export to Europe and a market for European manufactures. This economic dependency forms the context for the nineteenth-century Arab renaissance, the *Nahda,* during which Western ideas were assimilated.

There is some debate about the role of foreign capital in the new industrialization of Egypt after 1919, but certain aspects of this development seem incontrovertible. Firstly, it occurred under a British colonial domination that aimed "not to *prevent* Egyptian industrialization, but to *guide* it along lines favourable to England." [15] A major part was played not only by foreign capital, but also by some of the quarter of a million Europeans resident in Egypt at the time of the 1927 census. As an example, "when the Egyptian Federation of Industry was established in 1922, the eleven directors all lived in Egypt but only three were Egyptian citizens." [16]

This influence of foreign residents finds its reflection in the introduction of cinema. The first projections of the Lumière cinematograph took place in Alexandria in 1896 and in Cairo the following winter. The first film theater was set up (by an Italian) in 1900, and by the time of the first legislation on the cinema in 1911 there were eight theaters in Cairo and three in Alexandria, all showing American and European films. The number of theaters in Egypt continued to rise, and it was the cutting off of imported films during the 1914–18 war that led to the first production of films. But this film making was all the work of foreigners: the Frenchman De Lagarne, who commissioned a series of short actuality films on Alexandria, and the Italo-Egyptian Cinematographic Company (with backing from the Banco di Roma), which made half a dozen short dramas, all directed by Italians. The first truly Egyptian film seems to have been a thirty-minute short, *The Civil Servant / Al-bash-kateb*, made in 1922 by Mohamed Bayoumi, who later shot several newsreels. Four years later a feature film, *Kiss in the Desert / Qubla fil-sahara*, was made by two Chilean émigrés of Lebanese origin, Ibrahim and Badr Lama, but Egyptian critics generally consider the first real Egyptian feature to be a film released in 1927, when Istephane Rosti directed the stage actress Aziza Amir in her production of *Leila*. Of the thirteen silent features made in Egypt, the critic Samir Farid singles out Mohamed Karim's 1930 adaptation of Mohamed Hussein Heykel's novel *Zeinab* as indisputably the most important. [17]

Elsewhere in the Arab world, cinema developed only slowly. In Tunisia, Albert Samama (known as Chikly), who had arranged the first film showings in Tunis in 1897, later directed the first Tunisian national productions, the short *Zohra* in 1922 and the feature-length *The Girl from Carthage / Ain al-Gheza* in 1924, both starring his daughter, Haydée Chikly. Otherwise, production in the Maghreb was restricted to shooting by European companies, beginning with about 60 actualities (out of a total of 1,800) in the 1895–1905 Lumière catalogue and some footage of the French military campaign in Morocco shot by Félix Mesguich in 1907. The only silent feature film production apart from Chikly's pioneering effort was the location filming undertaken by European (mainly French) companies, beginning with Luitz-Morat's *Les cinq gentlemen maudits* in 1919. In Syria, where the first screenings took place in Aleppo in 1908 and the first regular film theater was set up in Damascus in 1912, three silent films were made between 1928 and 1937, the first of which was Ayyoub Badri's *The Innocent Victim / Al-muttaham al-bari* (1928). In Lebanon, production was even more restrained. The first Lebanese film, Jordano Pidutti's *The Adventures of Elias Mabrouk / Mughamarat Elias Mabruk* (1929), was an amateur effort that received no commercial distribution, and production in the 1930s was sporadic.

In general, Arab cinema outside Egypt only hit its stride after World War II, since it was only in Egypt that the sense of national identity was historically founded. As the struggle for Egyptian independence intensified following the popular uprising of 1919, an indigenous nationalism emerged in the 1920s and 1930s. This nationalism was reflected in the new laws governing the Egyptianization of corporations (even though these were "frequently ignored or obeyed in appearance only"), and it found its fullest expression in the Bank Misr, which was established by Egyptian nationalists in 1920 to foster local industry and which "dominated the entire Egyptian economy until its nationalization in 1960." [18] The outcome of the early-twentieth-century effort to industrialize was very similar to that in India, in that Egypt "was largely self-sufficient in most consumer goods even before World War II gave a great boost to local industry." [19]

Initially, the progress of a nascent Egyptian film industry lagged behind these general economic developments. Though Egyptian producers became interested in the possibilities of sound film making at the beginning of the 1930s, it was not until mid-decade that production passed double figures (13 films in 1934–35) to reach a peak of 25 in 1944–45, making a total of 170 features in all between 1927 and 1945. The first sound films were shot in Paris, and the use of foreign—especially Italian—directors for Egyptian-produced films was common in the early 1930s. The first two Egyptian sound films, Mario Volpi's *The Song of the Heart / Anshudat al-fuad,* with the singer Nadra, and Mohamed Karim's *Sons of Aristocrats / Awlad al-dhawat,* both released in 1932, explored the filmic potential of Oriental songs. But though this basis in song was later to become the formula for a successful industry, there were at first problems in adapting the slow rhythms of traditional vocal presentation to the cinema, and *The Song of the Heart,* for example, was a commercial failure. The bulk of the early sound film production in Egypt was theatrical in style and had the range customary in a Third World commercial industry: a series of farces by Togo Mizrahi, Bedouin tales of love and adventure by the Lama brothers, adaptations of stage melodramas by Youssef Wahby, and a number of films starring the great singer Mohamed Abdel Wahab directed by Mohamed Karim.

An important impetus came from Bank Misr. As early as 1925 its director, Talaat Harb, had set up the Misr Theater and Cinema Company and had called, in his inaugural address, for a company "capable of making Egyptian films with Egyptian subjects, Egyptian literature and Egyptian aesthetics, worthwhile films that can be shown in our own country and in the neighbouring oriental countries." [20] In fact, however, the company concentrated largely on theatrical ventures, though a film processing laboratory was apparently set up in the 1920s, and it was not until sound had firmly established itself that Talaat Harb's attention turned to film production. 1935 saw the opening of Misr Studios, equipped with imported European facilities and manned by staff who had been sent for training to France and Germany. These were the first real studios, in the modern sense, in either Africa or the Arab world, and they played a key role in establishing a base for the subsequent expansion of Egyptian film making.

It is from the immediate prewar period that one can date the customary gulf that comes to exist in a film industry between commerce and art. Samir Farid illustrates the aspiration to commercial success excellently when he quotes a 1936 book by one of the European-trained directors, Ahmed Badrakhane. Claiming that "the popular masses dream of seeing settings they do not know but sometimes read about in novels," he offers the following definition of a "good script": "It's a story of love and jealousy between three or four people set in a beautiful city, inside splendid palaces and needing a short time-span, with natural or accidental obstacles endangering the happiness and even the life of the heroes; the latter have to overcome these obstacles and finally enjoy a merited happiness."[21] Against this trend can be set a handful of films with more serious aspirations, of which the best known is Kemal Selim's *The Will / Al-azima* (1939), the first Egyptian film that "dealt realistically with a social problem drawn from real life and conditions in Egypt."[22] Obviously, the precise nature of this realism needs to be set against the prevailing attitudes and assumptions of Egyptian film makers, rather than be seen as a "source"

57. *Kemal Selim:* The Will / Al-azima *(Egypt, 1939)*

for a postwar Egyptian "neorealism," if its qualities are to be established. But the appearance of *The Will* did offer subsequent film makers a striking example of independent film making.

The years from the end of World War II to the 1952 revolution are characterized by Samir Farid as "the cinema of the war profiteers." As in India and elsewhere, the war had increased the urban labor force and offered the opportunity for enormous profits to unscrupulous local businessmen, who were subsequently prepared to invest heavily in a speculative operation like film production. Thanks to the convergence of three contingent factors—the very low cost of film making, the sudden increase in purchasing power, and the even more rapid constitution of "parasitic capital" accumulated by war profiteers—"the cinema became, in Egypt, the 'easiest, quickest and surest' way of making a fortune. Films costing 5,000–10,000 [Egyptian] pounds and bringing receipts of more than 100,000 can be counted by the dozen." [23] The number of film theaters, which had passed 100 when the Misr Studios were founded, reached 244 in 1949, when four other modern studios came into existence. Film production rose above fifty films a year from 1945 to 1950, a level of output that allowed Egyptian films to play an important part in neighboring Arab countries (though the control of this distribution tended to be in the hands of Beirut-based Lebanese entrepreneurs) but still left Egypt vulnerable to foreign imports in its domestic market.

Thus, while Egypt's films contributed to making the Egyptian dialect known and understood throughout the Middle East, its cinema had no strong roots among the mass of its own population. As late as 1973, the director Kemal el-Sheik observed that 60 percent of Egyptians "do not know Egyptian films or refuse to know them." [24] The home audience for Egyptian films is largely limited to the urban population of Cairo and Alexandria, who reserve fashionable acclaim for foreign—especially Hollywood—movies. The number of Egyptian directors doubled in the years 1945 through 1952, but they had to work within the tight censorship constraints of a 1947 law that largely precluded the depiction of poverty, peasant life, calls to revolt, and the questioning of traditional customs. Not surprisingly, the cinema—dominated by melodramas and farces and with a strong element of song and dance—was shunned by serious writers. A few important directors did make their appearance, however. Among these were Salah Abou Seif (b. 1915), who had worked at Misr Studios, gone to Europe for further training, and returned to serve as assistant to Kamal Selim on *The Will;* and Youssef Chahine (b. 1926; see chapter 12), who had studied in the United States and who showed a precocious talent from his first feature, made when he was just twenty-four.

The 1952 revolt by a group of young Egyptian officers under the nominal leadership of Gen. Mohammed Neguib may indeed have been "a seminal event of the mid twentieth century [which] profoundly influenced the other Arab states and much of the Afro-Asian world," [25] but its immediate economic consequences were muted. Though attempts were made at agrarian reform under Gamal Abdel Nasser, who took over unchallenged leadership in 1954, private enterprise was the first to receive government support. The Egyptian cinema of the early 1950s therefore shows a continuity with the organization that had been current under the deposed King Farouk, and output reached an all-time peak of eighty films in the 1953–54 season.

Although the decade of the 1950s saw a number of remarkable films from both Salah Abou Seif and Youssef Chahine, the concept of an Egyptian neo-realist movement is an exaggeration: for example, Abou Seif's *Raya and Sekkina / Raya wa Sekkina* (1953) was simply an all-action thriller with a virtually expressionistic style, and Chahine's productions of 1956–57 were two Farid el-Atrach musicals. But other works by these two directors, such as Abou Seif's *The Tough Guy / Al-futuwa* (1957) or Chahine's *Cairo Station / Bab al-hadid* (1958), do show a closer connection with the realities of lower-class life than had been customary in Egyptian cinema. These years also saw the appearance of a strikingly independent talent, Tewfik Saleh (b. 1926), who made his debut with the adaptation of a novel by Naguib Mahfouz, *Street of Fools / Darb al-mahabil* (1955). This was in fact a period during which prominent writers began for the first time to involve themselves with cinema, but in

58. *Salah Abou Seif:* Raya and Sekkina / Raya wa Sekkina *(Egypt, 1953)*

general the film making—like the 1952 revolution in its early years—remained an expression of petty-bourgeois nationalism.

Though Egypt had become largely self-sufficient in production of consumer goods by 1940, further development was limited, and the advance "beyond these industries into the technologically advanced and capital-intensive lines of production" occurred only "to a modest extent." [26] Nasser sought the solution to this economic stagnation through a greater involvement of the state, which in the aftermath of the Suez crisis in 1956 had acquired the substantial economic interests previously owned by Britain and France. The Nasser government "became progressively more dedicated to state-capitalism from the mid-1950s. In 1956–57 there was a dramatic shift in the state's involvement in the economy. From encouragement of private capital accumulation through infrastructure and through loans, the state moved to take complete control over production." [27] The Bank Misr, which controlled up to a fifth of all industrial output by this time, was nationalized in 1960, and by the end of the decade "the government effectively controlled Egyptian industry." [28]

These developments, which followed from Nasser's evolving concept of Arab socialism (as set out in his Charter of National Action in 1962), found their echo in the film industry. In 1957 a National Organization for the Consolidation of the Cinema was set up by the Ministry of National Culture and Guidance, with the aim of raising the standards of production and regulating working practices. The same period saw the introduction of film study at Cairo University and the foundation of the first ciné-clubs. In 1961, the creation of the General Organization of Egyptian Cinema set the basis for important state participation in the industry, and the first state-produced film appeared in 1963. Samir Farid, noting that "in effect the public sector produced all the films of any importance during the period 1963–71," [29] lists some of the major achievements as including *The Sin / Al-haram* (1965), by the prolific Henry Barakat (b. 1914); *The Postman / Al-bustagi* (1968), by a newcomer, Hussein Kamal (b. 1932); and Tewfik Saleh's *The Rebels / Al-moutamarridoun* (1968), Abou Seif's *The 68 Trial / Al-qadiya 68* (1968), and Chahine's *The Land / Al-ard* (1970). However, though some artistic success was achieved, the government failed to make the industry commercially viable. The 1960s saw the introduction of television into Egypt, and the number of film theaters began a steady decline, from 350 in 1955 to less than 250 twenty years later. The flood of foreign film imports remained and taxes on cinema receipts were kept at a high level, and as a result, losses by the state organization amounting to some five million Egyptian pounds had led to a virtual cessation of state production by the early 1970s, even before the effects of Anwar Sadat's new and very different policies were felt.

Despite the lack of commercial success achieved by the state-run film organization and the transfer of some commercial production activity to Lebanon in the late 1960s (to escape government control and influence), the Egyptian

59. Tewfik Saleh: The Betrayed / Al-makhduun *(Syria, 1972)*

film industry has maintained its level of output at around forty or fifty films a year into the 1980s. This continued activity has not, however, been symptomatic of a trouble-fee industry. The appearance in 1969 of *The Night of Counting the Years / Al-momia,* a complex study of modern and traditional values, the first feature of Shadi Abdes-Salam (b. 1930), seemed to herald a renaissance of Egyptian cinema, the appearance of a "new cinema" of the kind familiar throughout the world in the 1960s. Yet this proved to be Abdes-Salam's only feature-length film, though he has made a handful of short documentaries. When the new generation emerging from film schools and television production also failed to make any sort of real international mark, Egyptian cinema began to lose some of its preeminence. The situation was aggravated by the difficulties the older film makers experienced while working in Egypt during Sadat's rule: the three films Chahine made in the late 1970s were all co-produced with the Algerian state production company, ONCIC; Tewfik Saleh, after making *The Betrayed / Al-makhduun* (1972) in Syria (from Ghassan Kanafani's celebrated Palestinian story, *Men in the Sun*), went to Iraq to become head of the film institute in Baghdad; and Abou Seif's only feature film since 1978 has been *Al-qadissia,* made in Iraq in 1980. The experience of these distinguished directors points to the new importance of Arab cinema outside Egypt.

The Machreq

In the Machreq (the Arab East), an important role had traditionally been played by Lebanese financiers and distributors, and until the civil war, local cinema attendance in Lebanon was the highest in the Arab world. But in the absence of all government support, film production itself was slow to get under way, with just eight features in the period 1930–52. Production developed more strongly in the 1950s with a dozen more features; Lebanese film making remained artisanal in nature, though, as is reflected in the two first features of the pioneering Georges Nasser (b. 1927). It was not until the 1960s, when state intervention in the Egyptian industry drove many Egyptian producers into exile, that levels of production in Lebanon rose—indeed, some two hundred features were made in the decade up to 1975 alone. Writing in 1966, the Lebanese critic Farid Jabre noted the weakness of this international expatriate cinema: "The greatest problem of the Lebanese cinema is in its lack of national background; in fact, many of the technical directors, assistants and even actors are former Egyptians who have settled permanently in Lebanon and carry on their professions in the Lebanese studios." [30] The 1970s, however, saw the emergence of a number of talented, largely Western-trained

60. Heiny Srour: The Hour of Liberation / Saat al-tahrir daqqat *(Oman, 1973)*

61. Samir Zikra: The Half-Meter Incident / Hadithet al-nusf metr *(Syria, 1982)*

Lebanese directors who were involved in the political turmoil of their country: the Paris-trained Georges Chamchoum (b. 1946), responsible for *Lebanon . . . Why?* (1979), and two women documentarists, the journalist Jocelyn Saab (b. 1948) and Heiny Srour (b. 1945), director of *The Hour of Liberation / Saat al-tahrir daqqat* (1973), on the struggle in Oman, and *Leila and the Wolves / Leila wal-dhiab* (1984), about the role of women in the Palestine Liberation Movement. The most talented of the newcomers is Borhan Alawiya (b. 1941), who received his training in Belgium. Alawiya followed the truly remarkable somber feature-length study of the massacre of a Palestinian community by Israeli troops, *Kafr Kassem* (1974), with a UNESCO-produced feature documentary on architecture and the environment, made in both French and Arabic versions, *For God to Be on the Side of the Poor Is Not Enough / La yakfi an yakoun allah maa al-fuqara* (1976), which drew on the ideas of the veteran Egyptian architect Hassan Fathy.

In Syria, too, production has been intermittent. Following independence in the 1940s there was a brief flurry of film production activity, financed by profits made out of wartime trading, but these initial efforts were unsuccessful, and for a decade (1951–60) no features were completed. Since the 1963 revolution the Syrian film industry has had two faces: on the one hand, a purely commercial sector, often employing expatriate Egyptian film makers and echoing the standard Egyptian formulas; and on the other, a state organization with control over distribution and a limited production program of features and documentaries. Unlike the commercial sector, the state organization has since the early 1970s shown itself willing to offer backing to young directors making their first feature films. Two film makers, both born in 1945 and trained in Moscow, who have benefited from such support and had their work produced and shown abroad are Samir Zikra with *The Half-Meter Incident / Hadithet al-nusf metr* (1982) and Mohamed Malass with *City Dreams / Ahlam al-madina* (1984). The only Syrian film maker to have created a real international reputation with work made over the course of a decade is the documentarist Umar Amiralay (b. 1944) who studied at the IDHEC in Paris and made his only feature-length film, the remarkable documentary study *Daily Life in a Syrian Village / Al-hayat al-yawmiyya fi qaria suriyya,* in 1974. Since then he has worked largely on fifty-minute documentaries for television: *The Hens / Al-dajaj* (1976) and more recently, for French companies, *The Misfortunes of Some / Maius qaum* (1982) on Lebanon and *Video in the Sand / Vidéo sur sable* (1984) on television in Kuwait.

A more ambitious and sustained program of state-organized feature film production has been followed in Iraq. Though the first film show in Baghdad occurred in 1909, there seems to have been no production before World War II. Developments in the early postwar years follow a pattern familiar from the other countries of the Machreq. Limited by the wider incomprehensibility of the Iraqi dialect and lacking any strong theatrical tradition (the first theater was established in Iraq in 1927), Iraqi film production in the private sector was speculative and often mediocre in quality. In all (not including a couple of Egyptian coproductions in 1945–46), about twenty features were made before 1964. In a national production limited largely to the domestic market, the two best-known films prior to the establishment of a state sector were *The Night Watchman / Al-haris* (1968), by a leading actor, Khalil Shawqi (b. 1924), and *The Thirsty People / Al-zamiyun* (1971), directed by Mohammed Shukry Jamil (b. 1936), who received his training as a film editor working for the Iraqi oil companies.

The first of several successive attempts to restructure the cinema was made in 1959 by the Ministry of Culture and National Guidance. An organization grouping theater, dance, radio, television, and cinema was established in 1969, and five years later the Iraqi General Organization for Cinema achieved autonomy. It had produced some sixty documentaries by 1977 when its first feature, Faisal al-Yassiry's *The Head / Al-ras,* was produced. Though this was not particularly well received, three further features followed in 1978, and the early 1980s saw a further burst of film making, with half a dozen features completed (all with multimillion-dollar budgets), including Sahib Haddad's *Another Day / Yawm akhar,* Faisal al-Yassiry's *The Sniper / Al-qannas* (set in Beirut), and two films made by Shukry Jamil, *The Walls* (1979) and *Clash of Loyalties / Al-masala al-kubra* (1983). The latter film, made in English and

Arabic versions and starring Oliver Reed, shows the difficulties of reconciling big-budget international coproduction with an authentic national identity. The film tells the complex story of Iraq's emergence as a nation-state after World War I, but this is done from the perspective of the British, who form the central focus of the narrative; the historical subject is thus reduced to a clash of personal involvements among expatriates. Far from being a historian of his national culture, Shukry Jamil gives the impression of using Jack Hildyard's camerawork and Ron Goodwin's musical score in an attempt to emulate David Lean, and in the process the mass of the Arab people are reduced to mere extras dying spectacularly in epic desert battles. This tendency for Iraqi cinema to lose its national identity is also apparent in the early 1980s in the employment of the veteran Egyptian director Tewfik Saleh to make *The Long Days / Al-ayyam al-tawila* and of Salah Abou Seif for the epic *Al-qadissia*.

There are no national organizations to match those of Syria and Iraq elsewhere in the Machreq, and feature film production has not as yet really got under way in Jordan, Sudan, or the Gulf States. A few talented individuals have, however, made their appearance, and two of these demand special mention. In Kuwait, the talented Khalid Siddik (b. 1948), who studied at the Pune Film and Television Institute in India, returned to make a number of documentaries for television and government departments before finding backing for two well-received fictional features, *The Cruel Sea / Bas ya bahr* (1971)

62. *Khalid Siddik:* The Wedding of Zein / Urs Zayn *(Kuwait / Sudan, 1976)*

63. Michel Khleifi: Fertile Memory / Al-dhakira al-khasba *(Palestine, 1980)*

and a Kuwaiti-Sudanese coproduction, *The Wedding of Zein / Urs Zayn* (1976), from the novel by Tayeb Salih. A few years later, the struggle of the Palestinian Arabs, the subject of innumerable documentaries by foreign and Arab film makers, found an authentic local voice in Michel Khleifi, who was born in Nazareth in 1950 and studied cinema in Belgium. His first feature-length documentary, *Fertile Memory / Al-dhakira al-khasba* (1980), revealed a talent to set alongside Amiralay and Alawiya.

The Maghreb

Film making has followed a quite separate pattern of development in the Maghreb (the Arab West), as distinctive national cinemas have emerged in Algeria, Tunisia, and Morocco. French colonial policy here had created a minority of educated Arabs whose views were shaped by French cultural dominance. But despite the support given to settler communities in all three states, economic development was minimal: "Industry, apart from mining and building, remained rudimentary—manufactured products were supplied from *la mère patrie*—and the expanding population was heavily underemployed. Vast *bidonvilles,* or shanty-towns, grew on the outskirts of the major cities, and such industry as there was developed on the basis of an abundant supply of cheap but inefficient labour."[31] Despite these drawbacks, in the years since independence, levels of film production in the Maghreb have been higher than in the Arab East, with over 125 fictional features produced by the early 1980s, over half of them in Algeria.

In Tunisia, Chikly's pioneering efforts of the 1920s found a muted echo in two independently produced sound films, Abdelaziz Hassine's *Tergui* (1935) and J. A. Creusi's *Madman from Kairouan / Majnun al-Kairouan* (1937). The decade preceding independence in 1956 saw the beginnings of a film culture, with the founding of ciné-clubs, extensive amateur film making, and the creation of one or two film journals, but it was not until 1966 that the first post-independence feature film by a Tunisian was released.

By the mid-1960s, a modern cinema of the Maghreb had already come into existence in neighboring Algeria. The roots of this national cinema lie in the liberation struggle that was waged against increasingly ferocious French opposition from 1954 to 1962. The first film unit was established in 1957 by the Frenchman René Vautier in the context of the National Liberation Front (FLN), and the first administrative structures were evolved in 1960–61. At the time of independence in 1962, there were three organizations in existence: the Centre Audio-Visuel, organized by Vautier to produce agit-prop material, which remained in existence for just six months; the independent production company Casbah Film, run by Yacef Saadi, which specialized in coproductions such as Gillo Pontecorvo's *The Battle of Algiers / La battaglia di Alger* (1966), in which Saadi played his own historical role as a key resistance figure, and Luchino Visconti's adaptation of Albert Camus's novel *The Stranger / L'étranger* (1968); and the Office des Actualités Algériennes, a newsreel organization founded by Mohamed Lakhdar-Hamina that also produced features. In 1964, the first steps toward the complete nationalization of the film industry were taken, and by 1969 the Office National pour le Commerce et l'Industrie Cinématographique (ONCIC) acquired a monopoly of film production and distribution (triggering a five-year boycott by the U.S. majors). The only production outside ONCIC from this point was the ambitious program of feature films made by the state television organization, RTA.

Because of the centralization of control over the development of Algerian cinema, its output has a remarkable thematic homogeneity. In 1965, *The Dawn of the Damned / L'aube des damnés*, an excellent compilation film on the struggle against colonialism throughout Africa, by Ahmed Rachedi (b. 1938), and *The Wind from the Aurès / Assifat al-aouras*, a fictional story of the Algerian popular struggle, directed by Mohamed Lakhdar-Hamina (b. 1934), set the pattern for a full cycle of war films. Both these directors have aspired to reach a wide audience and deliberately adopted conventional Western forms—the epic and the adventure story—for their subsequent films, which have included Rachedi's *Opium and the Stick / L'opium et le bâton* (1970) and

Lakhdar-Hamina's *December / Décembre* (1972) and *Chronicle of the Years of Embers / Chronique des années de braise* (1975). The war for independence is given a more sober treatment by Slim Riad (b. 1932) in *The Way / La voie* (1968), an evocation of the six years the director spent in a French internment camp.

By 1972 a second cycle of films—this time dealing with agrarian reform— had begun. Key films here are *The Charcoal Burner / Al-fahham*, the first feature of Mohamed Bouamari (b. 1941), and two television films, Abdelaziz Tolbi's *Noua* and Lamine Merbah's *The Plunderers / Les spoliateurs*. The themes of war and agriculture dominated the first decade of Algerian national production, but a new tone is apparent in *Omar Gatlato* (1977), by a new director, Merzak Allouache (b. 1944), which offered a shrewd and humorous look at the lives of contemporary urban youths, at their open passion for music and their hidden fear of women. The assurance shown in this first film is echoed in Allouache's subsequent features, *The Adventures of a Hero / Les aventures d'un héros* (1978) and *The Man Who Watched the Windows / L'homme qui regardait les fenêtres* (1983). The late 1970s also saw a whole range of films looking, at times with sociological exactness, at diverse areas of Algerian society: the role of women, in Sid Ali Mazif's *Leila and the Others / Leïla et les autres* (1977); the colonial seizure of land from the peasants, in Merbah's *The Uprooted / Beni-hendel* (1976); the fishing community, in Ghaouti Bendeddouch's *The Fishermen / Echebka* (1976); and so on.

Because of the limitations of a national output that amounts to barely five films a year, no Algerian film makers have been able to make more than a handful of films, and these have generally been interspersed with long years of silence. However, the late 1970s and early 1980s have seen an attempt to widen the scope of Algerian cinema, as evidenced in the emergence of the first woman director, the novelist Assia Djebar, and in the provision of ONCIC funds for a sardonic and highly negative view of the revolution, *The Crazy Years of the Twist / Les folles années du twist* (1983), by Mahmoud Zemmouri, who had made his first feature in France.

Algerian critics have generally shown themselves to be harsh in their judgments on national output, complaining of the lack of formal innovation and criticizing the overt commercialism of some of the established directors. A particular focus of attention has been the work of Mohamed Lakhdar-Hamina, perhaps the most forceful of all Algerian film makers, whose *Chronicle of the Years of Embers* won the 1975 Grand Prize at Cannes and created a new international awareness for Algerian cinema. Lakhdar-Hamina, who received his training in Czechoslovakia, is a highly skilled technician with a penchant for working in color and with wide-screen format and stereophonic sound. *Chronicle,* together with his next (fifth) feature, *Sand Storm / Vent de sable* (1982), has a visual gloss to rival anything produced in Europe. While this in itself is a remarkable achievement in the context of a cinema with so

64. *Mohamed Lakhdar-Hamina:* Chronicle of the Years of Embers / Chronique des années de braise *(Algeria, 1975)*

short a history, it can only be achieved by echoing Western forms and expending an inordinate amount of money (critics argued that a dozen low-budget films could have been produced with the funds spent on *Chronicle*). But the principal questions about Lakhdar-Hamina's work stem less from costs than from his narrative stance. Works of this dimension can only be interpreted as epics of the national consciousness, but looked at in this light, their inadequacies are clear. They offer little political insight but are rather purely lyrical protests: the poverty and sufferings of the colonized generate lushly beautiful images that negate, or at the very least defuse, the films' anger. Despite Lakhdar-Hamina's eloquence and directorial self-assurance, nothing could be more mystifying than his depictions of the national revolution.

In Tunisia, no such clear government priorities as existed in Algeria were to be found at the time of independence. The national film organization, SATPEC, was poised ambiguously between the state and the private sector, and from the start its activities were handicapped by the costs stemming from the mammoth studios set up at Gammarth in 1965, which failed to produce their hoped-for revenue, being incomplete (lacking sound stages) and outdated (equipped only for black-and-white at a moment when color processing was increasingly required). No changes were made after independence to the high level of colonial taxation on cinema admissions (45 percent), and the chance of Tunisian films being able to recoup costs within the local market of just seventy or so film theaters was nil. As in Algeria, most of the ambitious international coproductions undertaken in collaboration with European production companies were both costly and culturally insignificant. Yet a sense of the cultural importance of cinema remains strong in Tunisia, typified by the biannual Journées Cinématographiqes de Carthage, one of the major African film festivals, in continuous existence since 1966. With output limited to one or two films a year, Tunisian cinema is the work of a handful of committed individuals who struggle for years to set up each long-prepared feature. The only two Tunisian film makers to have been able to create any sort of *oeuvre* are the commercially minded Omar Khlifi (b. 1934), who adopted a fairly conventional Western style in films like *The Dawn / Al-fajr* (1966) and *The Fellaheen / Fallaga* (1970)—which are among the very rare Tunisian films to deal with the liberation struggle—and Abdellatif Ben Ammar (b. 1943), whose features *Sejnane* (1974) and *Aziza* (1980) are among the most probing examinations of Tunisian society. Otherwise, Tunisian features have tended to be highly individual projects that constitute virtually their authors' sole output: here the range is considerable, from Brahim Babai's neorealist-inspired *And Tomorrow? / Wa ghadan?* (1972) to the Nouveau Théâtre de Tunis's collectively made Brechtian adaptation *The Wedding / Al-urs* (1978), and from Ferid Boughedir's intellectualism in the codirected *Murky Death / La mort*

65. *Ridha Behi:* Sun of the Hyenas / Shams al-dibaa *(Tunisia, 1977)*

trouble (1970) to Ridha Behi's very impressive and committed attack on the cultural impact of tourism, *Sun of the Hyenas / Shams al-dibaa* (1977). Given the weakness of the Tunisian domestic market, a promising development in the early 1980s has been a new wave of culturally more viable coproductions with European companies, ranging from Taieb Louhichi's look at rural life *The Shadow of the Earth / L'ombre de la terre* (1980) to Mohammed Ben Mohammed's sophisticated study of migrants in Europe, whose uprootedness is symbolized when they are trapped on a cross-channel ferry, *Crossings / Traversées* (1982).

Perhaps the most paradoxical development has taken place in Morocco. This country has by far the richest set of production facilities, with studios at Casablanca (since 1939), the Souissi studios in Rabat (founded 1944), and new facilities at Ain-Chok (opened 1968), and the distribution circuit of three hundred film theaters is four times that of Tunisia. Yet the level of production is the lowest of the three Maghreb states. This failing can be attributed to a large extent to the lack of political development in Morocco, for which independence in 1954 under Sultan Mohammed V did not imply any sort of social revolution. In terms of the film industry, it is significant that the state organization, the Centre Cinématographique Marocain (CCM), continues with forms and structures established when it was set up under colonial rule in 1944; in addition to producing government-sponsored documentaries, then, it offers no more than minimal coproduction assistance to producers. Furthermore, there is no state policy for the film industry, which is entirely in the hands of private entrepreneurs. These businessmen have supported some commercial film making, beginning with the first Moroccan feature, *Overcome to Live / Vaincre pour vivre* (1968) by Mohamed B. A. Tazi, but the most striking achievements of Moroccan cinema are a handful of somewhat esoteric works that show a formal innovation unmatched elsewhere in the Arab world: Hamid Bénani's *Traces / Wechma* (1970), Moumen Smihi's *El-chergui* (1975) and *Forty-four, or The Tales of Night / Quarante-quatre, ou Les récits de la nuit* (1982), and Ahmed Bouanami's *Hallucination / Le mirage* (1980).

The difficulties of sustaining a political stance in the Moroccan situation are revealed clearly in the career of Souhel Ben Barka (b. 1942), a highly talented film maker whose first feature, *A Thousand and One Hands / Mille et une mains* (1972), looked at the misery that goes into the manufacture of exquisite Moroccan carpets. The political commitment apparent in this film is to be found too in the choice of subject matter for subsequent features: the international politics of oil production, in *The Oil War Will Not Take Place / La guerre du pétrole n'aura pas lieu* (1975), and the South African state, in *Amok* (1982). Unfortunately, the treatment of these themes does not match their ambition. Like the García Lorca adaptation *Blood Wedding / Urs al-dam* (1977), featuring Irene Papas and Laurent Terzieff dubbed into Arabic, these films give only a detached, exterior view of their subjects. Political issues are

66. *Ahmed el-Maanouni:* The Days, the Days / Alyam! Alyam! *(Morocco, 1978)*

shaped not too convincingly into conventional-style thrillers, and Moroccan culture is reduced to mere folklore. *Amok* in particular, a kind of updated version of *Cry the Beloved Country,* fails totally to find the passion and authenticity demanded of any African account of the horrors of apartheid. While Ben Barka's career to date is depressing in its development toward a hollow echo of stale European commercial formulas, another European-trained film maker, Ahmed el-Maanouni (b. 1944), emerged in 1978 with *The Days, The Days / Alyam! Alyam!* to give a vivid and effective semidocumentary look at the contradictions of Moroccan society. Thus, although the twenty-year evolution of cinema in the Maghreb shows many gaps and setbacks, there is a continuing vibrancy as new voices unceasingly make themselves heard.

Black Africa

The low level of film production in black Africa is unsurprising in view of the fact that industrialization there has been extremely limited. A recent survey describes African entrepreneurs as operating "in a border area between petty producers and foreign firms, an area—one thinks of saw-milling, furniture-making, baking, building materials, motor transport, and the like—where the capital requirements for entry were fairly low and the technology relatively simple." [32] Black African industrialization has, moreover, certain features that distinguish it from developments elsewhere. Firstly, it has occurred extremely late: except for limited developments in Dakar in the 1930s, modern industry dates only from World War II, when a combination of circumstances—colonial governments seeking to diversify their economies, local European settlers aiming for greater autonomy, and foreign firms seeking commercial advantages—led to some change from the old reliance on the export of primary products and the import of manufactured goods. Secondly, unlike development in, say, Latin America or those economies that achieved a boost from the disruptions to the world economy during the war, such developments as have occurred in Africa were often not the work of indigenous capital—indeed, the earliest modern manufacturing firms in particular tended to be started by foreign capital. Thirdly, the onset of industrialization coincided with the achievement of independence by nationalist politicians, so from the start, a key role was played by the state. As a result, industrialization in black Africa has a double pattern of development: not only are there regional variations, as between West Africa, with "its entrepreneurs from artisanship and trade," and East and southern Africa, where entrepreneurs emerged "from the straddling process of Western education and modern sector employment," [33] but there are also divergencies arising from the attitude of the state, which have ranged from clear disapproval of all capitalist development, as in Nkruma's Ghana or Nyerere's Tanzania, to the enthusiastic encouragement of private business found in Kenya and Nigeria.

All these features—together with the echoes of colonial cultural dominance—have gone to shape the pattern of an emergent black African cinema, which is, even after twenty years, still in its infancy. Exiled film makers from the extreme east and west of black Africa have produced striking films. In the west, Med Hondo (b. 1936), a Paris-based émigré from Mauritania made a remarkable debut in 1970 with *Soleil O,* which reflected his ten years or so in France and his involvement there in avant-garde theatre. The film is notable for the eloquence of its attack on neocolonialism. The tone, though at times violent, is always assured, and there is a willingness to confront points of conflict and controversy. The richness of its audiovisual complexity makes *Soleil O* a major innovative work, and though its roots are in the theater, its style mixes narrative and reportage, dream or nightmare and actuality. Hondo's rich stylistic mix found a more uneven synthesis in his second feature, and first in color, *The Negroes, Your Neighbors / Les bicots-nègres, vos voisins* (1973). His feature-length documentary on the Polisario Front, *We'll Have the Whole of Death for Sleeping / Nous aurons toute la mort pour dormir* (1977), left no doubt about the sincerity of his commitment, but the style was almost classical in its restraint: a lyrical, rhetorical celebration of the popular struggle, lacking drama or contradiction, it seemed to address itself to an audience already converted to its cause. But the exuberant *West Indies* (1979), in which

67. Haile Gerima directing Harvest 3,000 Years / Mirt sost shi amit *(Ethiopia, 1974)*

he again sought inspiration in theater and dance and used a huge single set
(built in an old Citroën factory) for the slave ship on which the action occurs,
saw Hondo return to his expressive best. Though the action is largely sung,
danced, or acted out in symbolic fashion, there is no mistaking the clarity of
its analysis of the mechanisms of colonization, slavery, and collaboration.

In the east, Haile Gerima (b. 1946), who had left Ethiopia to study in the
United States, returned with a UCLA crew in 1974, on the eve of the downfall
of Emperor Haile Selassie, to shoot *Harvest 3,000 Years / Mirt sost shi amit,* a
film rooted firmly in Ethiopian culture and in Gerima's personal background.
Shot near the town where the director had grown up and using songs and
poems by his father, the film offers an impassioned attack on three thousand
years of oppression. It combines great formal complexity—much influenced
by the traditions of African oral literature—with a rare depiction of the time-
less rhythms of peasant life. The images of reality are shot through with
dream sequences, and the rich stylistic texture uses to full effect a whole array
of visual tricks. After this strikingly mature first work, Gerima went on to
become a leading black American film maker.

For film makers resident in black Africa, the crucial cultural shaping force
is the heritage of the colonial era. Despite the aspiration to Pan-African unity
typified by the continentwide Fédération Panafricaine des Cinéastes (FEPACI),
set up in 1970, the common languages of mutual communication remain those

of the former colonizers—English, Portuguese, and French. Many of the newly independent states of Africa, most of which acquired their freedom between 1957 and the mid-1960s, have adopted national policies toward cinema, in some cases attempting to nationalize local distribution networks. But in no case do they have the economic power to break the control of world film distribution held by the major U.S. corporations. Levels of film production remain extremely low, and in most cases the "national" production remains the work of a tiny handful of individuals. Training has generally been acquired in Europe, and film making reveals the imprint of the diverse patterns of cultural interaction between the African states and the former European rulers, who retain enormous cultural, economic, and often political influence. In the former British colonies, for example, the potential cultural role of film has been ignored almost as totally by the new governments as by the old British colonial administrations. Since such film production structures as existed at the time of independence were unambiguously located within ministries of information, those film makers who had received any sort of training were oriented toward documentary production. As a result, there has been extensive application of film to official developmental ends but virtually no feature production. Film is seen as a tool—as a medium of mass communication with enormous educational potential—but not as a means of expression for the national culture and identity.

An excellent example of this state of affairs is Kenya, where the Kenyan Institute of Mass Communication makes numerous films to support educational and agricultural programs and has both an efficient and well-organized distribution system for its documentaries and a film training program. However, no Kenyan feature films have yet been made. Ghana, too, has its state organization, the Ghana Film Industry Corporation, as well as a National Film and Television Institute for training young film makers. But all the sporadic feature film production that has occurred has been independently organized. The first feature film by a Ghanaian, Sam Aryetey's *No Tears for Ananse* (1968), was followed by several other features in the early 1970s, yet no regular output was established. It was not until the international success of Kwaw Paintsil Ansah's theatrical adaptation *Love Brewed in the African Pot* (1981) that a fresh impetus to Ghanaian production was given. The early 1980s have seen the production of several further features, including King Ampaw's *Kukurantumi* (1983), but these, like Ansah's film, show that the Ghanaian developments in theater and literature are not as yet matched by formal film making skills.

Much the same is true of Nigeria, which despite its vast size and wealth has as yet developed no film industry as such, though occasional features have been made since the early 1970s, when the American Ossie Davis filmed an adaptation of Wole Soyinka's play *Kongi's Harvest* (1971). In Ola Balogun (b. 1945), Nigeria has one of black Africa's most forceful and prolific film

68. Ola Balogun: Ajani ogun *(Nigeria, 1975)*

makers, with ten features to his credit in the decade since his debut with *Alpha* in 1972. Balogun is unusual in being fluent in French as well as English and in having studied film at the IDHEC in Paris. Lacking the documentary concerns typical of anglophone Africa, he sees as the first priority the establishment of a popular cinema; thus, the impetus behind such works as *Cry Freedom* (1980) and *Money Power* (1982) is essentially commercial. One of Balogun's early films, *Ajani ogun* (1975), was made with performers from the Yoruba theater, and in the 1980s such stage adaptations—legendary tales of village life, love, and magic—have become popular, including Bankole Bello's *Efunsetan President of the Women of Ibadan / Efunsetan aniwura iyalode Ibadan* (1981) and especially the film versions of Hubert Ogunde's plays: *Aiye* (1980), directed by Balogun, and *Jaiyesimi* (1980) and *Aropin Ntenia* (1982), both codirected by Ogunde and the Englishman Freddie Goode. All these are no more than filmed stage performances, and it is indicative of the artisanal level of Nigerian production (despite the existence of five hundred registered movie theaters and hundreds of unregistered ones) that these films can be profitably exploited by Ogunde himself on his theatrical touring circuit. With a mode of production and distribution echoing the early years of European cinema, Ogunde is his own producer, performer, and presenter, retaining full control over his work by personally supervising the projection of the single print. In 1983, on the eve of the coup that overthrew President Shegari, there were ambitious plans to set up an industrial base for a nascent

Nigerian film industry with a multimillion-pound film complex including studios, laboratories, and postproduction and location facilities, but these plans have now been shelved.

Whereas in general the former British colonies received their independence peacefully, the liberation movements in Angola and Mozambique had to fight on for their freedom from Portuguese rule until 1975. The newly developed cinematographic institutions of both states reflect the form of socialism developed within the liberation struggle. Though documentary work predominates in both countries, it is very different from the "neutral" informational style prevalent in anglophone Africa. The new approach was well defined by the Mozambican minister of information, Jorge Rebelo, in his opening statement to the Maputo conference on African cinema in 1977: "We have not as our objective simply to combat and neutralize enemy cinema. Our objectives are also to produce, project and develop a truly revolutionary cinema which participates in revolutionary transformation and is capable of promoting it." [34]

The Angolan liberation struggle was the subject of numerous foreign film and television reports and also of two films by one of the women pioneers of Third World cinema, the Guadeloupan Sarah Maldoror. Although she studied cinema in Moscow, in the short *Monangambee,* shot in Algeria in 1970, and especially in the feature-length *Sambizanga* (1972), made in the Republic of Congo, she adopted a Western style and gloss which to some extent detracted from the films' message. Both these films were adapted from stories by the Angolan novelist Luandino Vieira, who in 1977 became head of the newly established film institute (IAC). By this time Angolan production was already under way with a series of short films having as an overall title *I am Angolan, I Work Hard / Sou angolano, trabalho com força* (1975). The IAC's first feature-length film, Rui Duarte de Carvalho's *Courage, Comrade! / Faz la coragem, camarada!* (1977), followed, and a regular production program of short and medium-length documentaries continued into the 1980s. A first fictional film, *Nelisita* (1983), also by Duarte, drew on traditional storytelling techniques. *Nelisita* shows the enormous potential of a rethinking of African narrative cinema so as to give films a new social role and changed relation to the audience. All film activity in Angola is state-controlled, and though the number of movie theaters in active use has declined from eighty at independence to fifty, including thirteen in the capital, by 1983, these program the 150 features imported by the state organization, EDICINE, which selects 40 percent from the West, 40 percent from the socialist countries, and 20 percent from the Third World.

When the FRELIMO took over in Mozambique in 1975 there was already a considerable amount of film activity and some film facilities in Lourenço-Marques (now Maputo), since in 1973 "as many films were produced in Mozambique as in Portugal, including pornographic films co-produced with

69. Ruy Duarte: Nelisita *(Angola, 1983)*

South Africa." [35] Film was given a high priority by the new government, with the Instituto Nacional de Cinema (INC) set up as early as 1975. The facilities available for completing black-and-white films in both 16mm and 35mm were applied to new ends by the Ministry of Information, which saw the cinema as a valuable means of ideological propaganda. The production program—a regular newsreel, *Kuxa Kanema,* a dozen or so documentaries a year, and occasional features—is ambitious, and important contributions were made by Brazilian film makers. The films produced relate very directly to the development of a socialist state within Mozambique, but some have been shown abroad: *25* (1977), by the Brazilians Celso Lucca and Jose Celso Correa; Murilo Salles's *These Are the Weapons / Estas são as armas* (1978); and the collectively made *Mozambique, or The Treatment of Traitors / Os comprometidos* (1983). The best-known national production is *Mueda, Memory and Massacre / Mueda, memoria e massacre* (1979), shot by the Brazilian film maker Ruy Guerra, who was born in Mozambique. This is the record of a play about a massacre at the village of Mueda in 1960, before the popular struggle, when six hundred people were killed. First staged in a FRELIMO training camp in Tanzania in 1968–69, the play has been produced annually by the people of the region since 1976 on the site where the massacre occurred. Guerra's film, shot in black-and-white in just two days, mixes interviews with survivors and peasants with a record of the actual performance. It is shot as a "real" happening, in newsreel style using a handheld camera, and with a deliberate disregard for the rules of conventional cinema. It is exemplary of an approach to film making that gives weight to the popular experience of oppression and of the liberation struggle.

The national cinemas of Angola and Mozambique are totally rooted in the new societies being built there. This is not the case in francophone Africa, where one of the most remarkable and controversial production experiments in the entire Third World has occurred—the program of aid to black African film makers by the French Ministry of Cooperation, which operated for almost twenty years until it was abandoned in December 1980 in the face of African criticism. The ancestor of all black African cinema is arguably the short *Africa on the Seine / Afrique sur Seine,* shot in 1955 in Paris by a group led by Paulin Soumanou Vieyra (b. 1925), who went on to become the historian of black African cinema and a prolific documentary film maker (he made his first feature, the satirical study of African ruling classes *Under House Arrest / En résidence surveillée,* in 1981). Many African film students who studied at the IDHEC made their first shorts in Paris, and as early as 1967, Désiré Ecaré from the Ivory Coast made a classic medium-length study of the exile community, *Concerto for an Exile / Concerto pour un exil.*

Film production in Senegal, which was to have the most developed cinema in francophone Africa with some twenty-six features between 1968 and 1983, began in the early 1960s with a number of Ministry of Cooperation–aided short films shot in black-and-white, without synchronous sound recording but with an imaginative interplay of sound and image, including a French-language voice-over commentary. Among the film makers of varying ages who emerged in this extremely low-budget area of production are Ababacar Samb-Makharam (b. 1934), Mahama Johnson Traoré (b. 1943) and Djibril Diop-Mambety (b. 1945), and the best-known films are the early works of Ousmane Sembene, *Borom sarret* (1963) and *Black Girl / La noire de . . .* (1966). (Sembene's career is the subject of chapter 15.) During the same period, a fresh and individualistic voice was heard from two self-taught film makers in Niger, the eclectic Mustapha Alassane (b. 1942) and Oumarou Ganda (1935–81), who had appeared in Jean Rouch's *Me, a Black Man / Moi un noir*. Ganda offered his reflections on his service in the French army in his first film, *Cabascabo*, as early as 1969, but it was not until 1980, the year before his death, that he was able to make a film of full feature length, *The Exile / L'exilé*.

The first true black African feature film was Ousmane Sembene's *The Money Order / Mandabi*, made in color in 1968 without Cooperation assistance. But it was followed by a whole wave of low-budget fictional works, which were usually Cooperation-aided and with editing and postproduction work carried out in Paris. These works were made by film makers from all over francophone Africa. During the years 1970–74 the first Senegalese features of Traoré, Samb-Makharam, and Diop-Mambety were followed by those of Philippe Maury and Pierre-Marie Dong from Gabon, Sébastien Kamba from Congo, Djim Mamadou Kola from Upper Volta, Ignace-Sola Randrasana from Madagascar, and Pascal Abikanlou from Benin. All these features were highly personal films, structured more as works of self-expression than as acts of communication with a known audience, and on occasion they treat directly the problems of the film maker's personal identity. They were inevitably limited, by the circumstances of their making, to the "ghetto" of noncommercial distribution. Indeed, the choice confronting francophone African film makers was encapsulated by the two features made by Cameroon directors in 1976: Jean-Pierre Dikongue-Pipa's *Muna Moto*, a critically acclaimed 16mm black-and-white study of the pressures of dowry and arranged marriage that received little showing in Africa, and Daniel Kamwa's *Pousse-pousse*, a 35mm color film that was one of black Africa's biggest commercial hits, seen by an estimated four hundred thousand people.[36]

The impact of the Cooperation program was enormous. In the dozen years from 1963 to 1975, about 125 out of the total of 185 films of all kinds made in francophone black Africa received aid or technical assistance from the French ministry, and these films set the pattern for almost all production. The method of finance was to purchase at a much higher price than normal the noncommercial rights of the films in question—often before they had even been shot—for distribution in France and through French cultural centers abroad.

The result was the creation of a low-budget African fictional cinema, made by film makers who were of necessity complete authors of their work: script-writers, producers or coproducers, directors, and often even leading per-formers too.

Even though the Ministry of Cooperation was careful to avoid any kind of censorship, accepting all the projects put to it, the contradictions of this pro-gram of French cultural aid to film makers from over a dozen sovereign Af-rican states are self-evident. Far from being examples of indigenous cultural expression, the films were a personal form of "art" cinema, effectively con-ceived and completed in Paris and available in the film maker's home country only at the local French cultural center. This program of French aid existed quite independent and apart from the structure of the commercial distribution system in francophone Africa, through which audiences in the fourteen newly independent states of what had been French West and Equatorial Africa were exploited by two French companies, SECMA and COMACICO, who exer-cised a joint monopoly and excluded African films from African commercial cinema screens.

The French Cooperation scheme was an original and enlightened venture, but its inherent paternalism led inevitably to its eventual rejection by the Af-rican states. Although it produced a mass of interesting work, it is perhaps significant that the two greatest black African film makers, the Senegalese Ousmane Sembene and Souleymane Cissé (b. 1940) from Mali, both did their feature film work outside the confines of the French-aided scheme, just as they both learned the craft of film making in Moscow, not Paris. Sembene's work, which is considered in detail later, is matched for critical rigor and creative excitement by Cissé in three masterly features of increasing stylistic complex-ity: *The Girl / Den muso* (1975), *Work / Baara* (1978), and *The Wind / Finye* (1982). The cultural importance the French attached to cinema undoubtedly also influenced the African governments, many of which attempted to gain control over their own distribution and exhibition networks and in some cases set up national production organizations. The extreme instance of this activity is Burkina Faso (formerly Upper Volta), which, though one of the world's poorest countries and possessing just six movie theaters at the time of indepen-dence in 1960 (a figure that had doubled by 1981), can now justifiably claim to be the capital of black African film making, with its biannual film festival (FESPACO), its nationalized cinema organization (SONAVOCI), its film school (INAFEC), and even a privately owned studio complex (CINAFRIC). Despite the difficulties of interstate collaboration, the French distribution duopoly has been replaced by an African-controlled consortium (CIDC), which allows the showing of African films on African screens. In the late 1970s the scope of francophone African film making was widened with a handful of feature-length documentaries made in Senegal. Safi Faye (b. 1943), black Africa's sole woman film maker, who had trained as an ethnographer,

70. *Souleymane Cissé:* The Wind / Finye *(Mali, 1982)*

71. *Gaston Kaboré:* God's Gift / Wend kuuni *(Burkina Faso, 1982)*

applied her observational skills to her native village in *Letter from My Village / Kaddu beykat* (1975) and *Fadjal* (1979), while Moussa Bathily (b. 1946), a former assistant to Sembene, offered a lament for the passing of traditional ways in *Circumcision / Tiyabu biru* (1978). Though French aid has been withdrawn, new films by talented young directors continue to appear in the 1980s, such as *God's Gift / Wend kuuni* (1982) by Gaston Kaboré (b. 1951) from Burkina Faso and *Djeli* (1981) by Fadika Kramo-Laciné (b. 1948) from Ivory Coast. Black Africa may be the youngest of the film making regions, but it shows increasing strength and potential at the beginning of the 1980s as it celebrates the twentieth anniversary of its birth with Sembene's *Borom sarret*.

Part Four

Cinema Astride Two Cultures

An author who has carefully thought about the condition of production today . . . will never be concerned with products alone, but always, at the same time, with the means of production. In other words, his works must possess an organizing function besides and before their character as finished works. And their organizational usefulness must on no account be confined to propagandistic use. Commitment alone will not do it.

Walter Benjamin

One of the crucial elements in an evaluation of Third World film making is the location of the film maker astride two cultures, on the one hand using a Western-originated technology and often employing formal structures of narrative derived from the West, and on the other drawing on—and relating the work produced to—his or her own native tradition. The experience of the last thirty years has shown this situation to be of enormous creative potential for an artist. In this final part of the book, attention is paid to the achievements of just a handful of notable film makers of the Third World. This choice is limited but not random, for all the film makers selected meet two criteria. Firstly, they have all produced a series of feature films over a period of fifteen or twenty years and achieved a degree of notoriety and influence outside their own countries. Secondly, their work offers the opportunity to consider in greater detail the artistic implications of some of the issues raised in earlier chapters:

> the strengths and limitations of an approach akin to that of the Italian neorealists
>
> the possibility of creating a social and political cinema while retaining the favor of an audience shaped by Western concepts of entertainment
>
> the ambiguous impact of post-1960 European film modernism
>
> the ways in which a politically committed film maker can draw on the traditions of a local entertainment cinema
>
> the struggle necessary to create a filmic expression of national issues in the absence of any industrial infrastructure for film production

the potential of new cinematic forms that have grown directly out of the
social organization and culture of the oppressed

Of necessity, these discussions of individual Third World film makers are
shaped somewhat differently from customary director monographs. Just as
the conventional form of the history of a national cinema does not correspond
to the realities of Third World cultural production, so too the assumptions of
creative independence and universal comprehensibility that underlie auteurist
approaches to individual Western film directors need to be questioned when
one is dealing with film makers from the Third World. To assert no more than
the "universal humanity" of, say, Satyajit Ray's films is to ignore key aspects
of the director's work, and I have tried here, within the limits of my own
knowledge, to begin the task of setting these film makers in their specific social and cultural contexts. In each case, similar factors need to be taken into
account: the film maker's class position, his social and cultural context, his
relation to the existing local tradition of film making, and his attitude toward
the West. The preoccupations of the individual film makers range widely, but
the work of all six can only be fully understood when their work is related to
the contradictions of their particular national film making context and when
their individual modes of expression are seen in relation to the societies in and
for which they are working.

I am fully aware now, thanks to my Western critics, of the Western traits in my films. They have so often been brought to my notice that I can actually name them: irony, understatement, humour, open endings, the use of leitmotifs, a fluid camera and so on. These elements are never used consciously. It is not as if I find myself saying: Ah, now for a bit of British understatement. They are used intuitively to best serve the needs of the subject matter in hand.

Satyajit Ray

Satyajit Ray's social origins are within one of the Western-educated elites discussed earlier, the *bhadralok,* who, under the stimulus of European contact in Calcutta, "refashioned Bengali as a rich literary language, freely borrowing forms and techniques from English to enable them to grapple effectively with the intellectual issues introduced into their society by the European cultural intrusion. To the existing body of fine religious poetry, they added secular writing in a variety of forms." [1] In addition to the enrichment of Bengali language and literature, they felt compelled "to re-examine the philosophic basis of their culture," thereby spreading an intellectual ferment throughout Bengal. The bhadralok's proficiency in English made them the channel through which the new ideas from Europe (democracy, liberalism, nationalism, the liberation of women, and social equality) flowed into Indian society.

Ray's family was centrally concerned in this cultural renaissance. His grandfather was a pioneer printer and publisher who also composed Hindi songs, played the flute and violin, and wrote children's books. He was also one of those who joined the Brahmo Samaj, "a community of ardent social reformers who blended an ancient Vedantic Hindu content with a Christian form in their religion, and developed the driving force of a puritan ethic in their urge to change traditional Hindu society towards modern times." [2] Satyajit

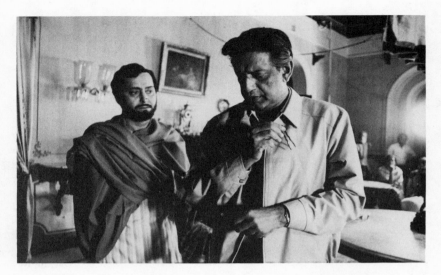

72. *Satyajit Ray (right), directing* The Home and the World / Ghare baire
(India, 1984)

Ray was later to capture the excitement of this moment of synthesis between Western ideas and traditional Hindu values in two of his finest films, *Devi* and *Charulata*. His father, who died when Satyajit was two, was well known for his children's verses, and he edited a children's magazine, *Sandesh,* which Satyajit was later to revive. Satyajit's own education followed a familiar bhadralok pattern, with study at Presidency College, Calcutta, where English was the language of tuition, followed by studies of art at the University of Santineketan, founded by Rabindranath Tagore, who had been a friend of the Ray family. Ray was later to pay tribute to Santineketan in his feature-length documentary *Rabindranath Tagore* (1961), and to his art teacher there, Binod Behari Mukherjee, in the short documentary *The Inner Eye* (1974).

In considering Ray's work as a film maker, it is important to remember that his work has no roots in the traditions of Indian film making. Thus, though Ray was deeply influenced by Indian culture through his studies at Santineketan, he was largely Western in his film tastes. As a child he devoured Hollywood movies—the silent comics and Tarzan, gangsters, and westerns. Later a crucial impact was made on him by Jean Renoir, who visited India in 1949 to make *The River,* and it was a viewing in London of De Sica's *Bicycle Thieves* that gave him the encouragement to begin work on *Pather panchali.*

There can be little doubt about the wisdom of the particular line of independence from the industry that Ray chose in the 1950s, since it has allowed him a prolific and uninterrupted career over almost thirty years. His output during this time is best considered in terms of a succession of overlapping stages. The first stage—that with which his name is indissoluably linked—comprises the films of the "Apu" trilogy: *Pather panchali* (1955), *The Unvanquished / Aparajito* (1956), and *The World of Apu / Apur sansar* (1959); *The Goddess / Devi* (1960), adapted from a story suggested to the author, Prabhat Mukherjee, by Rabindranath Tagore; and the first two episodes (*The Postmaster* and *Samapti*) in the set of Tagore adaptations that go to make up *Three Daughters / Teen kanya* (1961).[3] Here Ray's sympathies are most deeply involved in a loving recreation of the preindependence world of rural India. He creates a succession of young heroes, of whom the archetype is the actor Soumitra Chatterjee (the mature Apu, Umaprasad in *Devi,* and Amulya in *Samapti*), who find themselves torn between traditional values and their newly acquired Westernized education. All Ray's immense skill at tracing the relationships of characters among themselves and with their environments finds full expression here.

But already as early as 1957 Ray seems to have been consciously working to extend the range of his approach, and binding this first stage to a subsequent one, we find a whole series of films in which the characters are drawn from a much wider sphere. The films that fall into this category are the contemporary comic fantasy *The Philosopher's Stone / Parash pathar* (1957), the study of a declining aristocracy *The Music Room / Jalsaghar* (1958), and the ghostly tale

73. *Satyajit Ray:* The Unvanquished / Aparajito *(India, 1956)*

74. Satyajit Ray: The World of Apu / Apur sansar *(India, 1959)*

75. Satyajit Ray: The Goddess / Devi *(India, 1960)*

of obsessive avarice *Monihara,* which forms the third part of *Three Daughters.* To these may be added Ray's venture into the world of crime and drug smuggling, *Abhijan* (1962), and two striking films made in the mid-1960s from original scripts, *Kanchanjungha* (1962) and *The Hero / Nayak* (1966). Ray's consummate professionalism is shown in his mastery of the enormously wide range of tone here: from the rather clumsy comedy of *The Philosopher's Stone* to the atmospheric grotesqueries of *Monihara,* from the elegy of *The Music Room* to the fights and action sequences of *Abhijan.* Nowhere (except perhaps at times in *The Music Room*) does one feel that Ray is deeply involved with his characters: when Soumitra Chatterjee reappears as the taxi-driver hero of *Abhijan,* he gives a stiff and mannered performance, with his expressive face obscured by a long black beard and a permanently sour scowl. The settings, too, which had previously been a source of immediate pleasure in their own right, are here no more than locations for an action that unfolds with mathematical precision. Most interesting in this respect are Ray's two original scripts, *Kanchanjungha* and *Nayak.* Here, when he is released from the need to compress a sprawling novel (such as Bibhuti Bhushan's *Pather panchali*) into a ninety-minute narrative, the tight shaping power of Ray's imagination is most apparent. Both films are conversation pieces that observe to the full the classical unities of time (a single day in *Kanchanjungha,* the journey from Calcutta to Delhi in *Nayak*) and place (the terraces of the hill station of Darjeeling; the express train). Ray does not sympathize with either the autocratic head of the family in *Kanchanjungha* or the angst-ridden film star of *Nayak*—in both cases the portraits are pieced together from the externals of behavior; and though he is working from his own scripts, Ray's direction here has a quite impersonal tone, particularly compared to the "Apu" trilogy or the Tagore adaptations.

The Big City / Mahanagar (1963), *Charulata* (1964), and the first episode of the two-part *The Coward and the Holy Man / Kapurush-o-mahapurush* (1965) all star the actress Madhabi Mukherjee, and they form a set that complements the preoccupation of Ray's first films with the young educated male. Here Ray moves back to his central concerns to treat, in a variety of periods and social contexts, the problems of women in Indian society. As in the early films, his method is to use a mass of brilliantly observed and often very funny details to build up a single strand of plot. Both *Mahanagar* and *Kapurush* have a contemporary setting. In *Mahanagar,* Madhabi Mukherjee plays Arati, a hitherto sheltered housewife who takes her first timid steps toward earning a living and helping to support her family; the effect on both her and her husband when she finds that she actually enjoys working is beautifully and delicately traced. *Charulata,* one of Ray's undoubted masterpieces, is adapted from a story by Tagore and set at a period of particular significance to the director: the last quarter of the nineteenth century, when British ideas were beginning to make themselves felt on Bengali intellectuals, including the Tagores and Ray's own grandfather. Charulata, the sensitive but bored wife of a westernized newspaper publisher, finds herself drawn sexually to her husband's young cousin who comes to stay, and who shares her taste for literature. The film moves with beautiful precision from flirtation and almost childish competitiveness to near tragedy amid a beautifully reconstructed period setting. While Tagore's story ends in disaster, Ray in his adaptation is less conclusive, choosing to freeze the film's last frame as husband and wife are hesitantly on the point of coming together again.

As early as 1961—the Tagore centenary year—Ray had revived the children's magazine *Sandesh,* founded by his grandfather and edited by his father until his early death. Ray wrote and drew extensively for the magazine, composing and translating nonsense verse and writing short stories and a series of detective stories featuring the private detective Felu. In 1969, this interest found expression in the cinema with *The Adventures of Goopy and Bagha / Goopy gyne Bagha byne,* adapted from one of his grandfather's best-known stories. Subsequently, though his more serious films have had a mixed reception, his children's films—which never patronize their audience—have been

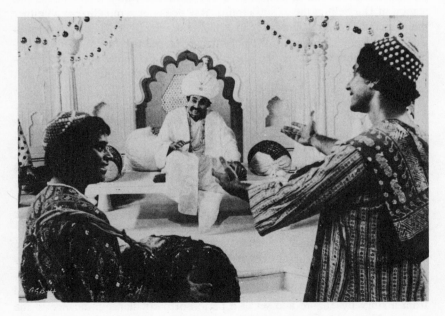

76. Satyajit Ray: The Adventures of Goopy and Bagha / Goopy gyne Bagha byne *(India, 1969)*

universally praised. To date, the series of films, all adapted from his own stories, includes two featuring the detective Felu—*The Golden Fortress / Sonar kella* (1974) and *The Elephant God / Joi baba felunath* (1978)—and a sequel to *Goopy and Bagha, The Kingdom of Diamonds / Hirok rajar deshe* (1980).

The early 1970s were in many ways a difficult period for Ray as he strove to respond to criticism of his work by confronting political issues and the post-independence Indian scene. Two characteristic works of the period are *Days and Nights in the Forest / Aranyer din ratri* (1970) and *Distant Thunder / Ashani sanket* (1973). In both he tackled new subject matter in an oblique fashion. *Days and Nights in the Forest,* a first real look at present-day Calcutta society, shows not life in the city but an excursion to the countryside by four young friends. There the limitations of both their sensitivity and their male identities are exquisitely brought out in their interaction among themselves and in their contact with three very different women. The film has an extremely precise structure, and the interweaving of the four individual stories with the fairground dancing at the end of the film is a masterpiece of editing. *Distant Thunder,* a return to the past and to rural India, is an equally distanced view, this time of the great Bengal famine of 1942–43. Typically, the subject is told at the level of the inhabitants of a remote village, for whom the famine is a catastrophe they can neither combat nor comprehend. The film's concentration—as always with Ray—is on the social interaction of the people, in the midst of whom is Soumitra Chatterjee as the tormented Brahmin priest. The formal and visual beauty of the film (Ray's first in color since *Kanchanjungha*) is striking, setting up great tensions in view of the horror of the subject (a final title tells us that an estimated five million Bengalis died).

Between these two obliquely angled films, Ray began what was to be a loosely linked trilogy of films in which he confronted the problems of Calcutta head-on, in an uncompromisingly contemporary, urban context. *The Adversary / Pratidwandi* (1970), in which the hero is a young man, Siddhartha, very much in the Apu tradition, illustrates Ray's difficulties with this kind of subject matter. The awkwardnesses of the film's narration (the dream sequences, the unconvincing flashbacks to an idyllic childhood) mirror those of the hero, who is unable to accept either his younger brother's firm political commitment or his sister's more complaisant westernization. For Siddhartha, the only source of authentic values seems to be the bird call he remembers from his childhood (and hears again at the end of the film), and inevitably his revolt against Calcutta, when he attacks the unfeeling bosses at a job interview, can be no more than personal outburst. In *Company Ltd. / Seemabaddha* (1971) there is a similar problem in the location of the film's moral judgment on the corrupt business world, though like all Ray's work of the period, it abounds in brilliantly chosen and often humorous detail. The film is narrated by an ambitious young executive, Shyamal, who is willing to sell out in order to achieve the directorship he seeks. But like so many potentially wicked

77. Satyajit Ray: The Adversary / Pratidwandi *(India, 1970)*

characters in Ray's work, Shyamal is personally attractive, and the condemnation of his actions by his young sister-in-law seems more a mark of her own
emotional maturity (she was in love with him as a child) than a solidly rooted
social judgment. *The Middleman / Jana aranya* (1975) is by far the bitterest of
Ray's indictments of the city, but it is also one of his more ambiguous films. It
is difficult not to side with the personable young hero, Somnath, as he attempts to make his way in the Calcutta business world against all the odds. His
struggles lead him unwittingly to pimp for his best friend's sister who, unknown to them both, has turned to prostitution. The difficulty Ray seems to
experience in showing any sort of positive aspect to the social involvement of
his contemporary heroes is emphasized by the inadequacies of the balancing
figure in the film, Somnath's retired father, who accepts everything uncom-
prehendingly. In any case, the force of this modern trilogy, despite its inner
contradictions, is remarkable, and the films are clearly the work of a major
director struggling to overcome his personal remoteness from the issues he is
tackling.

The new phase of Ray's career that opened with the making of *The Chess
Players / Shatranj ke khilari* (1977) is still difficult to define, but three new

impulses are apparent in Ray's work at the beginning of the 1980s. The first is the new willingness to work in Urdu or Hindi rather than his native Bengali, though he still remains understandably aloof from the dominant structures of the all-India movie. Despite the use of a large budget and very popular Hindi stars, *The Chess Players* is essentially an intimate film, viewing its ostensible subject—the unscrupulous British take-over of the state of Oudh in 1856—from the point of view of two noblemen who have virtually abandoned their wives and positions in society in order to indulge their passion for chess. *Deliverance / Sadgati* (1981), a fifty-minute drama filmed for television that tackles the issue of caste through a tightly structured tale of the oppositions within a village community, was similarly made in Hindi.

Ray's second concern, which these two films amply bear out, is to treat major social questions from a point of view detached from the particular awareness of his protagonists. This concern is particularly apparent in *Pikoo* (1981), a twenty-six-minute short made in Bengali for French television. Though it tells the story of a momentous day in the life of a lonely six-year-old boy, the perspective chosen is an adult one, and the film measures the child's limited awareness against the enormity of the actual occurrences (his father's discovery of the mother's adultery and the death of his grandfather).

The third impulse in Ray's recent work is toward the adaptation of major works of literature. While *Pikoo*, like the earlier films for children, was made from an original Ray story, both *The Chess Players* and *Deliverance* are adaptations of stories by the great Hindi writer Premchand; and Ray's subsequent feature (which was interrupted by a heart attack) is a version of a major novel by Rabindranath Tagore, *The Home and the World / Ghare baire* (1984).

The Home and the World is an adaptation for which Ray wrote a first draft in the late 1940s, long before he made his first feature. As so often happens with projects that have such a long gestation, the resultant film is somewhat laborious and, in this case, overloaded with dialogue. It is set in a key period for Ray—around 1907—and, like *Charulata* and *Devi,* traces the impact of Western ideas on the wealthy Indian intellectual elite. It is—also like *Charulata*—a triangular love story, but this time the tale is told not through the experience and viewpoint of a single character, but through the eyes of all three characters. Bimala the wife, Sandip the friend, and Nikhil the husband are successively the focus of narrative attention. In this, Ray follows the pattern of Tagore's novel, which tells, in the form of a diary with three equal voices, the story of a woman who is urged by her husband to leave seclusion and does so, only to fall in love with his best friend. As in Ray's own original scripts, the action is tightly compressed in time and space, set largely in a beautifully reconstructed Bengali palace. The film is an account of the clash of ideas, the pain of social and personal change (even for someone as strong in personality as Bimala), and the disillusionment of betrayed ideals. But despite the balance given in the narration to the three characters and the extreme sensitivity with which Bimala's changing perceptions are traced, there can be no doubt that Ray, like Tagore, adopts the perspective of Nikhil, the aristocrat who is drawn personally to change but rejects social revolution. The somewhat muted quality of the film stems indeed from the fact that Sandip, though played by one of Ray's favorite actors (Soumitra Chatterjee, here making his thirteenth appearance in a Ray film), is shown from the first to be a failed idealist and a man whose advocacy of social action never disguises his purely personal ambitions. With its sensitivity and eloquence almost masking the melancholy defeatism of author and film maker alike, *The Home and the World* is a powerful statement of the bhadralok ideals that Ray inherited from Tagore.

If Ray's films are so accessible to Western audiences, it is largely because his sense of narrative structure and economy of detail are essentially rooted in Western approaches. Although Tagore and the Bengali novelist Bibhuti Bhushan, author of the stories on which the "Apu" trilogy and *Distant Thunder* are based, have been major influences on him, Ray's craft derives in part from a special creative tension between the rambling, often open-ended narratives that he adapts and the tight shaping impulse of his imagination, a tension that produces narrative structures to match those of the most finely wrought classical Hollywood movies. It is here, perhaps, that the Western influence on his art is most apparent, since by his own account the conception of time in his films is not rooted in Indian tradition: "The concept of an art form existing in time is a Western concept, not an Indian one. So, in order to understand cinema as a medium, it helps if one is familiar with the West and Western art forms. A Bengali folk artist, or a primitive artist, will not be able to understand the cinema as an art form."[4] The rhythm that underlies Ray's shooting and editing is also very Western, and though he has written his own (Indian) musical scores since *Three Daughters,* his own musical training was in Western forms: it is a sense of rhythmic interplay consciously derived from Mozart that helps to shape, say, *Days and Nights in the Forest.*

This sense of narrative shape and closure is not, however, accompanied by a similar sense of finality where his characters are concerned. Even when, as in *Charulata,* the logic of the action points, seemingly inexorably, to a tragic conclusion, Ray shows himself reluctant to adopt this perspective: *Charulata* ends with frozen, ambiguous images of hands *about* to touch in attempted reconciliation. Similarly, as many commentators have observed, there are no villains in Ray's work. Even the imperialist General Outram, who engineers the deposition of the king in *The Chess Players,* emerges as a slightly baffled but not totally insensitive figure; likewise, the corrupt businessmen the hero meets in *The Adversary,* and even the unscrupulous so-called public relations man Mitter, emerge as richly drawn, somehow attractive personalities.

This acceptance of the corrupt as well as the virtuous is crucial to the impact of Ray's work, since moral judgments in his films are not rooted in some externalized code or social ethic. Indeed, the key to the impact of a Ray film is in the depiction of individual characters on a personal level. This is an area of film making in which Ray is marvelously successful: whether he is looking at parents and children (the "Apu" trilogy, *Devi, The Middle Man, Pikoo*), husbands and wives (*The World of Apu, Mahanagar, Charulata*), or groups of friends (*Days and Nights in the Forest, The Chess Players*), he paints meticulously detailed, often deeply humorous pictures of their interaction. Any wider social issues—questions of the role of women, changing religious beliefs, the workings of British imperialism—are filtered through such situations and are never allowed to lead to schematization. Characters are fully rounded human beings first, and social representations or symbols only on a secondary level: hence the fact that Ray's most profound insights into social issues are those where the approach is most oblique. Ray's most successful films are precisely those in which his sympathies are most deeply engaged by his characters—the "Apu" trilogy, *Devi, Charulata, Days and Nights in the Forest,* for example,—but even where he is handling material fundamentally alien to him—an autocratic father, a film star, a crooked businessman, a self-centered Brahmin—he cannot prevent himself from giving their views full weight or allowing them genuine human qualities. Indeed, part of the problem of the Calcutta "trilogy" lies in the fact that characters who should be condemned for their actions are allowed to engage us as people. This lenience limits the social impact of Ray's work. Even potentially socially determined actions are invariably given a purely personal motivation within the plot of any Ray film.

Ray's films mirror in cinema the achievements in painting and literature of the Bengal renaissance. For Ray, as for his artistic predecessors, the creation of a work of art is a means of rediscovering his own Indian heritage through the technical means and conceptual tools acquired from contact with Western culture. The ultimate strength of his work rests in those passages in which the sense of discovery is strongest: the rural village community in *Pather panchali,* the clash of cultures in *The Postman,* the first generation of westernized Indian intellectuals in *Devi,* the awakening of a woman's consciousness in *Charulata.* Here Ray's communication with his audience is direct and immediate. Even many of those films that approach their ostensible subject matter obliquely manage to convey Ray's own involvement as well: we feel in *Days and Nights in the Forest* that the director, too, is exploring the world outside Calcutta along with his heroes, and that *The Chess Players* is a personally researched analysis of the workings of imperialism. It is the sense of discovery that gives life to even the tiniest details, turning Ray into a film maker who, even when working as a miniaturist, is a major artist.

Ray's contribution to Indian cinema is incalculable. It is apparent from the preceding analysis that despite the accessibility of his work for Western audiences, his roots are profoundly Indian. Even though many aspects of his style are closer to Western cinema than to the all-India movie, the approach that underlies them can in fact be traced to an Indian source, Rabindranath Tagore. As Chidananda Das Gupta writes in his illuminating critical study of Ray (the most substantial by an Indian critic), "Ray's classicism, like so much else in his outlook, is derived from Tagore. It was in Tagore that the restless reformism of the 'Bengal Renaissance,' casting about for the right blend of East and West, found its equilibrium." [5] Ray's adaptation of Tagore's *The Home and the World* points both to the patrician origins of Ray's classicism and to the limitations of this classicism as a stance from which to view the contemporary world.

As Indian critics begin to probe more deeply into Ray's work, it becomes clear that the distinction between East and West needs to be supplemented by the distinction between classes within India itself. Raghumath Raina, in his foreword to Das Gupta's study, points out that the Bengal renaissance can be seen from another perspective, that is, as "the beginning of colonial culture," arising when the imperial power in Calcutta created a new middle class in nineteenth-century Bengal that accepted Western ideas, "as it were at second hand." Ray "inherited the world-view of his class. That explains why there are no villains in his films, there is an absence of anger, 'a sense of detachment, a distance from the event.' When Chidananda says that Ray's philosophical outlook is Indian, he ignores that it is the outlook of a particular Indian class." [6]

A closer consideration of Ray's widely proclaimed "universal humanity" leads to the same conclusion. Far from being a neutral artistic quality, this humanity, too, can be seen most properly as the product of a tradition created initially by a middle class that has come to terms with colonization. As Solanas and Getino remark in another context, "One of the most effective jobs done by neo-colonialism is its cutting off of intellectual sectors, especially artists, from national reality by lining them up behind 'universal art and models.'" [7]

Ray's enormous power and marvelous sensitivity in his reaction to the past—ranging from the decline of the Mogul rulers to the adulthood of Apu—should not serve to mask the ambiguities of his attitude to the present, typified by his preference in the 1970s for children's stories. Ray's films are very much contained within the conceptual framework of a preindependence approach, and it is here—in the denial of actuality, of the living presence of contemporary society—that they differ most profoundly from the Italian neorealism to which they may in so many other ways be usefully compared. A more appropriate analogy for Ray's approach would be the aristocratic Luchino Visconti, meditating on the passing of the old order in such films as *Senso* or *The Leopard*.

Je raconte une Alexandrie où il y avait une intelli-
gence de vivre entre les différentes races, les diffé-
rentes nationalités, les différentes religions, qui était
extraordinaire. Comment a-t-on pu la perdre? . . .
On a vécu cette intelligence. Alors, c'était dans l'in-
térêt de qui? Il faut dévoiler ça. Et qui est en train
d'y collaborer, de nous faire subir ça? Quelles sont
les classes qui dominent, qui dirigent?

Youssef Chahine

Youssef Chahine's work reflects a very different approach from that of
Satyajit Ray to the problems of past and present, though Chahine too comes
from a middle-class background and experienced an education shaped by the
realities of Britain's seventy-four-year occupation of Egypt. Chahine was born
in Alexandria in 1926, the son of a scrupulous but financially unsuccessful
lawyer. His father was a supporter of the nationalist Wafd party, but his sup-
posedly anti-British sentiments did not prevent him giving his son an education typical of the middle classes under colonialism. Chahine, who was
brought up as a Christian, was educated first at a religious school and then at
Victoria College in Alexandria, where the language of tuition was English.
After a year at Alexandria University, he persuaded his parents to allow him to
study drama abroad, and he spent two years at the Pasadena Playhouse, near
Los Angeles.

The cosmopolitanism inherited from his years in Alexandria remains a
constant feature of Chahine's work. He has a deep awareness of developments
in the West, helped by the fact that he speaks half a dozen languages fluently
(his command of accent and intonation in the English-language episodes of
Alexandria . . . Why? / Iskandarya . . . leh? [1978] is remarkable). Balancing this cosmopolitanism, however, is a strong local patriotism: there is no

78. *Youssef Chahine (center), directing* Alexandria . . . Why?/Iskandarya . . . leh? *(Egypt/Algeria, 1978)*

evidence that Chahine's Christian upbringing or English-language education made him feel any less of an Egyptian. On the contrary, while he is able in his later films to offer vivid portraits of Egyptians abroad, he seems far less at ease with non-Egyptian subjects and settings. His film on the Algerian war, *Jamila/Jamila al-jazairiyya* (1958), which was shot entirely in Egypt, was subjected to severe criticism in Algeria, despite the evident sincerity of his motives, and he himself counts the two films he made in Lebanon as being among his least important works. His best work is profoundly Egyptian— though this does not mean that he has been able to work easily in his native country. The three major films he completed in the late 1970s all had to be made in coproduction with the Algerian state film company, ONCIC; yet in each case the subject, settings, and actors were totally Egyptian.

Unlike Satyajit Ray, who spent five years preparing *Pather panchali* and who made his first feature away from the mainstream of Indian commercial cinema, Chahine entered the film industry as an assistant director immediately upon his return from the United States. By the age of twenty-four he had completed his first feature as a director, *Father Amin/Baba Amin* (1950), and throughout his career he has remained a highly professional film maker, concerned to keep working and to remain in touch with his audience. He has shown on several occasions that he feels the exclusion of Arab films from European screens very keenly, but he is understandably far more bitter about the 80 percent of screentime that foreign films traditionally enjoyed in Egypt. He knows all too well the defects of the traditional Egyptian commercial film, but at the same time he is emphatic in his insistence that it is the responsibility of Egyptian film makers to make works accessible to a mass audience. Symptomatic of his attitude is his acceptance of the commercial failure in 1958 of *Cairo Station / Bab al-hadid*—a remarkable film that is generally regarded as the best of his early works—and his subsequent resolve to work in a more popular style. Similarly, when it became difficult for him to set up projects in Egypt in the mid-1960s, he moved to Lebanon for two years, even though he dislikes working abroad.

While all Chahine's work shows his awareness of the commercial context, it is also intensely personal. Indeed, as his technical skills have increased, he has allowed more and more of his intimate emotions and attitudes to emerge—in this sense, *Alexandria . . . Why?* and *An Egyptian Story / Hadutha mis-riyya* (1982) are the culmination of his work over thirty years. From the first, he showed an interest in the psychology of the individual, and madness and schizophrenia are a constant feature of his work. At the same time he has shown an increasing concern, firstly to situate these traumas socially and then to attempt the more difficult task of offering an analysis of the interaction of the individual and society. The growth in sophistication from the straightforward social realism of *Cairo Station* to the much more complex (though perhaps less successful) allegory of *The Choice / Al-ikhtiar* (1970) at the beginning of the 1970s is significant in this respect. Although he admitted in 1970 that his politicization had "developed haphazardly," his concern with politics reaching its culmination with *The Sparrow / Al-usfur* (1973) in the early 1970s, this development has not led to the adoption of any abstract theory of society. His films continue to depict a living, contradictory reality: indeed, his latest, and arguably finest, films achieve a quite remarkable fusion of the political and the personal. Because of this sense of growth—of the development, change, and continuity of thought from one film to the next—Chahine's work demands a chronological treatment that relates the films to the social and political changes Egypt has undergone since the 1950s.

Chahine made his feature film making debut in 1950, that is, two years before the overthrow of King Farouk. Despite the social and political disorder of the country, this was a time of expansion for Egyptian cinema, and Chahine was able to work without too many constraints (as he later wryly admitted, "It wasn't at the beginning of my career that I made my worst films, but right in the middle"). Chahine's stance at this time seems to have been essentially apolitical, and his films were concerned largely with individual rather than social problems. He depicts himself in *An Egyptian Story* as having been obsessed with achieving fame abroad and with success on Hollywood's terms. Chahine did draw one lasting value from the Farouk era: the abiding stress on tolerance, so apparent in *Saladin / Al-nasir Salah al-din* and *Alexandria . . . Why?*.

Given his social origins, it was natural for Chahine to welcome the Nasser revolution of 1952, since at first this was essentially a bourgeois nationalist movement without an articulated ideology. In the spirit of national renaissance and renewed patriotism, the film industry flourished and took on a new seriousness. In the 1950s, serious writers such as Naguib Mahfouz (who worked with Chahine on *Jamila, Saladin,* and later, *The Choice*) and the socialist novelist Abderrahman Sharkawi (author of *The Land / Al-ard*) began to involve themselves with cinema for the first time, opening the way for the production of films reflecting the life of ordinary people. The problem for Egyptian intellectuals—Sharkawi apart—was their own lack of knowledge and contact with the peasants who formed three-quarters of the population. Chahine has been very honest about the limitations of his approach. He regards *Black Waters/ Siraa fil mina* (1956) as one of the best of his early films but admits its weaknesses: "For the first time I interested myself in the workers' world. Without understanding their problems, it's true. I really liked them, the workers. I found they were good guys and I wanted to tell a story taking place among them. But there were still many confusions in my mind and it's only later that I've come to see that it wasn't enough just to like the workers." [1]

Analogies can be found between Chahine's celebrated *Cairo Station* (1958) and the work of the neorealists. There is the same sympathy for the poor and oppressed and a like attempt to link personal problems to social conditions. Chahine admits a debt to the Italians: "De Sica and Zavattini, in one sense and without knowing it, helped us enormously since we were able to stress that it was only thanks to neorealism that the Italian cinema had achieved an international reputation." [2] Like *Bicycle Thieves, Cairo Station* was rejected by those whose problems it presented, and Chahine, like De Sica, was attacked in certain film circles for having shown aspects of reality that gave foreign audiences a bad impression of the Arab world. The crucial limitation of both the De Sica–Zavattini team and Chahine at this period is the inability to go beyond mere description of individuals and offer an *analysis* of society as a whole. Symptomatic of this is the concentration on social outcasts rather than on activists. Though one of the leading characters in *Cairo Station* is a trade union organizer, the labor theme is subordinate to the psychological breakdown of the crippled and sexually frustrated newspaper vendor, Kenawi, played with considerable force by Chahine himself. Nevertheless, the frankness of this portrayal is remarkable in the context of Arab cinema of the 1950s and anticipates the openness of the self-revelation of the two late autobiographical works.

The early 1960s in Egypt were marked by two developments: the formulation of the concept of Arab socialism by President Nasser, and Nasser's emer-

79. *Youssef Chahine:* Cairo Station / Bab al-hadid *(Egypt, 1958)*

gence as both a symbol and a leader in the quest for Arab unity. There seems little doubt that, despite his disagreements with Egyptian film censors, Chahine's politicization during the period between the Suez crisis in 1956 and the Six Day War of 1967 took the form of a commitment to Nasser's policies. Peter Mansfield, in his excellent study *The Arabs,* notes that Nasser "raised expectations in the Arabs which neither he nor Egypt could possibly fulfil. He was the new Saladin who would unite all the Arabs to liberate the land of Palestine from the Zionists. But this near great-power role was quite beyond Egypt's strength and ability." [3] Yet this was precisely the image that Chahine's Eastmancolor cinemascope epic *Saladin* (1963)—a film whose direction he took over at short notice—seeks to project. Saladin, charismatically played by Ahmed Mazhur, is the great leader who unites the Arabs and shows magnanimity to the foes he defeats as much by moral superiority as by tactical ingenuity. Chahine stresses that Saladin's army contains Christian as well as Muslim generals and claims that the Muslim faith respects all religions equally. By 1963, though, this equation of Nasser with Saladin was already wishful thinking, since the stresses pulling the Arab states apart were very apparent. Indeed, the film is doubly mystifying in that it is precisely this much-fostered blind allegiance to the seemingly invincible leader that was one of the chief reasons for the traumatic disasters suffered by Egypt and its army in 1967.

The socialist reforms initiated by Nasser from 1961 onward, in which major industries, banks, and insurance companies were nationalized, included moves to reduce the maximum land holding from two hundred to one hundred feddas (a fedda is approximately equal to an acre) and focused attention once more on the problem of the peasants. It apparently took Chahine eight years to set up the production of his masterly rural epic *The Land* (1969), adapted from the novel by Abderrahman Sharkawi. In this film, as in so much realist fictional film making, we are given a story of defeat, framed here by two strikingly contrasted images of hands: the hands of the old peasant tending his delicate young cotton plants in the opening shot, balanced by the same hands clinging desperately to the mature plants as the man is dragged to his death in the very last image. But *The Land* marks a considerable advance on *Cairo Station*. Not only is the technique more assured, the political focus is stronger. Chahine and Sharkawi are treating not marginal figures but a village group able to stand for the overwhelming majority of the Egyptian people. The basic conflict is between the villagers and the arrogant Bey, who deprives them of water for their fields and plans to seize much of their land in order to construct a road to his newly built mansion; it is within the community that the whole range of attitudes and particular interests working against unity is brought out. Nothing is more significant than the distinction the authors draw between the easy unity of the villagers saving a cow that has fallen down a well and the rivalries and squabbles that divide them when their shared water supply is threatened and their latent conflicts of interest as petty landowners emerge. In view of this implicit critique of Nasser's failure to extend his reforms to the nationalization of land, it is not surprising that the novel's setting of 1933 has been retained; nevertheless, the film emerges as of far more than merely historical interest.

The last year of Gamal Abdel Nasser's rule before his death in September 1970 was a difficult one, both for Egypt and for the Arab world. The civil war that had been threatening in Lebanon broke out in Jordan, and Arabs confronted each other in fratricidal strife. The president was a sick man, and his designated successor, Anwar Sadat, lacked his unquestionable authority. New problems and tensions were coming to the surface. It was at this point that Chahine made what is perhaps his most difficult film for Western audiences, *The Choice* (1970), coscripted with Naguib Mahfouz. Yves Thoraval records that Mahfouz's response to the 1967 defeat had been to "shut himself away in a silence broken only by a few symbolic stories,"[4] and certainly *The Choice* is a hermetic work. And although the psychoanalytic aspects of this story of madness and schizophrenia are characteristic of Chahine (the ending of the film in particular recalls *Cairo Station*), even on the level of simple narrative, this story of a cold but successful writer who kills his identical twin brother (who has real contact with ordinary people) and then takes on both their identities simultaneously is both showy and confusing. The symbolic dimension of the story—intended by Chahine as an indictment of the passivity of Egyptian intellectuals in the difficult "no peace, no war" situation following the 1967 defeat—is difficult to unravel, certainly at a single viewing.

The Sparrow (1973) is far more straightforward and successful. Here Chahine, once the ardent Nasserist, takes a lucid look at the reasons for the 1967 defeat at the hands of Israel, finding them not simply in specific errors by Nasser or weaknesses in army tactics but in the very structure of Egyptian society. The film was warmly received outside Egypt: the Algerian newspaper *El-mudjahid* described it as "the first Arab film which politically goes some way towards analysing a situation and determining the objective cause of that situation." [5] The fact that the film—along with another story of the 1967 war, the young Ali Abdel Khalek's *A Song on the Way / Ughniya al al-mamarr* (1972)—was banned for two years by the Sadat government, then at the height of its popularity after the successful 1973 offensive against Israel, is witness enough to the sharpness of the critical light it sheds on recent history and the extent to which Sadat wished to ignore the fundamental weaknesses to which it draws attention. Chahine does, however, shape, and to some extent distort, the historical facts so as to fashion a narrative capable of engaging a mass audience. The corruption and covert sabotage of public projects for private gain thus become a tale of mystery centered on an unseen bandit manipulated by hidden forces who arrange his death when capture seems imminent. Similarly, the initial accounts of the Egyptian army's defeat are omitted from the film for greater dramatic effect, so that the ordinary people of Cairo are shown moving without transition from the euphoria at the propaganda stories of the "great Egyptian victory" to dismay at Nasser's celebrated television speech of 9 July 1967, when he took full responsibility and offered his resignation. In the film's remarkable conclusion, it is an ordinary woman of the people, Baheya, who takes to the streets to lead what becomes a flood of humanity shouting "No!" to the resignation and hence to the acceptance of national defeat. In this way Chahine carefully balances his denunciation of high-level corruption with an affirmation of popular patriotic feeling.

In 1975, the year after the reopening of the Suez Canal, there was a wide gulf between the steadily more radical thinking of Chahine and the policies pursued by Sadat. There could be no question now of another paean of praise in the manner of *Saladin*. Of the situation in 1974, when Chahine began work on *The Return of the Prodigal Son / Awdat al-ibn al-dall* (1976), Peter Mansfield writes: "For the first time in twenty-two years articles appeared in the Egyptian press attacking the Nasserist revolution in all its aspects and even defending the *ancien régime* and the monarchy. There was talk of selling off the nationalized industries to the private sector, dismantling the Arab Socialist Union and restoring political parties. Could de-Nasserization go further than this?" [6] Indeed, one of the most tangible results of Sadat's policies was "the emergence of a new high-spending millionaire class. Some were *nouveaux riches;* others were members of the old régime who had recovered some of

80. *Youssef Chahine:* The Sparrow / Al-usfur *(Egypt / Algeria, 1973)*

their wealth as a result of the desequestration of property seized in Nasser's time. Their conspicuous consumption . . . was an insult to the poverty-stricken Egyptian urban masses." [7]

These nouveaux riches were the very people Chahine had indicted for the debacle of 1967 in *The Sparrow,* and his disillusionment can be clearly read from *The Return of the Prodigal Son,* in which the once idolized radical, Ali, returning home after ten years in prison, disappoints all who knew him with his prevarication and his eventual emergence as a technocrat indifferent to the demands of the workers. Stylistically, this new film needs to be seen against the traditions of Egyptian popular cinema, since Chahine has sought to give it a broad appeal by including songs and dances and a lurid blood-bespattered melodramatic ending (a combination he has termed "musical tragedy"). But the meaning of the film is clear, as all the sympathetic characters (the working-class family, and two students who represent the rising generation) leave for internal exile in Alexandria. Moreover, the framing of the film with shots of a Fellini-esque clown at the beginning and end seems a sign of Chahine's derision, his refusal to accept at its own evaluation of seriousness the bourgeois world he depicts.

After three increasingly bitter looks at contemporary Egyptian society, it is not surprising that Chahine, by nature an eclectic director, should turn his attention elsewhere. A heart attack when he was still in his early fifties led him to question his own life, and the first result was *Alexandria . . . Why?* (1978), his most openly autobiographical film to that date. It is a splendidly fluent picture of a vanished world—Alexandria in 1942, awaiting the arrival of Rommel's troops, who, it is hoped, will finally drive out the British—richly peopled with English soldiers and Egyptian patriots, aristocrats and struggling bourgeois, the enthusiastic young and their corrupt or disillusioned elders. Chahine openly mocks the nationalists (his terrorist patriots are mostly caricatures), leaves the condemnation of Zionism to a Jew, and tells love stories that cross the neatly drawn barriers separating Muslim and Jew, Egyptian aristocrat and English Tommy. The revelation of his own background and a few of his personal obsessions (with the crucified Christ, for example) seems to have released fresh creative powers in Chahine. His technique of intercutting the action with scenes from Hollywood musicals and 1940s newsreel footage from the Imperial War Museum is as successful as it is audacious, and the transitions of mood are brilliantly handled. But, by an irony which Chahine himself does not appreciate, this very personal statement of his belief in a tolerant society came to be seen elsewhere in the Arab world—thanks to the coincidence of its timing—as an opportunistic political

81. Youssef Chahine: Alexandria . . . Why? / Iskandarya . . . leh?
(Egypt / Algeria, 1978)

82. *Youssef Chahine:* An Egyptian Story / Hadutha misriyya *(Egypt, 1982)*

statement, a justification of President Sadat's policy of peace with Israel as formulated in the Camp David agreements.

The autobiographical concerns of *Alexandria . . . Why?* are continued and strengthened in *An Egyptian Story* (1982), a directorial self-revelation within the context of popular cinema to rank with anything by Fellini (especially in the fantasy sequences, which refuse all claims of realism, and in the concept of the artist struggling in a world of women: mother and sister succeeded by wife and daughter). The starting point is Chahine's heart attack—located here during the shooting of *The Sparrow*—and much of the film is a dream-cum-nightmare, acted out under the influence of the anesthetic during his operation in London (prompting oddly disconcerting echoes of Powell and Pressburger's *A Matter of Life and Death*). The full emotional and rhetorical side of Chahine's character is exposed in this self-portrait, in which elements of farce and melodrama abound. Coincidence is used with abandon: the young hero is involved in a riot against Farouk, is seduced by an older married woman, and attends his sister's wedding (which takes place only a day after the death of the groom's mother) all in a mere twenty-four hours or so. The zest with which Chahine recreates his own life is enormously engaging, and it is this lack of inhibition that allows him to fuse the personal story with the portrait of a society in transition, the studio-reconstructed settings of Cannes, London,

83. *Youssef Chahine:* Adieu Bonaparte / Wadaan ya Bonaparte *(France / Egypt, 1985)*

Moscow, and Algiers with the authentic clips from newsreels and Chahine's own earlier films. Above all, the portrait Chahine offers is archetypal of the situation of the Third World film maker: profoundly Egyptian but at the same time conceived in terms of *Hamlet*—to which this film, like *Alexandria . . . Why?*, makes frequent reference. *An Egyptian Story* in fact gives us (together with Ritwik Ghatak's bitter Bengali testimony, *Reason, Debate, and a Tale*) perhaps the fullest self-portrait yet achieved by a Third World film maker.

After two personal stories, Chahine turned his attention to the historical epic with an expensive French-Egyptian coproduction dealing with the French invasion of Egypt, *Adieu Bonaparte / Wadaan ya Bonaparte* (1985). Despite the title, Bonaparte is no more than a pretext, "a pretext to tell of the confrontation between the French imperialism of the time, with all its contradictions, and the unleashing in the Egyptian Arab people of a force to oppose a brutal occupation."[8] The central character is in fact not Bonaparte but Caffarelli (Michel Piccoli), an astrologer who characteristically finds himself caught between French and Arab culture and between his own aristocratic background and the peasants whose living conditions he tries to better.

Chahine's career makes a fascinating contrast with that of his contemporary Satyajit Ray, in that it shows an artist formed and educated under colonialism coming enthusiastically to terms with a postrevolutionary society.

Where Ray's work is characterized by all the distancing devices typical of the classical artist, Youssef Chahine parades his attitudes and enthusiasms with a romantic fervor. Though he has experienced many of the same pressures as Ray, his Egyptian context did not offer him a single tradition within which he might shape his approach to the present. Instead, the very diversity of the social and political developments through which he has lived has fostered an eclectic approach, and his work offers a kaleidoscopic view of a shifting society in which the individual is constantly pulled in diverging directions. Chahine's openness to external events and to his own moods and impulses means that his work is bound to be uneven. His work holds a great lesson, however: that it is possible for the Third World film maker to deal with social and political issues intelligently within the formal narrative structures of a cinema directed toward a mass audience and to combine this commercial concern with a totally personal style.

Le cinéma est, plus que la presse, la force des idées neuves au Brésil: les idées d'indépendance économique, politique et culturelle à l'égard de l'exploitation impérialiste.

Glauber Rocha

The situation of Glauber Rocha, who began his career in Brazil in the 1960s, comprises an interaction of forces and influences very different from those that characterize the work of Ray and Chahine. Both India and Egypt had rich, long-established cultural traditions, which, though variously dislocated or distorted during the years of colonization, had been drawn upon in the late nineteenth and early twentieth centuries to balance the modernizing forces from the West, thereby allowing the creation of a distinctive cultural synthesis. In Brazil, however, no such usable tradition existed. Portuguese colonists had simply brushed aside the existing Indian population, much as the settlers in North America did; but in Brazil, the immigrants created a new and extreme colonial society by importing Negro slaves from Africa—so many, in fact, that at the time of independence in 1822 slaves made up two-thirds of the population.[1] The paradoxes of this situation are spelled out by the Brazilian critic Paulo Emilio Salles Gomes:

> Brazil is a prolongation of the West. . . . The European "colonizer" found the native "colonized" inadequate and opted to create another. The massive importation of Europeans followed by widespread miscegenation assured the creation of a new colonized, although the incompetence of the colonizer aggravated natural adversities. The peculiarities of this process, by which the colonizer created the colonized in his own image, made the colonized, to a certain point, his equal. Psychologically, the colonized and the colonizer do not see themselves in these roles.[2]

The effect was to create a society remarkably homogeneous for so vast a territory: largely Portuguese-speaking and 90 percent Catholic. But this comparative stability, maintained despite massive immigration during the nineteenth century, was achieved only under regressive political structures. The monarchy, under which independence was proclaimed, persisted until 1889, and slavery was retained until 1888, just eight years before the coming of the cinematograph.

The lack of a local tradition that could serve as a "useful past" has had a determining impact on the development of Brazilian culture. The dynamic force of Brazilian literature, as Afrânio Coutinho shows, has been marked by the "struggle between an imported tradition and the search for a new tradition of local or native coinage" and by the "conflict in the relationship between Europe and America."[3] This conflict is not one that can be easily resolved, with the result that each writer has felt himself "obliged to begin from the beginning. . . . He is an exile in his own land."[4] In these circumstances Brazilian literary consciousness took a hundred years to reach maturity, and then only under an impetus derived from abroad: Coutinho singles out the Modern Art Week held in São Paulo in February 1922 as the key shaping impact.

Coutinho's account of the delayed emergence of a national literature in Brazil provides a helpful analogy for developments in cinema, where an authentic voice was likewise achieved only after decades of endeavor. Though Brazil had a continuous tradition of film making from the earliest silent days, the work that had been produced was not of a kind that could, of itself, lead to the emergence of a cinema of international standing. For this, foreign impetus was required and the *cinema novo* of the early 1960s drew on two quite distinct European sources. The first was Italian neorealism, which constituted a major shaping force on the early films of Nelson Pereira dos Santos, beginning with *Rio 40 Degrees / Rio 40 graus* (1955), which Glauber Rocha was later to describe as being "revolutionary in and for Brazilian cinema" and "the first really committed Brazilian film."[5] The second impetus came from developments in France, where the *nouvelle vague* and its attendant polemics were a further source of inspiration for Brazilian film production. The New Wave also provided the methodological tool, which Rocha used for his critical analysis of Brazilian cinema, *Revisão crítica do cinema brasiliero,* in 1963, in the shape of the *politique des auteurs* that the New Wave directors developed to help create a place for themselves within their own national industry.[6]

Glauber Rocha's work contains to the full all the paradoxes and contradictions that such a mixture of sources would imply. As Ismail Xavier has pointed out with specific reference to *Black God, White Devil / Deus e o diabo na terra do sol* (1964), "The film's densely metaphorical style virtually pleads for allegorical interpretation even while its internal organisation frustrates and defies the interpreter searching for a unifying 'key' or implicit 'vision of the world.' And this resistance to interpretation is by no means incidental; it structures the film and constitutes its meaning." [7] The difficulties of interpretation of Rocha's films stem from the constant play of oppositions. Characters tend to be symbolic figures, synthesized from a number of historical and legendary sources. But instead of forming consistent poles within which the narrative can operate, they themselves shift, vary, and even exchange position as the film unfolds. In a remarkable piece of analysis, René Gardies has shown that all of Rocha's first six features can be seen as variations on a single text, the myth of Saint George and the Dragon.[8] But as Randal Johnson notes, "Gardies's analysis would seem to suggest only one side of the coin. St. George himself is often the dragon resurrected and transformed. The difficulty of many of Rocha's films is that images, people, and things are rarely what they appear to be, or, better said, rarely *only* what they appear to be." [9] Constant metamorphosis characterizes the films at all levels: a single character is both God *and* Devil, the ostensible "message" of a film is negated by the manner in which the events are narrated, and so on. Rocha's work is therefore a key example of Third World film making, which, while drawing on Western source elements, inverts and distorts these same elements so as to produce meanings that are radically new. At the same time, the films' stylistic novelty is presented unambiguously as the output of underdeveloped film production structures. Again Ismail Xavier's comments on *Black God, White Devil* offer an insight into Rocha's work as a whole, which "attunes its style to its own conditions of production and thus marks its aesthetic and ideological opposition to the colonizing discourse of the film industry. Its very texture expresses the underdevelopment that conditions the films, transforming its technical precariousness into a source of signification." [10]

Glauber Rocha was born in 1938 in Vitoria da Conquista, in the Brazilian province of Bahia. There he studied law, worked in journalism as a film critic, and became a leading member of the artistically inclined young people of the province, participating in theatrical productions and film club activities. He also made two short black-and-white 35mm films, *The Patio / O patio* and *The Cross in the Plaza / A cruz na praça,* before moving in 1960 to Rio de Janeiro, where he became part of the group around Nelson Pereira dos Santos, whose first features are the most important forerunners of *cinema novo.* This period of the early 1960s—under the presidency of João Goulart, who had been vice-president from 1956 to 1961—was the culmination of a brief period of democracy that had begun in 1945 with the removal from power of the dictator Getulio Vargas. It was a time of optimism; Goulart's period of administration "was marked by the unleashing of popular forces and aspirations. The conservative forces came under threat, since their previous domination began seriously to be checked by successive electoral victories of the politicians and political groups representing the masses. The political conflict thus sharpened. New forms of popular and worker organization emerged at this stage." [11] Within this context, Paulo Emilio Salles Gomes tells us,

84. *Glauber Rocha:* The Turning Wind / Barravento *(Brazil, 1962)*

"*cinema novo* formed part of a broader and more profound current which also expressed itself through popular music, theatre, the social sciences, and literature. This current—composed of individual spirits of luminous maturity and the uninterrupted explosion of young talents—was the most polished cultural expression of a broad historical phenomenon." [12]

Glauber Rocha's role within these developments was crucial. His first feature, *The Turning Wind / Barravento,* made in 1962, marked the beginning of *cinema novo.* Perhaps because it was a project taken over by Rocha at short notice after the production had been set up by another director, it is uncharacteristically straightforward. The film adopts a basically realistic style to document the lives of a group of people normally excluded from the screen—in this case, the fishermen of the remote coastal region of Bahia. In its theme and meticulously composed imagery, the film is comparable with Luchino Visconti's *La terra trema* (a film Rocha had not seen at the time). Both films contain in their titles—Visconti's "quaking earth" and Rocha's "storm"—a reflection of the impact of political awareness on a fishing community as much as a chronicling of natural disaster. *Barravento,* in particular, is a lucid and committed questioning of traditional values. An outsider, Firmino, who has spent years in the city and is sought by the police as a troublemaker, returns to his native village and attempts to activate the fishermen, struggling to break their passivity and combat their fatalistic beliefs. To some extent, despite initial setbacks, he is successful. Though the landlord reveals his power and ruthlessness by depriving the fishermen of the net, their only source of income, when they question his profiteering, the natural leader of the community, Aruan, is eventually provoked into breaking free of the stranglehold of superstition. In the film's final images, Aruan sets off for the city to earn the money that will enable the village to own its own net and so profit by its own labor.

Already in *Barravento,* though the narrative flow forms the central core of the film, the complexity of Rocha's thought is apparent. The struggle of Firmino and Aruan takes on an allegorical meaning, and the use of music and dance lifts the film out of a naturalistic, documentary vein. Firmino is first introduced as a swaggering, dancing figure who stands out in his white city suit, and his encounters with Aruan take the form, not of realistic fights, but of stylized and danced ritual confrontations. Though its didactic political message is clear, the film shows too Rocha's fascination with semipagan religion and with the *macumba* (a dance in which the participants enter a state of trance or possession).

In Rocha's second film, *Black God, White Devil* (1964), released when he was only twenty-five, the links with neorealist cinema are still apparent. For Glauber Rocha, the pull of the rural past is as strong as it was for such urban-educated Italian neorealists as Giuseppe De Santis and Pietro Germi. As De Santis and Germi gave us the myth of southern Italy, its poverty and bandits, its mafia and its great landlords jealous of their privileges, so in Rocha's film we encounter the *sertão* of northeastern Brazil, a desolate scrubland and wilderness of rocks where peasants live in poverty, fear, and superstition. Like De Santis, Rocha absorbed the visual lessons of Eisenstein and Soviet political cinema of the silent era, which color his sense of composition and his cutting style. There is an even closer analogy with Germi's Sicilian films (*In the Name of the Law* and *The Path to Hope*): both directors admire John Ford, and their films embody an epic view of rural life that takes on odd and at times disconcerting echoes of the western. Here, in *Black God, White Devil,* we find the enigmatic Antonio-das-Mortes, the killer of bandits and hireling of church and landlords, a man without a past who strides through the film with the invulnerability of a Clint Eastwood hero. Though the opening of the film would not be out of place in a 1940s realist drama (the cowman Manuel kills

85. *Glauber Rocha:* Black God, White Devil / Deus e o diabo na terra do sol *(Brazil, 1964)*

86. *Glauber Rocha:* Black God, White Devil / Deus e o diabo na terra do sol *(Brazil, 1964)*

the cheating, physically abusive landlord and is from that moment a fugitive from the justice of the rich), Rocha soon shows his stylistic originality. After killing his pursuers, Manuel enters the realm of legend and nightmare with the first of two encounters that together symbolize the apparent range of possibility open to a peasant in revolt against society.

The black prophet Sebastião uses the crucifix as a weapon, to pin an adversary to the ground and to upturn the values of society. He advances like an avenging Christ through the countryside, preaching hatred of the republic and social upheaval—the rich to become poor and the poor to be saved. This aspect of his teaching, the first statement of the reiterated idea of the sea becoming the sertão and the sertão the sea, is the valuable part of his message, outgoing and revolutionary. But it is linked with a mystical element that demands a total submission, involving not only physical hardship but even the sacrificial killing of Manuel's child. Spared by Antonio-das-Mortes, who shoots down Sebastião's followers after Manuel's wife Rosa has herself stabbed Sebastião in her horror at his sacrifice of her child, the couple move on to come face to face with a second figure reacting violently to the backwardness and poverty that surround them. The bandit Corisco kills the poor to spare them from starving and metes out to the rich a justice that consists solely of rape, mutilation, and slow death. Rosa, too, is this time caught up by the message of hate, and she makes love to Corisco, shortly before Antonio arrives to kill him, in a scene of whirling close-ups of faces set to the music of Villa-Lobos, written for cellos and soprano. This scene is perhaps the most striking instance of Rocha's dynamic, operatic approach. After Corisco's death, Manuel plunges blindly across the bare landscape, which in the film's final image dissolves miraculously into the rolling breakers of the sea. The ambiguity of this image (for it is the film maker's vision, not Manuel's subjective viewpoint) indicates both Rocha's strengths as a poet of cinema and his refusal, as a political film maker, of dogmatism. Throughout the film his handling of his material is marvelously assured, and he moves effortlessly from the reportage-style shooting of the film's opening to a richer, more flamboyantly operatic style that allows him to present heroic gestures, legendary figures, and a desolate landscape without ever falling into bathos. Yet the demystification of the past is accompanied by a powerful sense of the force of backwardness. Antonio-das-Mortes destroys Sebastião and Corisco because they distort the truths they partially embody, but it is with their shared mystic vision of the sertão becoming the sea that Rocha ends his film.

Land in Anguish / Terra em transe (1967) marks a new stage in Glauber Rocha's work. After the fishermen of Bahia and the bandits of the Nordeste, he turns to the city and the struggle for political power. Conceived under the impact of the military coup of 1964, which proved the illusory nature of the Brazilian intellectuals' belief in the progress toward revolution, *Land in Anguish* is a work of deliberate chaos, a confusing welter of tumultuous images

87. Glauber Rocha: Antonio-das-Mortes *(Brazil, 1969)*

that reflect the thoughts, memories, and dreams of the hero, Paulo Martins, as he dies after willfully driving through a police roadblock. As Manuel was torn between the Black God and the White Devil, so Paulo veers erratically between the mystic conservatism of his first patron, Diaz, and the empty populism of the pseudorevolutionary leader Vieira. The turmoil of baroque imagery recalls the Eisenstein of *Ivan the Terrible* (especially in the "coronation" of Diaz) as much as the Sternberg of *Scarlet Empress*. Like Sternberg, Rocha scorns the primacy of narrative clarity and puts his faith in violent, expressive imagery, arranged in short sequences joined jaggedly and abruptly. Rocha has clearly put many of his own agonies and aspirations in the figure of the poet-politician Paulo, who is torn not only between Diaz and Vieira, but also between the two women associated with them: the enigmatic Silvia, who offers a delirium of the senses (as in the celebrated orgiastic party scene), and the lucid militant Sara. In the terms in which the film poses the issues, Sara is surely right when she tells Paulo that politics and poetry are incompatible, for he moves only at the level of the rhetoric of the leadership struggle. He is totally cut off from the people, a situation to which he responds by outbursts of furious violence directed toward the people's representatives, who earn his simple-minded contempt by their failure to respond in kind. Up to the moment of his death, Paulo is flailing in a void, lauding and abusing phantoms, turning

88. Glauber Rocha: Antonio-das-Mortes *(Brazil, 1969)*

endlessly into himself for answers that could only come from a direct contact
with reality, with the people.

After the apocalyptic despair of *Land in Anguish, Antonio-das-Mortes / O
dragão da maldade contra o santo guerreiro* (1969) offered suprising optimism and certainty. Returning to the world of *Black God, White Devil,* and
using color for the first time, Rocha complicates the symbolism and reverses
all the values of the earlier film as the myth of St. George's struggle against the
dragon, which in various forms is the poetic thread underlying all Rocha's
work, is here brought to the surface (the director originally called the film *The
Dragon of Evil Against the Warrior Saint*). Antonio-das-Mortes, the killer of
bandits, is now depicted as a true revolutionary force, and the source of all
evil is located in the landowner Horacio, who is usually seen in the company
of Laura, another of Rocha's enigmatically attractive but treacherous female
figures. In this realignment of values, a new importance is given to the forces
brushed aside as reactionary in the earlier films. Antonio still kills the bandit-
figure Coirana but then becomes, in a sense, Coirana's heir in the struggle.
Meanwhile, the "saint" and her followers, who represent primitive religion,
are now seen as positive figures aligned with a Catholic church that is also
depicted as on the side of the revolution. The new positive tone is emphasized
by the use of Orthon Bastos (who played Corisco in *Black God, White Devil*)

in the role of the disillusioned schoolmaster, redeemed from drink—like Dean Martin in *Rio Bravo*—to fight alongside the implacable and invincible Antonio.

Rocha's manifestos of the mid-1960s advocate an "aesthetics of violence" as a reaction to the hunger of Latin America: "Hunger in Latin America is not simply an alarming symptom; it is the essence of our society. Herein lies the tragic originality of *cinema novo* in relation to world cinema. Our originality is our hunger and our greatest misery is that this hunger is felt but not intellectually understood." The film maker's role is to create this understanding:

> *Cinema novo* reveals that violence is normal behaviour for the starving. The violence of a starving man is not a sign of a primitive mentality . . . *Cinema novo* teaches that the aesthetics of violence are revolutionary rather than primitive. The moment of violence is the moment when the colonizer becomes aware of the existence of the colonized. Only when he is confronted with violence can the colonizer understand, through horror, the strength of the culture he exploits.[13]

There is much violence in *Antonio-das-Mortes*—the massacre of the Saint's followers and the final shootout between Antonio and the landowner's hired killers—but the handling of it is always controlled, turning it into ritual. A fine example is the duel between Antonio and Coirana, a sword fight, the two men endlessly circling each other, held together by a pink scarf, an end of which each holds clenched between his teeth. Throughout the film the theatricality is extreme, with all traces of psychological depth removed from the characterization and replaced by a continuous interplay of image and music. There are echoes of American movies as well as of Brechtian drama. Laura and her cowardly lover Mattos sing their planned treachery, and the feats of Antonio are celebrated in the ballads, which have a key unifying function.

Rocha's first four features, all completed in Brazil before he was thirty-one, contain the essential part of his contribution to world cinema. To pretend that his later work in exile and after his return to Brazil has the same value would be to deny the unique beauty and originality of these early films. Though the same themes and stylistic preoccupations recur, the loss of contact with his national roots reduces the later works' power, as is shown by the two films made in 1970 as "a kind of self-criticism" while Rocha was under the direct influence of modernist European film making styles, principally those of Godard and Pasolini. *The Lion Has Seven Heads / Der leone have sept cabecas* was shot in Congo-Brazzaville and draws strength from contact with the African roots of Brazilian culture. Yet Rocha, while responding deeply to the sounds and colors of Africa, has imposed his own schematic allegorical structure on the film. The characters are all types—exploiters, collaborators, revolutionaries—but in most cases a precise meaning of what these characters rep-

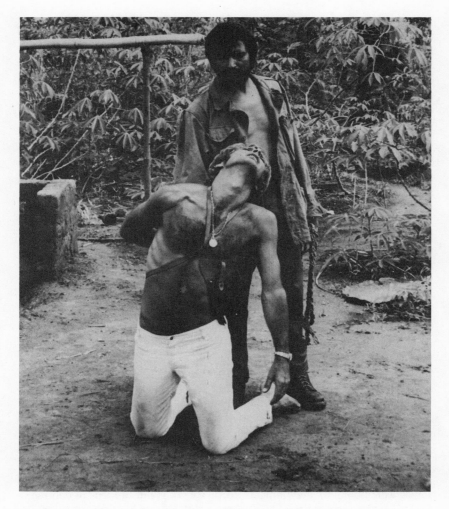

89. *Glauber Rocha:* The Lion Has Seven Heads / Der leone have sept cabecas *(Congo, 1970)*

resent is impossible to discern, and the relationship to political reality is unfathomable. The priest (played by Jean-Pierre Léaud), for example, corresponds to no definable white religious force in black Africa, and the central figure, the voluptuous blonde Marlene (Rada Rassimov), seems a mystifying embodiment of colonialism (though closely related to such earlier enigmatic Rocha figures as Silvia in *Land in Anguish* and Laura in *Antonio-das-Mortes*).

The film is as fragmentary and "ungrammatical" as its title would suggest, shot in long sequence shots during which isolated and largely incomprehensible symbolic actions are performed in interminable real time by characters lacking individualization and depth. The visual and aural richness of certain scenes offers, however, a purely aesthetic pleasure that is largely lacking in the confused and self-contradictory *Severed Heads / Cabezas cortadas,* made in Spain, also in 1972. Despite the efforts of Francisco Rabal as the dying ruler Diaz II and the presence of Pierre Clémenti as the Shepherd (and embodiment of death), the film remains the expression of a purely personal mythology. It never breaks through to real communication with an audience. Nor does it achieve either the surrealist impact of Buñuel or the synthesis of landscape and idea akin to that of Pasolini—to which it clearly aspires.

Rocha's statements at the time show that these two films of 1970 were intended merely as an interlude after a decade marked by a flood of films and projects. Instead they were followed by long years of silence, aborted plans, and failed hopes. In 1975, after completing a *History of Brazil / Historia do Brasil* in Italy, Rocha made his peace with the generals and returned to Brazil, where he completed one last major work, the government-backed *Age of the Earth / Idade da terra* (1980). Despite its length, its dazzling visual style, and its air of visionary authority, this is a deeply flawed work, preaching an unattainable union of Catholicism, revolution, and primitivism through a confusing action symbolically set against the indifferent backdrop of twentieth-century urban Brazil.

At the time of his death in Rio de Janeiro in 1981 at the age of forty-three, Rocha was, it seems, a deeply disillusioned man. But the frustrations of his later years should not be allowed to cloud the dazzling triumphs of the 1960s. Although a full critical reassessment of *cinema novo,* in which Glauber Rocha played such a key role, is beyond the scope of this volume, it is clear that the artistic richness of his work is closely related to the contradictions of the movement as a whole. These contradictions could be contained for a while—as in Rocha's major features—but eventually the wider social and cultural forces were bound to predominate. Rocha's work is thus a focus of contradictory impulses: an innovation denying the "old" cinema but fruitfully rooted in a reinterpretation of Brazil's film history; a national movement drawing its methodology and artistic stance from Europe; a committed cinema modeling itself on the French New Wave, which was at best politically ambiguous (when it was not positively reactionary); a cinema of supposed revolutionary awareness that was surprised and overtaken by an unanticipated series of military coups; a cinema for the people that never found a popular audience; a proclamation of artistic freedom that in fact heralded the purely commercial expansion of Brazilian film production, becoming, in the 1970s, the banner and reflection of the generals' "economic miracle." Paulo Antonio Paranagua is surely correct when he locates the source of these contradictions—for

Rocha as for *cinema novo* as a whole—in class terms: "*Cinema novo* presented itself as a political, revolutionary, popular cinema, while it in fact expressed the contradictions of the radical lower-middle classes, hoping to build a bridge between the disinherited masses and a national bourgeoisie which was entrusted with the task of leading the process of emancipation."[14] Seldom has the paradoxical situation of the innovative Third World film maker been revealed with greater clarity than in Rocha's work and career.

Le cinéma est un art qui a son propre langage, sa propre fonction. Je ne peux faire un film comme un article politique. Ça serait un abandon à la facilité. A l'inverse, ce que je ne peux pas raconter dans mes films, je l'écris dans des textes politiques. Les deux activités que je mène, art et politique, sont complémentaires, il n'y a pas de contradiction.

Yılmaz Güney

The work of Yılmaz Güney has been conditioned by the huge output of the Turkish film industry, which reached its peak of production (approaching three hundred films a year) during the period of Güney's activity as a director (1967–74). Güney himself made clear distinctions between his life and his films, and between film making and political activity, but his life was so dramatic that it is impossible to avoid considering it at least briefly before turning to an analysis of his work.

Of Kurdish descent, Güney was born in 1937, one of seven children of a seasonal worker in the region of Adana:

This South-Eastern part of the country, the great plain of Cukurova watered by the two rivers, the Seyhan and the Ceyhan, not only offers the ideal geographical conditions for a rich and fertile agriculture (it is a centre for cotton), but also, with its staggering demographic growth and climate of everyday violence (almost everyone is involved in some endless story of vendetta and carries a gun), it becomes a microcosm of the tumultuous society in transition that is Turkey today.[1]

Güney wrote poems and stories as a child and supported himself through his university studies by working as a laborer. In Istanbul, friendship with the director Atıf Yılmaz led to his debut as a film actor and scriptwriter in 1958. But

90. Yılmaz Güney, directing The Wall / Le mur *(France, 1983)*

after half a dozen films his career was brought to a temporary halt when, following the military coup of 1960, he was arrested and found guilty of "communist propaganda" in a story he had published at the age of eighteen. On his
release from prison in 1963, having served eighteen months, he immediately
took up his film career once more.

During the late 1960s he appeared in a dozen or so films a year, many of
them made from his own scripts, and he developed a connection with Turkish
film audiences that made him not only a film star in the conventional sense but
also something of a popular myth ("The Ugly King"), in whose sufferings
and ruthless quest for vengeance the poor and oppressed could see their lives
and aspirations reflected. When Güney turned to directing at the end of the
1960s, his first films followed the pattern of his earlier hits; then a new note
was struck by *Hope / Umut* in 1970. Seven films directed by Güney were released in 1971, including *Pain / Acı, Elegy / Ağıt,* and *The Father / Baba,* but
this burst of creativity was cut short by another military coup in 1971. Güney
was one-third of the way through a new film, *The Poor Ones / Zavallılar*
(finished by Atıf Yılmaz in 1975), when he was again imprisoned, this time
for over two years (April 1972–May 1974), on the grounds of "cooperation
with the communists" (in fact, for sheltering students sought by the police).
On his release he completed one of his most interesting films, *The Friend/
Arkadaş* (1974), and he had just begun *Anxiety / Endişe* (subsequently completed by his former assistant, Şerif Gören) when he was involved in a restau-

rant brawl. It seems that provocations by an anti-communist judge dining in the same restaurant as the film crew led to a scene in which guns were drawn by a number of those present, including Güney, and the judge was shot dead. Despite the forensic evidence and the confession of the person who actually fired the shot (Güney's nephew, who subsequently killed himself), Güney was sentenced to twenty-four years in jail, later reduced on appeal to eighteen.

Güney's situation in jail—during the early years at least—was paradoxical. He seems to have enjoyed fairly liberal treatment (to judge by Elia Kazan's account of their meeting, as published in the *New York Times*,[2] and by a German documentary film shot in the island prison of Imrali[3]). He was able to continue writing stories, novels, and scripts, and though the first two films produced from his prison scripts were unremarkable, the subsequent works— *The Herd / Sürü* (1978), *The Enemy / Düşman* (1979), and *The Way / Yol* (1982)—are major achievements. Moreover, he was able to maintain links with the world outside, and his Swiss coproducer on *Yol* records that he was able to contact Güney regularly by telephone from Zurich and to visit him freely when he was in Turkey. *The Herd* was released in parts of Turkey (though it was subsequently withdrawn by the censor), and the script of *Yol* was passed for shooting even though the director, Serif Gören, had himself just completed four months in jail for trade union activities.

At the same time, however, Güney's writings continued to be subject to action by the authorities, who condemned them and added to his sentence. After the military coup in September 1980, which was followed throughout Turkey by severe repression of all known communist sympathizers, Güney's films were banned and his freedom within prison severely curtailed. Finally, in October 1981, Güney made his escape to Switzerland, where he was able to finish postproduction work on *Yol*. He then moved to France, where he was able to make another feature, *The Wall / Le mur* (1983), funded in part by the French Ministry of Culture. But Güney did not take easily to exile, and none of his other projects came to fruition. In September 1984 he died of cancer in Paris, where he was buried. In all, of the twenty-six years since his debut in the film industry, he had spent twelve in jail, two doing military service, and three in exile.

The characteristic quality of Güney's work stems from the combination of elements drawn from the commercial entertainment cinema in which he made his name with his own response to a context that denied him the opportunity for open expression of his growing social concerns. The seventy or eighty films in which Güney appeared before becoming a director (about twenty of them from his own scripts) belonged to the mainstream of Turkish commercial cinema: shot on low budgets, largely on location, in a matter of days rather than weeks. Production was not merely influenced by Italian or Hollywood movies but often aimed squarely at remaking commercial successes: fifteen of the films Güney appeared in were direct imitations of foreign films—

91. Yılmaz Güney: The Hungry Wolves / Aç kurtlar *(Turkey, 1968)*

he played the Marlon Brando role in a reworking of *One-Eyed Jacks* and the Jack Palance role in an imitation of *I Died a Thousand Times,* and he starred in several James Bond–type films.[4] The stress was naturally on action rather than dialog, and plot veered inevitably toward melodrama. The early film *The Hungry Wolves / Aç kurtlar* (1968), his fourth as a director, shows many of the structural weaknesses of this kind of cinema: occasional inconsistencies caused by the inability of the editor to create a coherent geography out of the material shot on location, and confusions deriving from the fact that all scenes occurring in a single place seem to have been shot consecutively on the same day and with identical costumes and lighting, regardless of their position in the narrative. Similar constraints are apparent in *Elegy,* a far superior film made three years later, where the excellent setting of a mountain village virtually obliterated by rockfalls is used over and over again, until its dramatic impact is quite exhausted.

   Though Güney was the author of a number of stories and novels, scripting in this kind of cinema is in no sense a literary activity. As he himself said, "A script for me was hardly more than a pretext for a film. We could set out with the broad outlines of a script, but the film, in the end, is something quite different, and it may be totally different from what we had planned. So I left plenty of room for inspiration and improvisation during the shooting."[5] *The Father,* one of the Güney films released in 1971, shows the limitations of this approach. Though the central idea is striking, Güney found no inspiration for the early scenes of nightclub confrontations among the affluent (which are stilted and clumsily handled), and he then attempted to salvage the film, it would seem, by driving the melodramatic elements to extremes (in the end, the hero, having been offered a whore who turns out to be his own daughter, is shot dead by a gunman who turns out to be his son—and who recognizes him just too late). The counterbalancing strengths of Güney's approach lie in the sheer zest and excitement which he generates in his best work and in the numerous sequences in which the camera is allowed to follow an action without dialog, explanation, or comment: examples include Cabar following the cart that dumps his dead horse in an open field in *Hope*; the row of bandits, all carrying curiously feminine white sunshades, proceeding unawares toward an

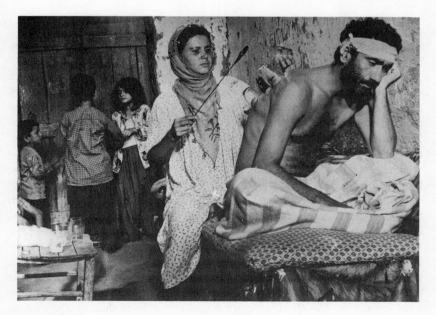

92. *Yılmaz Güney:* Hope / Umut *(Turkey, 1970)*

93. Yılmaz Güney/Atıf Yılmaz: The Poor Ones / Zavallılar *(Turkey, 1971–75)*

ambush in *Elegy;* and the faces of the group of down-and-outs encountered by
the three men just released from prison in *The Poor Ones.*

The choice of setting is also crucial to the impact of Güney's films, which
offer a wealth of varied images of Turkey today: the urban squalor of the bare
rooms inhabited by Cabar and his family in *Hope,* the deserted village
perched beneath the crumbling rocks in *Elegy,* the overcrowded prisons of
The Father and *The Poor Ones* (so much more convincing than the hys-
terically overdrawn prison of *Midnight Express*), the cotton pickers' camp—
which seems like an image from another century—in *Anxiety.* These settings,
however, are neither merely picturesque locales nor simply symbols (though
the crumbling village of *Elegy* is clearly that as well). Much of the dynamism
of Güney's work comes from the interplay of such settings, for his characters,
driven by poverty, are constantly on the move: seeking work in the town (*The
Enemy*) or buried treasure in the country (*Hope*), going to the hills to scratch
a living from smuggling and banditry (*Elegy*) or to the cotton fields to make a
meager living at a rate to be decided by the landowners (*Anxiety*). This theme
of internal emigration is nowhere more forcefully depicted than in the long
train journey in *The Herd,* or more poignantly defined than in *The Father,*
where the hero is so desperate that he can see no difference between spending

ten years in jail for a crime he did not commit and working in exile for ten years as a migrant laborer in Germany.

Crucial to the mass audience cinema in which Güney began his career is the central figure played by Güney himself (he starred in all the Turkish films he directed). Attilâ Dorsay has recorded the degree of audience involvement with Güney's roles in the 1960s: "His films are watched with as much attention and 'respect' as a religious ceremony. The audience is humiliated with him, suffers with him, and when, finally, he decides to revolt, they approve with applause and shouts of joy." [6]

In *The Hungry Wolves,* though the hero dies at the end, he is depicted throughout the film as an invincible figure with almost superhuman powers (the debt to the Clint Eastwood role in Sergio Leone's westerns is evident, emphasized by the imitated—or pirated?—Ennio Morricone musical score). In the later films it is largely through the transformation of the role of this hero that Güney's social concerns are expressed. What remains constant, however, is the role accorded to women, seen as inevitably subservient to men. There are moments in *Hope* where the cab driver and his wife, despite the screaming and blows to which both are driven by the effects of poverty, are depicted with the kind of delicacy characteristic of Satyajit Ray. But in general, Güney's view is harsher and very un-Western. Throughout his work women are stolen and abused, seduced and abandoned, sold, killed, or driven to suicide. To have a woman—as wife or daughter—is to be vulnerable: she will be killed or will betray you, and in either case the called-for response will be violent revenge—the vendetta that runs as an undercurrent through society in all Güney's work. Among the portraits of women, only two stand outside this generalization: the niece in *The Friend,* who is sympathetic and touching though fundamentally useless (as she is told, if you have not worked for a living, you can understand nothing), and the woman doctor in *Elegy.* The latter is the only active woman figure in Güney's work: she has created an independent life in a remote village and takes her own moral decision to help the bandits without telling the police; but even she is depicted as emotionally vulnerable to the forceful bandit leader (played by Güney himself).

In considering Güney's social concerns, it is important to consider the censorship context. Güney's puritanism in his attitude toward women and in his apparent opposition to Western attitudes (a young man is rebuked in *The Friend* for having long hair) is perhaps more explicable if we consider the pseudoliberalism of the then censorship laws. The interpretation of these laws allowed the production and distribution of material calculated to dull and degrade the minds of audiences through blatant sex and violence, but resolutely forbade the expression of left-wing views: "It was impossible for us to express our ideas clearly because of the censorship. We had to create a language which would allow us to communicate with the people, and this language was found. We were engaged in an illegal communication. . . . For example, we could

94. Yılmaz Güney: The Friend / Arkadaş *(Turkey, 1974)*

not say 'Organize yourselves,' but we showed the dead-end of individualism. The ideas which we wanted to transmit to the masses, I expressed in an elliptical way." [7] The bandit films, *The Hungry Wolves* and *Elegy,* are very significant in this sense in that they are both exciting adventure stories and also works that comment on Turkish society through their omissions: the lack of a concerned government bringing help or even defense to the villagers, the non-existence of religion as a positive force, the inability of women to achieve a real participation in life, and the failure of the bandits to offer a way forward beyond instinctive revolt (they remain bound by the retrogressive codes of honor, revenge, and vendetta).

The failure of the individual who acts alone is the uniting thread running through all Güney's features. Perhaps his major achievement as an actor-director is to have made the transition from heroic superman to vulnerable individual—and to have carried his audience with him. The advance that *Elegy* represents, relative to *The Hungry Wolves,* exemplifies this. Whereas the lone bounty hunter of *Hungry Wolves* is still a man invincible to all but an army, the bandit leader of *Elegy* is a demystified hero. His skills, force, and honesty are apparent, but so too are the limitations of his revolt: he has no set of ideas that can hold even his small band together, let alone establish the kind of contact with the peasants that alone can bring real social change. Together, the band can survive for a while; but the negative aspects of their vendetta-ridden code of values inevitably divide them, and they perish alone. Here there is no heroic end for the leader: he is merely gunned down from afar by a peasant excited at the prospect of a reward. In much the same way, the age-old beliefs of the father bring destruction to the family group in *The Herd.* In both *Hope* and *Anxiety,* the hero struggles desperately to obtain the money needed to survive and hold his family together, but in both cases the struggle is individualistic: Cabar, in *Hope,* turns his back on other cab drivers struggling to organize a political response and plunges into the lunatic scheme for hunting treasure, while Cevher, in *Anxiety,* has to break the strike organized by his fellow workers against their joint oppressors. In both cases the end is madness. Güney's world is unremittingly bleak: it is Cabar's best friend who proposes the insane treasure hunt, and the sincere commitment and heroic efforts of the main character in *The Father* to save his family merely trigger disaster for himself and all those he loves.

From a political point of view, *The Friend,* Güney's last completed film before his long imprisonment, is without question his most interesting work. Far from being (as Adrian Turner seems to assume) a mystical work in the manner of Pasolini's *Teorema,*[8] *The Friend* is a lucid analysis of the role of the educated elite in a developing country. The central figure of the friend, played by Güney, meets up with an old childhood acquaintance, Cemil, and goes to stay with him in a luxurious beach resort where the new bourgeoisie (of whom Cemil is a prime example) relax, drink, and fornicate. In the course of the film the friend brings Cemil to see the emptiness and failure of his life, when measured against the friend's own achievement in building roads to remote parts of the country and helping to bring progress and new ideas to the village where they were both born. Cemil commits suicide at the end, and the friend moves on, rejecting too the pampered niece. The film shows the possibility of new forms of social organization in the long discussions the friend has with workers and servants in the resort and with peasants in his home village, at which he preaches the need for discipline and study. Though Güney's most overtly didactic work, *The Friend* is by no means turgid or overly wordy. Moreover, it is no doubt false to attribute to Güney himself the precise sentiments expressed by the character he plays; in any case, there is, perhaps because of censorship problems, a certain ambiguity about the friend's specific message. But although his words to the poor and disorganized are often not

95. Zeki Öten/Yılmaz Güney: The Herd / Sürü *(Turkey, 1978)*

heard at all, there can be no doubt from the expressions on the faces of his listeners that a real communication has occurred and that the seeds of a new future for Turkey exist. Despite its didacticism, the film is shot through with striking images, of which perhaps the most startling and telling is the hallucinatory scene of ordinary workers watching an army convoy pass along the road bordering the resort.

A new stage of Güney's career opened with his arrest and long imprisonment in 1974. The first two scripts written in prison—*Permission / İzin* (directed by Temel Gürsu, 1975) and *One Day Certainly / Bir gün mutlaka* (directed by Bilge Olgaç, also 1975)—resulted in unimportant films, but the following three all achieved an international showing. If *The Enemy* (1979) made little impact (Güney later re-edited it in exile), *The Herd* (1978), which was directed by his friend Zeki Ökten, was a strikingly successful work. This film marked Güney's return in inspiration to the region in which he was born, but the story—of a family of nomadic shepherds destroyed by their contact with modern civilization as they transport a flock of sheep by train to Ankara—is not handled in a realistic, documentary fashion. Instead, Güney and Ökten have chosen to emphasize and stylize the clash of life-styles; their film thus becomes an epic of all rural communities facing the impact of technologically superior forces, rather than a particular, limited, case history.

The central figure in *The Herd* is the son who tries to heal the rifts caused by family vendettas and to adapt to modern society (and to find treatment for his dying wife). Eventually he is destroyed—driven to inarticulate revolt and then promptly beaten and arrested—just as the old patriarch is swallowed up in the anonymity of sprawling present-day Ankara. Through these figures, and by their excellent use of color, landscape, and music, Güney and Ökten have created a uniquely powerful image of the desperate plight of those living on the fringe of development in modern Turkey, and indeed, throughout the Third World. The film is full of striking scenes—not only the splendidly realized train journey itself, but also shots of a tractor remorselessly plowing up the traditional grazing grounds, and the rituals of the nomadic camp, punctuated by bursts of violence and public humiliation generated by the stresses of an authoritarian patriarchal society. Despite the production difficulties, which necessitated shooting on three different color stocks and allowed only a two-to-one shooting ratio, the film has fine visual authority and a well-sustained narrative drive.

Yol (1982)—shot by Şerif Gören just when the prison restrictions surrounding Güney were being tightened, and edited by Güney in Switzerland after his escape from prison—is a fascinating work, dealing with the fate of five prisoners released for a week to visit their families. The film follows in the tradition of *The Herd* and *The Enemy,* and despite Güney's own activities, it is not an overtly political film: it offers no solutions but merely chronicles the contradictions Güney sees in Turkish society. Again, like *The Herd,* it takes the form of a journey, which transports the spectator out of the westernized cities of Turkey and into the countryside, where attitudes are more feudal than modern. The dreams and hopes nourished by the five in prison are set against the grim realities that confront them outside, in a country dominated by the ever-present army, a disciplined twentieth-century force ruling brutally and unfeelingly over a population still animated by traditional patriarchal values and the codes of masculine "honor" that reduce women to objects and justify senseless vendettas and revenge killings. Here the resources of cinema are used to great effect to chronicle lives whose problems are not those of the immediate moment (Turkey after the last military coup) but of a whole historical era. All the characters of *Yol* are caught between the oppressive forces of modernization and feudalism, and although the film touches on such issues as the situation of the Kurdish minority, it is their relationships with women, not their political aims or ambitions, that motivate the five released men. Their backgrounds, courage, and resources vary enormously, and their stories raise a whole series of issues: marriage and sexuality, honor and responsibility, tradition and revolt.

Güney had succeeded in imposing his vision even when prevented from directing his elaborately conceived scripts, and he had managed to retain an essential optimism despite the endless years in prison. But exile was more difficult for him, since he was, as he lamented in his last interview, "cut off from my images, my visual background, and from my human background—a background that is linked to my land, my people, all of my past." [9] Perhaps as a result, the film made in exile in the year before his death, *The Wall* (1983), is a hermetic work. Though he was able to shoot in Turkish and enjoyed substantial French financial backing, Güney was unable to achieve the kind of impact created by *The Herd* and *Yol*. The camera never leaves the vast prison that is its single claustrophobic setting, and there is no relief from the mindless brutality of jail life. All Güney's films reflect the twin evils he saw coexisting in Turkey, capitalism and feudalism, the violence of which "contradicts human love and tenderness," so that "the violence of the social system is reflected in the lives of individuals." [10] But nowhere in his work is this oppressive force so powerful as in *The Wall*, in which there is no room for humor or irony, and hope has no place.

Though the narrative of *The Wall* lacks any directly autobiographical element, the film's overall mood is a clear reflection of its maker's state of mind in exile and hence cannot fail to color our immediate response to the film. Indeed, throughout his career Güney's personal history has served to distort the reception of his films, prompting a directly political reading that, for most of them—with the notable exception of *The Friend,* and perhaps *The Wall*—can be no more than partial. Güney himself never failed to make the distinction between his political activity, which was directed toward revolutionary change, and his film making, which, for him, was first and foremost a way of communicating with a mass audience. In the films he made from prison, as in his last work in exile, his use of the possibilities offered by the fictional feature film for stating and examining in a universally accessible way the contradictions that underlie contemporary Turkish society is exemplary. Despite all the barriers he encountered, there is an essential unity in his work over fifteen difficult years, which he himself defined admirably in his last interview as "a refusal of injustice, a call to resistance, the need for organisation and also the idea that individual liberation does not make sense, that it does not lead anywhere." [11] In Güney's world, only collective action of the kind he was denied the opportunity of depicting under Turkey's repressive censorship laws could lead to real social change.

Je conçois mes films comme des introductions à un univers que nous pouvons transformer.

Ousmane Sembene

Ousmane Sembene's work in Senegal—as both novelist and film maker—offers a rigorous response to the paradoxes of Third World cultural production.[1] The outstanding position occupied by Senegal among the states of West Africa in both novel and film is no doubt attributable in part to the impact of the political and cultural policies adopted by the French in the years preceding independence in 1960. It was in Senegal that the policy of "assimilation" was put into practice more thoroughly than elsewhere in Africa, allowing selected black Africans the full rights of French citizenship on condition that they underwent a totally French educational training (in which, for example, colonialists like Lyautey were the heroes of history and their African opponents no more than misguided rebels). The aim of this policy was to create an elite that would receive its university education in France and then return to the colonies to take over the reins of administration, thus demonstrating the indissolubility of the links with France. Though the system operated fully only in Senegal, the attitudes underlying it were expressed elsewhere in black Africa, and their impact can be felt in the work of a whole range of French-speaking African intellectuals and writers. The impact of these attitudes is particularly noticeable in the case of those film makers who have received their professional training in the West, at the IDHEC in Paris or the Centro Sperimentale in Rome.

Ousmane Sembene's career differentiates itself strongly from this all-too-prevalent pattern of development; indeed, the unique coherence and force of his creative work over thirty years derive from the unbroken links between his upbringing, his social beliefs, and the chosen subject matter of his novels and films. Unlike the supreme example of the "assimilation" system, the poet-

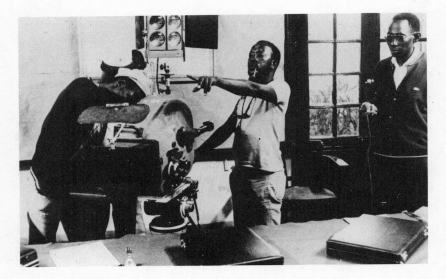

96. Ousmane Sembene (center), directing Xala *(Senegal, 1974)*

president Léopold Sédar Senghor (seventeen years Sembene's senior), the young Sembene was no scholar, and he went to work while still in his teens, first as a garage mechanic and then as a bricklayer. At nineteen he joined the French army—not as a conscript, but to escape hunger the only way he knew how—and served in the ranks in both Africa and Europe. Released after four years, he returned to Dakar in time to participate in the great railway strike of 1947, which forms the subject of his finest novel, *God's Bits of Wood*. Back in France, Sembene worked first at the Citroën factory in Paris and then, for some ten years, on the docks of Marseilles.

A Communist party member since 1950, Sembene played an active part in trade union organization and activity. By the mid-1950s his artistic talents were beginning to bear fruit: after dabbling in painting, he turned to writing, and published his first novel, *Le docker noir,* in 1956. This first work, though still immature and autobiographical, already contains the theme that Gerald Moore sees as central to all his novels: the need for change. It also expresses clearly the crucial dilemma of the black African novelist writing in French (which was ultimately to lead Sembene to turn to the cinema), the difficulty of reaching the audience the writer seeks. As Moore points out, the desire of the hero of *Le docker noir* to write "brings him up against the perpetual dilemma of the artist; the need for isolation and withdrawal in order to create seems at times a betrayal of that very comradeship in suffering which he seeks to celebrate. The generality of dockers do not read novels and cannot hence feel liberated by them."[2] A similar personal theme—in this case, the problems caused by the return to Africa of a young man who wishes to change the society into which he was born—is the subject of Sembene's second novel, *O pays, mon beau peuple!* (1957). But with his two major novels of the early 1960s—*God's Bits of Wood / Les bouts de bois de Dieu* (1960) and *L'harmattan* (1964)—Sembene gets beyond the limitations of the personal perspective. A key element in this progression (echoed later in the films) is the discovery of the female protagonist, that is, of the key role women play in changing society.

Sembene's published works of the 1960s and 1970s—the collection of stories *Tribal Scars / Voltaïque* (1962) and the short novels *The Money Order / Le mandat* (1965), *White Genesis / Vehi ciosane ou blanche-genèse* (1965), and *Xala* (1974)—all relate closely to his work in the cinema, being drafts or novelizations of themes and stories expressed in his films. Yet the appearance of *The Last of the Empire / Le dernier de l'empire* (1981), a satirical portrait of the African ruling class of politicians, shows that he has not abandoned the novel and that his status as a literary pioneer should not be underestimated. His originality can be measured by setting his work against the overall pattern of African fictional writing prior to independence. Then, as Claude Wauthier notes, "the meeting of two civilisations, the European and the African, the shock it caused both to the individual and to the society, narrated in the form of a semi-biography or a village chronicle, had been the favourite subject of African novelists."[3] These novelists "had begun by creating in their own image characters who set out, like Goethe's Wilhelm Meister, in search of knowledge." By contrast, in a work like *God's Bits of Wood,* which Moore characterizes as "the first epic novel to emerge in Africa," Sembene has moved on to work of wider significance. For Moore, his cardinal importance as an artist is that "his work was the first in Africa to move beyond 'protest' (whether satirical or indignant), to show people in the process of changing themselves, under the stress of oppression, into a force which can overthrow it."[4]

Despite this undoubted artistic success, it was perhaps inevitable that Sembene would eventually turn away from the novel. His lucidity as to the limitations of a book culture are shown clearly in *God's Bits of Wood* through the character of N'Deye, who has been to teacher training school:

> She lived in a kind of separate world; the reading she did, the films she saw, made her part of a universe in which her own people had no place, and by the same token she no longer had a place in theirs. . . . N'Deye herself knew far more about Europe than she did about Africa; she had won the prize in geography several times in the years when she was going to school. But she had never read a book by an African author—she was quite sure that they could teach her nothing.[5]

By the early 1960s, Sembene was becoming increasingly frustrated by the failure of his work—written in French and published in Paris—to reach

97. *Ousmane Sembene:* Taw *(Senegal, 1970)*

the mass of the people in his homeland. In Dakar and elsewhere in Africa, the
French language is that of the colonizer or bureaucrat, and his only potential
readers were precisely those members of the new black African elite whose
status he, like Frantz Fanon, most questioned. A scholarship from the USSR
in 1961–62 (when he was approaching the age of forty) took him to the Gorki
studios in Moscow, where he was able to study film making under such distinguished teachers as Mark Donskoi and Sergei Gerasimov. On his return to
Africa in 1963, film making began to take predominance over writing, and as
his confidence grew, he tackled subjects in greater depth and moved away from
reliance on the French language, making his films in such local languages as
Wolof and Diola instead.

But in moving away from literature and toward cinema, Sembene was turning to a medium that was still, in the early 1960s, virtually nonexistent in
black Africa south of the Sahara. Senegal itself had only seventy film theaters
for its three and a half million inhabitants, and there was no organizational
structure that would allow collaboration in film distribution between the various West African states. As Sembene was later to tell an interviewer, it was
easier for him to get his films shown in Paris than in Bamako, capital of neighboring Mali.⁶ Inevitably there was no commercially viable base for production

98. Ousmane Sembene: Black Girl /
La noire de . . . *(Senegal, 1966)*

in black Africa, and Senegal at that time possessed neither laboratories for processing films nor facilities for editing. Even in the field of short film production Sembene had few predecessors in Africa, and much of his energy in the 1960s and 1970s was of necessity devoted to the task of building up the basic structures of an African cinema. His productions are only the more visible aspect of a twenty-year struggle.

Ousmane Sembene's first film project, commissioned by the government of Mali and shot in 1963, was a documentary on the Songhai empire which has never been released. Also in 1963 Sembene completed *Borom sarret,* a highly successful twenty-minute fictional film that tells of the misfortunes of a cart driver in Dakar who is cheated by a client and then has his cart confiscated by the police. Based on an original idea never published in short story form, the film owes much to its well-observed detail and neat characterization. Turning the following year to a story he had written earlier (and which was published as *White Genesis* in 1965), Sembene tried to bring his writing and film making careers into unison. The resulting thirty-five-minute film, *Niaye,* is a complex but little-known work. Shot silent, its black-and-white images are accompanied by a web of stylized voice-over narration, which at some points comments on the action from without and at others addresses the characters directly. Music and newsreel footage are used discreetly in *Niaye,* which, though colored by the moralizing tone common in African cinema at this time, has a greater formal sophistication than either the source novel or any of Sembene's other early films. In contrast, Sembene's only other short film, *Taw,* a study of an unemployed black youth in Dakar shot in color for the National Council of the Church of Christ in 1970, is a simple tale that keeps to a basically realist recording stance.

Meanwhile Sembene had completed *Black Girl / La noire de . . .* (1966), arguably black Africa's first feature-length film. Shot in black-and-white and running to about sixty-five minutes, the film deals with the relationship between Africans and Europeans. It focuses on a young African girl, Diouana, who becomes maid to a French family; at first she is very happy, but then the family moves back to Antibes, taking Diouana with them. Far from being the land of her dreams, France turns out to be a place of utter solitude and exploitation, where she is denied real human contact and loses her personal identity. In despair, she kills herself. Sembene had found the subject in a report in *Nice Matin* and used it as the basis for one of the stories in the collection *Tribal Scars.* Adapting this text to the cinema, Sembene retained the French language of his original narration and dealt with the girl's sufferings by means of internal monologues. This separation of image and sound, inspired by the lack of synchronous sound recording equipment and emphasized by the use of another actress's voice for the monologues, gave the film—like *Niaye*—a superficial modernity, in the lineage of Melville's *Le silence de la mer* and Bresson's *Journal d'un curé de campagne.* In fact, its roots are more in the oral traditions of Africa and it adopts a basically moralizing stance. The film presents its case forcefully and with some nicely observed detail (such as the whites at a dinner party agreeing that "while Senghor's there, we've nothing to worry about . . ."). The clearest indication of the richness of Sembene's later style is the use made of the African mask that figures in the opening and closing images of the film. Purchased from a small boy by Diouana and given as a present to her employers, in Antibes it becomes her sole link with her homeland and the symbol of her degradation. Restored to the small boy at the end, it becomes a symbol of Africa that haunts the previously insensitive husband.

The Money Order / Mandabi (1968) shows a new confidence in the handling of the problems of adaptation, color, and full feature length. The film was financed partly by an advance from the Centre National de la Cinématographie Française, which necessitated that two separate language versions be made, one in French and one in the Wolof version preferred by Sembene. The production problems of the Wolof version point to the difficulty at this time of making specifically African films that use the language of the people. Sembene was working from a literary text written in French and published in 1965 as *Le mandat.* Since he was anxious to keep closely to his preplanned dramatic structure and pattern of dialogue, the Wolof version could

99. Ousmane Sembene: The Money Order / Mandabi *(Senegal, 1968)*

not simply be improvised; yet at the time, Wolof was not a written language, so there was no way of scripting the film except in French. In the end, Sembene had to rewrite his French dialogue using nonstandard French constructions: this approach allowed the actors to translate into Wolof at the moment of shooting.

The film as a whole is a slightly uncomfortable comedy, filmed with the great emphasis on the physicality of the players, particularly the gestures, burps, and grunts of its overweight hero. It recounts the misfortunes and humiliations of Dieng when he tries to cash a check sent him by his nephew in Paris. The style of *Mandabi* is realistic—it was shot on location with a largely nonprofessional cast—and it offers some sharp insights into the contradictions of Dakar society. Dieng himself, although pompous, conservative, and authoritarian, is nonetheless manipulated and maneuvered by his two wives. The tight little world in which he lives, where a check for a few pounds is a fortune, has its own petty greed and jealousy, but these weaknesses are far outweighed by the unfeeling arrogance and rapacity of a whole range of officials and businessmen, whose use of French indicates their distance from the people. Though *Mandabi* ends with a muted plea for change (muffled because of technical difficulties at the moment of shooting), it is a richly colored social study rather than a work of overtly political intent.

Emitai (1972) is set during World War II among the Diola people of the Casamance region of Senegal, where Sembene spent his childhood and worked as a fisherman while still a boy. It is a story of resistance by the peasant people of a small village to the French authorities, who have sent troops to requisition the community's vital harvest of rice and to enlist (by force if necessary) its young men. Sembene's handling of this subject avoids both false heroics and the psychologizing that would be typical of a Western approach (he does not, for example, deal with the —presumed—inner tensions of the young sergeant sent back as a colonial oppressor to his home village). Sembene's attitude toward the fetishist beliefs of the villagers is also significant: though himself a Marxist and atheist, he treats these beliefs with respect, without either romanticizing them (after the manner of Négritude) or reducing them simply to picturesque examples of primitive folklore. Instead, he traces a double pattern of reaction to oppression within the village: while the chief and the old men consult the tribal gods, prevaricate, and finally capitulate, the women of the village lead the resistance, hide the rice, and confront the French. When the elders are forced to surrender the rice, the women's attitude drives some of the men to attempt a stand against their oppressors, but to no avail—in the film's final images they are ruthlessly shot down. Once again, Sembene filmed on location, in a local language, with a largely nonprofessional cast; this time, though, he was working from an original script. The result is a work that lacks the tight dramatic unity and flow of *Mandabi* but that gets beyond a simple recording of African life to achieve a sharper critical insight into both traditional African culture and French colonial practice.

In *Xala* (1974), which also appeared in novel form the same year, Sembene's attention is turned to the neocolonialist era. Though this bitter satire is set in an unnamed African state, its relevance to Senegal is clear, and the film suffered eleven separate cuts before its release in Dakar was permitted. Here, Sembene moves away from surface realism: the film opens with a symbolic sequence of the takeover of power by the new black bourgeoisie. The central figure of the film, El Hadj Abou Kader, forms part of this new ruling group

100. Ousmane Sembene: Xala *(Senegal, 1974)*

and as the action opens is about to celebrate his affluence by marrying a third wife (younger than his daughter). But on his wedding night he is afflicted by *xala* (temporary sexual impotence), and his obsession with curing it finally brings financial ruin, the breakup of his new marriage, and his expulsion from the ruling elite.

Sembene's picture of the black bourgeoisie in *Xala* is harsh—he castigates its airs and pretensions, its corruption, and its misuse of privilege. The film also contains several marvelous moments of cultural confusion: Kader washes his limousine with imported mineral water and pays for his witch doctor's services by check; he sees himself as having an inalienable right to rule, yet his replacement on the council is a common pickpocket risen to affluence. As in *Mandabi,* the use of language—Wolof or French—is a measure of a character's complicity in the neocolonialist system. Against its gallery of corrupt officials, the film sets not an urban working population but a group of beggars, who collectively represent the people. The beggars, harassed by Kader when he is in power, take a fearful revenge in the film's ferocious Buñuelesque climax, when the hapless merchant is forced to strip and submit to the jeers and spitting of the beggars as a price for the lifting of the xala. Sembene does not offer easy answers, but his film is one that could not fail to make a forceful impression on the African mass audience toward which it was directed.

Ceddo (1977) marks a new departure in Sembene's work: it is a look at Africa's historical past, not in one particular time and place, but in an unspecified area of black Africa (though Wolof is spoken) and at a time that can be dated no more precisely than the eighteenth and nineteenth centuries. The film, structured as an allegory and deeply rooted in traditional culture and practice, deals with African response to alien intrusion. Though the characters include a Catholic priest and a European slave trader, the main emphasis is on the impact of Islam, in the person of an imam who eventually kills and supplants the king and imposes religious conversion on the people. As always, Sembene is anxious to avoid placing the blame for Africa's problems on anyone except the Africans themselves. As he told an interviewer at the time of the film's showing at Cannes in 1977: "Of course the West is responsible for much, but there is another kind of responsibility on the part of the blacks themselves, their involvement in the slave trade, cooperation with the colonialists on the part of tribal leaders." [7]

In the exemplary narrative of the film, then, focus is placed on the *ceddo*—the outsider who refuses to accept conversion and subordination, and who triggers the film's action by kidnaping the king's daughter. Though he is

101. Ousmane Sembene: Ceddo *(Senegal, 1977)*

eventually slain, the ceddo's spirit of revolt lives on in the princess, who on her return to her people kills the imam. This subject could hardly fail to be controversial in Senegal, where 70 percent of the people are Muslim, and almost inevitably the response of the government (which had supplied a substantial credit to the production) was to ban the film. The character of the princess—for Sembene, "the incarnation of modern Africa"—was also bound to provoke hostility, but it is in line with the film maker's reiterated belief (constant since his days as a novelist) that "there can be no development in Africa if women are left out of account." *Ceddo* is arguably Sembene's major film to date. In its stylization of action (as in the theatricalization of the confrontations of the king or the imam with the people) and its synthesis of several centuries of struggle, the film has certain similarities with the work of Pier Paolo Pasolini at the time of *Oedipus Rex* and *Medea*. But *Ceddo* is in no way derivative, and certainly, of all Sembene's films, it is the freest from literary form and influence. It is, rather, clearly patterned as an interplay of image and music (the sound track by Manu Dibango is remarkable): the rhythm is slow but perfectly judged and the film does full justice to its subject and to the traditional practices it depicts—though there is, of course, never a hint that a return to tribal culture would be either possible or desirable.

Ousmane Sembene's career as a film maker came to a temporary halt in 1977, and for many years he has been seeking backing for his long-planned, highly ambitious two-part study of the Almany Samori Touré, one of the leaders who put up the most stubborn resistance to the French imperialist forces at the end of the nineteenth century. His progress as a film maker from *Borom sarret* to *Ceddo* is nevertheless exemplary in its consistency and rigor. Though he never repeats himself in terms of theme or style, the films are unmistakably the work of a single creative personality confronting the full complexities of modern African life. From the very first he showed an innovative approach to the possibilities of working with tiny budgets that did not even allow synchronous sound recording. Yet despite such limitations, Sembene's early black-and-white films—*Borom sarret, Niaye,* and *La noire de . . .*—show considerable fluency and narrative ingenuity. Subsequently, Sembene moved on to a style of realist reconstruction of the surface of life that is very much akin to the practices of the Italian neorealists. Like the work of De Sica, *Mandabi* is essentially a social statement that limits itself to exposing the uncaring face of officialdom and the limitations of an isolated traditionalist (such as Dieng) faced with the need to conceive of social change. Certain literary influences are still apparent in *Mandabi*—a tightly scripted, well-made film—but in the 1970s Sembene's work has freed itself from such constraints, becoming more fluent and inventive while at the same time growing increasingly abrasive (as the difficulties he has experienced with the authorities show). Though the cinema has, in industrial terms, scarcely advanced at all over the past twenty years in black Africa, it has certainly advanced in

Ousmane Sembene, a progressive film maker who acknowledges the enormity of the problems to be faced and brings a keen critical sense to contemporary society. Against all the odds, Sembene refuses to be anything but determinedly optimistic about the future and constantly meets the challenge of finding new formal means to express his evolving concerns.

Revolutionary art will always be distinguished by what it shows of a people's way of being, and of the spirit of popular culture which embraces whole communities of people, with their own particular ways of thinking, of conceiving reality and of loving life. . . . By observing and incorporating popular culture we will be able to develop fully the language of liberating art.

Jorge Sanjinés

The English historian of Latin America, George Pendle, has written that visitors to the high plateau of Bolivia, the Altiplano, "are apt to feel oppressed by the mournfulness of the scenery. Bolivia's history, likewise, has been sad, and the prospects for the mass of the people . . . have often seemed almost hopeless." [1] A comparatively large but backward country, with some six million inhabitants occupying about 424,000 square miles, Bolivia was a Spanish colony from 1538 until the successful war of independence in 1825. Some 60 percent of its population is Indian, principally Aymara and Quechua, with 30 percent mestizo (mixed Spanish and Indian), and a mere 10 percent of pure Spanish descent. Despite social changes, illiteracy remains high, and the great bulk of the people are engaged in subsistence agriculture. Bolivia's principal natural resource is its minerals—it is one of the world's largest producers of tin—and some 65 percent of its exports are produced by the tiny portion of the population (3 percent) engaged in tin mining. Though the country takes its name from the great Latin American liberator Simón Bolívar, its political history since 1825 has been almost continuously disastrous, with absolutely no government stability. Bolivia has emerged as the loser from all the wars it has waged against its neighbors, and as a result its territory has been greatly reduced in extent: it was forced to cede its Pacific coastline to Chile after the war

102. Jorge Sanjinés (right, in dark glasses), directing The Courage of the People / El coraje del pueblo *(Bolivia, 1971)*

of 1879–83 and areas of the north to Brazil in 1903, and it lost further territory to Paraguay following an ill-fated push toward the Atlantic in the Chaco war of 1932–35.

Surprisingly, the 1952 coup—apparently the 179th in the country's short history—was one of the few genuine social revolutions of Latin America, as the Nationalist Revolutionary Movement (MNR), backed by the politically well organized tin miners, overthrew the military regime and allowed Paz Estenssoro, whom the people had elected president a year earlier, to return to the country following six years of exile in Argentina. The Paz Estenssoro government carried out wide reforms: the nationalization of the tin mines (80 percent of which were owned by just three companies, all controlled by absentee "tin barons"); the introduction of universal suffrage; land reforms; and steps to curb military power and influence. The weakness of this program lay in the fact that it was initiated from above and was not the product of viable *popular* movement for social change. The gaps thus remained: between the educated elite and the mass of the population and, more crucially still perhaps, between the highly politicized tin miners and the more tradition-minded peasantry. While Paz Estenssoro's achievements should not be underestimated, the willingness of the United States to develop an extensive aid program for his government indicates clearly the limitations of his reforms in practice, as opposed to the way they figured in presidential rhetoric. The contradictions of this U.S. aid program forms one of the principal themes of Jorge Sanjinés's work.

Although Paz Estenssoro proved himself an increasingly autocratic president, for twelve years Bolivia did enjoy a democratic government, and it was during this period that Sanjinés began his career. Born in 1936, Sanjinés studied philosophy at the Catholic University of Chile from 1958 to 1960, simultaneously following courses at the university's film institute. On his return to Bolivia, Sanjinés joined up with the writer Oscar Soria, and together they struggled to begin a film making industry. The lack of development in Bolivia as a whole was clearly reflected in the history of its cinema up to this point. The first films had been shown—and theaters established—in the early 1900s, and there were even some primitive documentaries shot around 1913. Though a first feature was completed in 1925, the first Bolivian sound film was not made until 1936. Subsequently, no more than a handful of features was produced, and no film industry was established. Indeed, there was no base for such an industry: film stock, rated among the luxury goods, was highly taxed, and no government help or support was forthcoming for film makers. Since no laboratories for processing film existed in Bolivia, all processing work had to be done abroad. This state of affairs was to be disastrous for Sanjinés in 1970, when the entire negative of a feature film, *The Paths of Death / Caminos de la muerte*, was mysteriously lost in a German laboratory.

In the early 1960s, Sanjinés and Soria began with two commissioned shorts, *Dreams and Realities / Sueños y realidades* (1961), for the national lottery, and *One Day, Paulino / Un dia, Paulino* (1963), made to mark the MNR's ten-year development plan. Then, together with Ricardo Rada, the pair were able to make their first independent short, the ten-minute *Revolution! / ¡Revolución!* (1963). The Bolivian critic Alfonso Gumucio-Dagron describes the film as "an x-ray of underdevelopment and a testimony on class struggle. In the first part it tells what poverty, infant mortality, unemployment, hunger, etc. are. In the second the people rise up in arms against the army of the dominant classes. The work was conceived as a call to struggle, an instrument for stirring up the people, a piece of 'agit-prop.'" [2] This celebration of the 1952 revolution won a prize at the Leipzig Festival in 1964, and the following year Sanjinés was invited to head the newly reopened Bolivian Film Institute. The years 1966 to 1971, during which Sanjinés made his Bolivian feature films, were a period during which the government was increasingly at the mercy of the military, as a succession of rightist generals jostled for power in a regular rhythm of coup and countercoup. The period was also one of failed revolutionary hopes, of which the most sensational and disastrous was that of Che Guevara, who, in 1967, attempted to repeat the success of the

Cuban Revolution in the mountains of Bolivia. But real contact with the Indians was never achieved, and the isolation of the small band of some fifty guerrillas, leading to the killing of Che, was comparatively easy for the Bolivian army and its CIA advisors. The same year, 1967, also saw, on 24 June, the "Night of San Juan," the brutal massacre of over a hundred people at the Siglo XX mining camp, one of the most savage acts of repression against the most militant sector of the community, the tin miners, that even Bolivia had known. This incident, too, was later to form the subject of one of Sanjinés's films.

During 1965–66, while director of the Bolivian Film Institute, Sanjinés was responsible for the production of twenty-seven newsreels, four documentaries, and a medium-length film, *Aysa* (1965), set in one of the mining communities of the Altiplano, all of which were occupied by the military by the time the film was ready for release. He also made his first feature, *Ukamau* (1966), a fictional tale made in one of the principal Indian languages, Aymara, telling of the murder of a young Indian woman and of her husband's long search for revenge. Sanjinés's response to the mixed reception of this film and the uneven impact of some of the stylistic experiments he had undertaken formed the basis of the intensive theorization of revolutionary cinema he undertook in the late 1960s and 1970s.

When the Film Institute was closed in 1966, Sanjinés, together with his close friends Oscar Soria and Ricardo Rada, formed the Ukamau collective; they were soon joined by Antonio Eguino (who, after acting as lighting cameraman for Sanjinés, went on to become a notable director in his own right in the 1970s). In all, the collective shot three features: the ill-fated *Paths of Death,* which was lost in a German laboratory; *Blood of the Condor / Yawar mallku* (1969), made in Quechua; and their best-known work, *The Courage of the People / El coraje del pueblo* (1971), made with funding from the Italian television company RAI. This last film, which dealt with the Night of San Juan massacre, was never released in Bolivia, since its completion coincided with the 1971 military coup that brought the brutally repressive Gen. Hugo Banzer Suárez to power. Sanjinés and Rada, in Italy completing postproduction work when the coup occurred, felt compelled to remain abroad. Despite this setback, however, Sanjinés was able to make two further films for and about the Latin American Indians in the 1970s, *The Principal Enemy / El enemigo principal* (1973, in Peru) and *Get Out of Here! / ¡Fuera de aquí!* (1977, in Ecuador). Popular opposition to the Banzer regime led in 1978 to a two-year period that was "one of the most confusing and turbulent in Bolivian history. Twenty-four months dedicated to the establishment of constitutional government saw no less than three elections, six presidents, three coups that succeeded and twice as many that failed to get off the ground, a notable worsening of the economic crisis and increasing polarization between the forces of left and right."[3] Sanjinés was able to return to Bolivia during this period to begin work on a new film, and the whole of his output to date was screened for the first time at the Bolivian Film Institute, except *The Courage of the People,* which, although public interest was great, was considered to be too powerful and was promptly banned by the military authorities. On 17 July 1980, this brief respite came to an end with a fresh coup, outstandingly brutal even by Bolivian standards, which brought Gen. Luis García Meza to power. Once again Sanjinés was forced into exile, and several years passed before he was able to return.

As Sanjinés himself makes clear, the concept of utility is fundamental to his work: he aims "to assist liberation struggles in Latin America."[4] All the feature film work of the Ukamau group has been submitted by its members to rigorous self-criticism, and their conclusions have resulted in fresh insights into the requirements of a cinema that is made for, as well as about, the people and that attempts to develop awareness as well as to entertain.

Though the aims of Sanjinés are different from those of the other film makers we have considered here, his starting point is in many ways similar, since he too belongs to a generation that was wholly oriented toward the United States. He was educated in a school where English was compulsory from the primary grades, and most of his classmates went to study in the United States. The effect of such an education is exemplified by Antonio Eguino, the cameraman on *Blood of the Condor* and *The Courage of the People,* who spent ten years in the United States and who, "when he came back, was almost a yankee in his thinking."[5] There was therefore a huge gulf between Sanjinés and the subject of his first feature, *Ukamau,* which depicted the clash of Indian and mestizo cultures, represented in the murder of an Indian wife by a mestizo villain, who is hunted down and killed by the husband. The gulf is apparent in the detached tone with which Sanjinés talks about this work, which

> shows the particular conflict of the Indian, his culture being constantly threatened from all sides by Western culture, by the *mestizos* who represent Western culture in a debased form. It can be seen that the Indian has a much more profound relationship with nature than the *mestizo* has with his own reality, because the *mestizo* is in fact preoccupied with flight from reality, whereas the Indian, with all the material primitivism of his way of life, with all his technical underdevelopment, "adheres" in a more authentic and human way to nature.[6]

It is interesting to note too that this film produced the very same sense of humiliation among the Bolivian elite as that which Paulo Emilio Salles Gomes sees as characteristic of Brazilian intellectuals faced with their own national culture. At the end of a screening at the Paris Cinémathèque, the Bolivian ambassador approached Sanjinés and whispered, "I am ashamed. Everyone will think we are just a race of Indians."[7]

The preoccupations of this first feature were developed further in *Blood of*

103. Jorge Sanjinés: Blood of the Condor / Yawar mallku *(Bolivia, 1969)*

the Condor, which is aggressively prefaced by two captions implicitly equating the racist views of Martin Boormann with those of U.S. government officials. The film combines a number of themes: the relationship between the Indians and the mestizo officials and police; the ruinous impact of U.S. Peace Corps workers, who bring alien values (and covert sterilization) to the Altiplano; the gulf between even the urbanized Indians and the wealthy bourgeois elite whose children are brought up to speak English. Like Sembene filming the animist rituals of the elders in *Emitai,* Sanjinés shows respect for the belief systems of the Indians, particularly the rituals by which the soothsayer uses cola leaves to uncover the truth about puzzling realities. *Blood of the Condor,* rooted as it is in actual events of 1960s Bolivia, is a story that depicts many defeats. The village headman, Ignacio, loses his three children and finds that his wife, Paulina, has been sterilized without her knowledge. When he raises a protest, he is shot down and left for dead by the police. Though his wife gets him to a hospital in La Paz and his brother Sixto seeks to help him, they cannot afford the blood for an urgently needed transfusion (it costs 350 pesos, when 200 pesos is a monthly wage). Although Ignacio dies, Sanjinés is not content with chronicling defeat, and he ends with two "victories": Sixto, who was first seen denying his Indian identity, returns to the Al-

104. Jorge Sanjinés: Blood of the Condor / Yawa mallku *(Bolivia, 1969)*

tiplano to take his dead brother's place; and, in a scene without basis in historical reality, the peasants seize and castrate the gringos who have sterilized their
women. The film's final image is of a mass of rifles raised on high.

Blood of the Condor sets the stylistic pattern of image-sound relationships
for the later films shot in exile. Filmed in black-and-white with a very mobile
handheld camera, it comprises a series of bleakly austere images that give a
powerful sense of physical toil. The shooting of the Indian ceremonials avoids
all trace of touristic folklore, and no humor is allowed to lighten the tone. The
visual style, backed up by sparse flute and drum music, makes great use of
held long-shot compositions, with montage effects (reminiscent at times of
Soviet revolutionary cinema) and distortions at moments of climax. The film's
narrative pattern is surprisingly complex, using flashbacks to illuminate previously shown events and constantly intercutting between Sixto's search for a
way to obtain blood in La Paz (neither he nor Paulina has the right blood
group) with Ignacio's earlier actions in the Altiplano. The Ukamau group was
able to choose this style because of the way they planned to take the film to the
people. As Sanjinés explained to an interviewer in 1970, "For the screenings
of *Yawar mallku* in the country regions we shall have a narrator present the
film who will first tell the story of the film and show photographs of the char-

acters, so carrying on the still-living tradition of the travelling storyteller which dates back to Inca times. After the screening we will talk with the people and then show the film again." [8]

Blood of the Condor was remarkably successful in several ways. Firstly, it reached a large audience—Sanjinés estimates that it was seen by 250,000 in Bolivia alone (equivalent to more than half the population of the capital, La Paz). It also contributed to change, in that the publicity it gave to the problems caused by the activities of the U.S. Peace Corps was certainly a factor in the government's decision to expel the Corps in 1971. But Sanjinés discovered that the impact of the film was limited to the urban petty bourgeoisie:

> When we showed it in the countryside to the Indians themselves, we realised that it did not communicate a great deal. It was not enough that the film was spoken in Quechua, that all the actors were peasants and that it took their side. . . . It was not that they could not understand what was being said; it was rather a formal conflict at the level of the medium itself which did not correspond to the internal rhythms of our people or their profound conception of reality. [9]

The lessons learned from *Blood of the Condor* helped shape the Ukamau group's next project, *The Courage of the People,* which, though shot in color and funded by the Italian television company RAI, shows no diminution of revolutionary fervor and commitment. The expression of this was possible thanks to the particular political circumstances of the period in which the film was shot: "The ten months of Torres' regime, from October 1970 to August 1971, was a period of perpetual crisis and extensive popular mobilization, and virtually devoid of effective government. Torres, although he occupied the residential *Palacio Quemado,* lacked real power." [10] Though he allowed right-wingers to occupy key military posts, General Torres also tried to placate the workers by raising miners' wages and embarking on a program of nationalization of foreign-owned mines—but he found himself unable to restrain the students and the parties of the left. It is this mood of popular militancy that *The Courage of the People* captures so well.

One of the lessons of *Blood of the Condor* was the potential power the authentic document and direct, firsthand testimony have. *The Courage of the People* marks a move away from the fictionalization of real situations and toward the reenactment of events by the surviving participants. The film opens with a long scene of striking miners and their families marching with banners across the desolate, windswept Altiplano—straight into an army ambush in which dozens are killed. There follows a sequence in which graphics, photographs, and newspaper clippings are used to document the successive massacres of miners by the army: December 1942 at Catavi (four hundred dead), January 1949 at Potosi (an unknown number dead), May 1949 at Siglo XX (eighty dead), May 1950 at Villa Vittorio Lapaz (two hundred dead), October

105. Jorge Sanjinés: The Courage of the People / El coraje del pueblo *(Bolivia, 1971)*

1964 at Sora Sora (an unknown number dead), May 1965 in the general occupation of the mines (eight hundred dead), September 1965 at Llallagna (thirty-two dead). In each case, Sanjinés names the political and military leaders responsible, including in one case his erstwhile patron, Paz Estenssoro.

This sequence forms a prelude to the film's central subject, the most recent massacre of miners, at Siglo XX on 24 June 1967, the Night of San Juan. Offering horrifying statistics about the disease and mortality rate in the mining community, the film then draws on the direct testimony of those involved in the 1967 incident, who reenact the events for the camera: the women's hunger strike, the arrest and torture of militants, the arrival of student representatives, the growing solidarity and general air of expectancy, leading to scenes of celebration with bands, bonfires, and songs. But this fiesta occurs within a mine surrounded by troops, and when the latter burst in, the anticipated slaughter takes place. At dawn, the women are left to count the cost in dead and wounded. The style of *The Courage of the People* is fragmentary and elliptical, reflecting a presumed awareness on the part of the audience of the background to the events recounted. There are no individual heroes—the community itself is the focal point, and, as Sanjinés says, the role of the camera team is to become a part of this community, "its instrument of expression, allowing the community to talk about itself through us." [11] This approach gives the film its strength and intensity of commitment but does not allow it to offer a critique of the miners' tactics or of the role of Che Guevara, with whom the miners plan to make contact. This is a celebration of popular struggle: the few militants who escape the slaughter will, we assume, continue the fight, and, after a fresh roll call of those responsible, the film ends with an echo of its opening images of workers displaying solidarity in face of military power. Two days after the film was completed, a fresh coup swept General Torres from power. As General Banzer began his work of repression, *The Courage of the People* was inevitably banned.

Sanjinés and the Ukamau group made two films in exile in the 1970s, *The Principal Enemy*, in Peru, and *Get Out of Here!*, in Ecuador. Both films build on the experience of the earlier films and offer a sharper focus to their political concerns. With these two works, the trajectory from an entertainment with a message made *for* the people (*Ukamau*) to an instrument of political awareness made *with* the people is complete. In *The Principal Enemy,* the action, presented by an old man who talks directly to the audience, has a three-part structure. In the first part, the still-unpoliticized peasants respond to a murder committed by their landlord by handing him over to the authorities for punishment. The result is predictable: the landlord is freed, while the witnesses are

106. Jorge Sanjinés: The Principal Enemy / El enemigo principal *(Peru, 1973)*

themselves imprisoned. In the central part of the film, the peasants come into contact with a guerrilla group that teaches them the lessons of armed struggle, and the landlord is executed after a popular trial. In the concluding part of the film, though, this action provokes a violently repressive response, in which defenseless peasants are thrown over a cliff. The identity of the "principal enemy" is now revealed: U.S. imperialism.

Stylistically, *The Principal Enemy* shows an interesting attempt to get away from the conventions of crosscutting and to rely instead on long-held sequence shots. The film can be accused of a certain schematism (the experiences of Che Guevara in Bolivia show that relations between guerrillas and peasants are not so straightforward as the film proposes), but it is a powerful indictment of the forces maintaining the status quo in Latin America as well as an eloquent incitement to revolt that does not disguise the likely human cost. *Get Out of Here!*, made under great practical and financial difficulties, but again in close collaboration with a rural community, is a similar exemplary tale of peasants struggling to keep their land after rich mineral deposits have been discovered. The film chronicles the ways in which the community is divided by foreign missionaries before being decimated by the hired army of the imperialists, and once more the strength of Sanjinés's respect for the Indian communal spirit is very apparent. Moreover, though given only a noncommercial

107. Jorge Sanjinés: Get Out of Here! / ¡Fuera de aquí! *(Ecuador, 1977)*

release, over the course of five years *Get Out of Here!* was apparently seen by a rural audience measured in the millions—far more than the number of viewers for the most popular "commercial" film in Ecuador.

The films of Sanjinés's exile, too, have been able to perform their intended task of contributing to the political education of the peasants. Like all the work of Sanjinés and the Ukamau group over almost two decades, they offer a striking example of work that moves away from Western models. In redefining cinema's social function and creating both a new mode of production and a new relation to the audience, the key element has been the relationship the film makers established with the Indians, who are both participants in the making of the films and the intended audience of the completed works. For Sanjinés and his colleagues, the contact with this audience was crucial in modifying the film makers' conception of cinema: "The language and objectives have become more defined. The spectators in turn have become creators of our work." [12] The films now reflect not the individualism of a Western-educated elite, but the ways in which the Quechua and Aymara people conceive of themselves:

> The organizing principle of this society is not the isolated individual but society in its totality: it is this society that must be formed collectively. They do not conceive of an individual living above or on the margins of society. This does not mean the negation of the individual; quite the reverse: the equilibrium of collectivity protects him, immunizing him against neuroses. For this reason history is lived collectively; what affects a member of the community affects the whole community both in life and death. [13]

In the work of the Ukamau group we have a rare example of a form of film making based on a radical rethinking of the stylistic pattern of film production that allows totally un-Western ways of seeing society and depicting the inter-relationships of individuals to their group to be expressed in a predominantly Western medium. As such, these films have an enormous practical and theoretical importance, and though Sanjinés's own career has been blocked in the 1980s, the work of the Ukamau group in the 1960s and 1970s remains an exemplary instance of a distinctively Third World cinema.

Conclusion

*The past should not be the object of mere contempla-
tion if the present is to be meaningful. For if the past
were viewed as a "frozen reality" it would either
dominate and immobilize the present or be discarded
as irrelevant to today's concerns.*

Renato Constantino

At the end of the present study of national film industries and individual
achievements still far too little known in the West, it is perhaps worthwhile to
attempt to pull together some of the threads of the argument and to explore
briefly what relevance the survey undertaken here might have for a study of
the worldwide development of cinema.[1] This survey has of necessity been a
general mapping out of the field and as such has inevitably led us into certain
byways. For example, though concern has focused on "developing countries
with a market economy," mention has been made of such Marxist states as
Cuba and Angola, whose cinemas are so obviously relevant to developments
in their strictly Third World neighbors in Latin America and Africa that to
have ignored them totally would have been to falsify the overall picture.
Equally, though the focus has been largely on the fictional feature film as the
key element in any film industry, some mention has been made too of documentary production, since the interrelationship of fiction and documentary is
often too close for neat distinctions to be made, and many interesting and relevant films involve an overlapping and blurring of such categories.

The emphasis throughout has been on the shaping impact of socioeconomic
factors in determining the development of non-Western cinema, and I am only
too aware of the distance this puts between the view of cinema advanced here
and that constructed in and through film theory in the 1970s. As a British
critic has recently lamented, the theoretical gains acquired in the past decade
implied certain losses, most regrettable among which was "any sense of the

305

film text as social object. In order to gain more rigorous insights into their internal workings, texts were wrenched out of history, given autonomy, cast adrift from context into a sea of contradictory interplay which need never be referred back to the historical specificities of the moment of production." [2]

What consideration of any aspect of Third World culture—including cinema—inevitably highlights is the absolute necessity of historical and contextual investigation. A national cinema in an underdeveloped country, like a literature under colonialism, can only be understood if the external shaping forces, and the ways in which individuals and social classes have responded to them, are also appreciated. What seems borne out by the present study is the extent to which it is possible to generalize about developments occurring in geographically disparate societies and over a time-span of several decades—despite the obvious distinctions of particular cultural traditions and the varieties of external pressure and dominance. Third World film making is not some inexplicable or unreachable "other" about which we in the West can have no opinion, but rather it is indissolubly linked to the forms of cinema we have known since childhood. This relation is a two-way one. The most important conclusion I should want to draw from this research is that the need to define Third World film making in relation to Hollywood (its principal external shaping force) calls for a complementary rethinking of Hollywood (and Western cinema in general) in terms of its international identity.

As we have seen, the history of cinema in the non-Western world—in terms of production as well as of distribution and exhibition—long precedes any definition of a distinctive Third World identity. Though we in the West were largely unaware of the fact, film production was flourishing in many parts of the non-Western world by the late 1920s, when India, for example, was already making more films than Great Britain. What is now apparent is the extent to which this production forms part of the common history of world cinema.

In economic analysis, the great contribution of Frank, Wallerstein, and the theorists of the "development of underdevelopment" was to show the inextricable links between metropolis and satellite, core and periphery. Their thesis is amply borne out by experience in cinema, for non-Western film production—like the spread of film exhibition outside the West—does not exist in a void: it is part of the attempt by capital in the periphery to assert itself and to obtain an increasing share of the domestic market. Except for isolated individual coproduction deals (particularly with Western television companies), the capital for film production has generally come from domestic sources; yet the product itself is shaped by the long-ignored factor of Western dominance of distribution. The pioneer film makers outside Europe, Japan, and North America have always worked in a context where foreign films dominate local screens, where local distributors are geared to circulate imported products, and where cinema is given a commercial entertainment function that may well be alien to local traditions. The difficulties experienced in establishing a local production industry are evidenced by the initial quotas established by governments in Mexico and Brazil, which required the showing of just one locally produced film a year by all film theaters. The disparity between Third World producers and the major international distributors is merely the most extreme example of the economic situation prevalent with regard to cinema everywhere outside the United States and underlines the importance of those economic factors so often ignored in Western accounts of film history. Similarly, the very different aims of local producers and distributors call into question the notion of a unified national film industry that is an unquestioned basis for most standard film histories.[3]

Because of our lack of real knowledge of developments in world cinema outside the West, there is a temptation to apply simple but unhistorical labels. Care needs to be taken in how we describe the various huge national cinemas that began to emerge in the 1930s and 1940s in various parts of Asia and Latin America, and that continue to be a feature of the "newly developing countries" of the 1970s and 1980s. These national cinemas are all as much a part of the world capitalist system as are those of Western Europe: all are financed by local capital impressed by the profitability of Hollywood and wishing to compete with it, and virtually all have modeled themselves on Hollywood's mode of production, concept of stardom, genre categorization, and style of publicity. Because of the unique degree of dominance exercised over world cinema by Hollywood, Third World national cinemas are likely to have needed strong government support to back up the linguistic barriers that have allowed them to come into existence in the first place, but they are rarely the direct expression of the state. Indeed, film makers working within such production structures are on occasion able to put forward views diametrically opposed to those of the ruling classes: the classic example is the Communist-inspired production in Kuomintang-dominated Shanghai during the early and mid-1930s. However, the Chinese example shows vividly the extent to which even this production is shaped in large part by Hollywood models, that is, by the films with which the dissenting works have to compete in the domestic marketplace. Generally, in fact, in terms of narrative structure or dramatic rhythm, there is likely to be little that is wholly distinctive or unfamiliar to a Western spectator in a Philippine thriller by Gerardo de Leon or a Mexican melodrama by Emilio Fernandez, and the makers of such films will have worked within production constraints not dissimilar to those experienced by mainstream film directors in the West. In some rare cases, as in India, local producers are able to dominate their own domestic market to such an extent that they can afford to be indifferent to imported films; then, and only then, is there the real possibility of an alternative mode of construction for commercial film making that is as individual and all-embracing in its codes of representation and expression as is, say, the Japanese industry.[4] But even then the cultural dominance of the West is such that the majority of local critics will turn their back on this domestic production, rejecting it *en bloc* in the name of more "mature" models drawn from Hollywood and particularly from Western Europe.

Where investigation of films produced wholly within the commercial system has been made, the result has often been the uncovering of work of real and lasting value. To take a single example, Indian cinema still has many largely unconsidered riches, but in the early 1980s it became possible to appreciate the outstanding talent of the Bengali director Ritwik Ghatak (1925–76), thanks to the efforts of the Indian National Film Development Corporation and a number of Indian critics and theorists.[5] Though Ghatak was to some extent influenced by foreign sources—Soviet silent cinema and Brecht's theorization of theater, for example—his work was done wholly within the traditions of Indian film melodrama. As Satyajit Ray, his exact contemporary, noted in a memorial address, Ghatak's films are entirely free of the influence of foreign cinemas:[6] they owe nothing to the styles of Hollywood or to the neorealism that had so profound an impact on Ray, and, totally rooted in the tradition of Bengali life and culture, they have a genuine strangeness for Western audiences. Ghatak completed only eight features, and the core of his work is a loose trilogy of films, all of which have as their starting point the human disasters caused by the partition of Bengal: *The Hidden Star* / *Meghe dhaka tara* (1960), *E Flat* / *Komal gandhar* (1961), and *Subarnarekha* (1962, released 1965).

At the level of plot events, these films are contemporary tales, but underlying this contemporaneity is a complex allegorical structure relating to the archetypes of Indian mythology in ways that constitute a critique of conventional Indian filmic approaches to myth. In this way, Ghatak strives to create an Indian national cinema—not by turning his back on popular forms, but by bringing the weight of his intellect to bear on them and incorporating them into his own work. Nowhere does he ape Western forms, and there is no sense of awkwardness or unease in his adoption of melodramatic elements or conventional patterns of songs and dances. Indeed, in *The Hidden Star* he deliberately drives the melodramatic situations to extremes, seeking a dramatic force adequate for his involvement regardless of the constraints of good taste. His profound sense of the need for a radically changed society, for a total transformation that cannot be achieved merely at a personal or domestic level, finds its stylistic expression in his emphatic use of close-ups, his dislocated, very un-Hollywoodian cutting, and his stridently exaggerated sound effects. Ghatak was a rebel within the system, and eventually his career was destroyed by alcoholism (though not before he had given one of the most remarkable and harrowing filmic self-portraits of the artist as alcoholic, *Reason, Debate, and a Tale* / *Jukti takko ar gappo* [1974]). Despite his revolt, Ghatak remains integrally a part of the Indian commercial cinema: to wrench his work out of this

108. Ritwik Ghatak: The Hidden Star / Meghe dhaka tara *(India, 1960)*

109. Ritwik Ghatak: Reason, Debate, and a Tale / Jukti takko ar gappo *(India, 1974)*

context would be as artificial as to consider it without reference to the history of his native Bengal.

Though Ghatak's level of achievement is by no means unique, it is of course not typical of non-Western film industries. In general, the industrial model of film making in the non-Western world that predates (or ignores) any concept of a distinctive Third World identity, when it is not merely imitative of the West, is at best parochial. But one of the paradoxes of the Third World situation is that any cultural production that wishes to be "national" in a more profound way—in the case of film, to move beyond the constraints of a production exercising a purely entertainment function in a constricted domestic market—must at the same time be influenced by yet other foreign models. To be aware of one's own Third World identity and the place of one's country in the world system implies a familiarity with the West that can hardly be acquired without education and travel, study of a foreign language or two, and acquaintance with Western thought and culture. None of the theorists of national cultural liberation advocates a simple return to the past. All, while stressing the importance of the people and of indigenous language and history, demand an awareness of modernity that is, in effect, a knowledge of the West. Developments in non-Western cinema since the notion of a Third World identity was born in the mid-1950s have all therefore been linked with developments in the West and form part of a still-unwritten history of world cinema in which Western and non-Western modes of expression are entwined.

In drawing attention to the key role of Italian neorealism as a catalyst in the development of the new styles of Third World film making that began to emerge in the late 1950s, one is not talking of a mere borrowing. Rather, a recognition of the affinity between, say, Satyajit Ray's explorations of Bengali village life and Luchino Visconti's commitment to Sicilian fishermen, or Roberto Rossellini's voyage through a war-ravaged Italy and Nelson Pereira dos Santos's vision of the Brazilian *sertão*, allows us to understand more clearly the nature of European postwar realism. The journey of discovery is simultaneously a journey of self-discovery, a positioning of the educated middle- or upper-class film maker in relation both to a previously unknown reality and to a hitherto unexpressed self. In terms of film history, what is truly significant is not that the Italians led the way, but that in the following decades their explorations found echoes and analogies throughout world cinema. This continuity can in no way be reduced to the level of a European "influence." If the explorations of Sicily and the *mezzogiorno* by Italian Marxist film makers precede by a decade or more those of the Brazilian *nordeste* by the protagonists of *cinema novo*, Ray was achieving world fame with his images of rural Bengal long before the London-based and socially committed heirs of the British Free Cinema were venturing into location-shot films adapted from their own stories by British regional novelists. To make the connection with Third World endeavors as well as with Italian neorealist "models" for British cinema is to begin to understand more clearly the gulf between Karel Reisz or John Schlesinger and their fictional material, and to find a basis on which social and stylistic investigation (into, say, the relation of character and landscape) can be constructed.

When we look at Third World achievements in the 1970s and early 1980s it is, of course, easy to pick out specific instances of direct Western influence—the impact of Robert Bresson on the young graduates of the Indian Film and Television Institute at Pune is a particularly striking example. But in terms of two further tendencies picked out in this study as major contributions of Third World cinema, it is clear that Third World film makers enter world film history on equal terms. Firstly, the theorization of a political cinema by Latin American critics in the late 1960s and early 1970s remains valuable today because it is a theory of film *practice*. As such, it provides a useful counterbalance to Western film theory of the 1970s, which has been well characterized by Dudley Andrew as "a verbal representation of the film complex."[7] This representation does not demand to be measured against some external criteria—the demands of production, for example; rather, it remains "an accumulation of concepts, or, rather, of ideas and attitudes clustered around concepts." Based on "the efficacy and import of *metaphors* about the film phenomenon," the Western discourse of film theory is "destined to remain in this literary world,"[8] whereas the Latin American theorization provides the basis for a whole range of committed and socially effective documentary and fictional film making.

Secondly, the role of Third World film makers in giving voice to peoples excluded from history and to ethnic minorities (or even majorities) normally denied expression—such as the Arabs of Israel or the Quechua Indians of Bolivia—calls into question the status of many Western cinemas as expressions of a *national* culture rather than simply as one-sided reflections of a purely metropolitan culture (be it that of Paris or London). Where, for example, are the films that would give us insight into the regional diversity of rural France? And why was it that the Wolof of Senegal and the Yoruba of Nigeria could find their filmic voice by the mid-1970s, while such "submerged" Western nations as Wales and Scotland had to wait until the 1980s for films in Welsh and Gaelic? To pose such questions is to undertake what seems to me the most urgent task of film history at the present time. Only when film history ceases merely to echo and justify by its inclusions and exclusions the Western commercial dominance of film distribution can it begin to draw attention to the diversity of voices that make up the true richness of cinema as a world phenomenon.

Notes

Part One. The Social, Cultural, and Economic Context

1. *Jump Cut* 27 (July 1982): 14.

Chapter 1. Third World Societies

1. Pierre Jalée, *The Third World in World Economy* (New York: Monthly Review Press, 1969), pp. 3–8.

2. Ibid., pp. ix–x.

3. Albert Memmi, *The Colonizer and the Colonized* (London: Souvenir Press, 1974), pp. 87–88.

4. Ibid., p. 107.

5. Ibid., p. 105.

6. Renato Constantino, *Neocolonial Identity and Counter Consciousness* (London: Merlin Press, 1978), p. 219.

7. Ibid., p. 110.

8. Memmi, *Colonizer and Colonized*, p. 91.

9. Constantino, *Neocolonial Identity*, p. 165.

10. Ibid., p. 36.

11. Memmi, *Colonizer and Colonized*, p. xiv.

12. Frantz Fanon, *Black Skins, White Masks* (New York: Grove Press, 1967), p. 18.

13. Geoffrey Kay, *Development and Underdevelopment: A Marxist Analysis* (London: Macmillan, 1975), p. 55.

14. James M. Petras, "New Perspectives on Imperialism and Social Classes in the Periphery," in *Neo-Marxist Theories of Development*, ed. Peter Limqueco and Bruce McFarlane, pp. 204–20 (London: Croom Helm, 1983).

15. Abdallah Laroui, *La crise des intellectuels arabes: Traditionalisme ou historicisme* (Paris: François Maspéro, 1978), p. 201.

16. Ibid., p. 202.

17. Ibid., p. 200.

18. Jock McCulloch, *In the Twilight of Revolution: The Political Theory of Amilcar Cabral* (London: Routledge and Kegan Paul, 1983), p. 91.

19. Ibid., p. 140.

20. Ali A. Mazrui, *The African Condition: A Political Diagnosis* (London: Heinemann, 1980), p. 63.

21. Stanley J. Stein and Barbara H. Stein, *The Colonial Heritage of Latin America* (New York: Oxford University Press, 1970), p. 160.

22. Ibid., p. 152.

23. Constantino, *Neocolonial Identity*, p. 53.

24. Ibid., p. 122.

25. Ibid., p. 124.

26. Premen Addy and Ibne Azad, "Politics and Culture in Bengal," *New Left Review*, no. 79 (May–June 1973): 77.

27. Ibid., p. 79.

28. Dorothy S. Blair, *African Literature in French* (Cambridge: Cambridge University Press, 1976), p. 8.

29. Gerald Moore, *Twelve African Writers* (London: Hutchinson, 1980), pp. 19–20.

30. Abiola Irele, *The African Experience in Literature and Ideology* (London: Heinemann, 1981), p. 71.

Chapter 2. Culture and National Identity

1. Cedric Robinson, "Domination and Imitation: *Xala* and the Emergence of the Black Bourgeoisie," *Race and Class* 22 (Autumn 1980): 147–48.

2. Jalée, *The Third World*, p. 117.

3. Gérard Chaliand, *Revolution in the Third World* (Harmondsworth: Penguin, 1978), p. 27.

4. Arghiri Emmanuel, "White Settler Colonialism and the Myth of Investment Imperialism," *New Left Review*, no. 73 (May–June 1972): 48.

5. Ousmane Sembene, in *African Writers on African Writing*, ed. G. D. Killam (London: Heinemann, 1973), p. 150.

6. Amilcar Cabral, *Return to the Source* (New York: Monthly Review Press / Africa Information Service, 1973), p. 47.

7. Ibid., p. 42.

8. Ibid., p. 43.

9. Frantz Fanon, *The Wretched of the Earth* (Harmondsworth: Penguin, 1967), pp. 178–79.

10. Ibid., p. 179.

11. Afrânio Coutinho, *An Introduction to Literature in Brazil* (New York: Columbia University Press, 1969), p. 45.

12. See William Lawson, *The Western Scar* (Athens: Ohio University Press, 1982).

13. Blair, *African Literature*, p. 182.

14. Jorge Luis Borges, "The Argentine Writer and Tradition," in *Labyrinths* (Harmondsworth: Penguin, 1970), pp. 214–15.

15. Terence Ranger, "The Invention of Tradition in Colonial Africa," in *The Invention of Tradition,* ed. Eric Hobsbawm and Terence Ranger (Cambridge: Cambridge University Press, 1983), p. 262.

16. Ibid., pp. 249–50.

17. Renato Constantino, "Notes on Historical Writing for the Third World," *Journal of Contemporary Asia* 10 (1980): 234.

18. Mazrui, *The African Condition,* p. 63.

19. Memmi, *Colonizer and Colonized,* p. 110.

20. Richard M. Morse, "The Americanization of Languages in the New World," *Cultures* 3 (1979): 28.

21. George Pendle, *A History of Latin America* (Harmondsworth: Penguin, 1963), pp. 187–88.

22. Larzer Ziff, *Literary Democracy: The Declaration of Cultural Independence in America* (Harmondsworth: Penguin, 1982), p. 301.

23. Irele, *The African Experience,* p. 44.

24. Ibid., p. 54.

25. See "Kenya: The Politics of Repression," special issue, *Race and Class* 24 (Winter 1983).

26. Erik Barnouw and S. Krishnaswamy, *Indian Film* (New York: Oxford University Press, 1980), p. 13.

27. Ola Balogun, "Traditional Arts and Cultural Development in Africa," *Cultures* 2 (1975): 159.

28. Arlette Roth, *Le théâtre algérien* (Paris: François Maspéro, 1967), p. 13.

29. A. C. Scott, *Literature and the Arts in Twentieth Century China* (London: George Allen and Unwin, 1965), pp. 36–37.

30. S. Theodore Baskaran, *The Message Bearers: Anglo-Indian Nationalist Politics and the Entertainment Media in South India, 1880–1945* (Madras: Cre-A, 1981), p. 41.

31. Ebun Clark, *Hubert Ogunde: The Making of Nigerian Theatre* (London: Oxford University Press, 1979), p. xi.

Chapter 3. Cinema and Capitalism

1. Alfred Cobban, *A History of Modern France,* vol. 3: *1871–1962* (Harmondsworth: Penguin, 1965), p. 71.

2. Douglas Gomery, "Rethinking U.S. Film History: The Depression Decade and Monopoly Control," *Film and History,* no. 10 (May 1980): 35.

3. V. F. Perkins, *Film as Film* (Harmondsworth: Penguin, 1972), p. 162.

4. David McLellan (ed.), *Karl Marx: Selected Writings* (Oxford: Oxford University Press, 1977), p. 416.

5. Paul A. Baran and Paul M. Sweezy, *Monopoly Capital* (New York: Monthly Review Press, 1966), p. 12.

6. Andre Gunder Frank, *Capitalism and Underdevelopment in Latin America* (Harmondsworth: Penguin, 1971), p. 11.

7. Ibid., p. 33.

8. Paulo Emilio Salles Gomes, "Cinema: A Trajectory Within Underdevelopment," in *Brazilian Cinema*, ed. Randal Johnson and Robert Stam (Rutherford, N.J.: Fairleigh Dickinson University Press, 1982), p. 247.

9. Immanuel Wallerstein, *The Capitalist World-Economy* (Cambridge: Cambridge University Press), p. 23.

10. Ferid Boughedir, "Report and Prospects," in *Cinema and Society*, ed. Enrico Fulchignoni (Paris: ITFC / UNESCO, 1982), p. 101. Amended Translation.

11. Alphonse Quenum, "Leisure in a Developing Country: The Case of Lower Dahomey," *Cultures* 1 (1973): 82.

12. Djingarey Maiga, in *Cinéastes d'Afrique noire*, ed. Guy Hennebelle and Catherine Ruelle, special issue, *CinémAction*, no. 3 (1978): 86.

13. Haile Gerima, interview with Paul Willemen, *Framework*, nos. 7–8 (Spring 1978): 32.

14. Ousmane Sembene, in Hennebelle and Ruelle (eds.), *Cinéastes d'Afrique noire*, p. 115.

15. Quoted in *Cinema Vision India* 1 (January 1980): 67.

16. *Report of the Indian Cinematograph Committee 1927–28* (Madras: Government of India Central Publications Branch, 1928), p. 201. [Hereafter *1928 Report.*]

17. Ibid., p. 103.

18. Ibid., p. 99.

19. Emmanuel, "White Settler Colonialism," pp. 35–57.

20. Pierre Roitfeld, *Afrique noire francophone* (Paris: Unifrance Film, 1980).

21. Harry Magdoff, "Imperialism Without Colonies," in *Studies in the Theory of Imperialism*, ed. Roger Owen and Bob Sutcliffe (London: Longman, 1972), pp. 144–70.

22. H. W. Morgan, *America's Road to Empire* (New York: John Wiley, 1965), p. ix.

23. Urho Kekkonen, in *Television Traffic: One-Way Street?* ed. Kaarle Nordenstreng and Tapio Varis (Paris: UNESCO, 1974), pp. 44–45.

24. Peter Harcourt, "Introduction: The Invisible Cinema," *Ciné-Tracts*, no. 4 (Spring–Summer 1978): 48–49.

25. Sylvia Lawson, "Towards Decolonisation: Some Problems and Issues for Film History in Australia," *Film Reader*, no. 4 (1979): 66.

26. Thomas Guback, "Hollywood's International Market," in *The American Film Industry*, ed. Tino Balio (Madison: University of Wisconsin Press, 1976), p. 394.

27. Jack Valenti, quoted in ibid., p. 396.

28. Richard Maltby, *Harmless Entertainment: Hollywood and the Ideology of Consensus* (Metuchen, N.J.: Scarecrow Press, 1983), p. 80.

29. Nicholas Garnham, *The Economics of the U.S. Motion Picture Industry* (London: Commission of the European Communities, n.d.), p. 6.

30. Thomas Guback and Tapio Varis, *Transnational Communication and Cultural Industries* (Paris: UNESCO, 1982), p. 50.

Part Two. Theory and Practice of Third World Film Making

1. Bill Warren, *Imperialism: Pioneer of Capitalism* (London: Verso, 1980), p. 9.

Chapter 4. The Beginnings of Non-Western Film Production

1. Julianne Burton, "Cuba," in *Les cinémas de l'Amérique latine,* ed. Guy Hennebelle and Alfonso Gumucio-Dagron (Paris: Lherminier, 1981), pp. 259–60.

2. Jay Leyda, *Dianying: Electric Shadows—An Account of Films and Film Audience in China* (Cambridge, Mass.: MIT Press, 1972), pp. 7–8.

3. Carl J. Mora, *The Mexican Cinema* (Berkeley and Los Angeles: University of California Press, 1982), p. 9.

4. Barnouw and Krishnaswamy, *Indian Film,* p. 14.

5. Salles Gomes, "Cinema: A Trajectory," p. 246.

6. Ibid., pp. 246–47.

7. Barnouw and Krishnaswamy, *Indian Film,* p. 15.

8. Satish Bahadur, "The Context of Indian Film Culture," in *New Indian Cinema,* ed. Shampa Banerjee (New Delhi: Indian Directorate of Film Festivals, 1982), pp. 8–9.

9. Tom Kemp, *Industrialization in the Non-Western World* (London: Longman, 1983), pp. 105–6.

10. Utpal Dutt, keynote address, *Symposium on Cinema in Developing Countries* (New Delhi: Ministry of Information and Broadcasting, 1979), pp. 8–9.

11. Jean-Claude Bernardet, quoted in Hennebelle and Gumucio-Dagron (eds.), *Les cinémas de l'Amérique latine,* pp. 130–31.

12. Abdallah Laroui, quoted in Yves Thoraval, *Regards sur le cinéma égyptien* (Beirut: Dar el-Machreq, 1975), p. 12.

13. Baskaran, *Message Bearers,* p. 102.

14. Ibid., p. 100.

15. Salles Gomes, "Cinema: A Trajectory," p. 248.

16. Paulo Emilio Salles Gomes, quoted in Hennebelle and Gumucio-Dagron (eds.), *Les cinémas de l'Amérique latine,* p. 129.

17. Erika Richter, *Realistischer Film in Ägypten* (Berlin: Henschel Verlag, 1974).

18. Henri Micciolo, *Guru Dutt* (Paris: Anthologie du Cinéma, 1975), p. 166.

19. Richard Dyer, "Entertainment and Utopia," *Movie,* no. 24 (Spring 1977): 3.

20. Paulo Emilio Salles Gomes, "Cinéma brésilien: Une trajectoire dans le sous-développement," in *Cinéma brésilien 1970–1980,* ed. Paulo Antonio Paranagua and José Carlos Avellar (documentation prepared for the 1983 Locarno International Film Festival), p. 7.

Chapter 5. Individual Authorship

1. Fernando Birri, "Cinema and Underdevelopment," in *Twenty-five Years of the New Latin American Cinema,* ed. Michael Chanan (London: British Film Institute / Channel Four Television, 1983), p. 12.

2. Nelson Pereira dos Santos, interview with Federico de Cardenas and Max Tessier, in *Le "cinéma novo" brésilien,* vol. 1, ed. Michel Estève (Paris: Lettres Modernes, 1972), p. 62.

3. Humberto Solas, interview with Marta Alvear, *Jump Cut,* no. 19 (December 1978): 28.

4. Ruy Guerra, interview with Jean A. Gili, in Estève (ed.), *Le "cinéma novo,"* p. 98.

5. Antonio Eguino, "Neorealism in Bolivia" (interview with Udayan Gupta), *Cineaste* 9 (Winter 1978–79): 29.

6. Satyajit Ray, interview, *Montage* (Bombay), nos. 5–6 (July 1966): n.p.

7. Santos, *Le "cinéma novo"* interview, p. 62.

8. Ray, *Montage* interview, n.p.

9. Eguino, "Neorealism in Bolivia," p. 29.

10. Jorge Fraga, interview with Zuzana M. Pick, *Ciné-Tracts,* nos. 7–8 (Summer–Fall 1979): 23.

11. Fernando Solanas and Octavio Getino, "Towards a Third Cinema," in Chanan (ed.), *Twenty-five Years,* p. 22.

12. Barnouw and Krishnaswamy, *Indian Film,* p. 69.

13. Ousmane Sembene, "Observations," *Symposium on Cinema,* p. 15.

14. Satyajit Ray, text for B. D. Garga's documentary film *Creative Artists of India: Satyajit Ray,* in *Montage* (Bombay), nos. 5–6 (July 1966): n.p.

15. Shyam Benegal, interview, in *Indian Cinema Superbazaar,* ed. Aruna Vasudev and Philippe Lenglet (New Delhi: Vikas, 1983), p. 159.

16. Salah Abou Seif, quoted in Guy Hennebelle, "Arab Cinema," *Merip Reports,* no. 52 (November 1976): 4.

Chapter 6. "Third Cinema"

1. Chaliand, *Revolution,* p. xv.

2. Julio García Espinosa, "For an Imperfect Cinema," in Chanan (ed.), *Twenty-five Years,* pp. 28–29.

3. Ibid., p. 28.

4. Ibid., pp. 29–30.

5. Ibid., p. 30.

6. Ibid., pp. 31–32.

7. Ibid., p. 32.

8. Ibid.

9. Ibid.

10. Ibid., p. 33.

11. Solanas and Getino, "Towards a Third Cinema," p. 23.

12. Ibid., p. 17.

13. Ibid., p. 18.

14. Ibid., p. 24.

15. Ibid., p. 22.

16. Ibid., pp. 22–23.

17. Ibid., p. 23.

18. Ibid.

19. Ibid., p. 27.

Chapter 7. The Indian Subcontinent

1. Ranjit Sau, *India's Economic Development: Aspects of Class Relations* (London: Sangam Books, 1983), p. 36.

2. Neil Charlesworth, *British Rule and the Indian Economy, 1800–1914* (London: Macmillan, 1982), p. 13.

3. Ibid., pp. 36–37.

4. Raghunath Raina, "The Context: A Socio-Cultural Anatomy," in Vasudev and Lenglet (eds.), *Indian Cinema Superbazaar*, p. 5.

5. M. A. Oommen and K. V. Joseph, *Economics of Film Industry in India* (Gurgaon, India: Academic Press, 1981), p. 21.

6. *1928 Report*, p. 32.

7. Ibid., pp. 35–36.

8. Ibid., p. 37.

9. Ibid., p. 26.

10. Ibid., p. 35. ·

11. Baskaran, *Message Bearers*, p. 81.

12. *1928 Report*, p. 23.

13. *Report of the Film Enquiry Committee 1951* (New Delhi: Government of India Press, 1951), p. 125. [Hereafter *1951 Report*.]

14. D. K. Fieldhouse, *Colonialism 1870–1945* (London: Macmillan, 1981), pp. 94–95.

15. Ardeshir M. Irani, "The Making of *Alam Ara*" (interview with B. D. Garga), *Cinema Vision India* 1 (April 1980): 12.

16. Barnouw and Krishnaswamy, *Indian Film*, p. 87.

17. *1928 Report*, p. 36.

18. *1951 Report*, p. 115.

19. Tariq Ali, *Can Pakistan Survive?* (Harmondsworth: Penguin, 1983), p. 35.

20. Sau, *India's Economic Development*, p. 50.

21. Ibid., p. 33.

22. S. Viswam, "The Asian Press: An Overview," *Vidura* (New Delhi), no. 20 (December 1983): 344.

23. Ibid., p. 345.

24. Barnouw and Krishnaswamy, *Indian Film*, p. 137.

25. See Oommen and Joseph, *Economics of Film Industry in India*.

26. Chidananda Das Gupta, "The 'New' Cinema: A Wave or a Future?" in Vasudev and Lenglet (eds.), *Indian Cinema Superbazaar*, p. 41.

27. Satchi Ponnambalam, *Sri Lanka: National Conflict and the Tamil Liberation Struggle* (London: Zed, 1983), p. 67.

28. Alamgir Kabir, *The Cinema in Pakistan* (Dacca: Sandhani Publications, 1969), p. 81.

29. Ibid., p. 34.

30. Philip Coorey and Amarnath Jayatilaka, "Sri Lanka (Ceylon)," in *International Film Guide 1974*, ed. Peter Cowie (London: Tantivy Press, 1974), p. 303. [Hereafter *International Film Guide*.]

31. Kabir, *Cinema in Pakistan*, p. 55.

32. Javed Jabbar, "Pakistan," *International Film Guide 1978*, p. 261.

33. Kabir, *Cinema in Pakistan*, p. 83.

34. Derek Elley, "James Lester Peries," *International Film Guide 1983*, p. 28.

35. Jabbar, "Pakistan," pp. 261–62.

Chapter 8. East and Southeast Asia

1. Kapila Malik Vatsyayan, "Aesthetic Theories Underlying Asian Performing Arts," in *The Performing Arts in Asia*, ed. James R. Brandon (Paris: UNESCO, 1971), p. 15.

2. Scott Meek and Tony Rayns, "Before the Cultural Revolution," *Sight and Sound* 49 (Autumn 1980): 216.

3. C. P. Fitzgerald, *A Concise History of East Asia* (Harmondsworth: Penguin, 1974), p. 122.

4. Joseph Needham, quoted in Leyda, *Dianying*, p. 21.

5. Fitzgerald, *History of East Asia*, p. 136.

6. Leyda, *Dianying*, p. 16.

7. Ibid.

8. Ibid., p. 20.

9. Tony Rayns and Scott Meek, *Electric Shadows: Forty-five Years of Chinese Cinema* (London: British Film Institute, 1980), p. A3.

10. Leyda, *Dianying*, p. 49.

11. Ibid., p. 50.

12. Ibid., p. 61.

13. Meek and Rayns, "Before the Cultural Revolution," p. 216.

14. "Present Program for Action," quoted in Leyda, *Dianying*, p. 74.

15. Leyda, *Dianying*, p. 71.

16. Régis Bergeron, *Le cinéma chinois. 1: 1905–1949* (Lausanne: Alfred Eibel, 1977), p. 103.

17. Leyda, *Dianying*, p. 64.

18. Ibid., p. 79.

19. Ibid., p. 86.

20. Ibid., p. 67.

21. Franz Schurmann and Orville Schell (eds.), *China Readings*, vol. 2: *Republican China* (Harmondsworth: Penguin, 1968), p. 52.

22. Rayns and Meek, *Electric Shadows*, p. A8.

23. Leyda, *Dianying*, p. 350.

24. Ibid., p. 140.

25. Ibid., p. 133.

26. I. C. Jarvie, *Window on Hong Kong: A Sociological Study of the Hong Kong Film Industry and Its Audience* (Hong Kong: University of Hong Kong Centre for Asian Studies, 1977), pp. 9–10.

27. Ibid., p. 10.

28. Rayns and Meek, *Electric Shadows*, p. A12.

29. All the information on Vietnamese cinema is taken from the dossier "Vietnamese Cinema": Pham Ngoc Truong, "Vietnamese Cinema from Its Origins to 1945," and Bui Phui, "The Seventh Goddess," in *Framework* 25 (1984): 63–70 and 71–83, respectively.

30. David Marr, "Vietnam: Harvesting the Whirlwind," in *Asia: The Winning of Independence*, ed. Robin Jeffrey (London: Macmillan, 1981), p. 165.

31. Truong, "Vietnamese Cinema," p. 65.

32. Phui, "Seventh Goddess," p. 71.

33. Benedict Anderson, *Imagined Communities: Reflections on the Origin and Spread of Nationalism* (London: Verso, 1983), p. 19.

34. D. A. Low, "Crux and Means: Some Asian Nationalisms Compared," in Jeffrey (ed.), *Asia*, p. 270.

35. Much of the material here is derived from the annual surveys published since 1964 in *International Film Guide*.

36. *1928 Report*, p. 34.

37. Tony Rayns, program notes for the Twenty-fifth London Film Festival (1981).

38. Grenfell Newell, *Switch On: Switch Off—Mass Media Audiences in Malaysia* (Kuala Lumpur: Oxford University Press, 1979), p. 152.

39. Constantino, *Neocolonial Identity*, p. 69.

40. Max Tessier, "Le cinéma philippin," *La revue du cinéma*, no. 375 (September 1982): 88.

41. Agustin Sotto, "Petite histoire du cinéma philippin," *Avant-scène du cinéma*, no. 287 (May 1982): 47.

42. Clive Hamilton, "Capitalist Industrialization in the Four Little Tigers of East Asia," in Limqueco and McFarlane (eds.), *Neo-Marxist Theories*, p. 138.

43. *Introduction to Korean Motion Pictures* (Seoul: Motion Picture Production Corporation, Republic of Korea [1980]), n.p.

44. Ibid.

45. Ibid.

46. Ibid.

47. Kai Hong, "Korea (South)," *International Film Guide 1981*, p. 214.

48. Derek Elley, "Taiwan," *International Film Guide 1982*, p. 296.

49. Jarvie, *Window on Hong Kong*, p. 43.

51. Ibid., pp. 3–4.

51. Ibid., p. 21.

52. Ibid., p. 37.

53. Ibid., p. 21.

54. Ibid., p. 32.

55. Ibid., p. 86.

56. Ibid., p. 87.

57. Li Cheuk-to (ed.), *A Study of Hong Kong Cinema in the Seventies* (Hong Kong: Eighth International Film Festival, 1984), p. 9.

Chapter 9. Latin America

1. This section owes much to *Les cinémas de l'Amérique latine*, ed. Guy Hennebelle and Alfonso Gumucio-Dagron (Paris: Lherminier, 1981). I have included numerous quotations from contributors to that volume, since they give a unique impression of the cinema of Latin America as seen through the eyes of Latin American critics.

2. Luis G. Urbino, writing in *El mundo ilustrado* on 9 December 1906, quoted in Carl J. Mora, *Mexican Cinema*, p. 8.

3. Emilio García Riera, "Mexique," in Hennebelle and Gumucio-Dagron (see n. 1), p. 365.

4. Hernando Salcedo Silva, "Colombie," in Hennebelle and Gumucio-Dagron, p. 238.

5. Juan Verdejo, Zuzana Mirjam Pick, and Gaston Ancelovici, "Chili," in Hennebelle and Gumucio-Dagron, p. 197.

6. Arturo Arias, Leonor Hurtado, and José Campang, "Guatemala," in Hennebelle and Gumucio-Dagron, p. 333.

7. Rodolfo Izaguirre, "Venezuela," in Hennebelle and Gumucio-Dagron, p. 481.

8. Stein and Stein, *Colonial Heritage*, p. 192.

9. Johnson and Stam, "The Shape of Brazilian Film History," in Johnson and Stam (eds.), *Brazilian Cinema*, pp. 26–27.

10. Maria Rita Galvão, "Vera Cruz: A Brazilian Hollywood," in ibid., p. 271.

11. Octavio Getino, "Argentine," in Hennebelle and Gumucio-Dagron (see n. 1), p. 40.

12. Ibid., p. 38.

13. Isaac Leon Frias, "Pérou," in Hennebelle and Gumucio-Dagron, p. 431.

14. Rodolfo Izaguirre, "Venezuela," p. 482.

15. Emilio García Riera, "Mexique," p. 391.

16. Randal Johnson, *Cinema Novo × 5: Masters of Contemporary Brazilian Film* (Austin: University of Texas Press, 1984), p. 3.

17. Jean-Claude Bernadet, quoted in Hennebelle and Gumucio-Dagron (see n. 1), p. 161.

18. Rui Guerra, "Popular Cinema and the State," in Johnson and Stam (eds.), *Brazilian Cinema*, p. 102.

19. Fidel Castro, "Words to the Intellectuals," in *Radical Perspectives in the Arts*, ed. Lee Baxandall (Harmondsworth: Penguin, 1972), p. 276.

20. Malcolm Coad, Nora Marcano, and Igor Barreto, "Venezuela," *International Film Guide 1980*, p. 324.

21. Alfonso Gumucio-Dagron, "Cameras are Dangerous," *Index on Censorship* 10 (August 1981): 31.

22. *Young Cinema and Theatre* (Prague), no. 4 (1980): 35.

23. The specific aims of the Salvadorean Film Institute are set out in Ann Lamont, Richard Walker, and Michael Chanan, *Film in El Salvador Has Been Born with War* (London: Salvadorean Film Institute Support Group, n.d.).

Chapter 10. The Middle East and Africa

1. This section is based on Lyle Pearson's articles in *International Film Guide 1978* and *1980–83*.

2. Fred Halliday, *Iran: Dictatorship or Development* (Harmondsworth: Penguin, 1979), p. 14.

3. Farrokh Gaffary, *Le cinéma en Iran* (Teheran: High Council of Culture and Art, Center for Research and Cultural Coordination, 1973), p. 2.

4. Ibid., p. 7.

5. Halliday, *Iran*, p. 148.

6. Ibid., p. 15.

7. John Motavalli, "Exiles—Iran: Cinema in Flames," *Film Comment* 19 (July–August 1983): 57–58.

8. *Post-Revolutionary Iranian Cinema* (Teheran: General Department of Cinematic Research and Relations, 1982), p. 8.

9. Berch Berberoglu, "Turkey: The Crisis of the Neocolonialist System," *Race and Class* 22 (1981): 278.

10. Yılmaz Güney, "From Isolation" (interview with Tony Rayns), *Sight and Sound* 52 (Spring 1983): 89.

11. Dennis Giles and Haluk Sahin, "Revolutionary Cinema in Turkey: Yilmaz Güney," *Jump Cut,* no. 27 (July 1982): 35.

12. Güney, "From Isolation," p. 89.

13. Samir Amin, *The Arab Nation* (London: Zed, 1978), p. 30.

14. Patrick Clawson, "The Development of Capitalism in Egypt," *Khamsin* (London), no. 9 (1981): 85.

15. Ibid., p. 93.

16. Ibid., p. 90.

17. Samir Farid, "Les six générations du cinéma égyptien," *Ecran* (Paris), no. 15 (May 1973): 38.

18. Clawson, "Capitalism in Egypt," p. 92.

19. Ibid., p. 91.

20. Talaat Harb, quoted in Farid, "Les six générations," p. 40.

21. Ahmed Badrakhane, in ibid., p. 42.

22. Galal el-Charkawi, "History of the UAR Cinema—1896–1962," in *The Cinema in the Arab Countries,* ed. Georges Sadoul (Beirut: Interarab Center for Cinema and Television / UNESCO, 1966), p. 84.

23. Farid, "Les six générations," pp. 42–43.

24. Kemal el-Sheik, interview with Khémais Khayati, *Cinéma 73,* no. 182 (December 1973): 65.

25. Peter Mansfield, *The Arabs* (Harmondsworth: Penguin, 1979), p. 286.

26. Clawson, "Capitalism in Egypt," p. 105.

27. Ibid., p. 99.

28. Ibid., p. 100.

29. Farid, "Les six générations," p. 47.

30. Farid Jabre, "The Industry in Lebanon 1958–1965," in Sadoul (ed.), *Cinema in Arab Countries,* p. 177.

31. Mansfield, *The Arabs,* p. 270.

32. John Iliffe, *The Emergence of African Capitalism* (London: Macmillan, 1983), pp. 75–76.

33. Ibid., p. 67.

34. Jorge Rebelo, quoted in *Cinémas noirs d'Afrique,* ed. Jacques Binet, Ferid Boughedir, and Victor Bachy (Paris: CinémAction, no. 26 / L'Harmattan, 1983), p. 42.

35. Victor Bachy, "Panoramique sur les cinémas africains," in ibid., p. 42.

36. Jean-René Debrix, interview with Guy Hennebelle, in Hennebelle and Ruelle (eds.), *Cinéastes d'Afrique noire,* pp. 154–55.

Chapter 11. Satyajit Ray

1. J. H. Broomfield, *Elite Conflict in a Plural Society: Twentieth Century Bengal* (Berkeley and Los Angeles: University of California Press, 1968), p. 10.

2. Chidananda Das Gupta, *The Cinema of Satyajit Ray* (New Delhi: Vikas, 1980), p. 15.

3. The full three-episode film runs to 165 minutes, and the first version released in the West (as *Two Daughters*) was confined to the first two episodes.

4. Satyajit Ray, "The Politics of Humanism" (interview with Udayan Gupta), *Cineaste* 12 (1982): 24.

5. Das Gupta, *Cinema of Satyajit Ray*, p. 68.

6. Raghunath Raina, foreword to Das Gupta, *Cinema of Satyajit Ray*, p. iv.

7. Solanas and Getino, "Towards a Third Cinema," p. 21.

Chapter 12. Youssef Chahine

1. Youssef Chahine, interview with Guy Hennebelle and Heiny Srour, *Cinéma 3* (Casablanca), no. 3 (September 1970): 38.

2. Ibid., p. 39.

3. Mansfield, *The Arabs*, p. 303.

4. Thoraval, *Regards sur le cinéma égyptien*, p. 41.

5. Quoted in *Algerian Cinema*, ed. Hala Salmane, Simon Hartog, and David Wilson (London: British Film Institute, 1976), p. 54.

6. Mansfield, *The Arabs*, p. 456.

7. Ibid., p. 457.

8. Youssef Chahine, interview with S.S., *La presse* (Tunis), 18 October 1984.

Chapter 13. Glauber Rocha

1. Stein and Stein, *The Colonial Heritage*, p. 148.

2. Salles Gomes, "Cinema: A Trajectory," p. 245.

3. Coutinho, *An Introduction to Literature in Brazil*, pp. 26–27.

4. Ibid., p. 41.

5. Glauber Rocha, quoted in Paulo Antonio Paranagua, "Brésil," in Hennebelle and Gumucio-Dagron (eds.), *Les cinémas de l'Amérique latine*, pp. 139–40.

6. Ibid., p. 145.

7. Ismail Xavier, "*Black God, White Devil:* The Representation of History," in Johnson and Stam (eds.), *Brazilian Cinema*, p. 134.

8. René Gardies, *Glauber Rocha* (Paris: Seghers, 1974), pp. 49–67.

9. Johnson, *Cinema Novo*, p. 120.

10. Xavier, "*Black God, White Devil*," p. 139.

11. *Brazil: State and Struggle* (London: Latin American Bureau, 1982), p. 33.

12. Salles Gomes, "Cinema: A Trajectory," p. 250.

13. Glauber Rocha, "The Aesthetics of Hunger," in Chanan (ed.), *Twenty-five Years*, p. 13.

14. Paranagua, "Brésil," p. 152.

Chapter 14. Yılmaz Güney

1. Attilâ Dorsay, "Yılmaz Güney: Son cinéma, sa création, sa personne," *Cinéma 80*, no. 262 (October 1980): 52.

2. Elia Kazan, "A View from a Turkish Prison," *New York Times Magazine*, 4 February 1979; translated in *Positif*, no. 227 (February 1980): 36–45.

3. *Besuch auf Imrali: Eine Begegnung mit Yılmaz Güney* (directed by Hans Stempel and Martin Ripkens, Federal Republic of Germany, 1979).

4. Tony Rayns, "From Isolation," *Sight and Sound* 52 (Spring 1983): 90.

5. Yılmaz Güney, interview with Attilâ Dorsay, *Cinéma 80*, no. 262 (October 1980): 61.

6. Dorsay, "Yılmaz Güney," p. 53.

7. Yılmaz Güney, interview, *Positif*, no. 234 (September 1980): 49.

8. Adrian Turner, "Présentation de Yılmaz Güney," *Positif*, no. 227 (February 1980): 29–35.

9. Yılmaz Güney, interview with Carl Gardner, *Stills*, no. 13 (October 1984): 49.

10. Ibid., p. 50.

11. Ibid.

Chapter 15. Ousmane Sembene

1. There is some confusion over the name, since all the films are listed as directed by Ousmane Sembene, while the novels were issued under the name Sembene Ousmane. Perhaps the best solution would be to follow the example of Paulin Soumanou Vieyra's valuable study of the director, which bears the title *Sembène Ousmane cinéaste* on the cover and *Ousmane Sembène cinéaste* on the title page! I have followed Vieyra's internal usage here, Sembene being the patronymic.

2. Moore, *Twelve African Writers*, p. 70.

3. Claude Wauthier, *The Literature and Thought of Modern Africa* (London: Heinemann, 1978), p. 304.

4. Moore, *Twelve African Writers*, p. 83.

5. Ousmane Sembene, *God's Bits of Wood* (London: Heinemann, 1970), pp. 57–58.

6. Ousmane Sembene, interview with Guy Hennebelle, in Hennebelle and Ruelle (eds.), *Cinéastes d'Afrique noire*, p. 125.

7. Ousmane Sembene, interview with Ulrich Gregor, *Framework*, nos. 7–8 (Spring 1978): 35.

Chapter 16. Jorge Sanjinés

1. Pendle, *A History of Latin America*, p. 210.

2. Alfonso Gumucio-Dagron, "Bolivia," in Hennebelle and Gumucio-Dagron (eds.), *Les cinémas de l'Amérique latine*, p. 78.

3. *Bolivia: Coup d'Etat* (London: Latin American Bureau, 1980), p. 51.

4. Jorge Sanjinés, "Language and Popular Culture," *Framework*, no. 10 (Spring 1979): 31.

5. Jorge Sanjinés, interview with Guy Braucourt, *Afterimage*, no. 3 (Summer 1971): 43.

6. Ibid., p. 42.

7. Ibid., p. 45.

8. Ibid., p. 46.

9. Sanjinés, "Language and Popular Culture," p. 31.

10. *Bolivia: Coup d'Etat*, p. 36.

11. Sanjinés, "Language and Popular Culture," p. 31.
12. Ibid.
13. Ibid.

Conclusion

1. My starting point was set out in a paper, "The Possibility of a History of World Cinema," in *Problems of Film History,* ed. Roy Armes, pp. 7–24 (London: Middlesex Polytechnic / British Film Institute, 1981).

2. Andy Medhurst, "*Victim:* Text as Context," *Screen* 25 (July–October 1984): 22.

3. My own histories of British and French cinema are certainly not immune from these strictures.

4. See Noël Burch, *To the Distant Observer: Form and Meaning in the Japanese Cinema* (London: Scholar Press, 1979).

5. See, particularly, Ashish Rajadhyaksha, *Ritwik Ghatak: A Return to the Epic* (Bombay: Screen Unit, 1982).

6. Satyajit Ray, quoted in *Ritwik Ghatak,* ed. Shampa Banerjee (New Delhi: Indian Directorate of Film Festivals, 1982), p. 2.

7. Dudley Andrew, *Concepts in Film Theory* (New York: Oxford University Press, 1984), p. 3.

8. Ibid., p. 9.

Bibliography

In view of the disparity of the areas of film history, politics, economics, and sociology on which this book draws, a single alphabetical listing of all bibliographical references would seem to have only limited value. The following set of references is therefore divided into sixteen parts, corresponding to the chapters of this book. Within any given part, references to film are listed separately from background material. While the listings of books and articles dealing specifically with Third World films and their makers are intended to be comprehensive, those dealing with background material are inevitably selective. Normally only English and French sources are given, but in the case of Latin American cinema I have included some references in Spanish and Portuguese. Where titles of books and articles included in the background sections are not self-explanatory, a brief annotation is included. The arrangement of material is basically alphabetical within any section, except in the bibliographies to chapters 11 to 16, where film makers' interviews, published scripts, and other writings are listed in the customary chronological order.

Chapter 1. Third World Societies

Addy, Premen, and Ibne Azad. "Politics and Culture in Bengal." *New Left Review,* no. 79 (May–June 1973): 71–112. [A Marxist critique of the *bhadralok* as a collaborating class under colonialism.]

Alavi, Hamza. "The State in Post-Colonial Societies: Pakistan and Bangladesh." *New Left Review,* no. 74 (July–August 1972): 59–81. [A key analysis of class formation with implications for postcolonial states throughout the Third World.]

Beji, Hélé. *Désenchantement national: Essai sur la décolonisation.* Paris: François Maspéro, 1982. [An account of contemporary Tunisian society stressing the limitations of the nationalist ideology which led to independence.]

Bottomore, T. B. *Elites and Society.* London: C. A. Watts, 1964. [A pioneering account.]

Broomfield, J. H. *Elite Conflict in a Plural Society: Twentieth-Century Bengal*. Berkeley and Los Angeles: University of California Press, 1968. [A sober academic assessment of the strengths and limitations of *bhadralok* culture.]

Chandra, Bipan. "Colonialism, Stages of Colonialism, and the Colonial State." *Journal of Contemporary Asia* 10, no. 3 (1980): 272–85. [A useful introduction to a controversial area.]

Constantino, Renato. *Neocolonial Identity and Counter Consciousness*. London: Merlin Press, 1978. [An impassioned Marxist attack on the effect of successive colonizations on the Philippines.]

————. "Notes on Historical Writing for the Third World." *Journal of Contemporary Asia* 10, no. 3 (1980): 233–40. [A key statement of the principles governing the writing of history from the perspective of national liberation.]

Fieldhouse, D. K. *Colonialism 1870–1945*. London: Macmillan, 1983. [A useful introduction from a non-Marxist perspective.]

JanMohamed, Abdul R. *Manichean Aesthetics: The Politics of Literature in Colonial Africa*. Amherst: University of Massachusetts Press, 1983. [An illuminating study of the relationship between colonial society and the literature arising from it, drawing on the work of both black and white writers.]

Laroui, Abdallah. *The Crisis of the Arab Intellectual: Traditionalism or Historicism?* Berkeley and Los Angeles: University of California Press, 1976. [A classic analysis of the situation of the Third World intellectual, caught between Western influences and traditional forces.]

Mazrui, Ali M. *The African Condition: A Political Diagnosis*. London: Heinemann, 1980. [The 1979 BBC Reith Lectures, full of perceptive insights into Africa's position in the world today.]

Memmi, Albert. *The Colonizer and the Colonized*. London: Souvenir Press, 1974. [The classic study by a Tunisian Jew of growing up under colonialism—a personal account with universal implications.]

Paz, Octavio. *The Labyrinth of Solitude*. New York: Grove Press, 1961. [Meditations on the relationship of culture and society in Mexico.]

Petras, James M. "New Perspectives on Imperialism and Social Classes in the Periphery." In *Neo-Marxist Theories of Development*, edited by Peter Limqueco and Bruce McFarlane. London: Croom Helm, 1983. [Some original thoughts on the processes of underdevelopment and their impact on social formation.]

Robinson, Ronald. "Non-European Foundations of European Imperialism: Sketch for a Theory of Collaboration." In *Studies in the Theory of Imperialism*, edited by Roger Owen and Bob Sutcliffe. London: Longman, 1972. [Useful insights into the role of local elites in mediating between colonizer and colonized.]

Stein, Stanley J., and Barbara H. Stein. *The Colonial Heritage of Latin America*. New York: Oxford University Press, 1970. [A set of essays tracing social and economic factors since 1500 that have shaped contemporary Latin America.]

Smith, Anthony D. *State and Nation in the Third World*. Brighton, England: Wheatsheaf Books, 1983. [An original and thought-provoking analysis of the development of the nation-state in Africa.]

Chapter 2. Culture and National Identity

Amirthanayagam, Guy, ed. *Writers in East-West Encounter: New Cultural Bearings*. London: Macmillan, 1982.

————. *Asian and Western Writers in Dialogue: New Cultural Identities*. London: Macmillan, 1982. [Two useful anthologies of personal reflections on East-West cultural relations, comprising papers delivered at a Honolulu conference.]

Anderson, Benedict. *Imagined Communities: Reflections on the Origin and Spread of Nationalism*. London: Verso, 1983. [Fascinating speculations on the contradictions of nationalism, drawing on a wealth of mainly Asian examples.]

Aziza, Mohamed, ed. *Patrimonie culturel et création contemporaine en Afrique et dans le monde arabe*. Dakar and Abidjan: Les Nouvelles Editions Africaines, 1977. [An invaluable collection of six essays by Arab and African scholars on shared traditions and contemporary problems of creativity.]

Balogun, Ola. "Traditional Arts and Cultural Development in Africa." *Cultures* 2, no. 3 (1975): 145–76. [By the noted Nigerian film maker, whose work often draws on traditional sources.]

Blair, Dorothy S. *African Literature in French*. Cambridge: Cambridge University Press, 1976. [A detailed history, better as an account of individual writers than as speculation on the wider issues of African literature in European languages.]

Bowers, Faubion. *Theatre in the East*. London: Nelson, 1956. [An enthusiastic pioneering account.]

Brandon, James R., ed. *The Performing Arts in Asia*. Paris: UNESCO, 1971. [Contains many valuable essays, including some on cinema.]

Butcher, Maggie, ed. *The Eye of the Beholder*. London: Commonwealth Institute, 1983. [Papers of a conference held in London on Indian literature in English.]

Cabral, Amilcar. *Revolution in Guinea*. New York: Monthly Review Press, 1969.

————. *Return to the Source*. New York: Monthly Review Press / Africa Information Service, 1973.

————. *Unity and Struggle*. London: Heinemann, 1980. [These three volumes contain the major work of Cabral available in English translation.]

Caute, David. *Fanon*. London: Fontana / Collins, 1970. [A short critical account in the Modern Masters series.]

Chabal, Patrick. *Amilcar Cabral: Revolutionary Leadership and People's War*. Cambridge: Cambridge University Press, 1983. [Cabral's work in the context of the liberation struggle in Portuguese Guinea.]

Clark, Ebun. *Hubert Ogunde: The Making of Nigerian Theatre*. London: Oxford University Press, 1979. [Historical survey of the work of a dramatist who began to interest himself in cinema during the 1980s.]

Coutinho, Afrânio. *An Introduction to Literature of Brazil*. New York: Columbia University Press, 1969. [A particularly illuminating study of the issues involved in the emergence of a distinctive Latin American culture.]

Donoso, José. *The Boom in Spanish American Literature*. New York: Columbia University Press, 1977. [An account, by a young novelist, of the eruption of Latin American literature onto the world scene.]

Emmanuel, Arghiri. "White Settler Colonialism and the Myth of Investment Imperialism." *New Left Review,* no. 73 (May–June 1972): 35–37. [Iconoclastic discussion of the distinctive interests of settler communities.]

Etherton, Michael. *The Development of African Drama.* London: Hutchinson, 1983. [The best account to date of its subject.]

Fanon, Frantz. *The Wretched of the Earth.* New York: Grove Press, 1964; Harmondsworth: Penguin, 1967.

———. *Studies in a Dying Colonialism.* New York: Monthly Review Press, 1965.

———. *Black Skin, White Masks.* New York: Grove Press, 1967.

———. *For the African Revolution.* New York: Monthly Review Press, 1967. [These four volumes contain Fanon's major writings.]

Franco, Jean. *The Modern Culture of Latin America.* Cambridge: Cambridge University Press, 1967. [A wide-ranging classic survey.]

Frantz Fanon. London: Panaf, 1975. [One of a series of assessments of African revolutionaries, this book examines Fanon's work with relation to the FLN struggle.]

Gendzier, Irene L. *Frantz Fanon: A Critical Study.* London: Wildwood House, 1973.

Hobsbawm, Eric, and Terence Ranger, eds. *The Invention of Tradition.* Cambridge: Cambridge University Press, 1983. [Contains the essays "Representing Authority in Victorian India" and "The Invention of Tradition in Colonial Africa."]

Irele, Abiola. *The African Experience in Literature and Ideology.* London: Heinemann, 1981. [Contains the best account of the language issue in contemporary African literature.]

Jad, Ali B. *Form and Technique in the Egyptian Novel 1912–1971.* London: Ithaca Press, 1983.

Jeyifo, Biodun. *The Truthful Lie.* London: New Beacon Press, 1985. [Essays by a Nigerian critic on the sociology of African drama.]

Jones, Eldred Durosimi, ed. *Drama in Africa.* African Literature Today, no. 8. London: Heinemann, 1976. [A collection of articles of variable quality.]

al-Khozai, Mohamed A. *The Development of Early Arabic Drama: 1847–1900.* London: Longman, 1984.

Laundau, Jacob M. *Studies in Arab Theatre and Cinema.* Philadelphia: University of Pennsylvania Press, 1958. [A pioneering account; weak on cinema.]

Lawson, William. *The Western Scar.* Athens: Ohio University Press, 1982. [A treatment of the theme of the clash of cultures in West African fiction.]

Le Page, R. B. *The National Language Question: Linguistic Problems of Newly Independent States.* London: Oxford University Press, 1964. [An introductory study with a wide range of examples.]

McCulloch, Jock. *In the Twilight of Revolution: The Political Theory of Amilcar Cabral.* London: Routledge and Kegan Paul, 1983.

Mackerras, Colin. *The Performing Arts in Contemporary China.* London: Routledge and Kegan Paul, 1981. [Contains a chapter on cinema.]

Moore, Gerald. *Twelve African Writers.* London: Hutchinson, 1980. [Perceptive essays by one of the finest critics of African literature.]

Morse, Richard M. "The Americanization of Languages in the New World." *Cultures* 3, no. 3 (1976): 28–53.

Nairn, Tom. *The Break-up of Britain.* London: Verso, 1981. [Though the subject is Britain, these reflections on nationalism have a far wider application.]

Ngugi wa Thiongo. *Writers in Politics*. London: Heinemann, 1981.
———. *Barrel of a Pen*. London: New Beacon Books, 1983. [Two collections of essays by a leading novelist, now in exile, on "the resistance to repression in neo-colonial Kenya."]
Obiechina, Emmanuel. *Culture, Tradition, and Society in the West African Novel.* Cambridge: Cambridge University Press, 1975.
Ostle, R. C. *Studies in Modern Arabic Literature*. Warminster, England: Aris and Phillips, 1975. [Papers of a conference held in London dealing with many aspects of language and creativity in twentieth-century Arabic literature.]
Roth, Arlette. *Le théâtre algérien*. Paris: François Maspéro, 1967. [A survey of the years 1926 to 1954.]
Said, Edward W. *Orientalism*. London: Routledge and Kegan Paul, 1978.
Scott, A. C. *Literature and the Arts in Twentieth Century China*. London: George Allen and Unwin, 1965. [Introductory, with a chapter on cinema.]
Taiwo, Oladele. *An Introduction to West African Literature*. London: Nelson, 1967. [A wide-ranging survey by a Nigerian academic.]
Wauthier, Claude. *The Literature and Thought of Modern Africa*. London: Heinemann, 1978. [An examination of African thought since the eighteenth century, covering 150 writers.]
Whittingham, Ken. "Egyptian Theatre." *Merip Reports,* no. 52 (November 1976): 13–19. [A brief introduction.]
Zahar, Renate. *Frantz Fanon: Colonialism and Alienation*. New York: Monthly Review Press, 1974. [A study of Fanon's political thought.]
Ziff, Larzer. *Literary Democracy: The Declaration of Cultural Independence in America*. Harmondsworth: Penguin, 1982. [An excellent account of the emergence of North American literature to set against the difficulties experienced in the Third World.]

Chapter 3. Cinema and Capitalism
The Economics of Third World Film Making

Bächlin, Peter. *Der Film als Ware*. Basel: Burg, 1945. Translated into French, and abridged, as *Histoire économique du cinéma* (Paris: La Nouvelle Edition, 1947). [The major pioneering study of the economics of the film industry as a whole.]
Bachy, Victor. "La distribution cinématographique en Afrique noire." *Film Echange,* no. 15 (Summer 1981): 31–44.
Balio, Tino, ed. *The American Film Industry*. Madison: University of Wisconsin Press, 1976.
Boulanger, Pierre. *Le cinéma colonial*. Paris: Seghers, 1975. [Study of French film making in North Africa prior to independence.]
Chanan, Michael. "The Economic Condition of Cinema in Latin America." In *Third World Studies 1985,* edited by Raana Gauhar. London: Third World Foundation for Social and Economic Studies, 1985.
Cheriaa, Tahar. *Ecrans d'abondance . . . ou cinémas de libération, en Afrique?* Tunis: Société Tunisienne de Diffusion, 1979. [The pioneering study of film distribution in Africa.]

Conant, Michael. *Antitrust in the Motion Picture Industry.* Berkeley and Los Angeles: University of California Press, 1960.

"Ecrans colonisés." Dossier. *FilmAction,* no. 2 (February–March 1982): 23–97.

Garnham, Nicholas. *The Economics of the U.S. Motion Picture Industry.* London: Commission of the European Communities, n.d.

Gomery, Douglas. *The International Film Industry.* Bloomington: Indiana University Press, 1969. [Study of Hollywood's dominance of Europe.]

———. "Hollywood's International Market." In *The American Film Industry,* edited by Tina Balio. Madison: University of Wisconsin Press, 1976.

———. "Film as International Business." In *Communication and Class Struggle,* edited by Armand Mattelard and Seth Siegelaub. New York and Paris: International General, 1979.

———. "Economic Struggle and Hollywood Imperialism: Europe Converts to Sound." *Yale French Studies,* no. 60 (1980): 80–93.

Guback, Thomas, and Tapio Varis. *Transnational Communication and Cultural Industries.* Paris: UNESCO, 1982.

Harcourt, Peter. "Introduction: The Invisible Cinema." *Ciné-Tracts,* no. 4 (Spring–Summer 1978): 48–49. [The status of Canadian cinema.]

Huettig, Mae D. *Economic Control of the Motion Picture Industry.* Philadelphia: University of Pennsylvania Press, 1944. Reprint. New York: Jerome S. Ozer, 1971. [A fascinating, pioneering account.]

Kindem, Gorham, ed. *The American Movie Industry: The Business of Motion Pictures.* Carbondale: Southern Illinois University Press, 1982. [A very useful anthology.]

Lawson, Sylvia. "Towards Decolonisation: Some Problems and Issues for Film History in Australia." *Film Reader,* no. 4 (1979): 66–71.

Maltby, Richard. "The Political Economy of Hollywood: The Studio System." In *Cinema, Politics, and Society in America,* edited by Philip Davies and Brian Neve. Manchester, Eng.: Manchester University Press, 1982.

Mattelart, Armand. *Multinational Corporations and the Control of Culture.* Sussex, England: Harvester Press, 1979.

Nordenstreng, Kaarle, and Tapio Varis, eds. *Television Traffic: A One-Way Street?* Paris: UNESCO, 1974.

Notcutt, L. A., and G. C. Latham. *The African and the Cinema.* London: Edinburgh House Press, 1937. [Very revealing of 1930s racist attitudes.]

Pendakur, Manjunath. "Cultural Dependency in Canada's Feature Film." In *The American Movie Industry: The Business of Motion Pictures,* edited by Gorham Kindem. Carbondale: Southern Illinois University Press, 1982.

Rachety, Gehan, and Khalil Sabat. *Importation of Films for Cinema and Television in Egypt.* Paris: UNESCO, n.d.

Richards, Jeffrey. *Visions of Yesterday.* London: Routledge and Kegan Paul, 1973. [More a celebration than a critique of imperial cinema.]

———. "Patriotism with Profit: British Imperialist Cinema in the 1930s." In *British Cinema History,* edited by James Curran and Vincent Porter. London: Weidenfeld and Nicolson, 1983.

Roitfeld, Pierre. *Afrique noire francophone.* Paris: Unifrance Film, 1980. [A commercial survey of distribution in francophone black Africa.]

Samé N'Gosso, Gaston, and Catherine Ruelle. *Cinéma et télévision en Afrique: De la dépendance à l'interdépendance.* Paris: UNESCO, 1983.

Schiller, Herbert I. *Mass Communications and American Empire.* New York: Augustus M. Kelley, 1970.

Smith, Anthony. *The Geopolitics of Information: How Western Culture Dominates the World.* New York: Oxford University Press, 1980.

Smyth, Rosaleen. "The Central African Film Unit's Images of Empire, 1948–63." *Historical Journal of Film, Radio and Television* 3, no. 2 (1983): 131–47.

———. "Movies and Mandarins: The Official Film and British Colonial Africa." In *British Cinema History,* edited by James Curran and Vincent Porter. London: Weidenfeld and Nicolson, 1983.

Staiger, Janet, and Douglas Gomery. "The History of World Cinema: Models for Economic Analysis." *Film Reader,* no. 4 (1979): 35–44.

Stam, Robert, and Louise Spence. "Colonialism, Racism, and Representation—An Introduction." *Screen* 24, no. 2 (March–April 1983): 2–20.

Thompson, Kristin. *Exporting Entertainment: America in the World Film Market 1907–1934.* London: British Film Institute, 1985.

Tulloch, John. *Australian Cinema: Industry, Narrative, Meaning.* Sydney: Allen and Unwin, 1982.

Tunstall, Jeremy. *The Media Are American.* London: Constable, 1977.

Usabel, Gaizka S. de. *The High Noon of American Films in Latin America.* Ann Arbor, Mich.: UMI Research Press, 1982. [A survey of Hollywood distribution dominance.]

Williams, Raymond. *Television: Technology and Cultural Form.* London: Fontana/Collins, 1974. [A lucid analysis of the relation of technology and society, with great relevance to Third World developments.]

Third World Film: The Social and Economic Contexts

Alavi, Hamza, and Teodor Shanin, eds. *Introduction to the Sociology of "Developing Societies."* London: Macmillan, 1982.

Amin, Samir. *Accumulation on a World Scale.* New York: Monthly Review Press, 1974.

Baran, Paul A., and Paul M. Sweezy. *Monopoly Capital.* New York: Monthly Review Press, 1966. [A work that has had great influence on recent economic studies of Hollywood.]

Bravermann, Harry. *Labour and Monopoly Power: The Degradation of Work in the Twentieth Century.* New York: Monthly Review Press, 1974. [Another work that has had great influence on studies of film industry organization.]

Brewer, Anthony. *Marxist Theories of Imperialism.* London: Routledge and Kegan Paul, 1980. [A survey of existing literature.]

Chaliand, Gérard. *Revolution in the Third World.* Harmondsworth: Penguin, 1978.

Cipolla, Carlo. *European Culture and Overseas Expansion.* Harmondsworth: Penguin, 1970.

Emmanuel, Arghiri. *Unequal Exchange.* New York: Monthly Review Press, 1972.

Frank, Andre Gunder. *Capitalism and Underdevelopment in Latin America*. Harmondsworth: Penguin, 1971. [The first of Frank's many influential studies of the "development of underdevelopment."]

Jalée, Pierre. *The Pillage of the Third World*. New York: Monthly Review Press, 1968.

Jones, Gareth Stedman. "The History of U.S. Imperialism." In *Ideology in Social Science,* edited by Robin Blackburn. London: Fontana/Collins, 1972. [A useful brief survey.]

Kay, Geoffrey. *Development and Underdevelopment: A Marxist Analysis*. London: Macmillan, 1975.

Kemp, Tom. *Industrialization in the Non-Western World*. London: Longman, 1983.

Lens, Sidney. *The Forging of the American Empire*. New York: Thomas Y. Cromwell, 1974. [An impassioned attack on U.S. imperialism.]

Magdoff, Harry. *The New Imperialism: The Economics of U.S. Foreign Policy*. New York: Monthly Review Press, 1969.

Petras, James. *Critical Perspectives on Imperialism and Social Class in the Third World*. New York: Monthly Review Press, 1978.

Rodney, Walter. *How Europe Underdeveloped Africa*. London: Bogle-L'Ouverture, 1972.

Roxborough, Ian. *Theories of Underdevelopment*. London: Macmillan, 1979. [A survey of existing literature.]

Wallerstein, Immanuel. *The Modern World System*. New York: Academic Press, 1974. [Perhaps the most accessible of Wallerstein's numerous books on underdevelopment.]

Warren, Bill. *Imperialism: Pioneer of Capitalism*. London: Verso, 1980. [A polemical attack on the Frank-Wallerstein-Amin thesis.]

Worsley, Peter. *The Three Worlds: Culture and World Development*. London: Weidenfeld and Nicolson, 1984.

Chapter 4. The Beginnings of Non-Western Film Production

General studies of Third World cinema are virtually nonexistent, and analytic accounts of individual commercial cinemas are also rare. The following are therefore of particular interest.

Armes, Roy. "Ending Western Dominance in Third World Cinema." In *Third World Affairs 1986,* edited by Raana Gauhar. London: Third World Foundation for Social and Economic Studies, 1986.

Baskaran, S. Theodore. *The Message Bearers: Anglo-Indian Nationalist Politics and the Entertainment Media in South India, 1880–1945*. Madras: Cre-A, 1981.

Colina, Enrique, and Daniel Diaz Torres. "Ideology of Melodrama in Old Latin American Cinema." In *Latin American Film Makers and the Third Cinema,* edited by Zuzana M. Pick. Ottawa: Carleton University Press, 1978.

Galvão, Maria Rita. "Vera Cruz: A Brazilian Hollywood." In *Brazilian Cinema,* edited by Randal Johnson and Robert Stam. Rutherford, N.J.: Fairleigh Dickinson University Press, 1982.

Hennebelle, Guy. *Quinze ans de cinéma mondial*. Paris: Cerf, 1975.

————, ed. *Le tiers-monde en Films*. Paris: CinémAction / Tricontinental, 1982.

International Film Guide. Edited by Peter Cowie and published annually (since 1964) by the Tantivy Press, London.

Kabir, Nasreen. "Made in Bombay: Les films populaires en langue hindi." In *Le cinéma indien*, edited by Jean-Loup Passek. Paris: Centre Georges Pompidou / L'Equerre, 1983.

————, ed. *Les stars du cinéma indien*. Paris: Centre Georges Pompidou / Centre National de la Cinématographie, 1985.

Mishra, Vijay. "Towards a Theoretical Critique of Bombay Cinema." *Screen* 26, nos. 3–4 (1985): 133–46.

Osiel, Mark. "Bye Bye Boredom: Brazilian Cinema Comes of Age." *Cinéaste* 14, no. 1 (1985): 30–35.

Ricard, Alain. "Du théâtre au cinéma yoruba: Le cas nigérien." In *Cinémas noirs d'Afrique*, edited by Jacques Binet, Ferid Boughedir, and Victor Bachy. Paris: CinémAction, no. 26 / L'Harmattan, 1983.

Sadoul, Georges. *Histoire du cinéma mondial*. 9th ed. Paris: Flammarion, 1972.

Stern, Henri. "Défense et illustration du cinéma commercial indien." In *Le cinéma indien*, edited by Jean-Loup Passek. Paris: Centre Georges Pompidou / L'Equerre, 1983.

Third World Affairs. Edited by Raana Gauhar and published annually by the Third World Foundation for Social and Economic Studies, London.

Thomas, Rosie. "Indian Cinema—Pleasures and Popularity." *Screen* 26, nos. 3–4 (1985): 116–31.

UNESCO. *Statistics on Film and Cinema, 1955–1977*. UNESCO Statistical Studies and Reports, no. 25. Paris: UNESCO, 1981.

————. *World Communications*. Paris: UNESCO, 1964, 1975.

Chapter 5. Individual Authorship
Issues of Third World Film Making

"Banned Films." Special issue. *Index on Censorship* 10, no. 4 (1981).

Boughedir, Ferid. "Report and Prospects." In *Cinema and Society,* edited by Enrico Funchignoni. Paris: IFTC / UNESCO, 1982.

Burton, Julianne. "Marginal Cinemas and Mainstream Critical Theory." *Screen* 26, nos. 3–4 (1985): 2–21.

"Cinéma arabe—Cinéma dans le tiers monde—Cinéma militant." Special issue. *Dérives* (Quebec), nos. 3–4 (January–April 1976).

Gabriel, Teshome H. *Third Cinema in the Third World: The Aesthetics of Liberation*. Ann Arbor, Mich.: UMI Research Press, 1982.

————. "Towards a Critical Theory of Third World Films." In *Third World Affairs 1985*, edited by Raana Gauhar. London: Third World Foundation for Social and Economic Studies, 1985.

Georgakas, Dan, and Lenny Rubenstein, eds. *Art Politics Cinema: The Cineaste Interviews*. Chicago: Lakeview Press, 1984.

"Other Cinemas, Other Criticisms." Special issue. *Screen* 26, nos. 3–4 (1985).

"Racism, Colonialism, and Cinema." Special issue. *Screen* 24, no. 2 (1983).

"Situation du cinéma du tiers-monde." *Cinéma 75*, no. 194 (January 1975): 85–96.

Steven, Peter, ed. *Jump Cut: Hollywood, Politics, and Counter Cinema*. Toronto: Between the Lines, 1985.

Symposium on Cinema in Developing Countries. New Delhi: Ministry of Information and Broadcasting, 1979.

Taylor, Clyde. "Decolonizing World Cinema." In *Third World Affairs 1985*, edited by Raana Gauhar. London: Third World Foundation for Social and Economic Studies, 1985.

"Third World Film." *Jump Cut*, no. 27 (July 1982): 14–40.

Yearwood, Gladstone, ed. *Black Cinema Aesthetics*. Athens: Ohio University Center for Afro-American Studies, 1982.

Italian Neorealism and the European Realist Context

Armes, Roy. *Patterns of Realism*. New York: A. S. Barnes; London: Tantivy Press, 1971.

Overbey, David, ed. *Springtime in Italy: A Reader on Neorealism*. London: Talisman Books, 1978.

Williams, Christopher, ed. *Realism and the Cinema*. London: Routledge & Kegan Paul / British Film Institute, 1980.

Chapter 6. "Third Cinema"

Major theoretical books and articles on Third Cinema, omitting those by Glauber Rocha and Jorge Sanjinés, which are listed in the bibliographies to chapters 13 and 16, respectively:

Alvarez, Santiago, et al. *Cine y revolución en Cuba*. Barcelona: Editoria Fontamara, 1975.

Birri, Fernando. *La escuela documental de Santa Fe*. Santa Fe, Argentina: Universidad del Litoral, 1964.

——. "Cinema and Underdevelopment." In *Twenty-five Years of the New Latin American Cinema*, edited by Michael Chanan. London: British Film Institute / Channel Four Television, 1983. (Originally published as "Cine y subdesarrollo," *Cine cubano*, nos. 42–44 [1967]).

——. "For a Nationalist, Realist, Critical, and Popular Cinema." *Screen* 26, nos. 3–4 (1985): 89–91.

Chanan, Michael, ed. *Twenty-five Years of the New Latin American Cinema*. London: British Film Institute / Channel Four Television, 1983.

García Espinosa, Julio. "For an Imperfect Cinema." *Afterimage*, no. 3 (Summer 1971): 54–67. (Originally published as "Por un cine imperfecto," *Cine cubano*, nos. 66–67 [1970]. Revised translation in *Jump Cut*, no. 20 [May 1979]: 24–26; and in *Twenty-five Years of the New Latin American Cinema*, edited by Michael Chanan. London: British Film Institute / Channel Four Television, 1983.)

——. *Por un cine imperfecto*. Caracas: Rocinante, 1973; Madrid: Castellote, 1976.

————. "In Search of the Lost Cinema." In *Latin American Film Makers and the Third Cinema*, edited by Zuzana M. Pick. Ottawa: Carleton University Press, 1978. (Originally published as "En busca del cine perdido," *Cine cubano*, nos. 69–70 [1971].)

————. *Una imagen recorre el mundo*. Havana: Editoria Letras Cubanas, 1979.

————. "Meditations on Imperfect Cinema . . . Fifteen Years Later." *Screen* 26, nos. 3–4 (1985): 93–94.

Gumucio-Dagron, Alfonso. *El cine de los trabajadores: Manual de apoyo teórico y práctico a la generación de talleres de cine super 8*. Managua: n.p., 1981.

Gutiérrez Alea, Tomás. "The Viewer's Dialectic." Parts 1, 2. *Jump Cut*, no. 29 (February 1984): 18–21, and no. 30 (March 1985): 48–53.

Hennebelle, Guy, ed. "Amérique latine: Théories pour des cinémas de libération." Dossier. *La revue du cinéma—Image et son*, no. 340 (June 1979): 53–107.

Johnson, Randal, and Robert Stam, eds. *Brazilian Cinema*. Rutherford, N.J.: Fairleigh Dickinson University Press, 1982.

Pick, Zuzana M., ed. *Latin American Film Makers and the Third Cinema*. Ottawa: Carleton University Press, 1978.

Salles Gomes, Paulo Emilio. "Cinema: Trajetoria no subdesenvolvimento." *Argumento*, no. 1 (October 1973): n.p. (Reprinted in part as "Cinema: A Trajectory Within Underdevelopment," in *Brazilian Cinema*, edited by Randal Johnson and Robert Stam. Rutherford, N.J.: Fairleigh Dickinson University Press, 1982.)

————. *Humberto Mauro, cataguases, cinearte*. São Paolo: Perspectiva, 1974.

————. *Cinema: Trajetoria no subdesenvolvimento*. Rio de Janeiro: Paz e Terra / Embrafilme, 1980.

Solanas, Fernando, and Octavio Getino. "Towards a Third Cinema." *Afterimage*, no. 3 (Summer 1971): 16–35. Also in *Movies and Methods*, edited by Bill Nichols. Berkeley and Los Angeles: University of California Press, 1976. (Originally published as "Hacia un tercer cine," *Tricontinental* [Havana], no. 13 [October 1969]. Revised translation in *Cineaste* 4, no. 3 [1970–71]: 1–10; and in *Twenty-five Years of the New Latin American Cinema*, edited by Michael Chanan. London: British Film Institute / Channel Four Television, 1983.)

————. *Cine, cultura y descolonización*. Mexico City: Siglo XXI, 1978.

Chapter 7. The Indian Subcontinent
Developments in Film Production

References to Satyajit Ray are listed separately in the bibliography to chapter 11.

Abbas, K. A. *I'm Not An Island*. Delhi: Vikas, 1977.

Banerjee, Shampa, ed. *New Indian Cinema*. New Delhi: Indian Directorate of Film Festivals, 1982.

————, ed. *Ritwik Ghatak*. New Delhi: Indian Directorate of Film Festivals, 1982.

Barnouw, Erik, and S. Krishnaswamy. *Indian Film*. New York: Columbia University Press, 1963; 2nd ed.: New York: Oxford University Press, 1980.

Baskaran, S. Theodore. *The Message Bearers: The Nationalist Politics and the Entertainment Media in South India, 1880–1945*. Madras: Cre-A, 1981.

Benegal, Shyam. *The Churning* (script). Calcutta: Seagull Books, 1984.

Burra, Rani, ed. *Indian Cinema 77/78*. New Delhi: Indian Directorate of Film Festivals, 1978.

————. *Looking Back: 1896–1960*. New Delhi: Indian Directorate of Film Festivals, 1981.

Cinema Vision India (Bombay), six issues, 1980–83.

Cinewave (Calcutta), seven issues to March 1985.

Da Cunha, Uma, ed. *Indian Cinema 78/79, Indian Cinema 79/80, Indian Cinema 80/81, Indian Cinema 83/84*. New Delhi: Indian Directorate of Film Festivals, 1979, 1980, 1981, 1984.

————. *The New Generation: 1960–1980*. New Delhi: Indian Directorate of Film Festivals, 1981.

Das Gupta, Chidananda. *Talking About Films*. New Delhi: Orient-Longman, 1981.

Datt, Gopal, ed. *Indian Cinema: The Next Decade*. Bombay: Indian Film Directors' Association, 1984.

Dharap, B. V. *Indian Films*. Pune: Motion Picture Enterprises, annually 1972–78.

Gopalakrishnan, Adoor. *The Rat Trap* (script). Calcutta: Seagull Books, 1985.

Gaur, Madan. *The Other Side of the Coin: An Intimate Study of Indian Film Industry*. Bombay: Trimurti Prakashan, 1973.

International Film Guide (London), annually since 1964. [Valuable, if irregular, surveys of production: Bangladesh—1978–81, 1986 (Alamgir Kabir and Fred Marshall); India—1969–70, 1972–86 (Chidananda Das Gupta and Uma da Cunha); Pakistan—1971, 1978, 1985–86 (Alamgir Kabir, Javed Jabbar, Edward H. Johnson, Ian McAuley, and Ijaz Gul); Sri Lanka—1974–78, 1980–86 (Philip Coorey, Amarnath Jayatilaka, and D. B. Warnasiri).]

Jabbar, Javed. "Preconditions for a Healthy Cinema in Pakistan." *Sequence* (Dacca), no. 2 (1970): 7–8, 39.

Jain, Rikhab Dass. *The Economic Aspects of the Film Industry in India*. Delhi: Atura Ram & Sons, 1960.

Kabir, Alamgir. *The Cinema in Pakistan*. Dacca: Sandhani Publications, 1969.

————. "A Study of the Pakistani Cinema." In *The Performing Arts in Asia*, edited by James R. Brandon. Paris: UNESCO, 1971.

————. *Film in Bangladesh*. Dacca: Bangla Academy, 1979.

————. "Twenty-five Years of Bangladesh Cinema." *Kino* (Calcutta) (April 1983): 9–15.

Kabir, Nasreen Munni. *Indian Cinema on Channel Four*. London: Channel Four Television, 1984.

Koch, Gerhard. *Franz Osten's Indian Silent Films*. New Delhi: Max Mueller Bhavan, 1983.

Micciolo, Henri. *Guru Dutt*. Paris: Anthologie du Cinéma, 1975.

Oommen, M. A., and K. V. Joseph. *Economics of Film Industry in India*. Gurgaon: Academic Press, 1981.

Parrain, Pierre. *Regards sur le cinéma indien*. Paris: Cerf, 1969.

Passek, Jean-Loup, ed. *Le cinéma indien*. Paris: Centre Georges Pompidou / L'Equerre, 1983.

Pearson, Lyle. "Sri Lankan Cinema." *Sequence* (Dacca) 4, no. 1 (1978): 21–23.

Raha, Kiranmoy, ed. *Indian Cinema 81/82*. New Delhi: Indian Directorate of Film Festivals, 1982.

Rajadhyaksha, Ashish. *Ritwik Ghatak: A Return to the Epic*. Bombay: Screen Unit, 1982.

Ramachandran, T. M., ed. *Seventy Years of Indian Cinema (1913–1983)*. Bombay: Cinema India International, 1985.

Rangoonwalla, Firoze. *Guru Dutt*. Pune: National Film Archive of India, 1973.

———. *A Pictorial History of Indian Cinema*. London: Hamlyn, 1979.

———. *Indian Cinema: Past and Present*. New Delhi: Clarion Books, 1983.

Report of the Film Enquiry Committee 1951. New Delhi: Government of India Press, 1951.

Report of the Indian Cinematograph Committee 1927–28. Madras: Government of India Central Publications Branch, 1928.

Sarkar, Kobita. *Indian Cinema Today*. Delhi: Sterling Publishers, 1975.

Sen Mrinal. *Views on Cinema*. Calcutta: Ishan Publications, 1977.

———. *In Search of Famine* (script). Calcutta: Seagull Books, 1983.

———. *The Ruins* (script). Calcutta: Seagull Books, 1984.

Shah, Panna. *The Indian Film*. Bombay: Motion Picture Society, 1950.

"Sri Lanka." Dossier. *Cinéma 76*, no. 216 (December 1976): 74–80.

Vasudev, Aruna. *Liberty and Licence in the Indian Cinema*. New Delhi: Vikas, 1978.

———. *The Role of the Cinema in Promoting Popular Participation in Cultural Life in India*. Paris: UNESCO, 1981.

———. *The Film Industry's Use of the Traditional and Contemporary Arts*. Paris: UNESCO, 1982.

———. *Indian Cinema 82/83*. New Delhi: Indian Directorate of Film Festivals, 1983.

Vasudev, Aruna, and Philippe Lenglet, eds. *Indian Cinema Superbazaar*. New Delhi: Vikas, 1983.

Willemen, Paul, and Behroze Gandhy, eds. *Indian Cinema*. London: British Film Institute, 1980.

Social and Economic Background

Alavi, Hamza. "India and the Colonial Mode of Production." In *The Socialist Register 1975*, edited by R. Milibrand and J. Savile. London: Merlin, 1975.

Ali, Tariq. *Can Pakistan Survive?* Harmondsworth: Penguin, 1983.

Charlesworth, Neil. *British Rule and the Indian Economy, 1800–1914*. London: Macmillan, 1982.

Gardezi, Hassan, and Jamil Rashid, eds. *Pakistan: The Roots of Dictatorship*. London: Zed, 1983.

Gough, Kathleen, and Hari P. Sharma, eds. *Imperialism and Revolution in South Asia*. New York: Monthly Review Press, 1973.

Patnaik, Prabhat. "Imperialism and the Growth of Indian Capitalism." In *Studies in the Theory of Imperialism*, edited by Roger Owen and Bob Sutcliffe. London: Longman, 1972.

Ponnambalam, Satchi. *Dependent Capitalism in Crisis: The Sri Lankan Economy 1948–1980*. London: Zed, 1981.

————. *Sri Lanka: National Conflict and the Tamil Liberation Struggle.* London: Zed, 1983.

Sau, Ranjit. *India's Economic Development: Aspects of Class Relations.* London: Sangam Books, 1983.

Spear, Percival. *A History of India.* Vol. 2. Harmondsworth: Penguin, 1965.

Thapar, Romila. *A History of India.* Vol. 1. Harmondsworth: Penguin, 1966.

Chapter 8. East and Southeast Asia
Developments in Film Production

Bergeron, Régis. *Le cinéma chinois 1: 1905–1949.* Lausanne: Alfred Eibel, 1977.

————. *Le cinéma chinois 2: 1949–1983.* 3 vols. Paris: L'Harmattan, 1983.

"Cinéma philippin." Dossier. *L'avant-scène du cinéma,* no. 287 (May 1982): 45–50.

Cosandey, Roland. "Pour servir à l'histoire du cinéma chinois (1930–1982)." *Cahiers de la cinémathèque,* no. 37 (Summer 1983): 11–27.

Glaessner, Verina. *Kung Fu: Cinema of Violence.* London: Lorrimer, 1974.

International Film Guide (London), annually since 1964. [Valuable, if irregular, surveys of production: Burma—1979, 1983–86 (I. M. Sudan and Fred Marshall); Thailand—1979–81, 1983–86 (Fred Marshall, Michael Denison, and Krit Kounavudhi); Malaysia—1972–86 (Baharudin A. Latif); Indonesia—1975–76, 1981–86 (Baharudin A. Latif and Fred Marshall); Philippines—1979–86 (Oskar Salazar and Agustin Sotto); Hong Kong and Taiwan—1976–86 (Verina Glaessner and Derek Elley); Korea (Republic of)—1981, 1983–86 (Kai Hong, Fred Marshall, and Derek Elley); Singapore—1984–85 (Fred Marshall).]

Introduction to Korean Motion Pictures. Seoul: Motion Picture Production Corporation, Republic of Korea [1980].

Jarvie, I. C. *Window on Hong Kong: A Sociological Study of the Hong Kong Film Industry and Its Audience.* Hong Kong: University of Hong Kong Centre for Asian Studies, 1977.

Lau Shing-hon, ed. *A Study of the Hong Kong Martial Arts Film.* Hong Kong: Fourth International Film Festival, 1980.

————. *A Study of the Hong Kong Swordplay Film, 1945–80.* Hong Kong: Fifth International Film Festival, 1981.

Leyda, Jay. *Dianying: Electric Shadows—An Account of Films and Film Audience in China.* Cambridge, Mass.: MIT Press, 1972.

Li Cheuk-to, ed. *A Study of Hong Kong Cinema in the Seventies.* Hong Kong: Eighth International Film Festival, 1984.

Lin Niantong, ed. *Cantonese Cinema Retrospective, 1950–59.* Hong Kong: Second International Film Festival, 1978.

————. *Hong Kong Cinema Survey, 1946–68.* Hong Kong: Third International Film Festival, 1979.

"Made in Hong Kong." Special issue. *Cahiers du Cinéma,* nos. 362–63 (September 1984).

Newell, Grenfell. *Switch On: Switch Off—Mass Media Audiences in Malaysia.* Kuala Lumpur: Oxford University Press, 1979.

Ombres électriques: Panorama du cinéma chinois 1925–1982. Paris: Centre de Documentation sur le Cinéma Chinois, 1982.

Pinga, Ben G. "Cinema in the Philippines." In *The Performing Arts in Asia,* edited by James R. Brandon. Paris: UNESCO, 1971.

Quiquemelle, Marie-Claire, and Jean-Loup Passek, eds. *Le cinéma chinois.* Paris: Centre Georges Pompidou, 1985.

Rayns, Tony, and Scott Meek. *Electric Shadows: Forty-five Years of Chinese Cinema.* London: British Film Institute, 1980.

Schwab, Christophe. "Philippines 83." *Positif,* no. 268 (June 1983): 44–47.

Shu Kei, ed. *Cantonese Cinema Retrospective, 1960–69.* Hong Kong: Sixth International Film Festival, 1982.

———. *A Comparative Study of Postwar Mandarin and Cantonese Cinema.* Hong Kong: Seventh International Film Festival, 1983.

Tessier, Max. "Le cinéma philippin." *La revue du cinéma—Image et son—Ecran,* no. 375 (September 1982): 85–100.

Tobias, Mel. *Memoirs of an Asian Moviegoer.* Hong Kong: SCMP Publications, 1982.

"Vietnamese Cinema." Dossier. (Pham Ngoc Truong, "Vietnamese Cinema from Its Origins to 1945," and Bui Phui, "The Seventh Goddess.") *Framework,* no. 25 (1985): 63–93.

Social and Economic Background

Amin, Mohamed, and Malcolm Caldwell, eds. *Malaya: The Making of a Neocolony.* Nottingham, England: Spokesman Books, 1977.

Bandey, B. N. *South and Southeast Asia 1945–1970.* London: Macmillan, 1980.

Elliott, David. *Thailand: Origins of Military Rule.* London: Zed, 1978.

Fitzgerald, C. P. *A Concise History of East Asia.* Harmondsworth: Penguin, 1974.

Hamilton, Clive. "Capitalist Industrialization in the Four Little Tigers of East Asia." In *Neo-Marxist Theories of Development,* edited by Peter Limqueco and Bruce McFarlane. London: Croom Helm, 1983.

Jeffrey, Robin, ed. *Asia: The Winning of Independence.* London: Macmillan, 1981.

McCormack, Gavin, and John Gittings, eds. *Crisis in Korea.* Nottingham, England: Spokesman Books, 1977.

Schurmann, Franz, and Orville Schell, eds. *China Readings,* vol. 2: *Republican China.* Harmondsworth: Penguin, 1968.

Silverstein, Josef. *Burma: Military Rule and the Politics of Stagnation.* Ithaca, N.Y.: Cornell University Press, 1977.

Southwood, Julie, and Patrick Flanagan. *Indonesia: Law, Propaganda, and Terror.* London: Zed, 1983.

Williams, Lea A. *Southeast Asia.* New York: Oxford University Press, 1976.

Yin, Hua Wu. *Class and Communalism in Malaysia.* London: Zed, 1983.

Chapter 9. Latin America
Developments in Film Production

References to Glauber Rocha and Jorge Sanjinés are listed separately in bibliographies to chapters 13 and 16, respectively.

Alvarez, Santiago, et al. *Cine y revolución en Cuba.* Barcelona, Spain: Fontemara, 1975.

Ayala Blanco, Jorge. *La aventura del cine mexicano.* Mexico City: Ediciones Era, 1968.

———. *La busqueda del cine mexicano: 1968–1972.* Mexico City: UNAM, 1974.

Bernardet, Jean Claude. *Brasil en tempo de cinema.* Rio de Janeiro: Paz e Terra, 1977.

———. *Cinema brasileiro: Propostas para uma historia.* Rio de Janeiro: Paz e Terra, 1979.

Bolzoni, Francesco. *El cine de Allende.* Valencia, Spain: Fernando Torres, 1974. (Translated from the Italian: *Il cinema di Allende.* N.p.: Marsilio Editori, 1974.)

"Brasil Ano 1970." *Cinemantics,* no. 2 (March–April 1970): 9–16.

"Brazil—Post Cinema Novo." Special issue. *Framework* 28 (1985).

"Brazilian Renaissance." Parts 1, 2. *Jump Cut,* no. 21 (November 1979): 13–22, and no. 22 (May 1980): 15–24.

Burton, Julianne. "The Hour of the Embers: On the Current Situation of Latin American Cinema." *Film Quarterly* 30, no. 1 (1976): 33–44.

———. "Cultural Context and Selective Perception: *Memories of Underdevelopment* in the Land of Overdevelopment." *Cineaste* 5, no. 1 (1977): 16–21.

———. "*Chuquiago* (The Unspoken and the Unspeakable)." *Cineaste* 9, no. 3 (1979): 50–53.

———. "Film Making in Nicaragua from Insurrection to Incine." *Cineaste* 10, no. 2 (1980): 28–31.

———. *The New Latin American Cinema: An Annotated Bibliography 1960–1980.* 2d ed. New York: Smyrna Press, 1983. [The indispensable reference work on Latin American cinema.]

Chanan, Michael, ed. *Chilean Cinema.* London: British Film Institute, 1976.

———. *Santiago Alvarez.* London: British Film Institute, 1980.

———. *The Cuban Image.* London: British Film Institute, 1985.

"Chilean Cinema." Dossier. *Ciné-Tracts,* no. 9 (Winter 1980): 18–55.

"Chili: Le cinéma de l'unité populaire." *Ecran 74,* no. 22 (February 1974): 13–20.

"Cinéma d'Amérique latine." *Cinéma 74,* no. 187 (May 1974): 38–61.

Coad, Malcolm. "Rebirth of Chilean Cinema." *Index on Censorship* 9, no. 2 (1980): 3–8.

Contreras y Espinosa, Fernando. *La producción, sector primario de la industria cinematográfica.* Mexico City: UNAM, 1973.

Contreras Torres, Miguel. *El libro negro del cine mexicano.* Mexico City: Editora Hispano-Continental Films, 1960.

de los Reyes, Aurelio. *Los origenes del cine en México: 1896–1900.* Mexico City: UNAM, 1973.

de los Reyes, Aurelio, et al. *80 años de cine en México.* Mexico City: Imprenta Madero, 1977.

de Paula Araujo, Vicente. *A bela epoca do cinema brasileiro.* São Paulo: Perspectiva, 1976.

Estève, Michel, ed. *Le cinéma novo brésilien,* vol. 1; and vol. 2: *Glauber Rocha.* Paris: Lettres Modernes, 1972.

Frias, Isaac Leon, ed. *Los años de la conmoción, 1967–1973: Entrevistas con realizadores sudamericanos.* Mexico City: UNAM, 1979.

Galindo, Alejandro. *¿Qué es el cine?* Mexico City: Nuestro Tiempo, 1975.

Galvão, Maria Rita Eliezer. *Crónica do cinema paulistano.* São Paulo: Atica, 1975.

García Riera, Emilio. *El cine mexicano.* Mexico City: Ediciones Era, 1963.

————. *Historia documental del cine mexicano.* 8 vols. Mexico City: Ediciones Era, 1969–74.

Gardies, René. *Glauber Rocha.* Paris: Seghers, 1974.

Getino, Octavio. *Cine y dependencia: El cine en la Argentina.* Buenos Aires / Lima: Cine Liberación, 1976–78.

Giudici, Alberto. *El cine argentino; Hollywood: Del esplendor al ocaso.* Buenos Aires: Acción, 1976.

Godoy Quesada, Mario. *Historia del cine chileno.* Santiago: N.p., 1966.

Gumucio-Dagron, Alfonso, ed. *Cine, censura y exilio en América latina.* La Paz: Ediciones Film / Historia, 1979.

————. *"Chuquiago:* X-Ray of a City." *Jump Cut,* no. 23 (October 1980): 6–8.

Guzmán, Patricio, and Pedro Sempere. *Chile: El cine contra el fascismo.* Valencia, Spain: Fernando Torres, 1977.

Hennebelle, Guy, and Alfonso Gumucio-Dagron, eds. *Les cinémas de l'Amérique latine.* Paris: Lherminier, 1981.

Heuer, Federico. *La industria cinematográfica mexicana.* Mexico City: Federico Heuer, 1964.

Hijar, Alberto, ed. *Hacia un tercer cine.* Mexico City: UNAM, 1972.

Johnson, Randal. "Brazilian Cinema Today." *Film Quarterly* 31, no. 4 (1978): 42–45.

————. *Cinema Novo × 5: Masters of Contemporary Brazilian Film.* Austin: University of Texas Press, 1984.

Johnson, Randal, and Robert Stam, eds. *Brazilian Cinema.* Rutherford, N.J.: Fairleigh Dickinson University Press, 1982.

Keel, Erich. "From Militant Cinema to Neorealism: The Example of *Pueblo Chico.*" *Film Quarterly* 19, no. 4 (1976): 17–24.

Lamont, Ann, Richard Walker, and Michael Chanan. *Film in El Salvador Has Been Born with War.* London: Salvadorean Film Institute Support Group, n.d.

"Latin America—Cinema as Social Practice—Havana Film Festival—Interviews." Dossier. *Undercut,* no. 12 (Summer 1984): 1–21.

"Latin American Dossier." Parts 1, 2. *Framework,* no. 10 (Spring 1979): 11–38, and no. 11 (Autumn 1979): 18–27.

"Latin American Film." Dossier. *Jump Cut,* no. 30 (March 1985): 44–61.

"Latin American Militant Cinema." Special issue. *Cineaste* 4, no. 3 (1970–71).

Littin, Miguel. *Cine chileno: La tierra prometida.* Caracas: Rocinante, 1974.

————. *El chacal de Nahueltoro: La tierra prometida.* Mexico City: UNAM, 1977.

Mahieu, José Agustin. *Breve historia del cine argentino.* Buenos Aires: EUDEBA, 1966.

Martin, Marcel. "Le cinéma cubain à la croisière des chemins." *La revue du cinéma— Image et son,* no. 360 (April 1981): 111–20.

Martínez Pardo, Hernando. *Historia del cine colombiano.* Bogotá: Guadalupe, 1978.

Martínez Torres, Augusto, and Manuel Pérez Estremera. "Chile: Introduction to the Chilean Cinema." *Cinema-TV Digest,* no. 33 (Fall 1972): 31–32.

————. *Nuevo cine latinoamericano.* Barcelona, Spain: Editorial Anagrama, 1973.

Mesa G., Carlos D. *El cine en Bolivia.* La Paz: Don Bosco de la Laz, 1976.

Mesa G., Carlos D., Beatriz Palacios, Jorge Sanjinés, Arturo Von Vacano, et al. *Cine boliviano: Del realizador al crítico.* La Paz: Gisbert, 1979.

Meyer, Eugenia, ed. *Cuadernos de la cineteca nacional: Testimonios para la historia del cine mexicano*. Mexico City: Secretariat of the Interior, Directorate of Cinematography, 1976.

Michel, Manuel. "Mexican Cinema: A Panoramic View." *Film Quarterly* 18, no. 4 (1965): 46–55.

Mora, Carl J. *The Mexican Cinema*. Berkeley and Los Angeles: University of California Press, 1982.

Myerson, Michael, ed. *Memories of Underdevelopment—The Revolutionary Films of Cuba*. New York: Grossman, 1973.

Nevares, Beatriz Reyes. *The Mexican Cinema—Interviews with Thirteen Directors*. Albuquerque: University of New Mexico Press, 1976.

Oms, Marcel. *Leopoldo Torre Nilsson*. Lyons, France: Serdoc, 1962.

Palacios More, Rene, and Daniel Mateus. *El cine latinoamericano*. Madrid: Sedmany, 1976.

Paranagua, Paulo Antonio, José Carlos Avellar, eds. *Cinéma brésilien 1970–1980*. Documentation for the International Film Festival, Locarno, 1983.

Pick, Zuzana M. "Latin American Cinema: A View Towards the Future of Documentary Practice." *Ciné-Tracts*, nos. 14–15 (Summer–Fall 1981): 64–70.

Por un cine latinoamericano. Caracas: Rocinante, 1978.

Proppe, Hans, and Susan Tarr. "Cinema Novo: The Pitfalls of Cultural Nationalism." *Jump Cut*, nos. 10–11 (June 1976): 45–48.

"Quinze ans de cinéma cubain." *Ecran 77*, no. 54 (January 1977): 19–36.

Schnitman, Jorge A. *Film Industries in Latin America: Dependency and Development*. Norwood, N.J.: Ablex, 1984.

"Spéciale Amérique latine." *Cinéma 70*, no. 144 (March 1970): 36–102.

Stam, Robert. "Brazilian Avant-Garde Cinema: From *Limite* to *Red Light Bandit*." *Millennium Film Journal*, no. 5 (Summer–Fall 1979): 32–42.

———. "*Hour of the Furnaces* and the Two Avant-Gardes." *Millennium Film Journal*, nos. 7–9 (Fall–Winter 1980–81): 151–64.

Stam, Robert, and Ismail Xavier. "Brazilian Avant-Garde: Metacinema in the Triste Tropiques." *Millennium Film Journal*, no. 6 (Spring 1980): 82–89.

Sutherland, Elizabeth. "Cinema of Revolution—90 Miles from Home." *Film Quarterly* 16, no. 2 (1961–62): 42–49.

Thevenet, Homero Alsina, ed. *Reportaje al cine argentino: Los pioneros del sonoro*. Buenos Aires: América Norildis, 1978.

"Third World Cinema." Dossier. *Afterimage*, no. 3 (Summer 1971): 8–77.

Trémège, Bernard, and Roland Cosandey, eds. *Semaine nationale du cinéma mexicain*. Documentation for the International Film Festival, Locarno, 1982.

Trevino, Jesús Salvador. "The New Mexican Cinema." *Film Quarterly* 32, no. 3 (1979): 26–37.

"Twenty Years of Revolutionary Cuban Cinema." Parts 1–3. *Jump Cut*, no. 19 (December 1978): 17–33; no. 20 (May 1979): 13–29; and no. 22 (May 1980): 25–34.

Valverde, Umberto. *Reportaje crítico al cine colombiano*. Bogotá: Toronuevo, 1978.

Vega, Alicia, ed. *Re-vision del cine chileno*. Santiago: Aconcagua, 1979.

Vianey, Alex. "Brazil: In Step with a Latin Beat." *Films and Filming* 10, no.2 (1963): 51–53.

Social and Economic Background

Bolivia: Coup d'Etat. London: Latin American Bureau, 1980.
Brazil: State and Struggle. London: Latin American Bureau, 1982.
Burns, E. Bradford. *Latin America: A Concise Interpretative History.* 3d ed. Englewood Cliffs, N.J.: Prentice-Hall, 1982.
Cardoso, F. H., and E. Paletto. *Dependency and Development in Latin America.* Berkeley and Los Angeles: University of California Press, 1979.
Clissold, Stephen. *Latin America—A Cultural Outline.* London: Hutchinson, 1965.
Dunkerley, James. *Rebellion in Their Veins: Political Struggle in Bolivia 1952–1982.* London: Verso, 1984.
Furtado, Celso. *The Economic Growth of Brazil.* Berkeley and Los Angeles: University of California Press, 1965.
———. *Economic Development in Latin America: From Colonial Times to the Cuban Revolution.* Cambridge: Cambridge University Press, 1970.
Galeano, E. *The Open Veins of Latin America.* New York: Monthly Review Press, 1973.
Griffiths, John, and Peter Griffiths. *Cuba—The Second Decade.* London: Writers and Readers Publishing Cooperative, 1979.
Lambert, Jacques. *Latin America: Social Structures and Political Institutions.* Berkeley and Los Angeles: University of California Press, 1967.
Paraguay: Power Game. London: Latin American Bureau, 1980.
Pendle, George. *A History of Latin America.* Rev. ed. Harmondsworth: Penguin, 1976.
Uruguay: Generals Rule. London: Latin American Bureau, 1980.

Chapter 10. The Middle East and Africa
Developments in Film Production

References to Yılmaz Güney and Ousmane Sembene are listed separately in the bibliographies to chapters 14 and 15, respectively.

Adhoua (Paris), four issues, 1980–81.
"African Dossier: Hondo, Gerima, Sembene." *Framework,* nos. 7–8 (Spring 1978): 20–37.
Arab Cinema and Culture: Round Table Conferences. 3 vols. Beirut: Arab Film and Television Center, 1965.
Armes, Roy. "Black African Cinema in the Eighties." *Screen* 26, nos. 3–4 (1985): 60–73.
Awed, Ibrahim M., Hussein M. Adam, and Lionel Ngakane, eds. *Pan-African Cinema . . . Which Way Ahead?* Proceedings of the First Mogadishu Pan-African Film Symposium. Mogadishu, Somalia: Mogpafis Management Committee, 1983.
Bachy, Victor. *Le cinéma de Tunisie.* Tunis: Société Tunisienne de Diffusion, 1976.
———. *Le cinéma au Mali.* Brussels: OCIC, 1982.
———. *Le cinéma en Côte d'Ivoire.* Brussels: OCIC, 1982.
———. *La Haute Volta et le cinéma.* Brussels: OCIC, 1982.

Balogun, Françoise. *Le cinéma au Nigéria*. Brussels / Paris: OCIC / L'Harmattan, 1984.

Berrah, Mouny, et al. *Cinémas du Maghreb*. Paris: *CinémAction*, no. 14 / Papyrus Editions, 1981.

Binet, Jacques, Ferid Boughedir, and Victor Bachy, eds. *Cinémas noirs d'Afrique*. Paris: *CinémAction*, no. 26 / L'Harmattan, 1983.

Bosséno, Christian. "Le cinéma en Algérie." *La revue du cinéma—Image et son*, no. 327 (April 1978): 55–96.

———. "Le cinéma tunisien." *La revue du cinéma*, no. 382 (April 1983): 49–62.

Boujedra, Rachid. *Naissance du cinéma algérien*. Paris: François Maspéro, 1971.

Boughedir, Ferid. "Report and Prospects." In *Cinema and Society*, edited by Enrico Fulchignoni. Paris: ITFC / UNESCO, 1982.

———. "Le cinéma en Afrique et dans le monde." *Jeune Afrique plus*, no. 6 (April 1984).

Brossard, Jean-Pierre. *L'Algérie vue par son cinéma*. Documentation for the International Film Festival, Locarno, 1981.

Calder, Angus, et al. *African Fiction and Film: Three Short Case Studies*. Milton Keynes, Eng.: Open University Press, 1983. [Open University course book.]

Centre d'Étude sur la Communication en Afrique (CESCA). *Camera nigra—Le discours du film africain*. Brussels / Paris: OCIC / L'Harmattan, 1984.

"Le cinéma iranien." Dossier. *CinémArabe*, no. 9 (June–July 1978): 10–22.

CinémArabe (Paris), twelve issues, 1976–79.

Cinémas des pays arabes. 3 vols.: *Le cinéma en Egypte*, *Les cinémas marocain, tunisien, mauritanien*, and *Le cinéma algérien*. Algiers: Cinémathèque Algérienne / Cinémathèque Française [1977]. Photocopy.

Cinéma 3 (Casablanca), three issues in 1970.

Cluny, Claude-Michel. "Cinéma de Bahrein." *Cinéma 73*, nos. 178–79 (July–August 1973): 18–19.

———. "Actualité du cinéma arabe." *Cinéma 77*, no. 222 (June 1977): 31–40.

———. *Dictionnaire des nouveaux cinémas arabes*. Paris: Sindbad, 1978.

Cluny, Claude-Michel, and Salah Dehny. "L'expérience du cinéma en Syrie." *Cinéma 75*, no. 197 (April 1975): 98–115.

Dadci, Younes. *Dialogues Algérie-cinéma*. Paris: Editions Dadci, 1970.

Les deux écrans (Algiers), issued monthly from 1978.

Diawara, Manthia. "African Cinema: FESPACO, an Evaluation." In *Third World Affairs 1986*, edited by Raana Gauhar. London: Third World Foundation for Social and Economic Studies, 1986.

Farid, Samir. "Les six générations du cinéma égyptien." *Ecran*, no. 15 (May 1973): 38–48.

———. *Arab Cinema Guide*. Cairo: Arab Cinema Guide, 1979.

Festival du film arabe, Paris. Documentation issued for the annual festivals held since 1983.

Gaffary, Farrokh. *Le cinéma en Iran*. Teheran: High Council of Culture and Art, Center for Research and Cultural Coordination, 1973.

Goux-Pelletan, Jean-Pierre. "Petite planète du cinéma: Liban." *Cinéma 71*, no. 161 (December 1971): 97–104.

Haffner, Pierre. *Essai sur les fondements du cinéma africain.* Paris: Nouvelles Editions Africaines, 1978.

Haustrate, Gaston, et al. "Le cinéma algérien." *Cinéma 76,* no. 207 (March 1976): 36–92.

Hennebelle, Guy, ed. *Les cinémas africains en 1972.* Paris: *L'Afrique littéraire et artistique,* no. 20 / Société Africaine d'Édition, 1972.

———, ed. "Le cinéma syrien." Dossier. *L'Afrique littéraire et artistique,* no. 36 (1975): 87–98.

———. "Arab Cinema." *Merip Reports,* no. 52 (November 1976): 3–12.

Hennebelle, Guy, and Janine Euvard, eds. *Israël-Palestine: Que peut le cinéma?* Paris: *L'Afrique littéraire et artistique,* no. 47 / Société Africaine d'Édition, 1978.

Hennebelle, Guy, and Khemaïs Khayati. *La Palestine et le cinéma.* Paris: E 100, 1977.

Hennebelle, Guy, and Catherine Ruelle, eds. *Cinéastes d'Afrique noire.* Paris: *CinémAction,* no. 3 / *L'Afrique littéraire et artistique,* no. 49, 1978.

International Film Guide (London), annually since 1964. [Valuable, if irregular, surveys of production. For the non-Arab Middle East: Afghanistan—1978, 1980–83 (Lyle Pearson); Iran—1973–82, 1986 (Hagir Daryoush); Turkey—1969, 1974–81, 1983 (Attilâ Dorsay, Giovanni Scognamillo, and Vecdi Sayar). For Egypt and the Arab world: Egypt—1974–81 (Abel Moneim Saad); Iraq—1979–82 (Mohammed Rida); Lebanon—1976, 1978 (Leon Torossian and Mohammed Rida); Syria— 1976, 1978–79 (Mohammed Rida); Algeria—1972, 1976, 1979, 1986 (Viggo Holm Jensen, Mohammed Rida, and Lizbeth Malkmus); Morocco—1979, 1983, 1986 (Mohammed Rida, Lyle Pearson, and Lizbeth Malkmus); Tunisia—1973, 1979, 1986 (Viggo Holm Jensen, Mohammed Rida, and Lizbeth Malkmus). For black Africa: general dossier—1975 (Viggo Holm Jensen); Cameroon—1986 (Roy Armes); Congo—1984 (Roy Armes); Gabon—1984 (Roy Armes); Guinea—1972 (Viggo Holm Jensen and Vibeke Pedersen); Ivory Coast—1972, 1974, 1984, 1986 (Viggo Holm Jensen, Vibeke Pedersen, and Roy Armes); Mali—1984 (Roy Armes); Mozambique—1979 (Alfonso Gumucio-Dagron); Niger—1972–74, 1984 (Viggo Holm Jensen, Vibeke Pedersen, and Roy Armes); Nigeria—1986 (Roy Armes); Senegal—1972–74, 1976, 1983, 1985 (Viggo Holm Jensen, Lyle Pearson, and Roy Armes); Upper Volta (Burkina Faso)—1974, 1984 (Viggo Holm Jensen and Roy Armes).]

Isitan, Ishak. "Turquie: Le cinéma du peuple." *CinémArabe,* no. 12 (July–August 1979): 30–31.

Kamphausen, M. "Cinema in Africa: A Survey." *Cineaste* 5, no. 3 (1972): 28–41.

Khan, M. *An Introduction to the Egyptian Cinema.* London: Informatics, 1969.

Khlifi, Omar. *L'Histoire du cinéma en Tunisie.* Tunis: Société Tunisienne de Diffusion, 1970.

Maarek, Philippe J., ed. *Afrique noire: Quel cinéma?* Paris: Association du Ciné-Club de l'Université Paris X, 1983.

McMullin, Corinne, Gérard Courant, and Gaston Haustrate. "Dossier: Révolution de l'image—Images de la révolution en Iran." *Cinéma 81,* no. 270 (June 1981): 57–75.

al-Mafraji, Ahmed Fayadh. *The Cinema in Iraq.* Baghdad: Research and Studies Center, General Establishment for Cinema and Theater, Ministry of Culture and Information, [1978].

Maherzi, Lofti. *Le cinéma algérien: Institutions, imaginaire, idéologie.* Algiers: Société Nationale d'Edition et de Diffusion, 1980.

Malkmus, Lizbeth. "A Desk Between Two Borders." *Framework,* no. 29 (1985): 16–29.

———. "Arab Cinema: Avoiding the Ghetto." *Third World Affairs 1986,* edited by Raana Gauhar. London: Third World Foundation for Social and Economic Studies, 1986.

Mar'a (New York), three issues as supplements to *Cineaste,* 1979–80.

Martin, Angela. "Four West African Film-Makers," *Framework,* no. 11 (Autumn 1979): 16–21.

———. *African Films: The Context of Production.* London: British Film Institute, 1982.

———. *Africa on Africa.* London: Channel Four Television, 1984.

Motavalli, John. "Exiles—Iran: Cinema in Flames." *Film Comment* 19, no. 4 (1983): 56–59.

Naficy, Hamid. "Iranian Feature Film: A Brief Critical History." *Quarterly Review of Film Studies* 4, no. 4 (1979): 443–64.

Opubor, Alfred E., and Onuora E. Nwuneli. *The Development and Growth of the Film Industry in Nigeria.* Lagos: Third Press International, 1979.

Otten, Rik. *Le cinéma au Zaïre, au Rwanda et au Burundi.* Brussels / Paris: OCIC / L'Harmattan, 1984.

Pommier, Pierre. *Cinéma et développement en Afrique noire francophone.* Paris: Pedone, 1974.

Post-Revolutionary Iranian Cinema. Teheran: General Department of Cinematic Research and Relations, 1982.

Sadoul, Georges, ed. *The Cinema in the Arab Countries.* Beirut: Interarab Center for Cinema and Television / UNESCO, 1966.

Salmane, Hala, et al. *Algerian Cinema.* London: British Film Institute, 1976.

Scognamillo, Giovanni, et al. *The Turkish Cinema.* Istanbul: IDGSA, 1979.

"Séminaire sur le rôle du cinéaste dans l'éveil d'une conscience de civilisation noire— Ouagadougou 8–13 avril 1974." Dossier. *Présence africaine,* no. 90 (1974): 3–203.

SeptièmArt [formerly *Goha*] (Tunis), fifty-two issues, 1964–Autumn 1984.

Thoraval, Yves. *Regards sur le cinéma égyptien.* Beirut: Dar el-Machreq, 1975.

Turkish Cinema with Stills, from Its Beginnings up to Date. Istanbul: Cinema and Television Institute, 1979.

Unir-Cinéma (Saint-Louis, Senegal), fifteen issues to December 1984.

"Vers un 'cinema novo' égyptien." Dossier. *Ecran,* no. 73 (May 1973): 34–53.

Vieyra, Paulin Soumanou. *Le cinéma et l'Afrique.* Paris: Présence Africaine, 1969.

———. *Le cinéma africain des origines à 1973.* Paris: Présence Africaine, 1975.

———. *Le cinéma au Sénégal.* Brussels / Paris: OCIC / L'Harmattan, 1983.

Weaver, Harold. "The Politics of African Cinema." In *Black Cinema Aesthetics,* edited by Gladstone L. Yearwood. Athens: Ohio University Center for Afro-American Studies, 1982.

Social and Economic Background

Ajami, Fouad. *The Arab Predicament: Arab Political Thought and Practice Since 1967*. Cambridge: Cambridge University Press, 1981.

Allen, Chris, and Gavin Williams, eds. *Sociology of "Developing Societies": Sub-Saharan Africa*. London: Macmillan, 1982.

Amin, Samir. *The Maghreb in the Modern World*. Harmondsworth: Penguin, 1970.

———. *Neo-Colonialism in West Africa*. New York: Monthly Review Press, 1974.

———. *The Arab Nation*. London: Zed, 1978.

———. *The Arab Economy Today*. London: Zed, 1982.

Asad, Talal, and Roger Owen, eds. *Sociology of "Developing Societies": The Middle East*. London: Macmillan, 1983.

Berberoglu, Berch. "Turkey: The Crisis of the Neocolonialist System." *Race and Class* 22, no. 3 (1981): 277–91.

Calvocoressi, Peter. *Independent Africa and the World*. London: Longman, 1985.

Cartney, Wilfred, and Martin Kilson, eds. *The Africa Reader: Independent Africa*. New York: Random House, 1970.

Clawson, Patrick. "The Development of Capitalism in Egypt." *Khamsin*, no. 9 (1981): 77–116.

Davidson, Basil. *The African Past*. Harmondsworth: Penguin, 1966.

———. *The Africans: An Entry into Cultural History*. Harmondsworth: Penguin, 1973.

———. *Africa in Modern History*. Harmondsworth: Penguin, 1978.

Dodd, C. H. *Democracy and Development in Turkey*. Walkington, Eng.: Eothen Press, 1981.

François, Pierre. "Class Struggles in Mali." *Review of African Political Economy*, no. 24 (May–August 1982): 22–38.

Halliday, Fred. *Arabia Without Sultans*. Harmondsworth: Penguin, 1974.

———. *Iran: Dictatorship or Development*. Harmondsworth: Penguin, 1979.

Hourani, Cecil, ed. *The Arab Cultural Scene*. London: Namara Press, 1982.

Hussein, Mahmoud. *Class Conflict in Egypt: 1945–1970*. New York: Monthly Review Press, 1973.

Iliffe, John. *The Emergence of African Capitalism*. London: Macmillan, 1983.

Lloyd, P. C. *Africa in Social Change*. Harmondsworth: Penguin, 1967.

Mansfield, Peter. *The Arabs*. Harmondsworth: Penguin, 1979.

Minter, William. *Portuguese Africa and the West*. Harmondsworth: Penguin, 1972.

Oliver, Roland, and J. D. Fage. *A Short History of Africa*. Harmondsworth: Penguin, 1962.

Said, Edward W. *The Question of Palestine*. London: Routledge and Kegan Paul, 1980.

Vatikiotis, P. J. *The History of Egypt*. London: Weidenfeld and Nicolson, 1980.

Chapter 11. Satyajit Ray
Ray's English Publications

Ray has published extensively in Bengali: twenty-two children's books, three screenplays, and a book on film aesthetics. In English, his publications include a novel, a collection of articles on cinema, some individual essays, and two scripts.

Our Films, Their Films. New Delhi: Orient Longman, 1976. [Collection.]
"I Wish I Could Have Shown Them To You." *Cinema Vision India* 1, no. 1 (1980): 6–7.
"The New Cinema and I." *Cinema Vision India* 1, no. 3 (1980): 14–16.
Pather panchali. Script. Bombay: Cine Central, 1984. Translated into French in *L'avant-scène du cinéma*, no. 241 (1 February 1980).
"Under Western Eyes." *Sight and Sound* 51, no. 4 (1982): 268–74.
"The Education of a Film Maker." *New Left Review*, no. 141 (September–October 1983): 79–94.
Phatik Chand. Delhi: Orient Paperbacks, 1983. [Novel.]
The "Apu" Triology. Script. Calcutta: Seagull, 1985.

Interviews

"The Growing Edge" (interview with Hugh Gray). *Film Quarterly* 12, no. 2 (1958): 4–7.
Interview with Guy Gauthier. *Image et son*, no. 178 (November 1964): 69–78.
"A Director's Perspective." *Montage* (Bombay), nos. 5–6 (July 1966): n.p.
Interview with James Blue. *Film Comment* 4, no. 4 (1968): 4–17.
"How I Make My Films" (interview with Lindsay Anderson). *Film World* (Bombay) 5, no. 4 (1969): 80–82.
"Rencontre avec Satyajit Ray" (interview with Jacques Aumont). *Cahiers du cinéma*, no. 216 (October 1969): 9–10.
Interview with Peter Cargin and Bernard Cohn. *Positif*, no. 112 (June 1970): 19–34.
"Conversation with Satyajit Ray" (interview with Folke Isaaksson). *Sight and Sound* 39, no. 3 (1970): 114–20.
"Ray's New Trilogy" (interview with Christian Braad Thomsen). *Sight and Sound* 42, no. 1 (1975): 31–33.
"A Voyage in India" (interview with John Hughes). *Film Comment* 12, no. 5 (1976): 52–54.
"Dialogue on Film." *American Film* 3, no. 9 (1978): 39–50.
Interview with Michel Ciment. *Positif*, no. 218 (May 1979): 9–21.
Interview with Karen Jaehne. *Positif*, no. 219 (June 1979): 33–36.
"From *Kanchanjungha* to the *Land of the Diamond King*" (interview with Bhaskar Chandavarkar). *Cinema Vision India* 1, no. 4 (1980): 20–21.
"Towards an Invisible Soundtrack?" (interview with Dhritiman Chatterjee). *Cinema Vision India* 1, no. 4 (1980): 12–19.
"You May Call Me Also a Commercial Producer" (interview with K. A. Abbas). *Film World* (Bombay) 17, no. 1 (1980): 28–31.
Interview with Wendy Allen and Roger Spikes. *Stills* 1, no. 3 (1981): 40–48.
Interview with Danièle Dubroux and Serge Le Peron. *Cahiers du cinéma*, no. 320 (February 1981): 7–12.
Interview with Emmanuel Decaux and Bruno Villien. *Cinématographe*, no. 82 (October 1982): 72–76.
Interview with Derek Malcolm. *Sight and Sound* 51, no. 2 (1982): 106–9.
"A Conversation with Satyajit Ray" (interview with Andrew Robinson). *Films and Filming*, no. 335 (August 1982): 12–22.

"The Politics of Humanism" (interview with Udayan Gupta). *Cineaste* 12, no. 1 (1982): 24–29. (Reprinted in *Art Politics Cinema—The Cineaste Interviews,* edited by Dan Georgakas and Lenny Rubenstein. Chicago: Lakeview Press, 1984.)

"Bridging the Home and the World" (interview with Andrew Robinson). *Monthly Film Bulletin* 51, no. 608 (1984): 292.

"From *Pather Panchali* to *Ghare Baire*" (interview with Jayanti Sen). *Cinewave* (Calcutta), no. 5 (January–March 1984): 7–20.

Critical Articles and Books

Banerjee, Ranjan K. "Satyajit Ray: Why One of the World's Greatest?" *Film World* (Bombay) 8, no. 6 (1972): 41–43.

Bassan, Raphaël. "Satyajit Ray: Cinéaste des contrastes." *La revue du cinéma—Image et son—Ecran,* no. 372 (May 1982): 71–84.

Ciment, Michel. "Le monde de Satyajit Ray." *Positif,* no. 59 (March 1964): 29–34.

Das Gupta, Chidananda. "Ray and Tagore." *Sight and Sound* 36, no. 1 (1966–67): 30–34.

———. "Ray and his Work." *Film Frame* (Ceylon) 1, no. 1 (1969): 43–45.

———. *The Cinema of Satyajit Ray.* New Delhi: Vikas, 1980.

———. "Western Response to Satyajit Ray." *Film World* (Bombay) 17, no. 1 (1980): 32–34.

———. *Satyajit Ray.* New Delhi: Indian Directorate of Film Festivals, 1981.

Houston, Penelope. "Ray's *Charulata.*" *Sight and Sound* 35, no. 1 (1965–66): 31–33.

Krupanidhi, Uma, ed. "Satyajit Ray." Special issue. *Montage* (Bombay), nos. 5–6 (July 1966).

"La longue patience du regard dans l'oeuvre de Satyajit Ray." Dossier. *Cinéma 81,* no. 267 (March 1981): 38–63.

Menon, M. R. "The Art and Films of Satyajit Ray: A Study." *Close-Up* (India), nos. 7–8 (1971): 5–17.

Micciolo, Henri. *Satyajit Ray.* Lausanne: L'Age d'Homme, 1981.

Ostor, Akos. "Cinema and Society in India and Senegal: The Films of Satyajit Ray and Ousbene Sembene." *Cinewave* (Calcutta), no. 7 (October 1984–March 1985): 8–18.

Peries, Lester James. "Satyajit Ray and the Critics." *Film Frame* (Ceylon) 1, no. 1 (1969): 13–20.

Positif, no. 218 (May 1979): 3–24, and no. 219 (June 1979): 17–36. [Dossiers on Ray.]

Rangoonwalla, Firoze. *Satyajit Ray's Art.* Delhi: Clarion Books, 1980.

Ray, Bibekananda. "Ray Off Set." *Sight and Sound* 53, no. 1 (1983–84): 52–55.

Rhode, Eric. "Satyajit Ray: A Study." *Sight and Sound* 30, no. 3 (1961): 132–36.

Robinson, Andrew. "Satyajit Ray at Work." *American Cinematographer* 64, no. 9 (1983): 72–80.

Seton, Marie. "Satyajit Ray's *Kanchanjungha.*" *Sight and Sound* 31, no. 2 (1962): 73–75.

———. *Portrait of a Director: Satyajit Ray.* London: Dobson, 1971.

Sinha, Rathin. "Whither the Traveller: Satyajit Ray at Sixty—A Reappraisal." *Maadhyam* (Bombay) 1, no. 6 (1981): 5–8.

Stanbrook, Alan. "The World of Ray." *Films and Filming* 12, no. 2 (1965): 55–58.
Wood, Robin. *The "Apu" Trilogy.* London: Studio Vista, 1972.

Chapter 12. Youssef Chahine
Chahine's Publication

Alexandrie pourquoi? Script. *L'avant-scène du cinéma,* no. 241 (June 1985). [The one script published in French.]

Interviews

"Vers une 'révolution culturelle' du cinéma égyptien" (interview with Guy Hennebelle). *L'Afrique littéraire et artistique,* no. 8 (December 1969): 80–84.
Interview with Guy Braucourt. *La revue du cinéma—Image et son,* no. 238 (April 1970): 56–64.
Interview with Guy Hennebelle and Heiny Srour. *Cinéma 3* (Casablanca), no. 3 (September 1970): 31–52. (Reprinted in part in *Cinéma 71,* no. 159 (September–October 1971): 127–30.
"D'où vient et où va Youssef Chahine" (interview with Guy Hennebelle). *L'Afrique littéraire et artistique,* no. 15 (February 1971): 72–84.
Interview with Claude Michel Cluny. *Cinéma 73,* no. 180 (September–October 1973): 96–99.
Interview with Guy Gauthier. *La revue du cinéma—Image et son,* no. 291 (December 1974): 62–66.
"Aller aussi loin qu'on peut" (interview with Noureddine Ghali). *Jeune cinéma,* no. 83 (December 1974–January 1975): 15–17.
"Le nationalisme démystifié" (interview with Andrée Tournès). *Jeune cinéma,* no. 119 (January 1979): 28–30.
Interview with Serge Daney and Serge Le Peron. *Cahiers du cinéma,* no. 310 (April 1980): 21–25.
"Youssef Chahine . . . Pourquoi?" (interview with Catherine Ruelle and Bruno Duval). *Cinéma 80,* no. 256 (April 1980): 48–55.
"Je rougissais en tournant" (interview with Jean-Pierre Peroncel-Hugoz). In "The Arab Cultural Scene," supplement to *The Literary Review* (1982), pp. 115–16.
"Le plus grand cinéaste égyptien vient d'être révélé à Paris" (interview with Patrice Barrat). *Les nouvelles littéraires,* 11 February 1982, p. 51.
Interview with Antonio Rodrig. *Cinématographe,* no. 112 (July 1985): 28–30.
"La bonté, l'arme la plus forte . . . Chahine parle d'*Adieu Bonaparte*" (interview with Anne Kieffer). *Jeune cinéma,* no. 168 (July–August 1985): 6–8.

Critical Articles and Books

Amghai, Mohammed. "Le cinéma arabe: Il s'impose enfin." *El-Moudjahid* 3, no. 102 (1973): 8–10.
Bosséno, Christian, ed. *Youssef Chahine l'Alexandrin.* Paris: CinémAction, no. 33 / Cerf, 1985.

Bosséno, Christian, Khaled Osman, and Mona de Pracontal. "Youssef Chahine." Dossier. *La revue du cinéma*, no. 400 (December 1984): 103–18.

Cluny, Claude-Michel. "Chahine Yûssif." In *Dictionnaire des nouveaux cinémas arabes*, pp. 161–72. Paris: Sindbad, 1978.

Ghali, Noureddine. "Reflets et mirages du cinéma égyptien." *Jeune cinéma*, no. 83 (December 1984–January 1985): 1–8.

Hajjaj, Nasreddine. "Youssef Chahine: The Experience of a Leading Film Maker." *Index on Censorship* 10, no. 4 (1981): 39–40.

Hennebelle, Guy. "Youssef Chahine, ou la quête d'un style nouveau." In *Les cinémas africains en 1972*, edited by Guy Hennebelle. Paris: *L'Afrique littéraire et artistique*, no. 20 / Société Africaine d'Edition, 1972.

Jonassaint, Jean, ed. "Chahine et le cinéma égyptien." Special issue. *Dérives* (Montreal), no. 43 (1984).

Khayati, Khémais. "Bonaparte et le Moineau." *Télérama*, no. 1814 (20–26 October 1984): 30–33.

Kieffer, Anne. "Youssef Chahine: Un homme du dialogue" and "*Adieu Bonaparte, ou le respect de l'autre*," *Jeune cinéma*, no. 168 (July–August 1985): 1–5.

Samak, Qussai. "The West as Seen Through the Arab Cinema." *Mar'a* 1, no. 2 (supplement to *Cineaste* 9, no. 4 [Fall 1979]): 32–35.

Thoraval, Yves. "Youssef Chahine, ou le renouveau permanent." In *Regards sur le cinéma égyptien*, edited by Yves Thoraval. Beirut: Dar el-Machreq, 1975.

Toubiana, Serge. "Chahine à la conquête de Bonaparte." *Cahiers du cinéma*, no. 364 (October 1984): 60–66.

Walid, Mohamed. "Youssef Chahine: Le pari de l'intelligence." *Adhoua*, no. 3 (January–March 1981): 9–15.

Zalaffi, Nicoletta. "Sous le signe de Shakespeare." *Image et son*, no. 298 (September 1975): 15–16.

Chapter 13: Glauber Rocha
Rocha's Publications

Several of the articles listed below have been published in English in anthologies edited by Pick, Chanan, and Johnson and Stam. These collections are referenced here by short title; the full citations appear in the bibliography to chapter 6.

Revisão crítica do cinema brasileiro. Rio de Janeiro: Editora Civilização Brasileira, 1963. Spanish translations: Havana: ICAIC, 1965: Madrid: Fundamentos, 1971.

"Humberto Mauro and the Historical Position of Brazilian Cinema." From Rocha, *Revisão crítica do cinema brasileiro*. In English: *Framework*, no. 11 (Autumn 1979): 5–8.

Deus e o diabo na terra do sol. Script (in Portuguese). Rio de Janeiro: Editora Civilização Brasileira, 1965.

"The Aesthetics of Hunger" (also known as "The Aesthetics of Violence"). In Portuguese: *Revista civilização brasileira*, no. 3 (July 1965). In French: *Positif*, no. 73 (February 1966): 22–24; *Cinéma 67*, no. 113 (February 1967): 32–33. In Spanish: *Cine cubano*, nos. 42–44 (1967): 57–58. In English: *Afterimage*, no. 1 (April

1970): n.p. Reprinted in Pick (ed.), *Latin American Film Makers;* Johnson and Stam (eds.), *Brazilian Cinema;* and Chahan (ed.), *Twenty-five Years.*

"La morale d'un nouveau Christ." *Positif,* no. 272 (October 1983): 17–19. [1966 text on Luis Buñuel.]

"Hunger Aesthetics versus Profit Aesthetics." In Italian: *L'avanti,* 15 October 1967. In English: *Framework,* no. 11 (Autumn 1979): 8–10.

"The Tricontinental Film Maker: That Is Called the Dawn." In French: *Cahiers du cinéma,* no. 195 (November 1967): 39–41. In English: Johnson and Stam (eds.), *Brazilian Cinema.*

"Cinema Novo and the Adventure of Creation." In Italian: Press documentation for the International Film Festival, Pesaro, 1968. In Spanish: *Cine cubano,* nos. 52–53 (1968): 25–40. In English: *Cinemantics,* no. 2 (March–April 1970): 12–16; *Framework,* no. 12 (1980): 18–27; an extract appears in Chanan (ed.), *Twenty-five Years.*

Terre en transe. Script (in French). *L'avant-scène du cinéma* (Paris), no. 77 (January 1968).

"Beginning at Zero: Notes on Cinema and Society." In English: *The Drama Review* 14, no. 2 (1970): 144–49.

"From the Drought to the Palm Trees." In French: *Positif,* no. 114 (March 1970): 42–47. In English: Pick (ed.), *Latin American Film Makers;* and Johnson and Stam (eds.), *Brazilian Cinema.*

Glauber Rocha y cabezas cortadas (with Augusto Martínez Torres). Script (in Spanish). Barcelona, Spain: Editorial Anagrama, 1970.

"Carta de Glauber Rocha." *Cine cubano,* nos. 71–72 (1972): 1–11.

"Lights, Magic, Action." In French: *Positif,* no. 164 (December 1974): 20–23. In Spanish: *Hablemos de cine,* no. 69 (1977–78): 30–31.

O século do cinema. Rio de Janeiro: Editora Alhambra, 1983.

Interviews

Interview with Guy Gauthier. *Image et son,* no. 175 (July 1964): 33–35.

Interview with Guy Allombert. *Image et son,* no. 212 (January 1968): 6–7.

Interiew with Piero Arlorio and Michel Ciment. *Positif,* no. 91 (January 1969): 19–36.

Interview with Michel Delahaye, Pierre Kast, and Jean Narboni. *Cahiers du cinéma,* no. 214 (July–August 1969): 22–41. In English: *Afterimage,* no. 1 (April 1970): n.p.

"Cinema Novo versus Cultural Colonialism." *Cineaste* 4, no. 1 (1970): 2–9,35. (Reprinted in *Art Politics Cinema—The Cineaste Interviews,* edited by Dan Georgakas and Lenny Rubenstein. Chicago: Lakeview Press, 1984.)

Interview with Gordon Hitchens. *Filmmakers Newsletter* 3, no. 2 (1970): 20–25.

Interview with Glenn O'Brien. *Interview* 2 no. 3 (1970): 24–25,38.

Interview with Noël Simsolo. *Revue du cinéma—Image et son,* no. 236 (February 1970): 104–10.

Interview with Miguel Torres. *Cine cubano,* nos. 60–62 (1970): 68–83.

Interview with Enrico Viani (press documentation for International Film Festival,

Pesaro, 1970). *Cinéma 70,* no. 151 (December 1970): 74–76. In English: *After-image,* no. 3 (Summer 1971): 68–77.

"The Way to Make a Future" (interview with Gordon Hitchens). *Film Quarterly* 24, no. 1 (1970): 27–30.

Round table discussion. *Cinema* (Great Britain), no. 5 (February 1970): 15–20.

"Les deux vagues du cinéma novo" (round table discussion). *Cinéma 70,* no. 150 (November 1970): 60–74.

"The Industry and European New Cinema" (round table discussion). *Cinematics,* no. 3 (July 1970): n.p.

"Brazil—The Next Vietnam?" *Time Out,* no. 74 (16–22 July 1971): 10,12.

Interview with Marcel Martin. *Cinéma 71,* no. 160 (November 1971): 26–29.

"Somos los heraldos de la revolución." *Cine cubano,* nos. 73–75 (1972): 40–45.

Quotations from interviews with Marcel Martin and Joaquin G. Santana. *Ecran,* no. 6 (June 1972): 38.

"La historia de Brasil según Glauber Rocha." *Cine cubano,* nos. 86–88 (1975): 95–98.

Interview with Manuel Carvalheiro. *La revue du cinéma—Image et son,* no. 376 (October 1982): 65–76.

Critical Articles and Books

Bruce, Graham. "Music in Glauber Rocha's Films." *Jump Cut,* no. 22 (May 1980): 15–18. (Reprinted in *Brazilian Cinema,* edited by Randal Johnson and Robert Stam. Rutherford, N.J.: Fairleigh Dickinson University Press, 1982.

Callenbach, Ernest. "Comparative Anatomy of Folk Myth Films: *Robin Hood* and *Antonio das Mortes.*" *Film Quarterly* 23, no. 2 (1969–70): 42–47.

Carlson, Terry. "*Antonio das Mortes.*" In Johnson and Stam (eds.), *Brazilian Cinema.*

Carvalheiro, Manuel. "Glauber Rocha: Un Ulysse moderne en quête de l'absolu." *Cinéma 82,* no. 281 (May 1982): 90–98.

Ciment, Michel. "Glauber Rocha." In *Second Wave,* edited by Ian Cameron. London: Studio Vista; New York: Praeger, 1970.

Dahl, Gustavo. "Dieu et le diable à l'age de la terre en transes." *Cahiers du cinéma,* no. 329 (November 1981): 14–17.

Dantas, Vinicius. "Obsceno e national." *Filme cultura* 15, no. 40 (1982): 40–50.

Estève, Michel, ed. *Le cinéma novo brésilien.* Vol. 2: *Glauber Rocha.* Paris: Lettres Modernes, 1972.

Fisher, Jack. "Politics by Magic: *Antonio das Mortes.*" *The Film Journal* 1 (Spring 1971): 32–47.

Gardies, René. *Glauber Rocha.* Paris: Seghers, 1974.

———. "Structural Analysis of a Textual System: Presentation of a Method." *Screen* 15, no. 1 (1974): 11–31. (Originally published in French in *La revue du cinéma—Image et son,* no. 271 [April 1973]: 65–90.)

"Glauber Rocha: Metamorfoses de um Roteiro." Dossier on script versions of *Deus e o diabo na terra do sol. Filme Cultura,* no. 43 (January–April 1984): 57–63.

Guibbert, Pierre. "Pour une lecture de Antonio das Mortes." *Cahiers de la cinéma-thèque,* no. 2 (Spring 1971): 2–20.

Hollyman, Burnes Saint Patrick. *Glauber Rocha and the Cinema Novo.* New York: Garland, 1983.

Johnson, Randal. "Glauber Rocha: Apocalypse and Resurrection." Chapter 4 in *Cinema Novo × 5: Masters of Contemporary Brazilian Film.* Austin: University of Texas Press, 1984.

Kavanaugh, Thomas. "Imperialism and the Revolutionary Cinema: Glauber Rocha's *Antonio das Mortes.*" *Journal of Modern Literature* 3, no. 2 (1973): 201–13.

Losada, Carlos, and Jose L. Lopez del Rio. "Rocha en dos films." *Cinestudio,* no. 87 (July 1970): 24–27.

MacBean, James Roy. "*Vent d'est,* or Godard and Rocha at the Crossroads." *Sight and Sound* 40, no. 3 (1971): 144–50.

Martin, Marcel. "Epitaphe pour Glauber Rocha." *La revue du cinéma—Image et son—écran,* no. 366 (November 1981): 89–98.

Martínez Torres, Augusto. "Echoes d'une conversation: Luis Buñuel et Glauber Rocha." *Cinéma 68,* no. 123 (February 1968): 48–53.

"La Mort de Glauber Rocha." Dossier. *Cinéma 81,* no. 274 (October 1981): 69–75.

Pierre, Sylvie. "Glauber Rocha par coeur, de tête et dans un corps." *Cahiers du cinéma,* no. 329 (November 1981): 9–13.

Senna, Orlando. "Roteiro tricontinental de Xanglauber." *Filme Cultura* 15, no. 40 (1982): 40–50.

Stam, Robert. "*Land in Anguish:* Revolutionary Lessons." *Jump Cut,* nos. 11–12 (June 1976): 49–51. (Reprinted in Johnson and Stam, [eds.], *Brazilian Cinema.*)

Van Wert, William F. "Ideology in the Third World Cinema: A Study of Sembène Ousmane and Glauber Rocha." *Quarterly Review of Film Studies* 4, no. 2 (1979): 207–26.

Xavier, Ismail. "*Black God, White Devil:* The Representation of History." In Johnson and Stam (eds.), *Brazilian Cinema.*

Chapter 14. Yılmaz Güney

None of Yılmaz Güney's novels, stories, or scripts have been translated into English.

Interviews

Positif, no. 234 (September 1980): 46–49.

Interview with Attilâ Dorsay. *Cinéma 80,* no. 262 (October 1980): 61–63.

Framework, nos. 15–17 (Summer 1981): 7–8.

Jeune cinéma, no. 144 (July–August 1982): 13–15.

Interview with Michel Ciment. *Positif,* no. 256 (June 1982): 34–41.

"Eye of the Tiger" (interview with Chris Auty). *City Limits,* no. 67 (14–20 January 1982): 11.

"Les hommes sont aussi paumés que les femmes écrasées" (interview with Michel Sidhom). *Ciné-critiques,* no. 7 (September 1982): 18–20.

"Propos de Yılmaz Güney" (interview with Marcel Martin). *Image et son,* no. 374 (July–August 1982): 88–96.

"Exile on Mainstream" (interview with Tony Rayns). *Time Out*, no. 647 (14–20 January 1983): 10–12.
"From Isolation" (interview with Tony Rayns). *Sight and Sound* 52, no. 2 (1983): 89–93. [Fuller version of the *Time Out* interview.]
"Güney's Last Journey" (interview with Carl Gardner). *Stills*, no. 13 (October 1984): 48–50.

Critical Articles and Books

Bassan, Raphaël. "Itinéraire escarpé de Yılmaz Güney." *Image et son*, no. 384 (June 1983): 16–19.
Cullingworth, Michael. "Behind the Mountains." *Sight and Sound* 53, no. 3 (1984): 208–10.
Dorsay, Attilâ. "Yılmaz Güney: Son cinéma, sa création, sa personne." *Cinéma 80*, no. 262 (October 1980): 52–60.
Ergün, Mehmet. *Bir sinemaci ve anlatici olarak Yılmaz Güney* (Yılmaz Güney as a Film Maker and Narrator). Istanbul: Dogrultu Yayinlevi, 1978. [Cited by Giles and Sahin.]
Finlayson, Eric. "Levantine Approaches: On First Looking into Güney's Turkey." *Monthly Film Bulletin* 51, no. 609 (1984): 324.
Giles, Dennis, and Haluk Sahin. "Revolutionary Cinema in Turkey: Yılmaz Güney." *Jump Cut*, no. 27 (July 1982): 35–37.
Gürkan, Turhan, ed. *Dunya basininda Yılmaz Güney* (Yılmaz Güney in the World Press). Istanbul: Güney Yayinlari, 1976. [Cited by Giles and Sahin.]
Gürsel, Nedim. "Yılmaz Güney: Miroir du peuple Turc." *Jeune cinéma*, no. 89 (September–October 1975): 17–20.
Heijs, Jan, ed. *Yılmaz Güney: Sein Leben—Seine Filme*. Hamburg: Buntbuch-Verlag, 1983. [The only book-length study of Güney's work.]
Kazan, Elia. "A View From a Turkish Prison." *New York Times Magazine*, 4 February 1979. (Translated into French in *Positif*, no. 227 [February 1980]: 36–45.)
Martin, Marcel. "Yılmaz Güney: Cinéaste militant." *Image et son*, no. 374 (July–August 1982): 82–87.
Rayns, Tony. "From Isolation." *Sight and Sound* 52, no. 2 (1983): 88–89.
Tournès, Andrée. "L'oeuvre de Yılmaz Güney à Berlin." *Jeune cinéma*, no. 134 (April–May 1981): 18–20.
Turner, Adrian. "Présentation de Yılmaz Güney." *Positif*, no. 227 (February 1980): 29–35.
Yalçin, Altan. *Yılmaz Güney dosyasi* (The Dossier of Yılmaz Güney). Istanbul: Güney Yayinlari, 1977. [Cited by Giles and Sahin.]
Weales, Gerald. "Istanbul Journal." *Film Comment* 11, no. 1 (1975): 4, 87.
"*Yol.*" Special issue. *Ciné-critiques*, no. 7 (September 1982).

Chapter 15. Ousmane Sembene
Sembene's publications

Le docker noir. Paris: Nouvelles Editions Debresse, 1956.
O pays, mon beau peuple! Paris: Amiot Dumont, 1957.

Les bouts de bois de Dieu. Paris: Le Livre Contemporain, 1960. In English: *God's Bits of Wood.* New York: Doubleday, 1962; London: Heinemann, 1970.

Voltaïque. Paris: Présence Africaine, 1962. In English: *Tribal Scars and Other Stories.* London: Heinemann, 1973.

L'harmattan. Paris: Présence Africaine, 1964.

Vehi ciosane, ou Blanche genèse, suivi du mandat. Paris: Présence Africaine, 1965. In English: *The Money Order, with White Genesis.* London: Heinemann, 1972.

Xala. Paris: Présence Africaine, 1974. In English: *Xala.* London: Heinemann, 1976.

Borom sarret. Script. *L'avant-scène du cinéma,* no. 229 (1 June 1979): 35–42.

Le dernier de l'empire. Paris: L'Harmattan, 1981. In English: *The Last of the Empire.* London: Heinemann, 1983.

Interviews

Interview with Guy Hennebelle. *Jeune cinéma,* no. 34 (November 1968): 4–9.

"Ousmane Sembene at the Olympic Games. *American Cinematographer* 53, no. 11 (1972): 1276, 1322.

Interview with Guy Hennebelle from *L'Afrique artistique et littéraire.* Reprinted in *Les cinémas africains en 1972,* edited by Guy Hennebelle. Paris: *L'Afrique artistique et littéraire,* no. 20 / Société Africaine d'Édition, 1972.

Interview with G. M. Perry and Patrick McGilligan. *Film Quarterly* 26, no. 3 (1973): 36–42.

"Film Makers Have a Great Responsibility to Our People" (interview with Harold D. Weaver). *Cineaste* 6, no. 1 (1973): 26–31.

"Les francs-tireurs sénégalais" (interview with André Pâquet and Guy Borreman). *Cinéma-Québec* 2, nos. 6–7 (1973): vii-xii.

"Carthage et le chemin de la dignité africaine et arabe" (interview with Tahar Cheriaa). *CinémArabe,* nos. 4–5 (October–November 1976): 15–17.

"Le cinéaste de nos jours peut remplacer le conteur traditionnel" (interview with Noureddine Ghali). *Cinéma 76,* no. 208 (April 1976): 83–95.

"Je refuse le cinéma de pancartes" (interview with Guy Hennebelle). *Ecran,* no. 43 (January 1976): 46–49.

"Un film est un débat" (interview with Jean Delmas and Ginette Delmas). *Jeune cinéma,* no. 99 (December 1976–January 1977): 13–17.

Interview with Jean-Claude Bonnet. *Cinématographe,* no. 28 (June 1977): 43–44.

Interview with Robert Grelier. *La revue du cinéma—Image et son,* no. 322 (November 1977): 74–80.

Interview with Ulrich Gregor. *Framework,* nos. 7–8 (Spring 1978): 35–37.

Interviews with Guy Hennebelle. In *Cinéastes d'Afrique noire,* edited by Guy Hennebelle and Catherine Ruelle. Paris: *L'Afrique Littéraire et Artistique,* no. 49 / *CinémAction,* no. 3 (1978).

Interview with Christian Bosséno. *La revue du cinéma—Image et son,* no. 342 (September 1979): 116–18.

"Africa Speaks Out" (interview with K. L. Arora). *Film World* (Bombay) 16, no. 3 (1979): 67–69.

"Le pouvoir, la parole, la liberté" (interview with Azzedine Mabrouki). *Les deux écrans,* no. 12 (April 1979): 19–21.

"A Propos de *Ceddo*" (interview with Françoise Pfaff). *Positif,* no. 235 (October 1980): 54–57.

"African Cinema Seeks a New Language." *Young Cinema and Theatre* (Prague), no. 3 (1983): 26–28.

Critical Articles and Books

Auguiste, Reece. "Sembene Ousmane and Afrikan [*sic*] Political Cinema." *Frontline* 2, no. 4 (1983): 114–16.

Bestman, Martin T. *Sembène Ousmane et l'esthétique du roman négro-africain.* Sherbrooke, Quebec: Editions Naarman, 1981.

Binet, Jacques. "Le sacré dans le cinéma négro-africain." *Positif,* no. 235 (October 1980): 44–48.

Coad, Malcolm. "Ousmane Sembene and *Ceddo.*" *Index on Censorship* 10, no. 4 (1981): 32–33.

Fisher, Lucy. "*Xala:* A Study in Black Humour." *Millennium Film Journal,* nos. 7–9 (Winter–Fall 1980–81): 165–72.

Gabriel, Teshome. "*Xala:* A Cinema of Wax and Gold." *Jump Cut,* no. 27 (July 1982): 31–33.

Gourdeau, Jean-Pierre. "Les bouts de bois de Dieu" de Sembène Ousmane. Paris: Bordas, 1984.

Landy, Marsha. "Politics and Style in *Black Girl.*" *Jump Cut,* no. 27 (July 1982): 23–25.

Minyono-Nkode, Mathieu-François. *Comprendre "Les bouts de bois de Dieu" de Sembène Ousmane.* Issy les Moulineaux, France: Les Classiques Africains, 1979.

Moore, Gerald. "Sembene Ousmane: The Primacy of Change." Chapter 3 in *Twelve African Writers.* London: Hutchinson, 1980.

Moriceau, Annie, and Alain Rouch. *"Le mandat" de Sembène Ousmane: Étude critique.* Paris: Fernand Nathan / Nouvelles Editions Africaines, 1983.

Ostor, Akos. "Cinema and Society in India and Senegal: The Films of Satyajit Ray and Ousmane Sembene." *Cinewave* (Calcutta), no. 7 (October 1984–March 1985): 8–18.

Pfaff, Françoise. "Three Faces of Africa: Women in *Xala.*" *Jump Cut,* no. 27 (July 1982): 27–31.

———. *The Cinema of Ousmane Sembene—A Pioneer of African Film.* Westwood, Conn.: Greenwood Press, 1984.

Pouillaude, Jean-Luc. "L'emblème: Sur *Ceddo.*" *Positif,* no. 235 (October 1980): 49–53.

Robinson, Cedric. "Domination and Imitation: *Xala* and the Emergence of the Black Bourgeoisie." *Race and Class* 22, no. 2 (1980): 147–58.

Serceau, Daniel. *Sembène Ousmane.* Paris: *CinémAction,* no. 34 / L'Afrique littéraire et artistique (1985).

Sevastakis, Michael. "Neither Gangsters nor Dead Kings: Ousmane Sembene's Five Fatalistic Films." *Film Library Quarterly* 6, no. 3 (1973): 13–23, 40–48.

Spass, Lieve. "Female Domestic Labour and Third World Politics in *La Noire de . . . .*" *Jump Cut,* no. 27 (July 1982): 26–27.

Turvey, Gerry. "*Xala* and the Curse of Neocolonialism." *Screen* 26, nos. 3–4 (1985): 75–87.

Van Wert, William F. "Ideology in the Third World: A Study of Sembene Ousmane and Glauber Rocha." *Quarterly Review of Film Studies* 4, no. 2 (1979): 207–26.
Vieyra, Paulin Soumanou. *Ousmane Sembène cinéaste.* Paris: Présence Africaine, 1972.

Chapter 16. Jorge Sanjinés
Sanjinés's publications

"Yawar mallku." *La revue du cinéma—Image et son*, no. 240 (July 1970): 96–100.
"Cinema and Revolution." *Cineaste* 4, no. 3 (1970–71): 13–14.
"A Militant Cinema." In Spanish: *Cine cubano*, no. 68 (1971): 45–47. In French: *Jeune cinéma*, no. 79 (June 1974): 4–5. In English: in *Latin American Film Makers and the Third Cinema*, edited by Zuzana M. Pick. Ottawa: Carleton University Press, 1978.
"Revolutionary Cinema: The Bolivian Experience." In Spanish: *Cine cubano*, nos. 76–77 (1972): 1–15; *Hablemos de cine*, no. 64 (1972): 20–27. In French: *Jeune cinéma*, no. 79 (June 1974): 7–10; *Positif*, no. 164 (December 1974): 27–30. In English: Pick (ed.), *Latin American Film Makers.*
"In Search of Popular Cinema." In Spanish: *Cine cubano*, nos. 89–90 (1974): 60–64. In English: in Pick (ed.), *Latin American Film Makers.*
"Pour un cinéma révolutionnaire et populaire." In French: *CinémArabe* nos. 4–5 (November 1976): 27–30.
"Problems of Form and Content in Revolutionary Cinema." In Spanish: *Ojo al cine*, no. 5 (1976). In English: in *Twenty-five Years of the New Latin American Cinema*, edited by Michael Chanan. London: British Film Institute / Channel Four Television, 1983.
Response to a questionnaire on the influence of Soviet silent cinema. *Cine cubano*, no. 93 (1977): 45–46.
"Language and Popular Culture." In English: *Framework*, no. 10 (Spring 1979): 31–33.
Sanjinés, Jorge, and Grupo Ukamau. Teoría y práctica de un cine junto al pueblo. Mexico City: Siglo XXI, 1979. [An important collection of theoretical articles and treatments for completed films.]
"El cine revolucionario en Bolivia." *Cine cubano*, no. 99 (1981): 80–83.
"Nuestro principal destinatario." *Cine cubano*, no. 105 (1983): 40–45.

Interviews

Image et son, no. 201 (January 1967): 58–62.
Venice press conference. *Jeune cinéma*, no. 41 (October 1969): 19–22.
Interview with Robert Grelier. *La revue du cinéma—Image et son*, no. 240 (July 1970): 92–96.
"La negación del Indigenismo" (interview with Isaac Leon Frias and Antonio Gonzales). *Hablemos del cine*, no. 52 (March–April 1970): 36–40.
"Ukamau and Yawar Mallku" (interview with Guy Braucourt). *Cinéma 70*, no. 144 (March 1970): 77–90. In English: *Afterimage*, no. 3 (Summer 1971): 40–53.
"A Talk with Jorge Sanjinés." *Cineaste* 4, no. 3 (1970–71): 12.

"*The Courage of the People*" (interview with Dina Nascetti). In Spanish: *Marcha* (Uruguay), 14 January 1971. In French: *Ecran*, no. 25 (May 1974): 49–65. In English: *Cineaste* 5, no. 2 (1972): 18–20.

Cine al día, no. 15 (June 1972): 9–10.

"Conversación con un cineasta revolucionario." *Cine cubano*, nos. 73–75 (1972): 1–9.

Interview with Fernando Perez. *Cine cubano*, nos. 71–72 (1972): 52–59.

Interview with Jean-René Huleu, Ignacio Ramonet, and Serge Toubiana. *Cahiers du cinéma*, no. 253 (October–November 1974): 5–21. In English: *Young Cinema and Theatre* (Prague), no. 2 (1975): 19–28.

Interview with Susana Seleme. *Ecran*, no. 34 (March 1975): 68–69.

"L'affrontement entre le tiers monde et l'impérialisme ne pourra être que violent" (interview with Evelyne July). *Cinéma 75*, no. 196 (March 1975): 81–85.

"Para ser verdaderamente bolivianos tenemos que estar integrados a la vida de las mayorías" (interview with Romualdo Santos). *Cine cubano*, no. 98 (1980): 56–61.

"Faire du cinéma un instrument de libération" (interview with Ginette Gervais). *Jeune cinéma*, no. 141 (March 1982): 1–5.

City Limits, no. 100 (2–8 September 1983): 17.

Critical articles

Alexander, William. "Class, Film Language, and Popular Culture." *Jump Cut*, no. 30 (March 1985): 45–48.

Dalton, Roque. "Yawar Mallku: Something More than Just a Film." In *Latin American Film Makers and the Third Cinema*, edited by Zuzana M. Pick. Ottawa: Carleton University Press, 1978.

Grant, Jacques, and Gerard Frot-Coutaz. "L'analyse d'un grand film: *L'Ennemi Principal*." *Cinéma 75*, no. 196 (March 1975): 68–79.

Ledgard, Melvin. "Jorge Sanjinés: El cine urgente." *Hablemos de Cine*, nos. 73–74 (June 1981): 25–28.

Pick, Zuzana M. "*The Courage of the People:* A Massacre of Tin Miners." In Pick (ed.), *Latin American Film Makers*.

Shedin, Michael. "Case Study versus Process Study: Two Films Made for Italian Television." *Film Quarterly* 27, no. 3 (1974): 27–39.

Sorel, Stéphane. "L'ennemi principal." *Téléciné*, no. 197 (March 1975): 10–13.

Zambrano, Oscar. "Un cinéma pour les paysans." *Cinéma 75*, no. 196 (March 1975): 86–89.

Sources for Photographs

Frontis. Contemporary Films. 1. National Film Archive. 2. Festival des Trois Continents. 3. National Film Development Corporation of India. 4. Festival des Trois Continents. 5. National Film Development Corporation of India. 6–8. National Film Archive. 9. Filmotsav 84. 10. The Other Cinema. 11. National Film Archive. 12. Association des Trois Mondes. 13. The Other Cinema. 14. Contemporary Films. 15. The Other Cinema. 16. Contemporary Films. 17. Association des Trois Mondes / Collection Ferid Boughedir. 18. The Other Cinema. 19–22. National Film Development Corporation of India. 23. Festival des Trois Continents. 24. Filmotsav 84. 25. Contemporary Films. 26. Filmotsav 84. 27. National Film Development Corporation of India. 28. Contemporary Films. 29. National Film Archive. 30. Festival des Trois Continents. 31–35. Tony Rayns Collection. 36. London Film Festival. 37. Festival des Trois Continents. 38. Association des Trois Mondes. 39–40. Festival des Trois Continents. 41. National Film Archive. 42. Tony Rayns Collection. 43. Festival des Trois Continents. 44–45. National Film Archive. 46. Festival des Trois Continents. 47. Contemporary Films. 48–54. The Other Cinema. 55. Contemporary Films. 56. Festival des Trois Continents. 57. Paul Willemen Collection. 58. National Film Archive. 59–60. The Other Cinema. 61. Festival des Trois Continents. 62. Association des Trois Mondes. 63. London Film Festival. 64–65. Association des Trois Mondes / Collection Ferid Boughedir. 66. Lizbeth Malkmus Collection. 67. Mypheduh Films. 68. British Film Institute. 69. Association des Trois Mondes/Collection Ferid Boughedir. 70. British Film Institute. 71. Gaston Kaboré. 72–77. Contemporary Films. 78–83. Association des Trois Mondes. 84. The Other Cinema. 85–88. Contemporary Films. 89. The Other Cinema. 90. Contemporary Films. 91–95. Cactus Films. 96. Contemporary Films. 97–99. The Other Cinema. 100. Contemporary Films. 101. Association des Trois Mondes / Collection Ferid Boughedir. 102–105. The Other Cinema. 106–107. Association des Trois Mondes. 108–109. National Film Development Corporation of India.

Index

Compositor: G&S Typesetters
Text: 10/12 Times Roman
Display: Helvetica Bold
Printer: Maple-Vail Book Mfg Group
Binder: Maple-Vail Book Mfg Group